JUSTICE
AS
TRANSLATION

JUSTICE
AS
TRANSLATION

An Essay in Cultural and Legal Criticism

JAMES BOYD WHITE

The University of Chicago Press
Chicago and London

James Boyd White is the Hart Wright Professor of Law, professor of English language and literature, and adjunct professor of classical studies at the University of Michigan. His books include *The Legal Imagination: Studies in the Nature of Legal Thought and Expression* (1973); *When Words Lose Their Meaning: Constitutions and Reconstitutions of Language, Character, and Community* (1984); and *Heracles' Bow: Essays in the Rhetoric and Poetics of the Law* (1985).

The University of Chicago Press, Chicago 60637
The University of Chicago Press, Ltd., London
© 1990 by The University of Chicago
All rights reserved. Published 1990
Printed in the United States of America
99 98 97 96 95 94 93 92 91 90   5 4 3 2 1

Library of Congress Cataloging-in-Publication Data
White, James Boyd, 1938–
Justice as translation : an essay in cultural and legal criticism
/ James Boyd White.
        p.   cm.
Includes bibliographical references (p. 271).
ISBN 0-226-89495-9 (alk. paper)
1. Law—Language.   2. Semantics (Law)   3. Judicial opinions—
United States—Language.   4. Law—Translating.   I. Title.
K213.W49   1990
340'.014—dc20   89-28358
                                                              CIP

To the memory of
Margaret Morgan (whom I never knew)
and
Mildred Hamler (whom I did)

CONTENTS

Introduction   ix

Part One: Looking at our Languages
1 Intellectual Integration   3
2 The Language of Concepts: A Case Study   22
3 The Language and Culture of Economics   46
   Appendix to Chapter Three   82

Part Two: The Judicial Opinion as a Form of Life
4 Judicial Criticism   89
5 "Original Intention" in the Slave Cases   113
6 "Plain Meaning" and Translation:
   The *Olmstead* Opinions   141
7 The Reading of Precedent: *United States v. White*   160
8 The Fourth Amendment as a Way of Talking About
   People: The *Robinson* Case   176
9 The Constitutive Character of the
   Exclusionary Rule   203
10 The Judicial Opinion as a Form of Life   215

Part Three: The Activity of Translation
11 Translation, Interpretation, and Law   229
12 Justice as Translation   257

   Notes   271
   Index   303

What is called our "experience" is almost entirely determined by our habits of attention.

—*William James*

INTRODUCTION

"To imagine a language means to imagine a form of life," said Wittgenstein, and that famous sentence may be taken as the text to which all that follows is addressed.

It means that our acts of language are actions in the world, not just in our minds. Even when we think we are simply communicating information, or being rigorously and exclusively intellectual, or just talking, we are in fact engaged in performances, in relation to others, that are ethical and political in character and that can be judged as such. This is true in the private world, as we talk with our friends in ways that promote or defeat our friendships, but it is true in the public world as well, as we know when we hear political campaign speeches that dignify, or demean, the process of election. It is especially true in the law, which is above all the creation of a world of meaning: a world with its own actors, its own forms and occasions of speech, and its own language. Whenever we talk we create a character for ourselves and a relation with others: we offer to constitute a community of a certain kind, for good or ill, and this is often the most important part of what we do.

How are our languages, our acts of language, and the characters and communities we create in our expressions to be understood and judged, in the law and elsewhere? That is the question to which this book is addressed.

* * *

To look at language in such a way is to work against the grain of our experience, for one of the deepest habits of our culture is to talk about language not as a field of action but as if it were transparent or neutral, merely a way of pointing to something outside of itself. In this mode we speak of language as a vehicle or container, as a technology, or as a code for the transmission of messages. What really counts, we seem to think, is external to language: in the mind as an idea or a feeling, or out there in the real world. In either case the function of language is to point to something, or label it, or, in the modern jargon, to signify it. As for us, we talk as if we lived for the most part outside of language and used it, as we might a telephone, to achieve our purposes, which are also outside language and do not have language as their object.

The habit of mind I am describing assumes that our most important uses of language are fundamentally propositional in character, indeed that any meaningful piece of discourse asserts (or denies) that such and such is the case; it is a statement that depends for its acceptance on chains of reasoning, deductive or inductive in character, that are external to itself and its context. It follows that any text can be recast into the propositions it affirms, indeed that rationality itself often requires such recasting. These propositions are not language-bound but are in principle translatable into any language whatever; this is in fact necessary if we are to claim, as so many want to do, that our knowledge is universal.

This is the image that is at work in most of our customary talk about thought and language; it is certainly the understanding out of which the great majority of academic books and articles are written. Perhaps it has its first modern manifestation in Hobbes, who told us that words are but names, that discourse is the joining together of names, and that all reason consists of adding and subtracting.[1] We see it at work in the way courts talk about the first amendment as protecting the expression of "ideas," in courses that define excellence in writing as "clarity," in works of analytic philosophy that assume that all meaning is conceptual and propositional, in the way scientific linguistics imagines language as a code for the transfer of information, and so on. This image is built at a deep level into all social science of the positivist kind—one thinks especially of economics, and of quantitative political science, psychology, and sociology—for the very operations of these disciplines require both reader and writer to pretend that language is transparent or neutral, able to describe without distortion what is out there in the world or in here in the reasoning mind. The fact that these commitments may be unconscious does not lessen, in fact it may intensify, their force.

What we call "logic" actually depends upon the view that language is a set of names: our idea of rational coherence requires that, for any state of affairs described as "X," it either be the case or not be the case that "X" exists; for this to work, "X" must have the same meaning across the discourse, and a meaning determined by something external to the discourse itself. "You can define 'raining' any way you want, but it must be the case, at any point in space and time, either that it is 'raining' or that it is not. The rule of noncontradiction requires no less." This kind of reason works algorithmically, by a series of binary choices.

When we talk this way—and no one among us can entirely avoid doing so—we talk as if it does not much matter what particular language we use, or what form of language, because whatever we want to say can be said, more or less efficiently, in any language at all. Once our auditors perceive the objects we are naming in the real or conceptual world, language has done its job and can—and should—disappear.

* * *

But we have another way of thinking about language, drawn from our experience of ordinary life and from our reading of literature. Here we find uses of language, and a sense of language, that deny virtually everything that has been said in the preceding paragraphs. For language can be seen not as transparent or neutral but as a real force of its own.[2] Language does much to shape both who we are—our very selves—and the ways in which we observe and construe the world. There is no nonlinguistic observer, no nonlinguistic observed. "The man is only half himself," said Emerson (in *The Poet*); "the other half is his expression."

This is a way of imagining language not as a set of propositions, but as a repertoire of forms of action and of life. Every utterance has meanings beyond the purely intellectual—meanings that are, just to begin the list of possibilities, political, ethical, cultural, aesthetic, social, and psychological in character—for, whether we know it or not, our every utterance is a way of being and acting in the world. Our purposes, like our observations, have no prelingual reality, but are constituted in language—in this sense they too are lingual in nature. Nothing human is free of language. As for logic and rationality, this sense of language denies that our words must mean the same thing every time they are used, indeed it denies that they can, for our words get much of their meaning from the gesture of which they are a part, which in turn gets its meaning largely from the context against which it is a performance.

Think of it this way: how little of what happens in any real utterance is reducible to the words uttered, let alone to the "propositions" they are supposed to express, and how much lies in the gesture, in the relations between speaker and auditor, in their material context, in the understandings they share—understandings about the natural world, about human motives and capacities and dangers, about what needs to be said and what does not. The meaning of a sentence lies not only in what we tend to think of as the sentence itself, in the words, but in the context, verbal and nonverbal, out of which it is constructed. Instead of thinking of language as a code into which nonlinguistic material is translated, or of language use as the manipulation of that medium for the expression of ideas, we can imagine languaging as a kind of dance, a series of gestures or performances, measured not so much by their truth-value as by their appropriateness to context.

* * *

The two views of language I have sketched out above do not exist in pure form, I suppose, for anyone in the world, but are at work in each of us all the time, in shifting and imperfect relation. It is no doubt sometimes right and helpful, indeed sometimes necessary, to act as if our language were transparent, merely a system of names, and so forth. We do it all the time, including, at moments, in the writing and reading of this book. It may even be useful to pretend for a moment that this is the right or only view of language, for to do this may permit a kind of analysis, of text-building, that has a value. But such a view is inherently reductive—it requires the repression of what, in another state of mind, we know—and like all reductive systems it will ultimately be pathological unless we can find a way to respond to what it leaves out. One could not found a life upon it.

What is required is to learn to shift the focus of our attention so that we come to see language as a reality of its own and its forms as forms of life, with all that entails. Not that we would, or could, ever come to see only language and nothing else; but we can hope that while we remain conscious of what we discern and desire in the world, and what we fear, we may become conscious as well of the languages through which we see these things, by which we act, in which we are ourselves embedded. To teach us how to do this has been one of the great tasks of imaginative literature from its beginnings. To do this completely is I think impossible, at least at the present stage of our intellectual development; but to try to do it is to move in the direction of completeness and inclusion, or what in the first chapter I shall call "integration." The writing of this book is itself meant to enact at least the beginnings of such a movement.

* * *

As this book is written out of a view of language so it is written out of a view of law, and they are related. At least until recently the image of law most widely accepted among legal academics, and especially students of jurisprudence, was that of a set of rules issuing from a political sovereign, and rules for the most part conceived of as plainly established and plainly accessible. Such are the rules passed by the legislature or articulated in judicial opinions; they (perhaps coupled with the more general rules called "principles" that inform the lesser ones) are the law itself. Even among those who would now no longer assert such a view as a theoretical matter, the law is often thought of as a means of social control—as a set of incentives, enablements, or punishments that will affect human behavior in such a way as to produce a state of affairs the lawmaker is thought to desire—and this can work, in the way imagined, only if the law is seen as a set of rules or directives, adequately plain. The view of "law as rules" is in fact an inescapable part of our own discourse as lawyers, for in talking about the choice of one rule over another we necessarily talk as if this choice really mattered, and we usually do so on the assumption that it will work as a means of social control.

But another strain in our thinking regards this view as simplistic and naive—as "formalist"—and instead looks through the tissue of laws and opinions and arguments, through the whole world of legal language, to what "really happens" in the world; here, in what officials actually do, or in the exercise of power by one group in society over others, is where the law is. The function of legal discourse, which purports to be neutral, to seek only the public good, to be concerned with justice, and so on, is actually to mask or obscure these realities, clouding them with high-minded talk; perhaps it does this accidentally or unconsciously, perhaps more malevolently, with the aim of inducing those most injured by the political process to acquiesce in it.

For me it is more valuable to think of law in a third way, as a culture—as a "culture of argument"—or, what is much the same thing, as a language, as a set of ways of making sense of things and acting in the world. So regarded, it is far more complex than the "law as rules" (or "law as rules plus principles") theory can begin to allow and far more substantial in its effects, actual and potential, than the "law as facade" theory would have it. The law is a set of ways of thinking and talking, which means, as Wittgenstein would tell us, a set of ways of acting in the world (and with each other) that has its own configurations and qualities, its own consequences. Its life is a life of art. This is, after all, how we learn law, not as a set of rules nor as the art of unmasking, as Swift might put it, but by participation in a culture, learning its language and how to live within it; and this is how we practice law too.

This culture is characterized, among other things, by its attention to the authoritative text—the rule, the case, the contract—which exists outside of and prior to the present dispute and is called upon by one side or the other, and sometimes both, to resolve it. The parties will argue about which texts count, about the nature of the facts upon which they bear, and about the meanings of both texts and facts. The law indeed works by argument, and does so under circumstances where agreement cannot be compelled by resort to logic or to data. It is thus a branch of rhetoric, conceived of both as the art of persuasion—necessary when intellectual or other compulsion is impossible—and as the art of deliberation, that is, as the art of thinking well about what ought to be done when reasonable people disagree. It can also be seen as a branch of rhetoric in a third sense, which can be called constitutive, for through its forms of language and of life the law constitutes a world of meaning and action: it creates a set of actors and speakers and offers them possibilities for meaningful speech and action that would not otherwise exist; in so doing it establishes and maintains a community, defined by its practices of language. At every stage the law is in this sense an ethical and political activity and should be understood and judged as such.

* * *

As its subtitle suggests, this book is meant as an essay in both cultural and legal criticism. Its aim is to work out a way of examining texts and languages (including legal ones) as forms of life, not merely as systems or instances of communication: to see discourses, that is, as ethical and political systems, as cultures in fact, and to see individual acts of expression as having meaning of these kinds as well. In doing this I build on the method of rhetorical and cultural criticism worked out in *When Words Lose Their Meaning*, to which this book can be taken as a sequel. Like that book, this one engages in the kind of philosophy that focuses on the meaning of our texts, languages, and practices; and it ultimately finds that meaning—as it finds justice and injustice—in the relations we establish with our languages and with each other, in our characters and our communities.

Part One—"Looking at our Languages"—is general in its scope. The aim of the opening chapter is to establish a theme for the whole by suggesting that what is called for in our life with language, and with each other, is an art of composition for which my name is "intellectual integration": the heart of it lies in making texts (and communities) in which place is given not merely to one, but to a variety of languages and voices. In the next chapter I pursue this theme by turning to the way of imagining language first referred to above, as a code or system of names, which I think obscures the variousness of our ways of being and acting in the world. I focus especially on our customary and easy talk about "concepts," which function as a set of names for intellectual entities that are assumed to exist apart from language. The idea is to work out a way of criticizing not only those familiar locutions but also the whole sense of language they imply, a sense of language that lies at the heart of most contemporary political and moral philosophy, and most academic talk more generally, and to contrast to it another sense of language, roughly sketched above, that is literary in character.

The following chapter turns to the discourse of economics, especially the form of neoclassical microeconomics associated with the "Chicago School" that has recently been so influential both in the law-and-economics movement and in the larger political arena. Here I focus upon the political and ethical implications of this discourse, the way it works as a culture, as well as upon the arts of language by which it might be more adequately controlled. But once again I wish this to serve as an example of something more general, namely certain mechanistic tendencies of thought that run very deep in our culture, forming many of our habitual ways of talking about the public world and the choices made within it. Against economics I pose the law, which—though it is now in danger of being swallowed up by economics—when properly understood seems to me to work on quite different principles to promise a different and far more admirable public culture.

Part Two, "Judicial Criticism," consists of a series of chapters on legal texts, specifically a set of Supreme Court opinions. The obvious reason for choosing judicial opinions is that they are central texts in our law. In them legal power is exercised before our eyes, through a decision that the writer seeks to explain and justify. The terms in which she does this become the terms in which other cases are thought about and argued out, not only in formal proceedings but in negotiations, planning sessions, and the like. They are the stuff of legal education, and from such opinions the culture of the law receives much, though not all, of its shape. My hope is to work out a way of talking about what we should admire and condemn in judicial opinions, which is also a way of asking more generally how we should criticize—how understand and judge—what judges do.

One way to criticize judicial opinions, natural for us, is to ask what we think of the result reached, that is, to approve or disapprove the outcome as we understand it in light of the relevant cases, statutes, constitutional provisions, and general understandings that govern it. "I would have decided it the same way (or differently)," one is saying. But we discover that we often find much to admire in an opinion with the result of which we disagree, and much to condemn in an opinion that "comes out" the way we would. To think of it in terms of the character of the judge, we can imagine ourselves having respect, admiration, and affection for a judge with whose votes we regularly differ, and contempt for one with whom we find ourselves often concurring.

What, then, are the excellences that we find ourselves admiring in judicial opinions with whose result we disagree, and perhaps strongly so? What do we condemn in an opinion that comes to the disposition of the case that we think proper but which we nonetheless regard as bad work? Our language for talking about these matters is extremely reduced and conclusory—bad opinions omit "relevant considerations," or "weigh them wrongly"; good opinions "marshal arguments impressively," and so forth. My hope is to work out a way of talking that is more responsive to what is actually at stake in our judgments of judicial excellence and the reverse. This is a question of some urgency, for it has become common for lawyers to feel that over the past twenty years there has been a serious deterioration in the quality of the work of the courts, especially the Supreme Court, yet common also to feel that our ways of defining both that deterioration and the excellence by which it can be seen as such are inadequate.

The cases I discuss are chosen from quite a wide historical range, but they all deal with one of two questions: the meaning of the language of the fourth amendment (which prohibits the government from engaging in "unreasonable searches and seizures") and the treatment of racial minorities. Both bodies of law deal with the disempowered and my hope is that this commonality of interest and concern will make more fruitful the comparison of one opinion with another.

I read these opinions as cultural and rhetorical texts, that is, with an eye to the kind of political and ethical community they build with their readers and to the contribution they make to the discourse of the law. My idea is not to make an exhaustive study of the judicial opinion in all of its manifestations, nor to analyze the whole field of law built upon the fourth amendment, but to read a series of opinions in such a way as to reflect, at least in outline and by performance, a way of thinking about judicial opinions more generally that can lead us to a fuller and more adequate criticism of this form of language and of life.

In all of this I find myself turning again and again to translation as a way of thinking about what we do with language in the law and elsewhere. Part Three, "The Activity of Translation," develops that thought at length. There is a sense, I believe, in which translation is the central practice of linguistic and social life; reflection upon its nature—its impossibilities and the arts they call for, the attitudes it engenders and requires—can lead to a useful way of thinking and talking about excellence in law, and excellence beyond it as well.

While there are some situations where translation seems as a practical matter to work well enough, there are others where it is in any full sense plainly impossible: think of translating a poem, for example, or a political speech, or an expression of love, from one language to another. In such cases the very activity of translation brings us again and again to face that which is particular or unique to the language and its context, to the speaker himself, and therefore cannot be translated, cannot be "set over," into another. Even to attempt to translate is to experience necessary but instructive failure. In this sense translation forces us to respect the other—the other language, the other person, the other text—yet it nonetheless requires us to assert ourselves, and our own languages, in relation to it. It requires us to create a frame that includes both self and other, both familiar and strange; in this I believe it can serve as a model for all ethical and political thought.

Acknowledgments

My thanks for their help in thinking about the questions raised here, and the texts that present them, go to many colleagues and friends, especially Milner Ball, Thomas Eisele, L. H. LaRue, Lawrence Lessig, Daniel Lucich, Donald McCloskey, Alfred McDonnell, Richard Pildes, Richard Posner, Frederick Schauer, James Scarboro, Cass Sunstein, Christina Whitman, and Mary White. Thanks beyond even these go to Wayne Booth, Kenneth Dewoskin, and Joseph Vining, for teaching me so much, respectively, about ethical criticism, about translation, and about the nature of authority, and to A. L. Becker, whose understanding of language and translation has influenced this book in the deepest ways.

The quotation from Wittgenstein with which this book begins is to be found in *Philosophical Investigations*, paragraph 19.

Earlier versions of several of the chapters have been published separately, in a somewhat different form, in the following journals, which have granted permission to reprint here. Chapter 1 appeared in 82 *Northwestern Law Review* 1 (1987); chapter 2 in 96 *Yale Law Journal*

1960 (1987) (Reprinted by permission of The Yale Law Journal Company and Fred B. Rothman & Company); chapter 3 in 54 *Tennessee Law Review* 161 (1987) (reprinted by permission of the Tennessee Law Review Association, Inc.); parts of chapters 4 and 5 in 20 *Georgia Law Review* 837 (1986); chapter 6 in 47 *Maryland Law Review* 239 (1987); chapter 8 in 1974 *The Supreme Court Review* 164 (© 1975 by The University of Chicago); and chapter 9 in 81 *Michigan Law Review* 1273 (1983). I am grateful for the permission to reprint. In addition scattered passages have appeared in the following pieces: "A Response to 'The Rhetoric of Powell's *Bakke*,'" 38 *Washington and the Law Review* 73 (1981); "Is Cultural Criticism Possible?" 84 *Michigan Law Review* 1373 (1986); and "What Can a Lawyer Learn from Literature?" 102 *Harvard Law Review* 2014 (1989). This is not, however, intended to be a collection of essays but a book with a shape of its own.

While I hope what I say will be of interest to specialists in law, linguistics, and philosophy, I have tried in this book to speak mainly to the general reader, and for that reason have kept the apparatus of scholarship to a minimum. For similar reasons I have, without particular indication, omitted footnotes in quotations taken from judicial opinions.

PART

1

LOOKING AT OUR LANGUAGES

1

Intellectual Integration

It is an aspect of modern life frequently remarked that we divide up our experience into separate compartments or categories, each of which has its own kind of validity, its own language, but which do not readily fit together into a meaningful whole. We do this internally, drawing a line say between reason and emotion, or mind and body, and externally too, as we separate home from work, or art from business, or one social or ethnic group from another. In our intellectual lives in particular we often proceed in this way, by isolating a single phenomenon or issue for observation and analysis. This is how science typically works, for example, and to think of the institution of the university as a whole, it seems to be built on the principle that each academic discipline has its separate methods, its separate truths, with very little sense that they fit together into an organic whole. When we look at the larger culture we inhabit it is very hard to see how it could be thought of as anything but fragmented.

In this chapter I want to think in a general way about the intellectual and social practices by which the divisions I speak of might be addressed. I ask what it might mean to integrate—to put together in a complex whole—aspects of our culture, or of the world, that seem to us disparate or unconnected; and what it might mean in so doing to integrate—to bring together in interactive life—aspects of our own minds and beings that we normally separate or divide from each other. I want to think of integration, that is—and its opposite, disintegration—as taking place on two planes of existence at once, the cultural and the individual. For what is at stake for us in the fragmentation of our culture is the fragmentation of our own minds and lives; and the integrative processes by which we resist this fragmentation on one plane of experience, as we try to bring things together to make new wholes, are simultaneously at work on the other as well.

To speak of "integration" may be a bit misleading, for this term may be thought to imply an ideal of perfect unity or coherence, a reduction to a dominant scheme or a single language in which every part has its proper and defined place. But I mean to use the term rather differently, to include a tolerance for, indeed a clarification of, diversity and difference. To put what I shall say in summary and somewhat Delphic form, what I mean by integration is a kind of composition, and that in a literal, and literary, sense: a putting together of two things to make out of them a third, a new whole, with a meaning of its own. In this process the elements combined do not lose their identities but retain them, often in clarified form; yet each comes to mean something different as well, when it is seen in relation to the other. In this sense each element is transformed, as it becomes part of something else, an entity existing at a new level of complexity. At the same time we ourselves are transformed as well, both as makers of the new object in the world and as those who engage with it.

I shall begin to give content to these generalities by talking about poetry, and about one short poem in particular; but by the end I shall have reached far beyond it to what we normally think of as quite different kinds of subjects, including law, the university, and the nature of our minds.

Poetry

I start with poetry because it seems largely built on the principle I have articulated, that we put two things together in such a way as to make a third—different from the others yet respectful of them—with a meaning of its own.

Think for example of the sounds of poetry. As Robert Frost said, the poem, or at least the English poem, is in large measure built upon the music that can be made by the tension between two different ways of organizing sound: the sound of the meter and rhythm, in English most naturally that of the iambic line, and the sound of the sentence as it would be spoken in living speech. In the poem these two principles of order begin and end together, but between those points they run in harmony and contrast to create a kind of music, almost as two melodic lines might do. The effect is to create something new in the space between mere musical prose on the one hand and mere sing-song versification on the other. Consider how this works in the following well-known and very short poem by Robert Frost:*

A Dust of Snow

The way a crow
Shook down on me

*Copyright 1923, by Holt, Rinehart and Winston, Inc. and renewed 1951 by Robert Frost. Reprinted from *The Poetry of Robert Frost*, edited by Edward Connery Lathem, by permission of Henry Holt and Company, Inc.

The dust of snow
From a hemlock tree

Has given my heart
A change of mood
And saved some part
Of a day I had rued.

If you read this poem aloud you will feel the tension between the force of its meter and rhyme, both of which work on the principle of recurring form and variations, and that of the long sentence of which it is made, which has its own shape, turning after "mood" to surprise us with what the iambic meter has continually promised us, a momentary uplift.

These two principles of order provide different energies for continuation and cessation as well. Thus at one point in the poem the syntactic sentence comes to an end—at "mood"—and we feel the necessity, or probability, of stopping there; but we also know that we can't, for we are only halfway through the rhyme scheme in the stanza, and this knowledge carries us forward two more lines. Or it works the other way: we come to the end of the first stanza, which is a kind of closure; but the sentence has not ended, and the force of our syntactical expectations carries us forward into the second. When the two systems close together at the end, they do so with reinforced finality. They become one not through merger, a loss of identity, but through interaction. Each is in fact heard with new distinctness as it is poised against the other, the sentence sound against the meter and rhyme, the meter and rhyme against the sentence sound. The reader holds both in his head at once.

To shift now from the sound of a poem to its images, think of what this poem asks us to imagine. The black crow is given visual significance by its juxtaposition with the white snow and the green hemlock (all the colors unstated but necessary, known to us); but they have necessarily symbolic significances too, for the crow and snow become images of death, at least when they are combined with hemlock, which necessarily reminds us of the poisonous root of which Socrates drank the liquor. The images thus fall simultaneously into two planes of meaning—the natural and the symbolic. In this poem they do not merge, in part because one kind of hemlock really is different from the other—you can make a perfectly drinkable hemlock tea from the tree in the poem—but remain in tension to create something new in the space between them. There are thus two systems of meaning simultaneously at work here: the image of the walk in the woods, with its minor catastrophe suddenly seen as a grace note, and the far more foreboding system of symbolism—death and redemption—which hints at Grace of a different kind altogether. Part of the art of the poem is keeping a distance between the two planes of meaning, so that both are held in the mind at once, each playing against the other to make a third.

The word "dust" from this point of view is lovely: it specifies the visual image with great exactness, as we imagine the snow so dry and crystalline that it bursts like shining dust in the air, while in the other plane of meaning it reinforces the images of death, for we all know that dust we are and unto dust we shall return.

With respect to the image-life of this poetry, then, just as with respect to its sounds, there are two principles of life and order, brought together not to merge but to interact, to make a third thing out of the life between them. There is a similar opposition in another respect as well, for this poem creates a tension between the sense that it represents an experience that is external to it—the fall of snow—and the sense that it is itself a new experience, in language, with a meaning of its own. Just as the viewer of a painting sees it now as a picture of the world, now as a composition in paint, the audience of the poem hears it now as an account of the world, now as a composition in words.

Much the same is true in the dimension of time, for the poem can be seen either as taking place in time or as an atemporal structure. That is, it can be thought of as it appears on the page, as a pattern that exists in two dimensions, spatially, to be described and explained by drawing connecting and contrasting arrows. Or it can be seen as taking place in time, as read aloud say, with a beginning and an ending, a moving from one place to another in a process of change.

This sort of transformation across time is in fact essential to the life of a poem. Think, for example, of the way a poem works on the experience that precedes it, turning autumn, say, into Keats's poem "To Autumn," just as apples are turned into cider, or the dust of snow down the neck into "A Dust of Snow," and just as the dust of snow turned the day from one thing into another. The poem converts what lies outside of it into its terms, and does this not only with such ordinary-world experiences as these, but with prior texts as well, such as those that give meaning to "hemlock" and "dust." And the poem itself is self-transformative, autopoetic, making itself—or being made by the poet and the reader together—out of its own origins, as a human life is made, line by line. For from its first utterance it establishes expectations that the rest of it will confirm or upset or modify, at each stage making new beginnings, giving rise to new expectations of its own.* It is only when we read the poem as taking place in time that we can experience the "surprise" that Frost thought essential to the poetic experience—here the surprise of discovering that the dust of snow did not ruin the day but saved it, saved it from an earlier "ruing."

On the other hand, no one fully reads a poem the first time through and our successive readings work to create a sense of the whole poem existing outside of time and space, in an ideal realm. These rereadings result in a kind of increasing appropriation of the verbal artifact to our own consciousness. Ultimately the "temporal" sense we have of the poem is not an accurate representation of any one actual reading, but a constructed reading, an ideal reading taking place in ideal time as well as ideal space, a world in which there is in fact no transformation, for the whole poem exists simultaneously. The poem comes to have both existences at once in our minds, the temporal and transformative poised against the atemporal and schematic, and much of its life is the play between them.

To speak even more generally for a moment, in each of the dimensions I have mentioned—of sound, image, and time—there is a tension between order and disorder: between the too regular, and thus singsong and dead, and the wholly irregular or chaotic; between

---

*Recall, for example, Keats's great poem "To Autumn," mentioned above. It begins with hyperfruition:

> Season of mists and mellow fruitfulness,
> Close bosom friend of the maturing sun

and ends in crispness and clarity. The art of the poem, or much of it, lies in how we get from one place to the other: the initial sense of excessive, distasteful fecundity, of deceit or conspiracy; the long rallentando of the second stanza, which delays the change of things and delays it further, making us impatient and reducing the world to the "last oozings" of the cider press; and the great pleasure afforded by the shift at the end to evening, to late autumn, and to sunset:

> Hedge-crickets sing; and now with treble soft
> The redbreast whistles from a garden croft;
> And gathering swallows twitter in the skies.

Similarly here, in Frost's poem, there is a transformation of the original trite event, the irritating fall of snow from the tree, into a moment laden with gentle ominousness, and then, by an act of poetic grace, into an emblem of grace itself, for it "saves" what we have every reason to "rue," or repent.

In all of this the poem is made of the same stuff as human life, the life of its maker and its audience: it takes place in time, it is autopoetic, made out of its own beginnings, and it converts what is outside of itself into internally determined, though always tentative, forms. As a form, then, the poem is inherently about the way we grow and live, about the processes of integration and transformation it exemplifies.

affirmation and denial; between what can be said and what is unsayable; and in all of this the poem puts together two things, two possibilities, in such a way as to create a life between them.

The poem thus brings to life, and integrates, several dimensions of speech at once: it places them in relation across space and time, and in so doing creates something new of its own. It cannot be reduced to a statement of this or that theory or message, to optimism or pessimism, or any other paraphrase. It is in fact a kind of speech with which "stating views" or "having a theory" or "delivering a message" is inconsistent; the very form of the poem is critical of the assumptions on which such speech rests.

Academic and Professional Discourse

What happens when we turn from the dense and concentrated form of speech we call the poem to the forms of speech we ourselves employ, especially in our academic and professional lives—as lawyers, scholars, or critics—but also in the rest of life as well; when we look to the texts, to the modes of discourse, we inhabit and create? What voices do we hear, and find ourselves using? What kinds of conversations make up our world? Are the texts we make and read integrative and transforming, as a poem is, and if not, could they be?

Voice

Here and in what follows I shall focus especially on the discourses that constitute the academic world, not to make fun of them—that is my world, too—but because they present certain important issues with great clarity and reasonable familiarity. What is true of the university is true, in a somewhat different way, of our larger culture as well.

Imagine, for example, that you are a professor in your office, littered with books and journal articles. With what hopes and expectations do you imagine that you turn to them? If you are at all like me you do so not with eager anticipation but with a feeling of guilty dread and with an expectation of frustration. For we live in a world of specialized texts and discourses, marked by a kind of thinness, a want of life and force and meaning. All too often we simply skim-read a text, and all too often we do so with the sense that nothing is lost.

But what do you think it says about the academic world, about the university, if this is true, if the literature we read and write, the literature that defines this part of our lives, can be skim-read with so little loss? What kind of intellectual or other community is defined by such a voice, directed to such an audience? If it can comfortably be skim-read, the text has a quality that is the opposite of poetic density, a kind of extraordinary dilutedness.

Sometimes, of course, a voice arrests us, we slow down, perhaps we move our chair and settle into a different position, or take something home and think it through, paying a different kind of attention to it altogether. But how rare that is.

Do I exaggerate? Perhaps I do, but as a way of checking that, let me ask you to suppose that you take a recent issue of the leading journal in an academic field—or for that matter a professional publication, like a state bar journal, or a general publication like the *New York Review of Books*—and read it through from cover to cover, then ask what minds, what discourse, what conversation, what intellectual community you could construct on the basis of that evidence, if it were all that you had. What would these imagined speakers be like, as minds and as people? What responses do they invite from you, what relationship do they seek to establish with you?

A wit once said of the highly oppositional and dramatic prose of Macaulay that it is "impossible to tell the truth in such a style." We can borrow that remark and ask: What truths can be said in the styles and voices and forms that characterize the academic world? Certainly anyone who has ever worked on a law journal must have wondered what could possibly be said in the form we call the "law review article," in the language and voice of that genre—anything, that is, in which any person could have any real interest. Of how many law review articles can one say, here is a mind really speaking to other minds?

I pick on the law, with which I am perhaps most familiar, but I think much the same could be said of professional discourse of other kinds. Part of the problem is what I have called thinness—so little life; but part of it is too much life of a certain kind, an insistent assertiveness, as if against something, against some other person who is denying what is said. This is how things are, we are told; a deafening note of demand. Yet am I insisting otherwise, or are you? Why then are we spoken to, why do we speak, in such a way? The academic text that is written against the views of others naturally seeks to meet every imagined objection in the language in which it might be made; but in doing this it too often loses its control over its own shape, its own language.

As I imagine the books and journals piled up in my office, then,

I want to ask: Where is writing that is about something that is actually important to the mind that composed it, regarded not as a professional agent seeking a new relationship with a professional community but as a mind, trying to make sense of life and of the texts that make it up? Where is the voice that compels attention by its authenticity, its urgency, its presence, and invites a similar response from another? Where is the voice that seeks to speak truth from the heart? Or—to think of this for the moment from the institutional or communal point of view—where is a conversation among a plurality of such voices? The university should be the place par excellence for disinterested and passionate talk of such a kind, but is it in fact? What kind of talk, among what kinds of voices, defines our profession, our university, our larger culture?

So far I have been speaking as if the problem were out there, in texts made by others, in them not us, in our reading not our writing, but of course this is not true. Those of us engaged in writing of this kind find that the worst and most painful consequences of the character of our discourse are those we suffer when we ourselves try to write, when we find that we are captured by voices, audiences, and languages that seem impossibly sterile or empty; diluted; defensive; full of static; in a deep sense unreal. If you do this kind of work, think of your own composing life and how often you feel, as you listen to your speech, that you are droning on and on, in a tone of insistent demand, or that your words are like broken chiclets in the mouth, impeding your talk to the point of inanity. Or how often you turn in dismay to the pages you have written, hearing in them the voice of Anyprof and wondering whether it is ever possible to say anything well. Our forms of speech, our very voices, seem to bleed what we have to say of half its life.

Sometimes of course we have the experience of feeling that our language is adequate to our situation, that the forms of speech available to us, or inventable by us, do what we want them to do, that we have voices we can live with. Many of these occasions are small ones: an exchange of familiar pleasantries on the sidewalk, when we get the tone just right; the sense that a conversation in class has suddenly taken off with a new life and in a new direction, a sense that may last only two or three minutes, and seldom lasts very much longer; or perhaps in writing a paper or giving a talk, when we strike a sentence that seems to us fixed and right, a sentence we can lean on. But this is not common anywhere in life and it happens I think more often in ordinary conversation and in classroom talk than it does in our professional discourse.

Why should this be?

Audience

Many of the properties of professional discourse—perhaps all of them—arise from our sense of the specialized audience we address and of ourselves with respect to that audience. In demonstrating our qualifications to speak, in striking one tone rather than another, in defining the question we address, and in assembling the materials we bring to bear upon it—in all of this we seek to meet, or perhaps confound, our audience's expectations. Professional articles and books are affirmations of the specialized discourse in which they are written, and beyond that of the specialized community to which they are addressed. This is in fact how fields or disciplines are constructed and maintained.

And of course this is not altogether a bad thing. In writing about Thucydides, say, it is important to be able to write on the assumption that your readers know Greek, and are familiar with the text, and that they can find the references that you make; similarly, in writing about law, it is important to be able to speak to those who can tolerate legal citations or the use of a term of art like "jurisdiction." Knowledge can advance only to the degree that it can be presumed in one's audience.

But while the existence of specialized audiences might explain the existence of specialized discourses, it does not explain the deadness or sterility of those discourses, nor does it tell us how to give them life.

I cannot wholly explain this phenomenon either, but I do think that there is something about our conception of professionalism—it may have to do with the use of a false image of science as a model of thought and discourse—that leads us to speak and write in ways that are false to the character of our own intellectual lives. I believe that we actually lead far richer and more complex lives, including professional lives, than one who knew us only through our professional writing would ever guess. We read more widely than our citations reflect; we think more variously than our arguments suggest; we pursue questions in ways that are more fully our own than we reveal; and our relations with prior texts are more rich and interesting than our bibliographic notes, in their often misleading claims to represent what we have read and thought about, are likely to suggest. (Suppose our references were not to the literature we think we are supposed to have read but to the texts we actually have read, and thought about, and wish to respond to: How different would our writing be, in voice and sense of audience, in shape and tone?) We have intellectual lives of mystery and puzzle, excitement and meaning, that are systematically bleached or obliterated by the formal styles of professional discourse. Yet all too often we write in ways that confirm and perpetuate that discourse, granting it unjustified authority over us and our minds.

The relative deadness of much of our professional discourse is I believe a function of what I earlier called the double segmentation of the culture and of the mind. Separate communities of discourse are established, more or less along subject-matter lines, which seem to have nothing to say to one another, or no way of saying it; in this sense the culture is divided. And since none of us is wholly defined by his or her professional discourse—we are all of us in this sense multi-lingual—there is a kind of corresponding internal segmentation, a division of our own experience, of our minds. Boundaries are thus drawn both among various professional or public forms of speech—horizontally, if you will—and vertically too, between our professional speech and the ways we talk in the rest of life.

Those of us engaged in this sort of work should not stop writing to each other, and ought not stop writing in ways that are more accessible to some audiences than to others. And no one would recommend the purely personal voice, which would be as empty in its way as the purely professional one is. But it seems to me right to ask: Can we find ways to talk that will reflect more fully what we actually know to be true of ourselves and our minds, of our languages and our cultures? Can we find or create voices that are more fully our own, speaking to audiences more fully recognized as the minds and people they actually are?

Or, to put it in the terms with which I began: What might it mean to integrate, to put together in a complex whole, aspects of our culture, or of the world, that seem to us disparate or unconnected, and in so doing to integrate, to bring together in interactive life, aspects of our own minds and beings that we normally separate or divide from each other? What kind of lives could we make for ourselves, what kind of communities with others?

Crossing Disciplines

One common and sensible response, especially in the university, is to think in terms of our segmented intellectual culture, the split-up academic world, and to try to address it through interdisciplinary work. This is particularly common for the law professor, who turns to one discipline or another in the hope that it will offer him what he feels his own to lack. But how are we to do this? How are we to imagine, how talk about, what we are trying to do?

"Findings" and "Methods"

When we look to the languages that are normally used to describe this kind of work, we find that they are full of difficulty. Take, for example, the common talk of "breaking down boundaries" or "establishing connections" between "fields"—as though there were entities out there in the world, perhaps like a patchwork quilt of agricultural fields seen from an airplane, among which connections—perhaps in the forms of wires, or pipes, or ditches—could be established. But what is this territorial metaphor of the "field" or "boundary?" And what can be meant by "connections?" It is all most unclear.*

A somewhat more developed language for conceiving of, and talking about, cross-disciplinary work is that of "findings." The idea is that the "findings" of one field should be made available to others, as though history or economics or philosophy, say, should pass a plate with the truth on it over to the law, which would then in some unspecified way put it to use (or vice versa). But this is of course far more difficult than such locutions suggest. In the first place, the image of the world created by one of these disciplines is not monolithic but full of variety and tension, not so much a set of established propositions as a set of questions and methods. The results of such work are normally not "findings" in any simple sense but tentative conclusions in a series of tentative conclusions, elaborated topics for argument and discussion of a certain kind. A discipline can for many purposes in fact be defined as a community of discourse organized around its disagreements, its ways of disagreeing, as well as its agreements. And even where a field does establish a particular view of the world, it does so only from its own point of view—its purposes and aims, its prior questions, and senses of method—and this makes the simple translation of findings impossible.

Consider, for example, the attempt of the law to rely upon the "findings" of psychiatrists as to the "sanity" of criminal defendants. While it is not true that psychiatrists have nothing useful to say to the law—not at all—it is true that their "findings" are not very usable by the law, for the reason that the two systems of discourse, and the two communities, operate on such radically opposed premises. Psychiatry thinks in terms of treatment and diagnosis and

---

*Perhaps the "field" is to be thought of as a force field, like those created by a magnet that forces a chaotic assembly of iron filings into an array between its poles. This image does catch some of the aggressiveness of modern academic life and its division of the world into those who act and those who are acted upon. But what relations could exist between such "fields," other than dominance, subjection, or indifference?

health; the law thinks in terms of guilt, blame, and punishment. There is a radical incompatibility between the discourses, between the conceptions of the human subject and the speaker's relation to him or her, that makes any transfer of "findings" problematic, to say the least, and renders the conversations in which that is attempted—recorded for us in courtroom transcripts—confused in ways that are at once highly comic and deeply tragic.[1] Or suppose it were established to the satisfaction of the psychological community that one group of human beings, defined by certain inheritable characteristics, scored less well on certain tests of mental facility than did another such group. The psychologists could, I suppose, tell us very little, as psychologists, about the value of the particular set of mental faculties that they tested for and nothing at all about the social consequences that might properly be thought to flow from this fact.

These are of course rather extreme examples but I think they establish a truth that applies in other cases as well. Think for example of the use of expert economic testimony, say on market share or the practical consequences of a particular administrative decision, where the law explicitly invokes economic criteria. Even there, as every practicing lawyer knows, the law does not, and cannot, simply sit back and let the experts tell us their "findings." The lawyer who participates in such a case must train herself in the presuppositions of the discipline, the hypotheses upon which the whole edifice rests, the kinds of tentativeness necessarily built into the conclusions, and so on. To prepare a witness of her own or to cross-examine the witness of another, the lawyer must in fact become something of an expert herself, in arguing to judge, jury, or hearing examiner, and she must be prepared to educate her audience into expertise as well. As lawyers we cannot simply accept the conclusions of others; we must make them our own, and to do that we must move out of the legal culture and into the other one. In doing this we are not picking up "findings," but learning a language; findings can in fact exist only in the terms of one language or another, not in a world beyond language.

Perhaps more advanced than the language of "findings" is that of "intellectual method." The idea here is that one learns from another discipline not its "findings" but its methodology, which can be brought like a machine to problems in one's own field, upon which it will go to work without itself undergoing any transformation. Thinking again of the law, this is the way that some people talk about the use of literary or critical theory, or philosophical hermeneutics; as though one simply learned an interpretive or critical technique and then turned to the law and put it to work. But the concerns of the literary critic are normally quite different from those of the lawyer. Any meaningful comparisons must take place by a process of translation that is based upon rather full knowledge of the practices that define each community, and this at the level of particularity and not merely that of theory or technique. Similarly, a certain branch of economics has been proposed to the law as the machine that will solve all its problems, this time with the power relations reversed: instead of the methodology being subordinated to the preexisting concerns of the lawyer, the claim is made that the method of economics can simply supplant law. But in either case the idea is of a discipline as a technology: you learn to run the machine of literary or economic analysis, then you wheel it up to the new object, called the law, and it goes to work, spitting out results as a log chipper spits out wood chips.

These are at bottom images of interdisciplinary work either as territorial spread or conquest, in which one "field"—or its inhabitants—simply absorbs or takes over another, or as a kind of mechanics. All of them assume that when you put two things together only one is in any meaningful way changed.

Communities of Discourse

This kind of talk is rooted, I think, in our false contemporary metalanguages about knowing, learning, and talking. Take, for example, our standard language of "communication": the idea is that I have in my head some idea or perception or fact which I wish to get across to you; if I am successful, you will wind up at the end of the process with exactly what I had in my mind, or at least a reasonable facsimile thereof. This is a model not only of expression but of knowledge, and the acquisition and institutionalization of knowledge too. I acquire bits of knowledge from experience and from others, which I then sort into various categories, where they are then available for communication. It is the organization of such bits of knowledge that makes up what we call a "field"; and the university is nothing but an assemblage of such fields.

This model is not only false to our experience of language and learning and talking, it creates an incoherent image of our collective intellectual life. If the university is to have a character of its own as a social and intellectual world, there must be some way of organizing these fields into a whole. But what could it be? This is the point at which we find it natural to speak about "connections," "bridges," the transmission of "findings" from one field to another, and the application of the "technology" of one discipline to the problems of another. It is all a bureaucratic, objectifying, and nominalizing vision of the world, operating on a cluster of related metaphors that ultimately imagine organization in terms of territories or machines and that are thus inadequate to real intellectual lives and communities.

What is most obviously missing from this mechanistic picture of the world is the individual human mind. In this image of life, people are inquirers and processors of knowledge, which they organize into structures. But how is this done? What is the life of the inquiring and investigating mind? What would happen if we began to think of what we do as if each of us were an independent mind, defining and pursuing questions of its own, motivated by interest and curiosity, by a sense of importance or urgency? This is to suggest that we think experientially, or phenomenologically, about human beings as human beings rather than as parts of machines. This leads us to a different conception of the intellectual community and of the conversational process by which it is maintained. For none of us acts alone: our minds, our questions, our sense of what needs to be said, of what can be said, are all shaped by interaction with others; and our aims are not statable in terms of attainable "goals" but rather in the kind of inquiring and conversing life we hope to make possible for ourselves and for others.

Suppose, then, we were to think of our minds as minds, and our selves as engaged with the perpetual questions: How to think? What to think? What to say and how to say it? What are "fields" to such a mind, and how real are the "boundaries" between them? How are we to talk about, how imagine, what we are doing when we talk to each other across these lines? If you think of "fields" not as terrains or machines, but as communities of discourse, groups of people defined by their willingness to talk in certain ways, the question becomes: What kind of relationships can we establish among these various ways of talking, and the communities they define? In so doing, what larger community can we create?

Law and Literature

As a way of thinking about the possibilities suggested by that question I would like now to turn to the relations between two "fields" I know something about, law and literature. I want to put aside both the "findings" conception of interdisciplinary work—which here mainly consists of using literature to establish truths about the inhumanity of law—and the "technology" conception—which here mainly consists of using the terminology developed in the current critical theory debates to carry on preexisting arguments about the way legal texts should be interpreted. Instead I want to ask how they might be put together in such a way as to change both and make a third.

In doing this I shall speak about what I have attempted to do in my own work, in part to give the reader some idea of the place I start from, in part simply because this represents one mind's effort to put two things together in a certain way.

When I went to law school from doing graduate work in English literature, I was startled to discover how similar the two enterprises were, and similar in ways that seemed generally unremarked. In particular, the habits of close reading and textual analysis developed in literary studies seemed very close to those required by legal training. This circumstance led me to think about the law as a kind of literature and my first book, *The Legal Imagination*, was aimed at working that idea out.

My initial question was: What happens if we look at the literature of the law as if it really were literature, as though it defined speakers and a world, a set of possibilities for expression and community? (Edmund Wilson in a famous essay gave a reading of Emily Post's *Etiquette* as though it were a novel:[2] What happens if you read the law as if it were a novel?) The context in which I asked this question was a course for law students, and there it is easy to make the answer appear disastrous. The law can be made to seem a dead, bureaucratic, overconceptualized, unfeeling language if any is, and the question can be brought home to the future lawyer with some vividness: What does it mean to devote your life to speaking such a language, in such forms, and with such voices?

The point of this comparison of law with literature, despite what I have just said, was actually not to maintain that literature is superior to law but to help the reader see that law can be regarded as a literary activity, and that so regarded it affords the composing mind, and the community more generally, a range of remarkable opportunities not otherwise available. The law not only has its limits as a discourse but, perhaps more surprisingly, affords resources that ordinary life lacks. My aim in this book was not to "connect fields," then, but to try to transform our sense of law by putting it together with something else: to try to see it as a compositional art, as a set of activities by which minds use language to make meaning and establish relations with others. This is to suggest the possibility of integration at the individual level too, for from this point of view an essential part of the task of the lawyer, and of the judge, can be said to be the establishment of a voice of his or her own in the law, a way of speaking that is both professionally excellent and individually authentic—indeed I think it cannot be the former unless it is the latter.

But how about literature? Is our sense of it transformed too when we put it together with the law? This is the question that started me on my next work, *When Words Lose Their Meaning*. I began with the idea of reversing the flow of *The Legal Imagination* and reading "literature" as if it in some very rough way were law. The first step in such an analysis, I thought, was to identify in the "nonlegal" work before us the cultural inheritance that is analogous to what we call the law: that set of resources of speech and thought that is in function like the body of cases, statutes, and other precedents that define a lawyer's situation by offering him certain occasions upon which, and certain materials with which, to speak (and by denying him others). In a sense, that is, we are all like lawyers, for we all act out of a particular linguistic inheritance and in a particular rhetorical situation, both of which can be subject to critical analysis and judgment; or, to put it another way, the situation of the lawyer in this respect is an exaggerated and clarified version of the situation of every speaker. This way of reading thus focuses attention first on the nature of the language a particular writer or speaker has inherited—the language that gives her some things to say and do with words and denies her others, the language that constitutes her natural and social world and gives it meaning. (This is a species of cultural and rhetorical criticism.)

But none of us simply replicates the materials of our culture in our speech or in our conduct. We act upon and modify our languages all the time. Once again the lawyer represents, in a clarified and somewhat exaggerated form, a universal human condition, for while he uses his materials he is always arguing for their reformation. In general terms what this means is that we can ask not only what a speaker's inheritance is, but how, by what art, and to what end, he acts upon it, giving new life to its central terms or reducing them to cliche, enriching or impoverishing it. (This is a species of aesthetic and literary criticism.)

The third focus of attention suggested by "reading as a lawyer" is upon the set of relations we enact in our speech, relations both with our audience and with those other people we talk about. This is again a feature of speech that is exaggeratedly clear for lawyers, who are required to address each other (and judges) in certain highly stylized ways, and clear too for the law more generally, which establishes the fundamental relations among the actors in our polity. But something like it is true whenever one person speaks to another. We all know what it is like to be patronized, flattered, manipulated, or, on the other hand, spoken to directly and honestly—in a way that recognizes our autonomy and freedom—and we know that the relations we create in our talking can be analyzed and judged. (This is a species of ethical and political criticism.)

I see the lawyer, then, as engaged in a set of linguistic and literary activities, just as the poet or novelist is, just as the priest, the politician, and ordinary citizen are. Likewise, I see the poet or novelist, the politician, priest, and ordinary citizen, as engaged in certain forms of political and ethical discourse—of "legal" discourse—just as the lawyer is, and on all sides whether they know it or not. The aim of the comparison is to see each in a new way by placing it next to the other, and in so doing to make something new that comprises both. This kind of work on law and literature is not the transfer of "findings" from field to field, nor the transportation of "method" (thought of as a kind of intellectual machine that can go to work on new subjects without itself being modified), but a bringing to consciousness of the nature of our own intellectual and linguistic practices, both literary and legal, with the hope of holding them in the mind at once in such a way as to change our sense of both.

The kind of comparison I mean need not be made with literature and need not be as general as this. To think of it in curricular terms, for example, and to continue to think of the law, I could imagine a course not in law *and* history, or sociology or economics or anthropology, but law *as* each of those things. Our initial question would be: How is this writer of a legal text functioning, whether he knows it or not, as an historian, sociologist, or anthropologist? And of course the direction could be reversed, and we could ask: How is this anthropologist or historian, say, functioning as a lawyer? In both cases the hope would be to bring together in the mind at once two systems of discourse, two sets of questions and methods and motives, with the aim of making new texts that would incorporate both, not to merge them into one but to recognize their differences as we sought their similarities. We would hope, for example, to reflect in what we said the ways in which the lawyer is a practical and moral actor in the world, whose speech is a speech of power; and the ways in which, on the other hand, the lack of power of this kind creates a difficulty and an opportunity for every poet, every critic. We would put ourselves, in short, in the position of translators, those who know that what is said in one language cannot simply be set over into another without loss or gain and who therefore conceive of their task as the creation of new compositions that will establish mutually respectful relations between them.

To do this we need to find ways to hold in our minds at once different vocabularies, styles, and tones—different discourse systems—not to merge them but to integrate them, that is, to place them in balance with each other, in order to make, in our talk and our teaching and in our writing, texts that have some of the life of poetry.

* * *

I have been writing in this chapter largely out of a sense of dissatisfaction: dissatisfaction with the languages I see available for my use (and with my own relation to them), with the forms of discourse I find myself using, with the conversations I engage in and observe, with the voices I hear myself and others using, with the texts and communities we make. This dissatisfaction is especially acute with specialized professional or academic discourses, but it is not confined to those. More generally it is with a bureaucratized culture, one that reduces human actors to very narrow roles, human speakers to very thin speech. For me the best response is what I have called integration and transformation, the attempt to put together parts of our culture, and corresponding parts of ourselves, in ways that will make new languages, voices, and forms of discourse possible. Part of this can take the form of "interdisciplinary work," but only of a certain kind; and the crossing of disciplinary boundaries is not essential to what I am talking about.

What in my view *is* essential is that we should insist upon seeing the world as made up of people talking to each other. For me the fundamental image of life is not that of economic production and exchange, nor that of knowledge acquisition and transfer, but that of composition: people seeking to make texts that will establish meanings and relations with others. We should conceive of the relevant world as a world of people speaking to each other across their discourses, out of their languages, out of their communities of knowledge and expertise, and speaking as people seeking to be whole. We should try to write that way ourselves.

The direction of thought I recommend is thus in large part introspective: we should direct our attention towards the practices we engage in, with the object of making them more self-conscious, and therefore amenable to more complete understanding and modification. The object of this kind of work can be defined partly in terms of voice: Can we find a wider range of voices, or ways of being, in our writing and offer a wider range to others? Can we be, for example, less assertive, or less continually assertive, more open and tentative and suggestive in our style? Can we find voices of our own that will reflect more fully what we know to be true of ourselves, our minds, our languages, and our cultures?

The object can also be defined in terms of the text itself, of the text we make, and here I return to the conception of poetic integration with which I began: Can we learn to produce texts that are more "integrated" in the sense that in them we put two things—two systems of discourse, two sets of practices—together in such a way as to make a third that transforms our sense of both? Can we become more fully conscious of what we, and our languages, leave out, and find ways to reflect that consciousness in our speech? Can we find ways to connect the way we talk professionally with the ways we talk in ordinary life? The object is not connection but integration: the integration of parts of our culture, and parts of ourselves, into new wholes.[3]

Of course these new wholes would not be units or integers but compositions, and the kind of integration of self and culture that it is possible for us to attain is not permanent but temporary: it must be achieved over and over again as we assemble fragments into new orders, each of which has within it the principles of tension and disorder. The clarification of life achieved by a poem, as Frost reminds us, is not permanent or absolute but temporary and incomplete—a "momentary stay against confusion."[4]

Finally let me say, as you have no doubt already guessed, that the image of integration I have been trying to get before us is an image not only of intellectual but of social and political life as well, a way of thinking about the relations between people and races and cultures as well as departments or fields. I shall return to this subject in later chapters; for now let me say only that here too our effort should be to put two things together not with the object of merging them into one but with the hope of making something new, a social composition, with a meaning of its own.

2

THE LANGUAGE OF "CONCEPTS":
A CASE STUDY

It is important to think not only about the ways our languages are put together in our compositions, as I have just been suggesting, but also about the qualities of those languages themselves—about what it means to talk one way rather than another. This chapter starts us off on this sort of criticism by examining one of our own ways of talking, and one that has great (and in my view unjustified) authority in our world—the authority indeed of naturalness, for we turn to it naturally, as if it were the only possibility, or even as if it embodied rationality itself. At its most general the discourse I mean is the kind of propositional and conceptual language, briefly described in the Introduction, that serves as the *lingua franca* of social and political theory, of analytic philosophy, indeed of academic and expository writing more generally. It sometimes takes language itself as its subject, both formally, as in scientific linguistics, and informally, when the linguistic presuppositions of talk on other subjects are exposed. But I want to stress that the tendency of mind with which I am concerned is not confined to certain disciplines, or certain speakers, but exists in all of us, and that my object is not so much to criticize others as to engage in a sort of self-criticism, to capture something of what I think is at stake when our minds start to move in this way.

Much of the quality of this discourse can be caught in a particular set of locutions involving the word "concept," and it is with these particulars that my analysis will accordingly begin. But first I shall say a word about why I think this kind of study of language matters.

The Reciprocity of Language and Character

In a famous passage in his *History of the Peloponnesian War* Thucydides says that during the wave of civil wars that followed the Corcyrean

22

revolution words themselves lost their meaning. In the Crawley translation the passage reads as follows:

> Words had to change their ordinary meaning and to take that which was now given them. Reckless audacity came to be considered the courage of a loyal ally; prudent hesitation, specious cowardice; moderation was held to be a cloak for unmanliness; ability to see all sides of a question inaptness to act on any. Frantic violence became the attribute of manliness; cautious plotting a justifiable means of self-defense. The advocate of extreme measures was always trustworthy; his opponent a man to be suspected. . . . [T]he moderate part of the citizens perished between the two, either for not joining in the quarrel or because envy would not suffer them to escape.[1]

Here Thucydides talks about social collapse in terms that will seem all too familiar to us—think of Lebanon, for example—but what is most interesting to me is that he focuses attention on a verbal or linguistic deterioration that he finds associated with the social and political one. He does not claim that the shift in language *causes* the change in behavior; on the other hand, for him that shift does reflect a change in culture that makes certain kinds of speech and conduct—those we associate with civilized life—increasingly impossible.

For me this passage is a kind of emblem, defining a topic and suggesting a view of life: a way of focusing attention on the relations between language and the individual self, between language and our collective life.[2]

The essential feature of our experience captured in this passage is the structural reciprocity between language and character (or what we call personality or identity). Each of us is partly made by our language, which gives us the categories in which we perceive the world and which form our motives; but we are not simply that, for we are users and makers of our language too; and in remaking our language we contribute to the remaking of our characters and lives, for good or ill. This remaking is necessarily a shared or collective process, for language itself is socially constructed. The reciprocity I speak of thus exists at the collective as well as at the individual level, for our community is defined by our language—our language *is* the set of shared expectations and common terms that enable us to think of ourselves as a "we"—and that language too can be transformed.

On some occasions at least we may be able to contribute to the remaking of our shared resources of meaning, and thus of our public or communal lives. This is obviously the case with great artists and thinkers—their work changes the terms in which we think and talk, the ways in which we imagine and constitute ourselves—and upon reflection we can see a similar process at work in ordinary life as well, as we make and remake our own languages in our conversations with one another. Language and the world it constitutes are thus forever changing—"moderate prudence" loses its force as an appeal and thus as a socially validated possibility—and we change with them, both as individuals and as communities. The ineradicable flux of language, and of the world, so recently discovered and lamented by the modernist who learns at last that the language and methods of "science" are after all not good for all forms of thought and life, is actually structural to human experience, a condition of life that has been addressed again and again by our predecessors. What is required to face it is not a science in the usual sense but an art—the art of reconstituting language, self, and community under conditions of fundamental uncertainty, an art that is literary and rhetorical in character and of which we ourselves are the most important subject.

From this point of view, the law offers an especially interesting form of life, for at its central moment, the legal hearing, it works by testing one version of its language against another, one way of telling a story and thinking about it against another, and by then making a self-conscious choice between them. It is an institution that remakes its own language and it does this under conditions of regularity and publicity that render the process subject to scrutiny of an extraordinary kind. As an ethical or political matter, then, the structure of the legal process entails remarkable possibilities—little enough realized in the event—for thinking about and achieving that simultaneous affirmation of self and recognition of other that many (I among them) think is the essential ethical task of a discoursing and differing humanity. These possibilities arise from the fact that the premises of the legal hearing commit it to a momentary equality among its speakers and to the recognition that all ways of talking, including its own, may be subject to criticism and change.

The larger public world provides a less formally structured version of the same process, for it is not true that one sphere of life, say the economic or the intellectual, determines all the others. There is no privileged ground of analysis upon which we can stand, no privileged subject by explaining which we can explain—or ought to try to explain—everything else. At the collective level, then, we face exactly the same reciprocity that exists in the relation between the individual self and its culture more generally. We are always making ourselves, as individuals and communities, always making our language; yet we are always being made by our language, by our past, and by the actions of others, and the line between the maker and the made is never clear. This means, among other things, that our own habits of mind, of perception, and of feeling are contingent and changeable; they are a central part of our proper subject of attention, and this is true for us not only as citizens, or cultural actors more generally, but in our professional lives, as lawyers and teachers and writers. Our work cannot claim to have a validity beyond culture, beyond language, but should be seen as a way of working with and within language.

Talking about ethics or politics, or the public world more generally, thus itself becomes a species of what it describes: How ought we to talk in our own performances? About those performances? These questions invite us to be self-reflective, to make our own process of thought and speech the subject of our critical attention—for whatever we claim to believe about others must also be true for us. They invite us to resist the fallacies of reductionist theories that can account for everything in the world but themselves.

This means that as we talk about ethics or politics or law we take positions, implicitly or explicitly, on certain large questions about the nature of language and its relation both to culture and to the individual self. To ask, "What are the proper expectations to bring to the political and linguistic activities of others?" is to ask also, "What are the proper expectations to bring to what we ourselves say and do?"

"Concepts"

I want to start to work out a line of response to that question by thinking of some of the implications of the word "concept" (and its cognates), especially as it is used in thought and writing about language, ethics, and politics. I choose this word both because it is a central term in much of our discourse and because it seems for most people to be completely unproblematic, a perfectly natural way to talk. But for me it is problematic in the extreme: it has overtones and implications that I find difficult, and it is these difficulties that I wish to address.

My hope is to identify certain assumptions about language and life that are often associated with this word—assumptions that I think false or misleading but that can exist, I hasten to add, without its help, and that can also be at least partly denied or resisted by one who uses the term with appropriate qualifications. I seek to use this word, that is, as a way into certain larger qualities of our culture, certain habits of our own minds that are so firmly fixed that they may easily seem to inhere in the nature of thought itself.*

In talking about this word and its associations I speak simply as a local informant about my own language, without any claims to knowledge beyond those of my reader, whose language it also is. I do not ask that what I say be taken on faith or authority, but that it be checked against the reader's own experience; and I speak out of the recognition not only that my account of my language may be wrong but that even if it is right it may not, indeed will not, wholly correspond with the experience of another person, for there is a sense in which all of our languages are different.

This said, let me begin with a statement of my own experience of this part of our language, while recognizing also that it has something of the character of an admission: the admission that as I have read articles, mainly in journals of law and philosophy, but in other fields too, that use the word "concept"—the "concept" of law, the "concept" of right, the "concept" of equality—I have found myself repeatedly saying that I simply do not know what this word means. I keep wishing that the writer would use another word (like "word") or just drop the term entirely. It is not my thought that the word "concept" and all its derivatives should be driven from the language: "conception" as a word for "understanding," as in " my conception" of law or legal argument or "my conception" of good teaching, seems to me useful; and I suppose I would use "concept" in mathematics and perhaps some other similar fields, as in the "concept of a triangle," or the "concept of a carburetor." And since it is part of my view that writers remake their languages all the time, there is no reason in principle why "concept" could not be used by one writer or another in a way that is adequately, even beautifully, controlled or qualified.

For all language, not just the language of "concepts," has its dangers. All languages threaten to take over the mind and to control its operation, with all that this implies for one's feelings, for one's sense of self, and for the possibilities of meaning in one's actions and relations. The art of all speech, all expression, thus lies in learning to qualify a language while we use it: in finding ways to recognize its omissions, its distortions, its false claims and pretensions, ways to acknowledge other modes of speaking that qualify or undercut it.

---

*Other terms could afford similar access to this region of our culture and our minds: the word "theory," for example, or "problem" or "knowledge" or "reason" or even "fact."

The art of expression is the art of talking two ways at once, the art of many-voicedness. So it is with the word "concept": its more appropriate uses, in science and mathematics say, might remain unchanged, for there perhaps it is properly qualified and controlled by the rest of the relevant discourse; but I think its use in linguistics, law, politics, and so forth, should be more fully and explicitly controlled by arts of qualification, including those of irony, ambiguity, and contrast, than is now usually the case. I am speaking, then, not of necessities but of tendencies, of the forces a particular mode of speaking seems to generate, the directions it moves us, or what might be called its cultural implications, or the pressures with which our art must come to terms.

Language as Culture

But to say this is to invite the question, What can I mean by the "pressures" of a particular form of speech, or its "moving us" in certain directions? As an example let us consider the language and culture of contemporary economics. Of course economics is a useful, legitimate, and interesting field of inquiry, but it is also a culture, and a culture shaped in part by the implications of its intellectual and verbal habits. Suppose you decided to study the way wealth is created by exchanges, and for purposes of analysis you posited a set of actors, of equal age and competence, each with some control over the material of the universe—called resources—and you assumed as a fundamental psychological principle an unlimited acquisitiveness on the part of each, and therefore, with respect to the resources, a severe structural scarcity. Suppose further you assumed that each agent was interested in its own welfare only, and thus perceived itself to be in permanent competition with all other agents (except those whom it chose to make the object of what economists call altruism). Next you assumed a medium in which surplus could be accumulated without limit. Then you began to see what flowed from these assumptions and tried to analyze real world events in these terms.

If you actually did this you would find yourself caught in a game, perhaps a fascinating game, testing your capacity to draw certain kinds of logical conclusions from the premises stated, a game with a force and life of its own. You would become a player, an economist; you would inhabit a world with its own values, its own realities, its own rewards. From such simplicity, such complexity! And such fun, too, though for me of rather an empty kind (at least until an attempt was made to connect the economic language and its culture to others). For good or ill, the language and its practices would gradually start to shape the way you saw the world and felt about it, your sense of yourself and of others. You might find yourself, for example, thinking and talking as if people really were the objects or calculating machines that economics assumes them to be; you might even find yourself accepting "GNP" as a measure of a nation's economic health.

Of course one could claim that the language of economics is a scientific theory and as such wholly value-neutral. "An economic theory is a simplified version of reality," one might say, "meant, as all such theories are, not to be a full picture of anything but to permit the organization of data in simplified forms so that predictions can be made, assumptions tested, and so on." (Not to worry, says Milton Friedman, economic theory is merely a "filing system," to be proved or falsified by experiment. We don't *mean* what we say: we speak always in hypotheses.[3]) It is also conceivable that the language and culture of contemporary economics, and the body of knowledge they generate, could be subordinated to another culture, another set of values—say concern for the environment or for the welfare of those who seem least able to help themselves. But to achieve such a subordination is for the economic culture as a whole impossible, and for the individual economist difficult indeed: the premises of the discipline to which she has given herself are inconsistent with the uses to which she wishes to put what she discovers.

In the end, despite its claims to be merely hypothetical, economic theory becomes a culture of its own and can be studied and judged as such. My present point is not to criticize economics—I will do that at some length in chapter 3—but to suggest how habits of thought and language have tendencies, pressures of their own, that can perhaps be checked or controlled, but ought certainly to be reckoned with: how language has real power over the mind that uses it, even the mind that contributes to its reformulation. The cultural implications of one's language can be addressed, perhaps even overcome; but the tendencies are there, and have a force of their own.

Talk About Concepts

What, then, are the cultural implications of the word "concept?"

The first pressure of the term is to direct attention away from language to something else: to the realm of ideas, to what is in the mind, or to some field of intellectual reality, and in each instance to something that is assumed to exist in a realm apart from language. "Concepts" are not words; they are the internal or intellectual phenomena that words are thought to label, as markers, or towards which words are thought to point. To talk about concepts is thus to take a step in the direction of talking as if words had no force of their own, as if they were in fact transparent or discardable once the idea or concept is apprehended. On this view, in its extreme form, the function of words is either to identify external phenomena that can be observed without the use of language—that rock, or tree, or person—or to define or clarify concepts, which are also thought to exist outside language and beyond culture.

One form of the kind of discourse that talk about concepts invites is definitional, deductive, and empirical in nature, and in this sense fashioned on a certain model of science. In this way of talking, we define our terms on the assumption that they can be reduced to phrases that could substitute for them. Rationality consists of manipulating these definitions in patterns of deductive coherence or hypothetical description that will be tested by reference to extralinguistic phenomena, which will in turn establish whether they are true or false. Rational discourse, so conceived, is propositional in character; and knowledge, whether factual or conceptual, is of necessity propositional too. Propositions are what we reason about and reason with. (Hence all the talk in the philosophy journals about P and P'.) This kind of discourse is structurally coercive, in the sense that the writer seeks to prove something even to an unwilling reader who resists with all his might until forced by factual or logical demonstration to yield. At its center is an image of language as transparent: our talk is about what is "out there" in the natural or conceptual world, to which it is the function of language to point. Language obtrudes on our notice only when it is imperfect or fuzzy: in its ideal form it disappears from view entirely.

As I say, this set of assumptions derives from the model of "science" that has so powerfully dominated our intellectual life in this century. But the habit of mind and language I wish to identify is far deeper in our intellectual culture than the disciplines that explicitly model themselves on science, as I think the use of the word "concept" itself reveals. For we see this tendency of mind also when a classicist talks about the Greek "concept" of honor; when an analytic philosopher talks about the "concept" of a right; when an anthropologist talks about the Hopi "concept" of time; when a linguist reduces utterances to propositions that have the "same," ultimately conceptual, meaning to be expressed variously in different languages (or "codes"); when a lawyer talks about the "concept" of freedom of speech; when a sociologist or psychologist represents social or psychological "types" as if they corresponded with reality; when someone establishes a department in "The History of Ideas"; or when a teacher of writing praises a text for the clarity with which it "gets its basic concepts across." People may of course resist the implications of their usage—by thinking of conceptual variety or change or instability, for example—but this can be done only against the force of the term itself.

Consider, for example, the following quotation from a writer I admire, composed as part of an effort that I also admire, namely, to insist that modern philosophy recognize the differences that characterize different cultures and languages:

> In fact, of course, moral concepts change as social life changes. I deliberately do not write "because social life changes," for this might suggest that social life is one thing, morality another, and that there is merely an external, contingent causal relationship between them. This is obviously false. Moral concepts are embodied in and are partially constitutive of forms of social life. One key way in which we may identify one form of social life as distinct from another is by identifying differences in moral concepts. So it is an elementary commonplace to point out that there is no precise English equivalent for the Greek word *dikaiosuné*, usually translated justice. And this is not a mere linguistic defect, so that what Greek achieves by a single word English needs a periphrasis to achieve. It is rather that the occurrence of certain concepts in ancient Greek discourse and of others in modern English marks a difference between two forms of social life. To understand a concept, to grasp the meaning of the words which express it, is always at least to learn what the rules are which govern the use of such words and so to grasp the role of the concept in language and social life. This in itself would suggest strongly that different forms of social life will provide different roles for concepts to play. Or at least for some concepts this seems likely to be the case. There certainly are concepts which are unchanging over long periods, and which must be unchanging for one of two reasons. Either they are highly specialized concepts belonging within stable and continuing disciplines, such as geometry; or else they are highly general concepts necessary to any language of any complexity. I have in mind here the family of concepts expressed by such words as *and*, *or*, and *if*. But moral concepts do not fall into either of these two classes.*

Even this writer speaks of "understand[ing] a concept," of "grasp[ing] the meaning of words which express it," and of "rules governing the use of such words." For me these formulations draw

---

* Alisdair MacIntyre, *A Short History of Ethics*, pp. 1–2 (1966).

attention away from the reality of text and language to another plane, which I think does not exist. I do not think that words "express concepts"; I think that utterances or texts made of words have meanings, a rather different thing. I do not think that the use of the words is reducible to "rules" (though of course we do have expectations, partly shared, to some degree expressible, which a particular use may confirm or disappoint). Finally, I think that even the key terms in our logic—"if," "and," "or"—shift from language to language too.

* * *

The central danger presented by our talk about concepts is that we may find ourselves speaking as if there were no reason why people in different cultures cannot have the same concepts, no reason why different languages cannot express the same concepts. To the part of our mind that works this way, indeed, variety of language may come to seem mainly a nuisance, a bother to be eliminated, if possible, in the interest of what we conceive of as "more efficient communication." For implicit in most talk of this sort is the premise or claim that concepts can be wholly restated, and restated in various languages. Underlying this is the assumption that "communication" occurs not when we speak the same languages—when we understand each other's utterances in the sense that we know how to respond to them—but when we have the same concepts. Although the conceptual world is communicable only *through* language, it is supposed to exist on a plane above and beyond language, which disappears when its task is done.

While the conceptual view is in principle neutral among languages, and would thus concede that the Chinese translation of our concepts could be as accurate as any statement of our own, in practice it is imperialistic. On this view of language there is no reason why we should learn any other language, any other habits of thought, than our own. At the practical level there is an implied claim that our own language is or can be a metalanguage, in which all propositions can be uttered, all truths stated. And the sense that our language—whether we mean by this English, or economics, or law—is the language into which all others can be translated presents the dangers of linguistic imperialism familiar to us from the experience of many colonial countries—the imposition, say, of English law on the Hindus or the Burmese or the insistence that all that really needs to be said in Indonesia can be said in Dutch.*

---

*Consider here Robinson Crusoe's account of the person he found on the island: "[I]n a little time I began to speak to him, and teach him to speak to me; and first, I made

One who uses the word "concept" in the way I mean, then, is on his way towards making the error of the bureaucrat who can only imagine the world in the terms of his institution; of the dean who thinks that the merits of any question can be made plain in the language of academic planning, without any shift of mind; of the lawyer who thinks that the world comes in legal categories; of the doctor who thinks that the definitions of disease in terms of physical cause and modes of treatment correspond perfectly to the experience of his or her patients; and so on.[4] It is the error of thinking that one's own habits of mind and expression are not to be questioned, that they simply define rationality and coherence. One cannot use a language of concepts, after all, to reflect upon and criticize any of the languages that shape one's mind and world.[5]

Attending to Language

Talk about concepts is also intimately, though perhaps not inextricably, tied to dichotomous and linear thinking, to a commitment to a kind of coherence that denies that our terms have shifting and contrasting uses. The most fundamental rule of logic, that of noncontradiction, requires it: Each term in a logical system must be used in such a way that it either is or is not the case that it applies to the world, and, if the system is to be coherent, the word must be used in ways that are at least consistent and preferably identical. This is a struggle for the univocal, for the proposition that is true or false, entailed or not entailed, and it works by propounding questions that must be answered yes or no. This mode of thought is thus not only dichotomous, it is inherently aggressive and defensive, for its claim is to mark out the terrain of truth.

But only one sort of truth. In ordinary language we use our words in richly overlapping, sometimes contrastive ways, and we know that we define our terms partly in the way we use them. The lawyer, for example, can use "jurisdiction," "equity," or "common law" in the most radically different ways without confusion. And, more deeply, poets have always known that life cannot be reduced to systems and schemes. It is in fact the point of certain kinds of poetry—the greatest, in my view—to capture assertion and denial at

---

him know his name should be Friday, which was the day I sav'd his life; . . . I likewise taught him to say Master, and then let him know, that was to be my name. . . ." Daniel Defoe, *Robinson Crusoe*, p. 150 (Everyman's Library ed. 1975). (I owe this reference to Lemuel Johnson.)

once, to carry the reader to the point where her languages break down. Toleration of ambivalence is an essential ingredient of intellectual, emotional, and political maturity: the capacity to see, with Virgil for example, at once the greatness of Rome and its terrible cost, or, with Wallace Stevens, at once the fictional character of the poetic world and its reality. Our artists repeatedly teach us that the comprising of contrary tendencies, the facing of unresolved tensions, is an essential part of the art of life. This is one reason why the poem or the drama or the novel, or any other piece of living speech, cannot be adequately represented in a paraphrase, which will normally speak with a single voice and with a confidence in its characterization that the poem itself undercuts or qualifies; to the extent that the paraphrase catches the contrasting forces of the poem, its multiplicity of voice and value, it approaches the status of a poem itself.

All this is something of a truism as said of poetry, but I think it is true of philosophy too. One of the great vices of much philosophic talk is the assumption that the texts made by Hobbes or Locke or Plato or Aristotle can on this point or that be reduced to an outline of an argument.[6] That of course is not what the writers wrote, but we are terribly tempted—one sees it in student papers and professional essays alike—to reduce intellectual texts to rationalistic outlines. Yet as Plato taught us, and Hobbes certainly knew, all philosophy must in part be about the language in which it is composed, and so too must all law, all history, all linguistics, all criticism. What we know of poetry, that it is not paraphrasable or subject to translation, is true as well of all of our texts, formal and informal. Each speech act has its own meaning.[7]

Under these circumstances the great task is to train the imagination to bring within its field of attention the language through which it functions. The central difficulty with talk about "concepts" is that it directs attention in just the wrong way, away from language to something that is thought to exist apart from language. And when attention is in fact directed to the problematic character of one particular term, or "concept," as it sometimes is, the rest of the language used is assumed to be of perfect stability and soundness. Actually all of our language, not just certain terms within it, is in constant flux. Our use of it, and our talk about it, should alike reflect this fact.

Literary Discourse

So far I have been criticizing some of the implications and tendencies of our talk about concepts. What other view is it possible to take of these matters?

The Way Words Mean

Let me start with the way words mean. Words are not discrete and definable entities, as much of our talk about concepts seems to assume. They do not carry their meanings like pieces of freight, which the competent reader can pick up perfectly, nor are they reducible to ideas that can be regarded as having some existence beyond or behind the language. Any use of language assumes a competence in the audience that the utterance itself does not confer. Much of the meaning of words therefore lies in silence, in the unstated but accepted background against which they have their meaning. Even mathematics is deeply cultural and communal, for its definitions rest on inherently unstable cultural assumptions—for example, about the meaning of the "shortest distance" in Euclid's famous definition of a straight line.

What is more, in our actual speech words normally do not exist as discrete units, as much of our talk seems to assume, but as parts of sentences or other expressions, each of which is located in a particular linguistic, intellectual, social, and cultural context.[8] It is not the words themselves but their various uses—or the ways they have been used—that have meaning; these uses occur in sentences and other gestures that serve the widest range of human purposes. The "proposition," which academics often assume serves as the standard form of thought, is in real speech more rare than one might think. Sentences are better thought of as "practices" than propositions—including sentences meant to be propositions, for they too exemplify a set of social and rhetorical practices, and do not merely succeed or fail to state the truth. (All this was well known by Samuel Johnson, the great lexicographer, who defined English words not only by substitutive phrases—"X means Y"—but much more richly by their actual and diverse uses in sentences made by eminent writers.)

Similarly, the metaphors of a "range of meaning" or a "semantic field," which suggest that words have meanings that can be represented as both two-dimensional and contiguous, like strips of tape or patches of cloth, are utterly misleading, for different uses appear in contexts that are socially, emotionally, and culturally different from each other. It is an abuse of language to try to reduce its meaning to the restatable, the propositional. Our talk about language should reflect the various ways in which it has simultaneous meanings in several dimensions. A better metaphor for the way words mean might be that of neurological ganglia, making up three-dimensional, organic, interactive patterns, which work by processes we know we do not understand, even though they directly coincide, as language also does, with our own processes of understanding.

Individuality of Meaning

Language has an ineradicably individual character. Words, and other language forms, simply do not mean—not ever—exactly the same things to all users of them, as the builders of intellectual systems must claim or at least hope to achieve. Each of us loads any expression with significances that derive from our prior experience of language and of life, an experience that is obviously different for each of us. And it is not only words that mean differently to different people, but the sentences or other utterances in which they appear, the cultural background against which they acquire their meaning, the silences into which they are intrusions. What is behind the shimmering and fluid world of language is not a world of potentially clear and in principle sharable ideas or understandings, as our talk about concepts assumes, but a world of private meanings, radical silences, incommunicable sensations, experiences and images. Each of us is a circle of experiences and meaning that can occasionally, through language, meet or overlap with others, at least at the edges. Talk about concepts seems to assume that language can be pierced and some underlying reality exposed. I think it cannot be done. What lies beyond language is real all right, but it is not communicable, certainly not in a language of concepts.

I do not mean that meaning is completely private, which would obviously make social and linguistic life impossible, but that for each of us there is always an element or dimension of meaning—perhaps a residuum, though from our point of view it doesn't feel like it—that is irremediably personal. It could hardly be otherwise when each of us brings to every utterance such widely differing sets of prior experiences, such different aims and wishes. What we call the self is in part the history of a perpetual, and in principle unstable, negotiation between the languageless experience of the organism and its language, a negotiation parallel to those between self and nature, self and other. This history will be different for each of us.*

---

*Think here of conversation and life on a law school or college faculty. We can if we are lucky create a world that we can inhabit with confidence and some comfort, upon which we can build much of our lives. Yet despite the sense we sometimes have that the shared world of meanings in such a place is permanent and natural, at moments we see that even this world will be maintained only by perpetual and imperfect negotiation. It can always collapse; and at its most healthy much of its meaning is radically different for its different members, and different in ways that never find expression. For one person the school may be a refuge, for another a cosmic challenge; for a devout Catholic the whole process would have meaning of a kind it could not for the atheist; and so on. Part of maintaining a community is maintaining the agreement not to speak

I have been saying that language is more personal or individual than conceptual talk allows, but there is one sense in which it is less so, for conceptual talk assumes that the speaker "has" a concept, indeed must have a concept in order to speak, as if the function of language is to express something that exists on an altogether different plane, in a languageless place called the mind. In fact, of course, much of the meaning of what we say is not to be found in our minds or intentions at all, but in the language itself.[9] We learn our languages in large part by imitation, often acting simply out of a sense of what is appropriate to specific kinds of occasions. We always say more than we know. This means that learning a language is partly learning from it the meaning of what we already know how to say, which has, without our knowing it, marked our world, our mind. This is why the study of our language is at once a study of ourselves and of our culture.

Definition: The Federalist Papers

I want to say that conceptual talk proceeds on the assumption that its terms can be stipulatively defined in phrases that could substitute for them, while literary definitions occur in the working of the text itself.

This is of course a commonplace with respect to poetry: we know that the poet creates webs of significance that define one thing in terms of another—the rose in sexual terms, for example, or the spider in theological ones. But the same thing can be seen in texts thought to be intellectual rather than poetic, including legal texts. The good writer knows that she cannot just use the word "privacy" or "foreseeability," for example, as though "everyone knows what it means," and also that a one-line definition will not do. She must give her terms meaning in her use of them, a meaning that will be somewhat different from the meaning that is given them in any other text.

---

or ask about the ways in which its language means differently for different members. And those differences can be so enormous that in listening to the talk one is often surprised that it can go on at all.

Or think of the formation of a friendship: how wonderful it is to find someone whose language speaks to you, and to whom your language speaks, below the explicit level. Or think of the lawyer interviewing a client: the story she has just been told makes sense of a kind, no doubt, it may even be compelling and vivid; yet the lawyer never accepts it in its first form but goes on to ask questions the function of which is to make explicit the language behind the language, the context that gives the utterances the meaning they have for the client. She tries to retrieve and make conscious as much of the context as she can in order to discover the range of ways the story can be told, its array of potential meanings.

The literary mind thus takes the words and sentences that surround it in the culture as defining incomplete possibilities for expression and action, ways of locating the self and the audience in relation to the culture; it then uses them in ways that transform them, for good or ill, in the relation that the text creates with its reader.

Think here, for example, of the first of the *Federalist Papers*. Its opening sentence reads as follows: "After an unequivocal experience of the inefficacy of the subsisting federal government, you are called upon to deliberate on a new Constitution for the United States of America." [10] The central word in that sentence is "deliberate," for this is what the text "calls upon" its reader to do; and for another reason too, since this invitation is also a promise, a promise that the text will participate in the deliberation, and do so in such a way as to exemplify its proper form. To this much at least the text is committed.

How is "deliberate" defined? Never by explicit description or distinction, never conceptually or stipulatively. The text does not say, for example, "by deliberation we mean the serious and sustained application of open-minded attention," or something equally thrilling, and then go on to use the term as if it automatically meant what the text declared it to mean. Instead, the term is given meaning by a kind of performance or enactment in the text itself.

The process of definition in fact begins in this very sentence, where we learn, perhaps disconcertingly, that "deliberate" does not mean open-mindedness on all topics, as we might be inclined to think. For the speaker takes it as a given that the existing government is "inefficacious." Even more striking, the text is willing to bury that assumption in a subordinate clause, almost as if hoping that the reader, in a hurry to reach the main subject, verb, and object, will slide over it without objecting. We are at once invited to "deliberate" and thrown off balance by the evident commitment of the writer on the question in issue.

But is this so bad? Just because we are undecided does not mean that everyone need be; indeed have we not something to learn from those whose opinions are settled, so long as they are put before us in a candid way? As the writer will say towards the end of the paper, "I frankly acknowledge to you my convictions, and I will freely lay before you the reasons on which they are founded." By this time, through a process described below, we have come to see the existence of "conviction" in our interlocutor not as a vice but as a deliberative virtue, as a benefit to us; and perhaps we have come to see as well that a similar state of conviction—based on "reasons"—is what we should aspire to ourselves.

This transformation begins in the opening paragraph, where the writer next tells us that what will be decided by this process of deliberation is "whether societies of men are really capable or not of establishing good government from reflection and choice, or whether they are forever destined to depend for their political constitutions on accident and force." Whatever "deliberation" is, then, it is of the gravest imaginable importance. We are also told that it is opposed to "accident and force," and that it involves "reflection," or as he soon says, a "judicious estimate of our true interests, unperplexed and unbiased by considerations not connected with the public good."

But "reflection" of this kind is most difficult indeed to attain, for the nature of mankind is against it; most obviously in the conduct of those selfishly opposed to the Constitution, who will resist it for reasons of interest or passion and not fairly participate in the debate on its merits. This the writer starts to say, but then corrects himself: many of the opponents are actually motivated by "upright intentions," though perhaps subject to "honest errors"; more than that, in fact, for there are often "wise and good men on the wrong as well as on the right side of questions of the first magnitude to society" and "we are not always sure that those who advocate the truth are influenced by purer principles than their antagonists." The fault is on both sides. The result will be that a "torrent of angry and malignant passions will be let loose." We can expect both sides to seek to persuade "by the loudness of their declamations and by the bitterness of their invectives."

The writer is here imagining a world in which the reader, like other citizens, will necessarily be confused: good men and bad on both sides of the question, everyone out of intellectual and rhetorical control, speakers proceeding by "declamation" and "invective," and so on. This gives rise to the felt need for something else, for what the text calls "deliberation"—for what it promises to offer us—and in doing so begins to give it meaning. In this context of uncertainty it is a real virtue for the voice of *The Federalist* to speak out of "conviction." Only the voice of this text, committed to the point of bias but self-corrective too, and utterly candid about its commitments, has the stability and maturity required to think its way through the questions before it. Thank heavens, the reader is led to say, someone knows his own mind and is willing to speak in such a way as to assist our own "deliberation" and to do so by explaining his "reasons," which are offered for our acceptance or rejection on the merits.

This is only the beginning of what could be said in this vein about *Federalist* No. 1, let alone about the *Papers* as a whole, one central achievement of which is to work out an extended definition by performance of "deliberation" and "reason" alike—a definition of a sort of rhetoric, in fact—but perhaps it suggests how such an analysis might proceed.

I might add one final point. In defining the conditions of its own utterance, *The Federalist* describes a discursive world dominated by selfishness, passion, short-sightedness, manipulativeness, and so on. This is what makes "deliberation" so necessary; it is also just the understanding of human nature more generally upon which *The Federalist*'s central argument for a strong national government ultimately rests. This is the premise upon which the authors resist the republicans, who believe in the practical possibility of civic virtue. In accepting this understanding as the condition of deliberation the reader is likely to be accepting it in deeper ways as well. The terms upon which *The Federalist* offers itself, that is, as a place and occasion for "reasoned" talk, distanced from the confusion and irrationality of ordinary life, are precisely the terms upon which it offers its reader the Constitution it wishes him to support. Both create the possibility of a new kind of community, based upon a new kind of conversation, of which one central term is "deliberation," as defined in this text. In this process, by which the raw material of human life and conflict is rhetorically transformed into an institution of thought and speech, a new intellectual and social place, *The Federalist* at once imitates and foreshadows the processes of law.

Consequences

What I think is called for, then, is not a conceptual but a literary understanding of the nature of language. The modern philosopher's question is, "What proposition are you advancing?" A better one would be, "What text are you making?" This question reaches the language used, its particular formulation, its relation to its context, the voice of the speaker, his or her definition of audience, and so on. "Who are you in this text, who am I, and what kind of conversation do you seek to establish between us?"

Because "concepts" are abstract, and because this chapter has opposed the "literary" to the "conceptual," it might be thought that for me literary discourse has to be concrete or particular. But a resolutely particular language would in its own way be as bad as a conceptual one, at least if it assumed the perfect adequacy of its terms and categories. It is the attitude towards one's language, as that shows up in one's use of it, and not the level of one's diction, that

counts most deeply. The heart of literary discourse is self-conscious-
ness of the language itself: of its social and cultural implications, of
its over-commitments and dead spots. As we saw in our reading of
Frost's poem, "A Dust of Snow," literary texts are characteristically
marked by a tension between languages (such as that between the
concrete and the abstract); the effect is to qualify each language while
using it. The art—it is the art of "integration"—lies in writing two
ways at once. In this respect law is naturally literary, for the legal case
as we normally think of it can be neither an exercise in abstract analysis nor the presentation of mere particulars, but requires the interaction of both modes of discourse; similarly, it requires attention to the
case not from one point of view or another—the plaintiff's or the defendant's—but from both at once.

Of course there will still be languages that are conceptual in nature, or, to put it another way, efforts to talk about particular terms in
particular discourses as if they stood for "concepts," and sometimes
this will have its uses. But it should always be regarded as a special
kind of language, not as a model for all language, and we should
require that its use be explained and justified, not taken as naturally
valid. It needs to be resisted, and this in two respects: both in the
false understanding of the mind and language upon which it proceeds and in its implicit imperialism, its erasure of other ways of talking. To see exactly how this might be done, and with what effects,
requires the study and composition of particular texts, but a part of it
surely will involve what I have called the integration of conceptual
discourse with other forms of speech, which affirm understandings
of a different kind. Conceptual talk would then sound like, what it is,
a structural metaphor, an artificial invention; it should be accepted by
its reader only when it appears in a text which finds a way to qualify
its larger implications as soon as they are uttered, and in this sense
has something of the character of literature.

Rationality

All of this has consequences for one's understanding of human reason, and for the expectations and standards that one should bring to
texts that purport to be "rational," including the present one. The
essence of rationality is not the manipulation or explication of ideas
or concepts, assumed to have some extralinguistic reality and force,
but using words well in accordance with the conditions of reality.
These include the limits of language and of our own minds; the reality
and contingency of the convictions out of which we function; and the

silence that bounds everything we say. Reason, on this view, is not reductive or schematic but an aspect of the art of integration: saying what we know to be true in light of all else we know to be true at the same time.

The tendency of theoretical and conceptual talk is to appeal to the part of ourselves that wants to be surrounded by linear arguments, always hypothetical and susceptible to summarization in logical outline; that wants to live without the personal or actual voice, and without the responsibility of conviction, in a world reduced to quantitative metaphors; that wants to render the world into certain abstract intellectual forms or claim it to be meaningless. It works by an ideal of the purely rational, where "rational" is given a special and rather bloodless significance. There may be occasions where this sort of rationality has its proper place, but it should never be taken as the model of rationality itself; and its use—like that of "concepts"—should always be qualified by reference to our larger understandings.

A proper language of reason, by contrast, and a proper language of justice too, would accept the literary conditions on which we live; that while we struggle for coherence in our expression, this coherence will always be tentative, always incomplete, for all that we say, all that we are, is in part a function of the context in which we live, always imperfectly perceived and always changing. For examples of literary discourse one can turn not only to poetry but, as I just suggested, to law, which has survived as well as it has—and has been as important as it has—because it is a discourse constantly in the process of its own transformation, not in part but all at once, a discourse in which the speakers recognize that their central terms must be defined anew as they are used in new contexts, that everything is in principle arguable, and that they are responsible for the definitions and arguments they make.

Ethics

A literary sense of language has an active ethical significance as well, for to acknowledge the limits of one's own mind and language is necessarily to acknowledge the existence of the other person, as well as the possibility of other languages. The norm of conceptual talk, indeed of much academic talk more generally, is by contrast inherently aggressive: the idea is to stake out certain intellectual terrain with the force of one's logic, or by the demonstration of certain facts, against an audience assumed to be hostile, who will be persuaded only if compelled. The literary method, on the other hand, knows that nothing can be said with certain truth or validity, that no one can be compelled to submit, and that compelled submission is worthless anyway. It proceeds instead on the assumption that our categories and terms are perpetually losing and acquiring meaning, that they mean differently to different people and in different texts. It is not a territorial claim but an invitation to reflection.

Literary texts are therefore not propositional, but experiential and performative; not language-free, but language-bound and language-centered; not reducible to other terms—especially not to logical outline or analysis—but expressing their meanings through their form; not bound by the rule of noncontradiction but eager to embrace competing or opposing strains of thought; not purely intellectual, but affective and constitutive, and in this sense integrative, both of the composer and of the audience, indeed, in a sense, of the culture. Texts of this sort are not coercive of their reader, but invitational: they offer an experience, not a message, and an experience that will not merely add to one's stock of information but change one's way of seeing and being and talking.

The implied standards for one's own expressions are thus authenticity, actuality, integration, a commitment to acknowledging the limits both of language and of mind. Concerning others a complementary ethic emerges with similar clarity and simplicity: respect for the other (grounded in a simultaneous recognition of similarity of situation and otherness of experience); allowing the other what we claim for ourselves, the authentic assertion of conviction and judgment; and a willingness to learn the other's language and to undergo the changes we know that will entail. What we ask from others is what we offer to them, a willingness to speak to them as they are actually situated and constituted, with recognition of their claims to a language and a world. The heart of this set of ethical practices is the art of simultaneous affirmation of oneself and recognition of the other.

Language as a Whole Way of Being and Acting

All this is known to the best writers of literature, of course: think of the languages of morals and manners in Jane Austen's *Mansfield Park*, for example. You could not make up a list of the rules of conduct she thinks proper, or express her sense of these things by exhaustively defining a set of central words. For Jane Austen language reflects the entire cultural and human situation; the art of life is an integration and mutual education of the capacities for right observation, right memory, and right speech—and the right speech that is called for is not rationalistic or conceptual, but an understanding simultaneously of social, ethical, and verbal reality. The experience of those who, like Mary and Henry Crawford, fail as moral beings is not a merely conceptual collapse or disintegration, but a failure and disintegration of their language, of their selves, a very different thing. For Jane Austen the right use of language is one way—the best way? the only way?— to expose and address internal incoherences and defects as they emerge in oneself and in others.[11]

By contrast our own language of morality and philosophy is badly impoverished. The attempt to convert moral and political distinctions into conceptual ones, merely intellectual statements rather than expressions of conviction, to make such choices "rational" in the computational sense that is now so natural to us, is to strip our central terms of much of their force and meaning and to destroy a cultural resource of great importance.

At any given point in time, and place in culture, certain appeals have force—people will listen, feel they must respond, and so on— while certain others do not. As time goes on these appeals, and the contexts from which they arise, shift and grow or wither. (Think for example of the different force of an appeal to the Gospels in the discourse of Harvard University made 100 years ago and today.) This is not merely a matter of intellectual or conceptual but of cultural change. We can understand much of what the words we translate as "honor" meant in the *Iliad*, or in the plays of Corneille, or what "honor" itself once meant in England, or in South Carolina, yet in our world these words cannot mean what they once did. The English word "honor," which once expressed the motives for which people would kill each other, or go to voluntary death, has now lost much of its meaning; and this loss is not merely, or primarily, a "conceptual" one but a loss of force and significance, a difference in relation to the unstated backgrounds and to the feelings of the speakers. Who today would ever ground a conviction on "honor?" This is really the point of the famous passage in Thucydides, quoted at the opening of this chapter: a resource is gone, and gone forever, except perhaps as it can be revived or recreated by individual speakers, exercising the kind of art that Thucydides himself, and other great writers, and perhaps our best judges too, can be seen to practice.

In our own thought and writing about the texts, practices, and cultures of others—and our own, too—we should be aware, then, not only of the reality but also of the insurmountability of the differences among languages. This means that we cannot simply construct versions of other people's central terms as if we could understand them perfectly. As with other translations, we have to recognize that the most we can attain is an imperfect understanding and approximation. What is called for is not an attempt to penetrate the other world at the level of idea, behind or beyond language, but the effort to learn the language ourselves, incomplete as that learning must of necessity be. One's main aim in learning a language—French or Burmese, say—should accordingly not be to discover how one can say this or that in French or Burmese, but to learn what one can say and be in those languages that one cannot in one's own.[12]

But, you may say, does this not mean the end of all attempts to generalize—to describe, count, weigh—and of all efforts to analyze the real worlds of different cultures, or the different stages of our own culture? My answer is both yes and no. I do think that it would mean the end of all attempts to treat political or cultural questions as if they were language-free—it would mean the end of pure behaviorism and of the view of individual and collective life that characterizes economics, at least in its unqualified form. But this does not mean that we can say nothing, describe nothing, about these important matters. We can give descriptive, analytic, and comparative accounts of the rhetorical and cultural situations of others; we can study and analyze their responses, creative or not, to their situations as we understand them. We can learn to see and judge their own reconstitutions of their own languages. We can, that is, describe with some accuracy the rhetorical facts (the claims that can and cannot be made); the literary facts (the ways in which individual speakers and writers remake their languages, for good or ill); and this will go far towards defining the essential ethical and political facts, the ways a particular community is constituted, in a text and in the world. We can identify the appeals and topics that characterize a particular world, and the way they are and can be elaborated. We can do in short what Thucydides has shown us how to do.

But this will not take the form of propositions about "concepts" or other parts of the nonlinguistic world, which can be elaborated and tested by deduction and induction; nor shall we assume that we can penetrate the minds and languages of others further than we in fact can do. An important part of our attention must always be given to our own language, to its preconceptions and its omissions. This is in a sense nothing new, for it has long been said that one of the points of all comparative studies is to make our own world accessible and criticizable in a new way. My point is that this truth is obscured by those aspects of our current discourse that assume that reality can be authoritatively described and understood in our language, whether on the theory that material reality can be described as well by "us" as by "them," or on the theory that nonmaterial reality can be represented and understood as concepts that can be translated without loss into our language.

For me the beginning of wisdom—this is what Plato teaches, for example—is to train the mind to be conscious of its formulations just as it is conscious of the intentions it seeks to realize through them, to be as aware of the language we use as we are of the world in which we use it. What stage of intellectual and ethical development such an awareness, properly disciplined and encouraged, might lead to is beyond our full imagining, but it could be as great a shift as the acquisition of language itself has been. What will lead us to it is not further conceptual elaboration nor an insistence on the transparency of our own languages nor a delight in meaninglessness but an art, slow to develop, of recognizing the other, an art of assertion within acknowledged limits—an art for which the best word, properly used to reflect its impossibilities, may be "translation."

3

THE LANGUAGE AND
CULTURE OF ECONOMICS

This chapter develops the suggestion made in the last, that economics, like law, can be examined as a form of life and language, or what I call a culture. With law, about which I shall here speak rather briefly, I am naturally familiar by training and experience. But with economics I am familiar only as an observer—as a general reader who reads the newspaper, as a lawyer who has followed a little of the law and economics literature, and as one who has lived among those interested in the field. I thus speak about it as an outsider, and, as you will see, I speak largely about features of economic thought that I find disturbing. What I say, then, should be taken as tentative, subject to correction and response from those who know what I do not. But it does reflect a good many years of thinking about these questions, and it says what I think. It is tentative, then, not in the sense that I do not mean what I say, for I do, but in the sense that I recognize that about much of this I might someday have to change my mind.

Economics and the Way We Think

To say that I shall speak about "economics" may be somewhat misleading, for I shall actually focus attention mainly on one branch of it, namely microeconomics of the neoclassical kind, especially upon the strong version associated with the "Chicago School." This is the economics in which the "Law and Economics" movement originated, and it is an important mode of thought among other economists as well. (It is the hope of many macroeconomists, for example, to be able to rest their work on a microeconomic foundation.) To use "economics" to refer to this particular branch of it, as I do, may be something of a solecism, but for a lawyer today it is an easy and perhaps forgivable one, since this is the terminology generally used by those who have been most energetic, and successful, in recommending this mode of thought to us.[1]

This branch of economics is interesting and important for additional reasons, since it exemplifies, in a rather pure and distilled form, certain larger dispositions of thought that are reflected as well in other forms of economics, in certain branches of political science, and in contemporary social thought both academic and popular. (The heart of this kind of thought is the sense that a certain, now somewhat outdated, image of science establishes universal criteria of meaning and validity.) While I shall mainly speak of neoclassical microeconomics, then, I also wish to draw attention to certain features of our culture, certain habits of thought and expression, that show up in the widest range of contexts. They are so natural to us that they may seem to be a part of nature itself, not cultural at all. But cultural they are, and my questions are how to identify, how to understand, and how to judge this part of our common life.

To put this another way, I think that this kind of microeconomics rests upon a broad base in our culture, to which it owes much of its intelligibility and appeal and which it can illuminate for us by presenting in stark form tendencies that are elsewhere more muted. It reflects, in sharpened form, a general view of human nature and human reason, of community and language, that goes back at least to Bentham, and that underlies the traditions in the law that we call Sociological Jurisprudence and Legal Realism, as well as Law and Economics. More immediately, the ground for what we now call an "economic" view of law was laid by those lawyers and academics of the twenties and thirties who, seeing that legal questions involved questions of policy as well as of rights, began to speak as though all legal questions were simply policy questions, and by those Supreme Court opinions, somewhat later in time, that began to resolve cases by "balancing" one "interest" against another, thus engaging in a crude form of the kind of cost-benefit analysis that is the grammar of modern economics.

Certain versions of the kind of thought I seek to identify are present not only in the law but in our public discourse more generally, and have been for a long time. Among philosophers the maker of the modern tradition in this respect I think is Hobbes, and this in two ways. First, in the famous opening paragraph of *Leviathan* he says that man is the creator of his social and political world in exactly the same way that God is the creator of the natural world and of man. This claim of human possibility, enormously important and liberating in its time, has a depreciated modern version that is our current dogma, namely that "we" can make ourselves and our world be whatever "we" want, a view that underlies much of the field of policy studies, of which economics is a branch. While economics has in some ways resisted these claims, insisting on the necessity of costs and the reality of scarcity, in a deeper and ethical sense its promise is similar, for it places the highest value on the human will. Secondly, as I suggested in the Introduction, Hobbes established a method of reasoning about social life that is still with us, and of which economics is perhaps the most fully elaborated form, namely, that of using the models of mathematics. Once our terms are defined with sufficient precision, all thought can be reduced to a kind of calculation: for Hobbes to what he calls subtraction and addition, and for the moderns, to forms of mathematical analysis that are more complex but that rest upon the same fundamental assumptions. Hobbes—or a part of him; there is the side that Leo Strauss made so much of, which is prudential and Thucydidean in character—thus forms a surprising and powerful alliance with Bentham, in other ways so different, for both think that language can be made transparent and that all intellectual activity can be reduced, or elevated, to a single form of thought, based on the methods of natural science. This attitude towards language—and hence towards culture and meaning, towards the role of the past, and towards the experience of others—is the deepest commitment of the view of life that finds expression in contemporary economics; it is also the point on which law most sharply differs from it.

So deeply rooted in our culture is this set of expectations and understandings that we are all in a sense economists now. My questions are what this has meant, what we can make it mean, and what we can keep it from meaning. My claim is not that the enterprise of economics ought to grind to a halt, but that the forms of language economists employ enact forms of life that entail certain intellectual and ethical dangers, which themselves should be understood more fully than they are both by economists and by those, especially in the law, to whom economics is recommended as a mode of thought. Economics should not be abolished, but neither should it be allowed, as some want it to be, to take over the law; and in all its forms those who use it should seek not the kind of exclusivity the language seems to call for but integration with, and subordination to, other forms of discourse.

Economics as a Total Culture

I shall begin with a kind of thought-experiment, an act of the imagination, in which we ask what things would be like if the language of economics of the sort I speak of, and the habits of perception, feeling, and thought that it realizes, were our only language, our only habits. Economics, after all, is among other things a way of imagining the world, and we can ask what life would be like on the terms it provides: Who are the actors in this universe, with what relations to each other and to the natural world? In what social and intellectual practices do they engage? What possibilities for meaning, for community, for self-understanding, for art—what motives for action, what conceptions of happiness—are enacted in this discourse? What, in short, would things be like if economics were our total culture?

I propose this experiment not to make the world turn in horror from what economics has to teach, or economists turn in horror from themselves—unlikely scene—but to identify certain dangers against which we, and they, should be on guard, to expose what it is we start to commit ourselves to when we think or speak in these ways. The idea is not that economics should be obliterated, but that it—like the language of "concepts" discussed in chapter 2—should be understood for what it is and placed in a proper relation to other languages, to other cultures, of quite a different kind.

When I speak of the "dangers" of a particular language or culture, I mean to point to nothing peculiar to economics but to a condition of all life, all language. Think, for example, of the language of the computer, or of arms control, or of medicine, or of the institution where you work: What would it mean to use that language to construct a whole world? What total culture would it make? These are the questions I asked about law in *The Legal Imagination*, and they could be asked of any discipline, any specialized set of linguistic and intellectual practices. Here I propose to ask them about economics. I am interested both in what happens to one's mind as one increasingly comes to speak the language of economics and in the nature of the world, and the community, that this talking makes.

Some would no doubt respond that nothing happens to the mind or to the community, that language is only a tool, and that economics does not make a culture but only adds to our knowledge in certain ways. Language no more affects the individual mind than the use of a hammer or a saw might do. Language is, or can be, purely instrumental; we look through it to the real world that it describes or manipulates. This book is written out of the view that this is not right either as to language or as to tools; that in important ways we become the languages we use—the language of computer analysis or military domination or economics; and that our habitual practices, whether with computers or jackhammers, rifles or fly rods, help to make us what we are, both as individuals and as communities.

In making this investigation, then, I start from the position set forth in chapter 2, that the languages we speak, and the cultural practices they at once reflect and make possible, shape our minds by habituating them to certain forms of attention, certain ways of seeing and conceiving of oneself and of the world. This is, in fact, why we learn them. I do not of course mean that every lawyer or doctor or economist or engineer or baseball scout or harbor pilot is the same as every other. The case is quite the reverse, for in each instance the full art of life involves the assertion and mobilization of what is individual in the actor. But it is true that the language and practices of a particular professional (or other) culture create many of the conditions upon which that part of life will be led; that these conditions are much, though not completely, the same for everybody within it; and that they can be made the object of attention and criticism.

For me, as I have said, the major art of intellectual life is accordingly to discover, and to try to control, the ways in which our languages capture and drive our minds, so that we may recognize what they leave out or distort, both in ourselves and in others, and subject them to the discipline of other forms of thought and expression. Control of such a kind is most difficult, for it is at heart a species of self-control: when we speak our languages we cannot help believing them, we cannot help participating, emotionally and ethically and politically, in the worlds they create and in the structures of perception and feeling they offer us. In time the soldier wants to go to war.

Many people think of economics solely as a scientific, conceptual, and cognitive system, apparently unaware that there are any other dimensions of meaning in economic talk. But all expression is loaded with values, ethical and otherwise; all expression defines a self and another and proposes a relation between them; all expression remakes its language (if only by repetition); in these senses all expression contributes to the creation of a community and a culture. All expression, in short, is ethical, cultural, and political, and it can be analyzed and judged as such. To claim that economics is a science is perhaps to claim that it cannot be judged in such terms. But "sciences" are cultures too, with their own created worlds and values. One way to describe my aim in this chapter, then, is to say that it reverses the usual flow: we are used to economic analyses of this or that aspect of our common life—voting, the family, war, and so forth. I propose here to begin what I would call a rhetorical (or cultural) analysis of a certain kind of economics.

Here let me stress again that what I call "economics" in the pages that follow is really only one form of it, and that form as practiced by those who are most eager to see it universalized as a mode of thought. This means that at least those economists who feel that they can distinguish what they do from what I portray will think that my account has a kind of exaggerated or caricatured quality. This is consistent with my purposes, however, for I am not trying to give a full account of a whole field but to identify certain pressures or forces in economic discourse with which its practitioners have to come to terms. For these purposes, the form of economics I have chosen has the great merit of a kind of extremism that presents these forces and pressures in highly clarified form. My object here is to bring to the surface, where they can be seen and studied, certain attitudes and assumptions that are latent but obscured in much of our public talk; that are explicitly at work in most economics, though in a qualified form; and that are made visible and accessible in the kind of micro-economics of which I shall speak. I hope I do not misrepresent what I describe, though I may of course unwittingly do so; but my main concern is not to attribute but to analyze the attitudes I discuss, and I will have no argument to make with those who wish to disown them.

You will notice that I do not take a particular text or person as representative of "neoclassical" economics or any of its sub-fields, nor for the most part do I cite particular writers on particular points. This is not an oversight. My concern is with structure and tendency rather than detail, and I am not interested in engaging in disputes about the representative character of a particular passage, text, or mind. Instead, I invite the reader to check what I say against what he or she knows of the ways this kind of economics works, the ways it is offered to us as a model, and the ways in which it is connected to larger or more widespread habits of mind and feeling, in economics and elsewhere. Rather than making a case that is meant to stand or fall by the degree to which the unwilling are compelled to assent to it, then, I mean to present a set of reflections, I hope in their own way persuasive, to be tested against the reader's own.

Economics as a Language of Theory

Neoclassical microeconomics imagines a social universe that is populated by a number of discrete human actors, each of whom is competent, rational, and motivated solely by self-interest. External to the human actors is a natural universe that affords what are called "resources," which are acted upon by human actors to create something called "wealth." Economic activity, and hence wealth, are defined in terms of the process of exchange by which one actor exchanges some item within his dominion for an item within the dominion of another, or, far more commonly, for money, which is the medium of exchange. To look at everything from the point of view of exchange is, naturally enough, to regard the universe as a collection of items for potential exchange, and in this sense to itemize it. When an exchange takes place, these items enter the economic system and become part of what we mean by productivity. Where no exchange actually takes place—as where wealth is created and consumed by the same person, or where leisure is chosen over work—the economic effect of the actor's decision is not disregarded by professional economists (as it often is in popular economic thought), but it is still measured by the value of an imagined exchange, the one the actor has forgone. The central principle of the system is that everything is at least hypothetically interchangeable and thus of necessity quantifiable in ways that permit meaningful commensuration, at any rate by the actors who are faced with the choices to which economics speaks.

As the natural universe is itemized by these real or imagined exchanges, the social world is atomized, conceived of as a set of actors of equal competence, without race, gender, age, or culture. Each actor is assumed to be motivated by an unlimited desire to acquire or consume.[2] Since each is interested only in its own welfare, each is in structural competition with all others. This in turn creates a severe scarcity with respect to the resources. Where there is no scarcity, as there once was not with respect to clean air or water, there can be no economics of this kind, and no value that the economist can recognize. ("All good things are scarce," says Judge Easterbrook in a revealing phrase.[3]) The final ingredient is money, a medium in which surplus can be accumulated with convenience and, in principle, without limit. So far as possible, all human interaction is reduced to the single model of exchange. Economics is the study of what life would be like on such assumptions.

Exchange is a method of determining value, which, tautologically, is said to be the price for which items are sold. This is the value that is put upon them by the economic system, and the only kind of value that economics can express. Obviously individuals may put different values on different items—indeed, this is ordinarily necessary for the exchange to occur in the first place—but although these private values drive the economic system, they are not directly expressible in its terms.

In the world of economics, individual actors function according to what economists call "rationality." This is a reasoning process that consists of identifying items of potential consumption or dominion in the world, calculating their value in dollar or other common terms, and estimating various kinds of positive and negative risks. Reason is thus reducible to calculation and risk assessment. This is, of course, a drastically reduced conception of thought. Compare, for example, the eighteenth-century view of reason as the intelligent and wise response to all the conditions of human and external nature, as the full attainment of intellectual maturity and wisdom.[4]

A Hypothetical Discourse?

Such is the image of life used as the basis for economic analysis. One common and not very surprising response of the non-economist is to claim that this picture is simply false because it does not accurately and completely reflect the processes of social life as we know them. People do not conceive of or organize their lives in this way: they are not fundamentally or exclusively self-interested, they have values other than those of acquisition and dominion, and they reason in ways that are both far more complex and multidimensional than economics suggests they do, and than economists themselves do.

To this the economist is likely to answer, as I said briefly in chapter 2, by saying something like this: "No, of course it does not reflect the truth of social life as one experiences it. We know that human beings are not social atoms or discrete agents, that they are not always rational in the sense we mean it, that they are not wholly self-interested, nor should they be. This theoretical structure is a system for the analysis and prediction of behavior, like those used by natural scientists. It can function as a theoretical system, indeed, only if it is in fact simpler than the phenomena it describes. By definition, therefore, it must be a reduction or simplification; this aspect of the theory is not a defect but a virtue." Economics is thus an attempt to apply something like the methods of physics to social phenomena, in the spirit of logical positivism.

On this view the value of the theoretical structure lies not in its stating truths about human nature, but in its permitting us to carry out empirical investigations into the nature of the world. In other words economic analysis should be regarded simply as an elaborate set of assumptions that can be used to generate hypotheses that will ultimately be tested by the study of specific transactions, either individual or aggregate. Economics is ultimately the study of behavior. "We think it will provide a better basis for predicting behavior than any alternative simplification," say the economists, "but we may be wrong, and in the spirit of science we will welcome correction as well as confirmation. And we want to stress that even if our theory is confirmed by the data, it will still not be an accurate and complete representation of the world. It will remain a deliberately reduced method of organizing data in order to make predictions—what Milton Friedman calls a 'filing system'[5]—not a picture of reality. By its nature this kind of theory is to be tested as a predictive tool, not as a description."

Real Commitments

You have heard one answer. But as one listens to economists talk, their view of their language as merely hypothetical often seems to disappear. I think it disappears in part because they really believe that it tells the truth about the world (or about their own feelings); this is why they talk this way and it is disingenuous to pretend that it is only a filing system. They think it is the right filing system, descriptively as well as predictively, or they wouldn't use it.[6] And it disappears for another reason too, a psychological one; even if they begin as skeptics it is impossible for them to remain so. As lawyers know—to their cost—it is very difficult to say things habitually, even things one doubts, without coming to believe them. I think this necessarily happens to economists as well, and to those non-economists who start speaking their language.

Consider, for example, the use of terms such as "self-interest" or "rich." The economist assumes that everyone is what he calls "self-interested." By this he does not necessarily mean "selfish," but only that each actor makes up his own mind about what his own values should be. These values may be altruistic, leading him to make charitable gifts to relieve the distresses of others or inspiring him to endow an institution that exists for the public benefit. Similarly they may be cultural, leading him to learn the cello, for example, or to become a greatly ambitious, if monetarily impoverished, artist. It is solely for the purpose of analyzing the activity of exchange that we assume that each person is "self-interested." Self-interest on this view is not the central human value (maybe not even a value at all) but simply the umbrella term that includes all the values, whatever they may happen to be, that individuals bring to their exchanges with others. Similarly, the word "rich" is used by economists to mean rich not only in money, but rich in "utility" or "happiness" too. It makes perfectly good sense that a person who is motivated by the desire to become "rich" in the latter sense might seek to imitate the life of Mother Theresa. The economist would say that such a person, however impoverished in material terms, is in fact "richer" than he would have been had he engaged in an alternative but more financially remunerative form of life. Likewise the clause "everything is for sale," or actually "sold," is said not to express a value, but to state what might be called an analytic fact: that we can analyze all transactions that actually occur between people, and those that do not, as if "sales" were contemplated and either consummated or not, even where the actor in question does not think of himself as willing to sell his honesty, his health, or his body for any price, or even where the two actors think of themselves not as self-interested negotiators but as friends eager to help one another.

In this way "self-interest" and "rich" and "for sale" and other similar terms can be claimed to be defined by the discourse in special ways, almost as if they were technical terms that should be understood in this special way and not taken to mean what they appear to mean. But can this work? I think not: One cannot habitually think of human action in such terms—especially in a culture like our own, which is so heavily dominated by the motive of self-interest in the usual sense, that of selfishness or self-centeredness—without tending to universalize their ordinary rather than their technical meanings.[7] The result is to validate both selfishness and the desire to acquire and consume. In the terms offered by this language, for example, one cannot criticize another for selfishness, or for wanting only to be rich (in the usual sense), for we are all "self-interested," we all want to be "rich." The use of "self-interest" to comprise all motives, including altruism, and the use of "wealth" to comprise all values, including ascetic ones, destroys distinctions that are essential to our ethical thought: between selfishness and generosity, for example, or between avarice and moderation. It is a very reduced idea of "altruism" to say that it is what apparently—but only apparently—serves someone else's interest rather than one's own. In such a language there can be neither the virtue nor the duty of charity.*

I think, then, that the language of economics cannot remain merely an abstract "filing system." It necessarily becomes a language

---

*One could go on. Think for example how this language affects the way in which someone who manufactures a product or sells a service—a "producer"—thinks about the meaning of what he does. He thinks of himself as meeting the desires of his "consumers," say for more sugar in the cereal or more poison on the lawn, and it is they, not he, who is responsible for what he produces. He is thus justified in making something shoddy, or ugly, or trivializing; indeed, he can take little satisfaction in making something sound, or handsome, or meaningful, because it is not he who determines what he makes. From the point of view of the "consumer," this language works similarly: to encourage him to think not of what is good, but of what he wants.

Or think of the way that baseball, say, is defined in economic terms: it becomes to which those who think in its terms are committed; it affects what they say, what they see, how they think, what they feel, and what they are. And one can imagine (if one does not know) economists who turn to this language as their way of talking about virtually everything—teaching, curriculum, vacations, politics, how to decide what to read, and so on—and who do so without examining the premises, the intellectual and ethical commitments, of that way of talking. One can readily see how this works: economics is a way of imagining what would happen if certain things were true; the economist lives among people who are interested not in the premises of the discourse but in tracing its implications, and that is what he will naturally want to do too. Indeed, as an economist he is in no better position than anyone else to think about the premises of his talk: this is how he talks, who he becomes. If we talk this way we too shall come to share the commitments that are implicit in the form of life and language we call economics.

Economics is not, as some might claim, politically or culturally "empty" but a powerful political and cultural system in its own right. It is an ideology as well as a method. It is offered to the law, by some at least, as the language in which legal analysis should proceed—as the language in which lawyers and judges should think and converse—and to the public more generally as the language in which the polity should organize its life. For some of its practitioners and admirers it holds out the promise of universality, of being or becoming the one system in which all social phenomena can rationally be talked about, analyzed, and judged.[8] Before agreeing to talk that way (more than we already do) we should think hard about what it promises, what it entails. Our question is, what kind of culture does it offer us?

Economics as a System of Value

We can start with the question of value. In its purest form economics claims to be a "value-free" social science. But as I suggested above I

---

entertainment, a purchase of pleasure, in no way to be distinguished from a pornographic film or a Mozart concert or a television sitcom. From the economist's point of view these activities are indistinguishable: the differences in their art and meaning simply disappear. Or think of what happens when education is talked about in economic terms (as has happened in Thatcher's Britain): the teachers are "selling a service" to the students and it is obviously right that the consumers of the good should determine what it is they want to buy. The existence of a university, based upon the premise that experience has something to teach youth, the past the present, becomes a grotesque malformation, a violation of the natural order of things—it is a "producer-dominated sector of the economy."

think it in fact enacts a set of values, including political ones, to which the speaker of this language cannot avoid finding herself at least in part committed.

In the World

Think, for example, of the way economics defines the economic actor and the processes by which he functions. He is for the most part assumed to be an individual of indeterminate age, sex, race, and cultural background, but of adequate competence at manipulating economic relations. He acts as one who is perfectly aware of his own wishes and wholly rational—in the special sense in which that term is used, to mean "calculating"—in his pursuit of them. He exists as an individual, not as part of a family, neighborhood, or other community, except insofar as he establishes contractual or exchange relations with others. He is assumed to be motivated by self-interest, which is defined in terms of competition, acquisition, and dominion, at least in relation to resources and other actors, for in the process of exchange the self is reduced to those desires.

Of course a particular individual may have other values— indeed the economist insists that he must, calling them "tastes" or "preferences"—perhaps including a "taste" for altruism, for peace and quiet, for heavy metal music, for appreciating nature unspoiled, for beautiful or ugly art, and so forth. These commitments will drive his participation in the exchange process, or his decision to withdraw from it. But in either case they are themselves valued by the method of exchange: either by an actual exchange that takes place or by a hypothetical or imagined exchange that is forgone (or in a more complicated case by a combination of exchanges made and forgone). In both cases what lies outside the system of discourse is converted by it into the acquisitive or instrumental values that all economic actors are assumed to have, for this is the only kind of motive about which economics can directly talk.

With respect to the external values in their original form, the system is purportedly "neutral." That is, it regards them as simply exogenous to the system itself. Economics of course recognizes that they exist, but it demeans them by calling them "tastes" or "preferences," names that imply that no serious conversation can proceed on such subjects.[9] And economics itself is by definition not about those values, but about the process by which they are reflected in the activity of exchange. This means that economics cannot, in principle, talk about any activity, any pleasure or motive or interest, other than the acquisitive or instrumental one that it universalizes. (Indeed it

does not talk about this either but merely assumes and acts upon it.)
This is not to be "value free," as its apologists claim, but to make
aggressive self-interest the central, indeed the only, value, for it is the
only one that can be talked about in these terms. To come at it the
other way, it is to claim that all motives and interests can be talked
about, at least for some purposes, as if they were selfish, quantifiable, and interchangeable; this is to erase all worlds of meaning except its own.

As I suggested earlier, an economist might here respond that
the commitments that lead the self to engage in acquisition might
themselves be altruistic or spiritual—for example, a desire to help the
poor or to make beautiful music—and that economics recognizes this
fact. It just regards choices of that sort as the domain of the actor, not
of the science of exchange. But this does not change my main point,
for it remains true that economics talks about such commitments in a
language of self-interested individualism, and this is to erase them, if
only for the time being, as what they are. The conventions of this
discourse necessarily habituate its user to thinking in terms of self-
interest as a central principle, and in practice the "time being" is
likely to stretch on forever. The reference to "altruistic selfishness" is
a disclaimer in its way as unconvincing as Milton Friedman's claim
that economics is only a filing system.

Economics is troubling not only for the self-interest that it directly asserts, but for the very neutrality, the "value freedom," that it
claims. To be neutral in principle on all questions of motive external
to the acquisitive and competitive ones enacted in the exchange game
is to be silent on all the great questions of human life: questions of
beauty and ugliness in art and music, sincerity and falsity in human
relations, wisdom and folly in conduct and judgment, and on the
greatest of all questions, which is how we ought to lead our lives.
Economic analysis assumes as a given the existence of "tastes" or
"preferences" which drive the system, but economics as a language
can provide no way of talking about them, whether in oneself or another, no way of thinking about which to prefer and which not.*

* * *

For the purposes of economic analysis all human wishes and
desires are thus reduced to a same level, as though no principled
choices could be made among them, as though it didn't matter what

---

*The only way an economist qua economist can judge the merit of a poem or a painting
or a work of philosophy—or even of economics?—is by asking how well it prevails in
the market place. The test of excellence in literature is what survives. See, e.g., Richard

choices one made. This in turn means that it is impossible to talk in these terms about our most important choices as individuals and communities, or about the education of mind or heart, for any impulse that we or others may happen to have is as good, or as valid, as the next and is as entitled to respect as any other.

Viewed as a recipe for life this is of course impossible, as philosophers have repeatedly shown since Plato's original destruction of Callicles' adoption of such a position in the *Gorgias*. Socrates asked Callicles how high the pleasure of scratching an itch ranked with him, or the pleasure of cowardice. Once these are demoted below other pleasures, one has committed oneself to a scale of value, and the only question is what it shall be. To claim that this is a wholly private question, not the proper subject of shared conversation, is either to say that the question is trivial or that we cannot help each other address it, both of which are impossible positions. We must and do have preferences, as the economist knows; and these necessarily commit those who have them to the inquiry of better and worse, as well as to that of greater and less. To refuse to engage in this inquiry—to "privatize" it—as economics in its neutral phase necessarily does, is to deny an essential and necessary aspect of human life. To reduce all value to self-interest, as it does the rest of the time, is intellectually and ethically intolerable. How could one educate one's children or oneself to live in a world that was neutral on all the great questions of life, except that it reduced them to acquisition, competition, and calculation? *

A. Posner, *Law and Literature*, pp. 71ff (1988). This may be true, in a trite way, but to say so does nothing to tell us how to judge the excellence of a particular work. It assumes out of existence the essential human task of judging better and worse. The critic, like the investor, becomes a predicter, not a judge.

*In this connection recall Thucydides' *History of the Peloponnesian War*, which traces the effects of the decision of Athens to refuse to consider questions of justice, in her relations with other cities, but to ground all public thought and conduct instead in pure self-interest. (This dramatized with great clarity in the famous Melian Dialogue in Book 5.) The result is the complete intellectual and moral collapse not only of the larger community of states but of the Athenian polity itself, and the consequent loss of Athens' capacity to function rationally at all.

One lesson of this text is that rational discourse about human choices must include the question of justice as well as that of expediency. Another might be that "self-interest" requires a different emphasis from the usual—"*self*-interest"—in recognition of the fact that coherence of character is essential to all success and that this coherence is always social in its origins and maintenance. A true "self-interest" would, then, require one to assert an interest in the culture and the community of which one is a part. (For fuller discussion, see *When Words Lose Their Meaning*, ch. 3 [1984].)

Among Economists

There is another dimension to economics, as a discourse among economists. Here too, in the discourse, values are of necessity enacted. For example, economics necessarily values the reduction of life to terms such as I describe, for this is what it achieves. It values thinking about human beings as self-interested creatures, each struggling to maximize its own "wealth"; it values quantitative reasoning and competition for dominance.

This last is especially so among economists, for it is ostensibly a premise of economic discourse, as a rule of proof appropriate to a science, that we will believe only what we are forced by logic and fact to believe. This means that economic conversations—like certain other academic discussions—are often attempts to compel others to submit to one's views, or to resist such submission. In doing so they necessarily perform, if only for a time, a claim that this is the most appropriate and valuable way to converse on these subjects, itself a most dubious position.

But the rule of proof just described applies only to conclusions reached from the assumed premises, not to the premises themselves. These are in fact chosen; economists talk the way they do not by compulsion but because in some sense they choose to live in the world that this discourse imagines and makes real. This choice expresses a wish or a value that should, like other choices, be subjected to critical examination. But in economics it is not and cannot be, for these are the premises of the discourse, its prior commitments, and they cannot be questioned in its terms. Another way to put this is to say that the precision and clarity of mathematical thought in a discipline like economics requires, as a condition of its existence, that a certain range of propositions about human nature and behavior be taken as true. These propositions themselves cannot be justified in terms of the discipline but are expressions of belief or faith.

In saying that "value-free" economics is actually committed to certain values, both in the assumptions it makes about the world and in the conventions by which its own discourse operates, I do not mean to suggest that the field is in this respect peculiar. Quite the contrary. Every discourse is a way of being and acting in the world, a way of constituting a character for oneself and a community with others; every discourse is a system of motive and meaning that commits its users to what we call "values," and it does so in both domains, that is, in one's account of the "other world" one talks about and in the here-and-now world one creates by talking. Science does this, and so do law and literary criticism too. Economics is not to be blamed, then, for having "values." But no one should be allowed to claim value-neutrality where it does not exist, and economics, like other discourses, can be praised or blamed for the values it has, or, more properly, for the forms of life it brings into existence.

All this is not to say that economics is wrong to do what it does, namely, to isolate the practices of exchange for study, especially when its results are applied to the spheres of life that are in fact characterized by exchanges that take place on conditions roughly matching the assumptions of the discourse. This is, after all, a good deal of the economic life of the investor or entrepreneur in a capitalist economy. But it is to say that this study would lead to insanity unless it were premised on a recognition that these activities, and the culture they and their study together create, require integration with the larger set of activities and cultures that make up our selves and our worlds.

Economics as a Political System

An economist might agree that the language and practices in which he engages as an economist must somehow be put together with the languages and practices that make up the rest of his life, both public and private. This would raise the interesting and important question, how this might be done, and with what effect on economics itself, a question to which I shall return at the end of this chapter.

But another line of response is possible as well, one that neither denies the political character of this discourse nor seeks to integrate it with other languages and practices but rather celebrates the politics and ethics that this kind of economics entails, at the center of which is the claim that the market is affirmatively desirable both as a model of life and as a political and social institution. Views that start out as hypothetical premises supporting the analytic method of economics, in other words, can end up being propounded as the proper grounds upon which to build a collective life.* In talking this way, the economist moves off the ground of purportedly pure science. He begins to use his language not as a "filing system" but as a way of ex-

---

*It is usual for economists to draw a bright line between "positive" and "normative" economics, and of course there are differences in emphasis between studies that set out to examine "what is" and those that ask "what ought to be." But this is a difference of emphasis only, not a radical shift of category: "Positive" economics enacts "norms," or what I have called values, and "normative" economics depends completely upon its claims that the world "is" a certain way.

pressing overt social and political attitudes. I should stress that not all economists take this step. But some do. They are of course perfectly entitled to do so, but only to the extent that their politics and ethics, not their economics, persuade us of the rightness of their vision.

Justifying the Market as a Model of Life

The institution of the market is celebrated by its proponents because in their view it is democratic—each person brings to the market his own values and can "maximize" them his own way—and because it is creative and open, leaving the widest room for individual choice and action. The market establishes a community based upon a competitive process which allows each person freedom to choose what to do with what is his. This means, for some economists at least, that all social institutions ought to be modified to approximate the market—to conform to the analytic model of life as exchange—or at least to be analyzed and judged on that presumption.

The market is further justified, when such justification is thought necessary, in either of two rather conflicting ways. The first is to say that the market is good because it promotes efficiency, that is to say, it maximizes the "welfare" of all participants in the process. It does this by definition, because each person participates in the process only because he thinks he gets more that way than he would any other way, and who are we to tell him differently? In maximizing the welfare of all participants it does the same for society as a whole, which is nothing more or less than the sum of all the participants in the market. One obvious trouble with this is that it reduces all social life to the process of exchange (as it reduces all social agents to human individuals); another is that it takes for granted not only the existing values (or "tastes") of the actors, but also the existing distributions among them of wealth, capacity, and entitlement, which it has no way of criticizing. Yet these may of course be eminently criticizable.

The "welfare" defense of the market would justify all transactions—including the sale of oneself into slavery or prostitution—that are not in an obvious sense "coerced" by another because they are marginal improvements for the actors involved. But an economy might provide a different set of starting points for of its actors, so that such degrading activities would no longer be "improvements" for anyone. We would all benefit from living in such a world. But the economist seems to have no way of saying this. On the premises I have described he cannot deny the desirability of redistribution, but he cannot affirm it either. Even to discuss the question requires a shift of discourse beyond this kind of economics.

The second ground upon which the market is justified is that not of its gross effects but of its fairness. This claim has two versions: the first rests upon the ethical standing of voluntary action and holds that the results of the market process are justified with respect to every actor because the choices by which it works are voluntary. The second version becomes the affirmative celebration of autonomy or liberty: whether or not it is efficient, the market is good because it gives the widest possible range to freedom of choice and action. Here the claim moves beyond justifying market results by the voluntary character of the choices upon which they rest to the point of asserting autonomy as the central social and political value. The obvious trouble with this line of defense, in both its forms, is that it assumes that all exchanges are for all actors equally voluntary and equally expressive of autonomy, a position that common sense denies.

Voluntariness and Autonomy

Let us begin with the "voluntariness" of the exchanges studied, which is essential both to the "welfare" and to the "autonomy" justifications. It is one thing to construct an analytic model that assumes voluntary choice as a way of working out what the consequences of such an exchange system would be if it existed, and for those purposes to write off constraints on conduct as one writes off abnormal incompetence and so forth. It is quite another to say that all human behavior not obviously coerced should be regarded as having the ethical or moral status of wholly free, autonomous action, which is entitled to our respect if anything is. Obviously most human choice is greatly constrained, some of it cripplingly so. It may be true that I sell my labor for the minimum wage, working at a noisy, ugly, demeaning, boring, and perhaps dangerous, job, but only because that is the best I can do. I do not want *that* choice to be given the sort of standing that an investor's choice to go for stocks rather than bonds, or my own choice to spend Saturday afternoon on the river or at the museum, should be given.[10]

Not only are we are differently situated financially, in ways that deeply affect the voluntariness of our choices; we are unequally situated psychologically as well. Some of us are much freer from conflicts, compulsions, and similar afflictions than others are. The choices of such people are entitled to a different kind of respect from, say, the decisions of an addict to continue a drug or of a prostitute to continue the life of abuse to which self-hatred commits him. And close inspection of criminal conduct makes it very hard to rest the validity of punishment comfortably on the basis of the free and autonomous moral choices made by those we punish. The "voluntary choice" model may be useful for analyzing certain kinds of conduct—especially that of the self-conscious and competent professional risk-taker who operates in a universe of quantitative symbols, such as the capitalist investor whose modes of thought so deeply shape the discourse of economics—but it does not adequately describe most human behavior.[11] In making ethical judgments, including judgments about social institutions, it is of central importance to keep vivid our sense of the different degrees and kinds of freedom that different actors have; and it is exactly these differences with respect to which the "voluntary choice" model is systematically blind.

* * *

To reduce the ideas of voluntary action, autonomy, and liberty to mere freedom from restraint, or, even more narrowly, to freedom from governmental restraint, as these justifications do, deeply impoverishes our thought. For us political liberty has not meant merely freedom from restraint but enablement or capacitation, and this is always social and communal in character. The question is not only how far people are free or restrained in their exercise of dominion over the assets that nature and society give them, but, far more importantly, what our community enables its people to do or to become. What range of responsibilities and participations, what opportunities for self-development and education, what roles in self-government, does this community offer its members? These are the serious questions about liberty—defining the kind of liberty one could imagine fighting and perhaps dying for, liberty as an aspect of community. To speak to such questions one needs a standard of human and political excellence of a kind that economics by its nature cannot have.

The Mathematical Image of the Person

The incapacity of economics to reflect degrees of voluntariness is actually a particular instance of a larger feature of the discourse, one that derives from its quasi-mathematical character. Its use of labels is inherently binary. One either is or is not "competent," an action is or is not "voluntary," because the formulas that are the stuff of economic thought require that a particular person, object, or event either be, or not be, an "A" or a "B" or whatever other label is used.[12] This is a ruling principle of the sort of logic upon which economics depends, and it marks it as an extreme form of the sort of conceptual discourse discussed in chapter 2. Of course, our actual experience is not of binary or dichotomous phenomena but of degree and of change. Our ordinary language, in its imprecisions and overlappings, reflects that fact. But none of this can be reflected in the language of economics.

The consequences are serious and reach beyond the issue of voluntariness to the very image of the human being that this discourse makes possible. I put aside for the moment the question of motive (reduced to self-interest) and intellectual process (reduced to calculation) and focus on something even more basic, the fact that in our actual lives all human beings are engaged in a never-completed process of growth and change, from infancy to old age. We start, and often end, in total dependence on others; our capacities gradually develop and shift, and some of them necessarily deteriorate; illness, in one form or another is nearly universal; and death lies always at the end. Our lives are a process of organic growth and decay. The development of wisdom, judgment, taste, and character; of the capacity for meaningful action and meaningful speech; of an intelligible identity in relation to others—this is the stuff of human life.

It makes no sense of this experience to speak as if each point in the curve of life is exactly the same as every other point, except for those before and after some arbitrarily chosen lines that determine "competence." Full competence is never attained; weakness and misunderstanding and internal conflict are parts of every human life. To speak of what we do as if all, or almost all, human conduct is equally competent, voluntary, and rational and entitled to respect as such, is to establish a vision that denies the central process of life, the transformation of the self through interactive experience with others. The human individual is not an integer, a feature of a mathematical system, as economics assumes, but—fortunately for us—is instead the locus of conflict, tension, and growth, a place where many selves live together, sometimes in harmony, sometimes not. On the economic view, however, the individual is reduced to a single unit, supposed to know its own values and how best to pursue them. This means, among other things, that education—for the rest of us the process by which character and value are formed—is reduced to the acquisition of information. True education of the mind and self is in such terms completely unimaginable; so too is the conception of the polity as a means of collective education.

To think of the human being as a developing person leads to an entirely different vision of human life and interaction from that supposed by the economist. If you think, for example, of how you have become whatever you are today, you will realize that it is largely through the innumerable gifts of other people. Not only the obvious ones, such as parents and grandparents, but the kindly aunt who could see that you were distressed when no one else could, or the second-grade teacher who saw in you capacities others had missed, or the music instructor whose habits of discipline and standards of excellence taught you something about the nature of achievement, or the kind-hearted custodian at your school who treated you as an equal, or the friends of both sexes who supported and criticized you. One could go on with thousands of instances of the way any human life has been formed by the gifts of others. For our own part, we too bring perpetual gifts to others in our relations with them, gifts that may be good or bad but in any case cannot be captured in the language of exchange.

* * *

It is not too much to say that the modern celebration of the market as the central social institution—as the most fair, most respecting of autonomy, and the most efficient—threatens to destroy the single greatest achievement of Western political culture: the discovery that a community can govern itself through a rule of law that attempts to create a fundamental moral and political equality among human beings. The great phrase in the Declaration of Independence—"all men are created equal"—is partly a theological statement about the conditions under which we are created and partly a political statement about the obligation of the government to acknowledge, indeed to create or re-create, that equality. This is the heart of what is meant both by equality under law and by our democratic institutions more generally, resting as they do on the premise that each person's vote is worth exactly what another's is.

The market purports to rest upon an assumption of the equality of all the actors in the system. In fact it rests upon a different assumption, the equality of every dollar in the system. Since some players have many more dollars, and through this fact are at a competitive advantage, it is a system that actively supports inequality among its actors. The ideology of the market, if it prevailed in its desire to convert all institutions into markets, would destroy this set of political relations and would create another in its stead, based upon the dollar.*

From the point of view of the market and its proponents the government is not what our legal and constitutional tradition insists it is, an institution of self-government, but an alien force, not express-

*For further discussion see the Appendix to this chapter.

ing the judgment of the people, not constituting them as a polity, but interfering in their affairs. To talk about "governmental intervention," for example, is implicitly to assume that there is a pre-governmental state of nature called the market, into which the government intrudes. But this is obviously silly. The entire process depends upon the protection of government, as the proponents of the market should know, for without it they could not hold on to what the social system gives them. Boiled down to essentials, then, the argument really is not that the government should not "intervene," but that it should do so solely on behalf of the market, to reinforce its methods and results, including its inequalities.

A related mythology is that the results of the market system are to be regarded as immutable because any "interference" with them would violate the rights of the possessors to the enjoyment and use of what they had acquired, including its further use in the market to increase their wealth and power. These rights are often spoken of as "natural rights," as though each of us had wrung his wealth from the soil by the sweat of his brow. But the truth is that wealth is always social, produced not only by one's own labors but by the contributions of many others, upon whom both its acquisition and retention alike depend. It is not I alone who have earned what I make, for I could not make it without the constant cooperation of others, who are often paid far less than I.

The market ideology claims to be radically democratic and egalitarian because it leaves every person free to do with her own what she will. But this freedom of choice is not equally distributed among all people. The market is democratic not on the principle of one person, one vote, but on the far different principle of one dollar, one vote. One could hardly make a greater mistake than to equate, as so much modern public talk carelessly does, the "free market" with democracy.

There are two distinct points here. First, the exchange transactions that the market celebrates are not entitled to the special respect claimed for them as free and voluntary, and hence fair, unless each person has roughly the same amount of money and the same competence and freedom in its use, which is demonstrably not the case. The accumulations of wealth it permits cannot thus be justified by the fairness of the transactions by which the accumulation occurs. Second, if the advocates of the market succeeded in converting other institutions into markets, the result would be to transfer to those who have wealth not only the economic power that inescapably follows it but also the political power that in our democratic tradition the people have claimed for themselves and have exercised through the institutions of self-government. This would validate and institutionalize private economic power held by one person over another, of the rich over the poor.[13] If we were to yield entirely to its claims, we would gradually find our traditional government, which operates by collective deliberation on a premise of fundamental equality of citizens, replaced by a private-sector government of the few over the many, wholly unregulated by collective judgment.

Economics as a System of Economic Analysis

But it is not only as a system of value and politics that this kind of economics, and the ways of thought it encourages, are troubling. I think that it is distorted and unrealistic as a way of imagining, thinking about, and shaping the processes of production and exchange that we think of as the economy itself.

The Social and Natural Matrix

The first distortion I wish to consider has to do with the relationship between the exchange system and the cultural and natural world that it necessarily presupposes. What I mean is this. The economic activity of exchange takes place under natural and cultural conditions that are absolutely essential to it, but about which economics has no way of talking except by itemization, quantification, and conversion into the material of actual or hypothetical exchange. All talk about exchanges, that is, necessarily presupposes that the exchangers live in the natural world of sun, air, and water, subject to the powers of growth and health and disease, a world the organization of which is complex far beyond our understanding. Each of the exchangers is part of that world in another sense as well, for each is himself an organism, and one that incompletely understands both himself and his relation to the natural world upon which he absolutely depends for existence. Each actor is also part of a society and culture that establishes a set of understandings and expectations upon which he can rely: that promises will normally be kept, that he can get his money home without being robbed, that it is worth thinking about the future, for oneself or one's children, and so on. The actor's character and motives (or "values"), or what the economists call his "preferences," are themselves formed by interactions both with his culture and with nature. This is how we are made as individuals and how we connect ourselves to the past and to the future.

But on all this economics is silent, for it begins to speak only when an actor has, at least in his own mind, identified some item in the world and begun to think of exchanging it for something else. It is his judgment of its worth, in exchanging it or in declining to do so, that is for the economist its value. But what confidence can we have in such judgments of worth, by actors necessarily imperfectly aware both of themselves and of the cultural and natural worlds they inhabit? To put it in epistemological terms, the economist assumes that there is nothing to be known about the natural or cultural world that cannot be known through the process of exchange itself. But in order to judge the value of an item now, or to predict one for the future, one must make estimates about possible changes in the social, cultural, and natural matrix in which all exchange takes place, about the effect of these exchanges upon that matrix. There is no reason to be especially confident in anyone's capacity to make such estimates.

Another way to put this point is to say that economics sees all value in terms of margins, comparisons, and differences and has no way of talking directly about the matters or items that it compares. Thus it sees the difference between what beans cost at the store and what they cost to grow, but it has no way to value either base upon which that difference rests, the socio-cultural base that enables the grocer to function securely or the natural base that produces the beans. Predictions of future value depend upon a continued stability in the base, which is not and cannot be measured by the value-as-margin method.

This is to talk about it in terms of knowledge, the knowledge that the economist assumes we have. But it can be cast in terms of value as well, for the language of economics assumes that the relation between humanity and nature should be one of dominion, that the expanded assertion of control by individual actors over nature— called "natural resources"—is inherently a good thing. But why should one grant such an assumption? As Wendell Berry repeatedly points out in his works on agricultural economics,[14] modern agriculture can be considered a great technological success only if one uses the measure of present-day output per man-hour, disregarding both the destructive effects of modern farming on the soil and the costs, natural and economic, of the fossil fuels used for both fertilizer and power. If productivity over decades or per acre is the test, as in a world of five billion perhaps it should be, our agriculture falls well below that of many more "primitive" peoples. If one includes the meaning of the kind of work the farmer does, its rhythms and its harmonies or disharmonies with nature, the picture is complicated further; still further if one asks how important it is in a nuclear age for a particular polity, or for humanity, that the capacity for fruitful and stable survival on a small scale be maintained. Economic language assumes, with what a theologian like James Gustafson might call a foolish pride,[15] that man's wants and wishes are the ultimate measure of value; it then claims that these wishes are constrained only in ways that traders can see and account for. These assumptions are dubious, to say the least.

The "non-economic background" that economics assumes to be stable, and which it does not regard as a form of wealth (for it cannot be appropriated and exchanged), is actually not stable at all but in perpetual flux. It is our most important form of wealth. It begins with soil and water and air, all of which we are now damaging in ways we cannot possibly understand. It includes the mysteries of vegetable and animal life, from microbes to mammals, and the value of differentiation into species, which on principle cannot be known until the crisis arrives—the change of weather or the spread of a virus—that will destroy one adaptation and make room for another. It extends to all the social instincts and habits that make collective life possible, including our respect for law, our sense of civic obligation, and our desire to cooperate with others. It includes our sense of the past and all that can be learned from it. In our own culture it includes the habits of self-government—of respect for the majority and minority alike—that run so deep in us, showing up as they do in our competence at organizing ourselves into self-governing communities.*

"Exchange," upon which economics focuses so much, is a secondary rather than a primary mode of life. It presupposes another world, in which it is embedded and which it can strengthen or weaken. Yet economics focuses only on exchange and has no way of talking about this larger world, which operates on such wholly different principles, let alone about the arts of social and communal life by which it is maintained and remade.[16] This is in turn to give the world itself a meaning of a new kind, reflected in the Japanese phrase for the blue sky that can rarely be seen over Tokyo these days: It is called a "recession sky."

And it drastically reduces the meaning of our activities as well. Think of this, for example, in connection with Thoreau's *Walden*, which expresses something of what a life of part-time agriculture meant to the person doing it, and consider how little of what that book and life are about could be expressed in economic terms. This is

---

*For further discussion see the Appendix to this chapter.

true not only of Thoreau's "non-economic" activities, but of the agricultural work itself, about which he is very explicit (especially in the first two chapters). In "The Bean Field" he says:

> When my hoe tinkled against the stones, that music echoed to
> the woods and to the sky, and was an accompaniment to my labor
> that yielded an instant and immeasurable crop. It was no longer
> beans that I hoed or that I hoed beans; and I remembered with as
> much pity as pride, if I remembered them at all, my acquaint-
> ances who had gone to the city to attend the oratorios.[17]

Or think of what Joseph Conrad, in his nautical novels and in his two volumes of autobiography, has managed to make of an activity—sailing a ship—which in economic terms is simply the transport of goods for a price. In *The Mirror of the Sea*, for example, he talks about the difference between sail and steam in these terms:

> History repeats itself, but the special call of an art which has
> passed away is never reproduced. It is as utterly gone out of the
> world as the song of a destroyed wild bird. Nothing will awaken
> the same response of pleasurable emotion or conscientious en-
> deavor. And the sailing of any vessel afloat is an art whose fine
> form seems already receding from us on its way to the overshad-
> owed Valley of Oblivion. The taking of a modern steamship
> around the world (though one would not minimize its responsi-
> bilities) has not the same quality of intimacy with nature, which,
> after all, is the indispensable condition for the building up of an
> art. It is less personal and a more exact calling; less arduous, but
> also less gratifying in the lack of close communion with the artist
> and the medium of his art. It is, in short, less a matter of love.[18]

* * *

The kind of economics I have been discussing naturally tends to value what it calls economic "growth," that is to say, the expansion of the exchange system by the conversion of what is outside it into its terms. It is a kind of steam shovel chewing away at the natural and social world. Another kind of economics might value not growth but conservation, not change or progress but stability, not reduction of nature to commodity but the maintenance of a harmonious relation between humanity and nature, between the domain of exchange and the other domains of human life.[19] It is a truism for economists that "we" are much "richer" than we were 30 years ago. But is that so obviously true if one takes into account the value of safe streets, healthy food, clean air and water, unspoiled scenery, a supportive community, or a sensible pace of life? What is really meant by the economist who says such things is that we have managed to turn more things into commodities. The "GNP" is no measure of true wealth: it positively values interference with nature, its transformation into commodities, and tells us that the richest nation is the one that interferes the most. But could we not have an economics that valued nature highly, and regarded interference with it as a bad thing? The richest nation might then be the one that managed to meet its people's basic needs, for food and shelter and culture and education, with the least interference with the world of nature.

The enormous matrix of productive human life and meaningful activity that lies outside the practices of exchange, like the matrix of the natural world, is simply excluded from the exchange mentality; or, if it is included, it is on terms that destroy its meaning.* Economics of the kind I have been discussing is thus defective even as an economics, for it in principle abstracts from a larger context a set of activities that depend upon, and interact with, that context. A proper economics—in its Greek root meaning household management— would respect and reflect the conditions, natural and cultural, upon which the exchange itself depends and would seek to value properly what that system by its nature radically undervalues.

The Only Possibility?

Are other kinds of economy, and of economic analysis, possible? The usual thing is to think of Marxism as the only alternative, but the kind of "Marxism" claimed by certain antidemocratic totalitarian states obviously offers no relief. In fact, in certain respects—I think of Marx's attitudes towards the relations between humanity and nature—the ideology of such economics closely parallels our own.[20]

But there are other possibilities. Here, for example, is E. F. Schumacher's brief description of Buddhist economic life as practiced in Burma:

> The Buddhist point of view takes the function of work to be at least threefold: to give a man a chance to utilize and develop his faculties; to enable him to overcome his ego-centeredness by joining with other people in a common task; and to bring forth the goods and services needed for a becoming existence. . . . [T]he

*For further discussion see the Appendix to this chapter.

consequences that flow from this view are endless. To organize work in such a manner that it becomes meaningless, boring, stultifying, or nerve-racking for the worker would be little short of criminal; it would indicate a greater concern with goods than with people, an evil lack of compassion and a soul-destroying degree of attachment to the most primitive side of this worldly existence. Equally, to strive for leisure as an alternative to work would be considered a complete misunderstanding of one of the basic truths of human existence, namely that work and leisure are complementary parts of the same living process and cannot be separated without destroying the joy of work and the bliss of leisure. . . . It is clear, therefore, that Buddhist economics must be very different from the economics of modern materialism, since the Buddhist sees the essence of civilization not in a multiplication of wants but in the purification of human character. Character, at the same time, is formed primarily by a man's work. And work, properly conducted in conditions of human dignity and freedom, blesses those who do it and equally their products.

* * *

While the materialist is mainly interested in goods, the Buddhist is mainly interested in liberation. But Buddhism is "The Middle Way" and therefore in no way antagonistic to physical well-being. It is not wealth that stands in the way of liberation but the attachment to wealth; not the enjoyment of pleasurable things but the craving for them. The keynote of Buddhist economics, therefore, is simplicity and non-violence. From an economist's point of view, the marvel of the Buddhist way of life is the utter rationality of its pattern—amazingly small means leading to extraordinarily satisfactory results.

For the modern economist this is very difficult to understand. He is used to measuring the "standard of living" by the amount of annual consumption, assuming all the time that a man who consumes more is "better off" than a man who consumes less. A Buddhist economist would consider this approach excessively irrational: since consumption is merely a means to human well-being, the aim should be to obtain the maximum of well-being with the minimum of consumption.[21]

I am not now concerned with the question whether this is an accurate description of Burmese attitudes but with the helplessness of modern economic language before patterns of this kind. Here we have described for us a life based upon desire not for objects or resources, for which there is competition and a market, but for meanings and relations. The "good" or excellence of life desired is not in principle limited in quantity; its "scarcity" is not to be reduced by increased production or managed by market exchanges, but must be dealt with by each person as he faces the limits of his mind and circumstances, alone or with others.

The key to the difference is perhaps the place given to the human will. For neoclassical microeconomics there is no higher value: the will is the source of the tastes and preferences that drive the machine of the social world and since it cannot be questioned save in its own terms it has nothing to learn except how to get what it wants. Another kind of economics might begin with the premise that the human will is often an engine of destruction; that its first need is not satisfaction but education, and this primarily an education into an understanding of the limited and dependent place the human being has in the world—limited in its own comprehension, even of itself, and dependent, both upon nature and upon others, for everything of value.

A true recognition of the equality of human beings would result not in the market economy, which is really a system of dominance and acquisition, but in an economy that achieved a far more equal sharing of the wealth, and did so by a severe curtailing of the desire to consume and expend. This would be an economics of education, freeing the self, and the community, from the false belief that what the human being wants or needs can be found in the Gross National Product. Meaning might instead be located in activities of love and art. But these are exactly the things—respect, love, art, education—about which economics of the standard kind cannot talk.

* * *

The language of neoclassical microeconomics is not a universal language of descriptive analysis, let alone of judgment, but is deeply rooted in the practices of a capitalist industrial and commercial economy. Much of its plausibility derives from the fact that the assumptions it makes about human behavior and reasoning fit rather well with the acquisitive values and calculating rationality of the economic sphere of our own larger culture. If one approves those aspects of our culture and wishes to extend them, as many do, there is perhaps no difficulty with this; but if one wishes to think about whether or not to approve them, this kind of economics does not afford a language in which one can do so, since it is by its very premises committed to them. There is thus a double relation between this method of economic analysis and our larger culture: the dissemination of this way of talking tends to confirm attitudes and conduct that conform to it, the prevalence of which are in turn taken to confirm the rightness of the method—all on the assumption that the premises of our own economy are built in to the nature of humanity. In this sense the "politics" of this kind of economic discourse is directly continuous with politics of another, more obvious, kind.

Controlling the Discourse

What has happened in this thought-experiment is that I have asked you to begin to think about a certain kind of economics as a total culture, about what it would mean to make one feature of our shared existence, namely economic exchange, the dominant metaphor for all of our shared existence. For me at least the results are impossible. I have described economics as a political system and as an economic system. A full account would go further, and describe it as a psychological system, a religious system, a linguistic system, a system of high culture and education, a system of reason, and so on. I have not done that in any detail, but you can perhaps see the lines along which such analyses would begin.*

*For helpful assistance in thinking about the psychology of this system, and of other social systems too, see Donald W. Winnicott, "Some Thoughts on the Meaning of the Word 'Democracy,'" in *Home Is Where We Start From: Essays by a Psychoanalyst*, p. 239 (1986), where he argues that democracy at once depends upon the emotional health and maturity of the citizen and contributes to those things. An ideology based on consumption, on strategies for maximizing, on a view of human tastes as of equal value and on their satisfaction as an unqualified good thing is hardly a recipe for health and maturity.

As for religion: One of the primary objects of religion is to draw our attention away from the apparent meaning of our activities towards something deeper, towards what in the view of the religion in question is "really going on" while we lead our daily lives of work and play. Religion speaks to what can be seen only from a distant point, from which life can be seen as a whole. It normally does this against our desires to deny certain features of our lives, especially the fact that we are mortal and that all object-oriented satisfactions are certain to end in failure. The idea is to bring us face to face with what we normally deny about our nature and our circumstances, with the idea of helping us live on those terms, that is to say, more truly. This is true of all religions with which I am at all familiar.

What would happen if one tried to make a religion of economics? It is true that the economist wants to penetrate the forms of life to reach a deeper truth, but economics works in the opposite way from religion, namely to narrow our range of vision, to increase our denials—it denies not only what we repress but what we know in our daily lives—with the effect of stimulating or increasing object-oriented behavior.

Similarly, while religious language is typically transcendental—a way of pointing or leading to a mystery in the world or in the self that cannot be described or reproduced in language, one that is beyond the reach of the "rational" mind—

Fortunately, as I said at the outset, the picture of economics as a total culture, even apart from any errors of understanding I may have made, is at most an extrapolation, an exaggerated rendition of certain implications of economic talk. No economist makes economics his only language; no one could. It must in the end bear some reciprocal relation to the rest of the culture, and the question is what that relation should be.

The economist, as insider, has to ask himself how this language, to which he is deeply committed, can and should be integrated with other languages, what other aspects of the culture should be mobilized and kept alive in his mind and talk, and whether, in consequence, the language of economics should itself be transformed. For us as comparative outsiders the question is both harder and simpler: harder because we know less about the language, but also simpler, for we are less committed to it. We can thus regard our main tasks as establishing habits of caution and circumspection before we consciously adopt its modes of thoughts and expression, as trying to become alert to the ways in which we have already unconsciously done so, and as learning to insist upon the regulation of this language by the practices of the larger culture, including the legal culture, of which we are a part.[22]

But how, and with what effect is this to be done?

A Problem of Writing

The forces against which one must work are powerful ones, for the conversion of theory into ideology, the movement from a set of obviously false assumptions to a picture of our social world thought to be

---

economics tends to claim not only that everything can be reduced to the power of reason but that reason can be reduced to a very small number of mental functions indeed. Instead of ennobling humanity by recognizing our every capacity and the limits beyond, it reduces humanity to a tiny slice of experience and thought. If economics were a total culture, then, and its language treated as adequate to all occasions, it would create an anti-religion, turning people away from trying to understand the meaning of their activities in a larger context, as fundamentally ethical and relational, towards a reduced understanding of them, as activities defined in terms of goals or objects.

This can of course be presented as a kind of hard-headed realism, an aversion to mushy talk about "meaning" and the like. But here as elsewhere, materialism is chosen for non-material ends that can themselves be seen and evaluated. Economic discourse, for example, expresses the deep desire to live in a world of objects and instruments, a world in which human actors compete for acquisition, prestige, and dominance.

true, is a natural process—anyone tends to universalize his language
and its assumptions—and one that it is hard to resist, perhaps impossible to resist completely. But I think I know where in the effort
one should focus one's attention, and that is on the attitude we have
towards the language we are using. The conversion of theory into
ideology works by a literary process, and I think the most important
method of resistance for economists and others alike is literary too: it
is to keep alive the recognition that not everything can be said in
economic terms, that to speak this language is to commit oneself in
ways that need to be resisted, that there are other languages, other
cultures, with which it must have a relation and to which it should
on many occasions submit.

This is not just a matter of saying, "Oh, yes, I know all that,"
and proceeding as usual. Sensitivity to the political and ethical significance of the discourse and to its intellectual limitations, if it is real,
will show up not merely in appendices or prolegomena but also in
one's actual writing and talking. This means that the discourse itself
will inevitably undergo transformation of kinds now impossible to
foresee. Not only, then, are those of us who stand in the general culture wise ourselves to resist the imperialism of economics; we can
properly insist as well that in speaking to us the economist integrate
what he knows as an economist with what he knows in the rest of life
and reflect this knowledge in the way he talks about the nature of our
community and its future. I am not trying to suggest that economists
should stop their trade but that they should be something else as
well, rhetorical and cultural critics of their own discourse. When they
are that, I believe they will find that their discourse itself will have to
be transformed.

It is not enough, that is, simply to confine economics to its
proper sphere or domain. It needs to be integrated with and transformed by the other discourses that make up our culture, by the rest
of what we know and value. For the political and other implications
of economics do not disappear when it is no longer regarded, as we
have been doing, as a total culture. They inhere in this language,
though in reduced form, even when it is used at its best, to analyze
those activities that proceed on its assumptions: where there is a market with easy exit and entry, where the itemization by which the
market proceeds involves no serious denial of complexity, where
there are adequate substitutes for the items exchanged (hence elas-
ticity of supply and demand), where the motives of the traders are in
fact wealth-maximizing, where most or all agree that the relevant values translate into dollars or some other medium of exchange, where

the actors are more or less equally situated with respect to wealth, competence, and other constraints, and so on. Even here, that is, economics has the political and ethical implications, and some of the economic failings, that I describe above.

This is true of neoclassical microeconomics of the "Chicago School" (or so I have been arguing), but how far is it true of other forms of economics and of our public thought more generally? Here we reach the limits of my own training to which I referred in the opening pages of this chapter. I do not know enough to say how far particular economists have been able to address in their writing the kinds of implications of their discourse that I have been tracing out, nor how far they have been able to create economic discourses of importantly different kinds. It has not been my object here to make such particular judgments, but rather to work out a method of analysis and criticism that can help us think about what is called for in such work, when we turn to it, and how it might be evaluated. (I do know that Schumacher is an economist, and he has obviously found other ways to think, and the same might be said of Amartya Sen and perhaps many others.) The study of the kind of economics I have been considering here is especially useful to this end, partly because that is the form of economics that has been most overtly imperialistic, especially with respect to law, partly because the very extremism of this form of economics brings into vision the forces and tendencies of the discourse with which more civilized forms of economics must find a way to come to terms.

I must also leave to the reader's own reflections how far what I have been saying is true not only of economics but of much of our public talk, that is, how far it is true, as I suggested earlier, that "we are all economists now." To try to establish that point would require a book of its own, or a series of them. But, for what it is worth, in my view it is not just this kind of economics that presents the dangers I describe, though it does so in extraordinarily stark form: all other attempts to isolate exchange and production from an understanding of our dependence on the natural world, all other attempts to apply to human life the language and methods of physical science, indeed all manifestations of the mechanistic assumptions of the modern world—that the world is a machine, that the mind is a machine, that human organizations are machines—present, in perhaps in diluted form, many of the same fundamental evils.[23] Our question is how to come to terms with the language of mechanism, particularly when there are occasions on which it seems to be of some real use. The answer is that we must develop what I earlier called the art of integration—of talking more than one way at once, as poets do—but this time in the hope not only that we can integrate this discourse with our others, but also that by doing so we may ultimately transform it into a language of a different kind, making possible an economics that will make sense of our situation and of the real character of our interactions with each other and with nature.

* * *

Whatever its merits, the language and practice of economics cannot be justified in its own terms. Whoever is to think and speak seriously about this matter must in the end turn to some other discourse, some other language, than economics. When that happens one necessarily affirms a view of self and language for which economics itself is insufficient. This is to take the single step I think most essential, to begin to think in more than one language, more than one voice, and thus to locate the particular practices of a discourse in the larger context of the rest of what we know and are.

To put my point slightly differently: When the economist speaks to us, he is acting not as an economic actor himself, engaging in arms-length exchanges designed to increase his utility, but as one mind speaking to another, seeking to persuade to particular conclusions, to a language, to a view of life. He speaks as a person asking to be believed. He is engaged, that is, in the rhetorical and communal practices of conversation in which he asks to be listened to as one who seeks the truth, and these are activities for the description and criticism of which his own language as an economist is wholly inadequate.

The Culture of the Law

The discourse of the law has its own dangers, especially those associated with the intellectual and social form we call the legal rule, which has a tendency to reduce people and events to caricature, and with the use of formulas to disguise exercises of power that are essentially authoritarian in nature. Some of these dangers will be examined in the chapters that follow. In addition to them there are those that exist whenever anyone thinks that the language he is speaking is the only language, and this is not a disease to which lawyers are immune.

But there are nonetheless real differences between economics and law, for law assumes an equality of actors and speakers, not of dollars; it provides a set of speaking-places where real differences of view and interest can be defined and addressed; it is not self-applying but leaves room for argument both ways; it is continuous with ordinary language and politics, and thus necessarily respects the culture it acts upon and out of; its methods of reasoning are not linear but multidimensional; its conversations take place among a plurality of voices; and it is inherently idealizing, taking as its constant subject what we ought to do, who we ought to be.

For what the law insists upon is that we are a discoursing community, committed to talking with each other about our differences of perception, feeling, and value, our differences of language and experience. The task of law is to provide a place and a set of institutions and methods where this conversational process can go on, as well as a second conversation by which the first is criticized and judged. Political power is divided up among separate actors under circumstances requiring that they talk to each other. This creates an occasion and necessity for deliberative and institutional politics, a method of collective thought, that is in principle wholly different from the expression of want or desire in the instant referendum of the market. This process is not reducible to the metaphor of exchange, to a conception of humanity as consisting of self-interested atoms trading at arm's length, or to a view of the institution—or "firm"—as such a trade set up on a permanent basis. For institutions are part of the culture that makes us what we are; they provide talking-places of special kinds and a kind of collective memory too.

The law requires us to attend to the past and what can be learned from it; it is indeed a system of collective self-education. The method for the analysis of this process is rhetorical, the standards ethical and political and cultural: Who are we to each other? How do we address our differences in language and situation? How can we best bring our inherited resources to bear upon this case, or this situation, and in so doing affirm and transform them? These are the questions, and this the view of law, that we shall bring to judicial opinions in the chapters that follow.

* * *

The difference between law and economics is perhaps most sharp on the central matter I have been addressing, the attitude towards one's own language and world. This I think can be posed as a question of attitude towards translation and translatability. Economics gets most seriously into trouble when its practitioners assume that everything can be said in its terms, that it is an adequate language for constructing the central metaphors of our social life. This is to speak as if this language has no force of its own. What is real to such a speaker are the objects in the world and the people who desire those objects and struggle with each other, one way or another, to obtain them. The function of language is to represent this world. It is thought to have no independent social or cultural or political reality. It is simply a transparent system for identifying the actors and those objects in the world that are the objects of desire or disdain, or for pointing towards the concepts,[24] existing above or beyond language itself, that create the mathematical entity called an economy. The language of economics is thus assumed to be a super-language, or an authoritative meta-language, and this in two dimensions: it describes the world the only way the world can be described; and it creates a set of conceptual structures which, if they meet the tests of economics themselves, are the only accurate conceptual structures for thinking about the world. Everything that is real can be said in, or translated into, this language.

What I have called the literary view of language—though many physicists and biologists would recognize it too—is that all languages are limited; that none says the whole truth; that full translation from one to the other is always in a deep sense impossible. This means that the most profound obligation of each of us in using his or her language is to try to recognize what it leaves out, to point to the silence that surrounds it—to acknowledge the terrible incompleteness of all speech, and thus to leave oneself open to hearing other truths, in other languages.

While lawyers can of course make the mistake of thinking that their language is the only one, the pressures of the law are against it, for the law is a constant linguistic competition. How to characterize the facts and the law, how to conceive of and feel about the case, and what, therefore, to do about it, are the central questions for the lawyer, who knows that her categories are those of argument and judgment, not simple factual description. The terms of her language itself are always arguable. The legal conversation must therefore proceed, if it is to proceed well, with a kind of structural tentativeness about itself. The law, at its best, is a system of translation that acknowledges its own inadequacies. It should listen to economics, regarding it as one language, one set of metaphors among many, and be willing to use it, when appropriate and with appropriate qualifications and transformations. But the last thing it should do is turn itself over to this other culture, working on such different linguistic, social, and political principles.

To think now of the most general version of my question and ask by what central metaphors we should conceive of our world, our motives and relations, I think we should turn to the traditional constitutional conception of humankind living in a natural world beyond our full comprehension, bound together by law, the first principle of which is the equal value of each human being, under a set of governments that democracy aims to make communities as well. We can conceive of human beings as living in time, in cultural and social contexts, as growing from childhood to maturity, as having children of their own; as people with a variety of languages and voices; and we can do so with a sense of the limits of their minds and ours. We can conceive of the material universe as one that is fundamentally organic and we can acknowledge our dependence, economically and otherwise, upon it. Law, as we have traditionally conceived and practiced it—as a rhetorical and cultural activity, as an art of language and of life—has been based upon such a view of human life. It has the great merit of drawing our attention constantly to the limits of our own point of view, of our own language, and towards the unknown merits of another. We should not abandon it.

APPENDIX

1. Dollar Democracy

I wish here to develop the point made in the text that the language of economics is blind to the differences of wealth among different actors in the real world and hence to what many of us would regard as the inherent unfairness of the transactions in which they engage. One response of the economist is to say that the distribution of wealth is not an economic but a political question, and that society ought simply to decide what it wants to do about unequal distribution and then do it. The economist as such has no special wisdom on that matter, and thus no objection in principle to any political decisions made, including those involving radical redistribution. If sincerely meant, this position is, so far, unobjectionable. But how can one continue happily to study and play the game and impliedly assert its fairness without ever asking what its premises are? If one cannot ask such a question "as an economist," one can ask it as an independent mind, and should not one's answer show up in one's work, one way or another?

Another response of the economist is simply to make the assumption formal, give it a name—the marginal utility of money—and claim that a dollar *is* worth the same to a rich man as a poor man, or at least that we cannot claim that it is worth less. This is said to be required by the primary assumption of the discourse that utility, or value, is individually determined, a matter on which therefore the economist, as an economist, cannot speak. If so, the transactions between rich and poor are not unfair in the sense claimed. This justification appears to rest on other-respecting agnosticism—Who am I to speak about the experience of others?—but I think it is so unrealistic that it must be rooted in desire, either in the desire not to think about such things or in the desire to see, and participate in, real differences in wealth and power. (Who am I to say that this chocolate éclair is not worth more to the fat rich man than this loaf of bread is to the poor woman with three hungry children?)[25]

The position on the marginal utility of money itself is easily refutable, and not only by appealing to one's capacity to imagine with sympathy the plight of others. Think, for example, of one voluntary institution that does in fact work by exchange and risk-assessment: the poker game. The poker game depends entirely upon the rough economic equality of the participants. Otherwise the process of bluffing and betting becomes both unfair and uninteresting and the poorer player quits. The rich man has the edge every time, for what he risks is worth less to him than the same amount to his poorer neighbor, and everyone knows it.[26] The same is true of the market itself. To the claim that the market is a fair game and its results entitled to ethical respect, one can respond that this game would be fair, if at all, only if the conditions on which we played it were roughly similar for all of us, which they patently are not.[27]

2. Permanent and Renewable Resources

Another way to approach the limits of economics is to assume for the moment the validity of the language of "resources" and "valuation," and ask how adequately the market values resources that have a long or indefinite life. I think that it systematically undervalues them and that the reason has to do with the nature of an exchange-for-money economy. Because for this kind of economics all value is ultimately exchange value and hence, in our world, money value; and because money has its own value, determined by supply and demand for present capital; and because money value is always a rent, that is, measured against time; and because the exchange method generates the conception of income over time as the definition of wealth; this kind of economics can have no way to measure any "resource" that has a permanent value. In an environment in which individuals can invest their capital in financial markets and obtain a return of so much per year, all other investments that do not produce that income per year are automatically unreasonable (unless they will produce some exploding balloon of income in the not-too-far distant future). The investment of money for a return thus becomes the model to which all other investments are assimilated. On this method the present value of anything that will come into possession very far in the future, say fifty years hence, is nearly zero, even though in ways not reflected in the income-over-time method of measuring wealth its value in fact may be enormous. This is true most obviously of the natural resources of the renewable kind (fisheries, forests, the soil itself, and so on), but certainly no less so of the social and cultural resources of which I spoke above.[28]

What is more, the value of money (or other medium of exchange) is itself completely dependent upon the larger social, natural, and cultural context of which economic exchange is only a part. This means that there is a kind of structural paradox: the possibility of money rent in a capitalist system forces all other investments to that model; but that model is itself parasitic upon other sources of value that are not accurately reflected in it.

3. Erasing Community

Economics has the greatest difficulty in reflecting the reality of human community and the value of communal institutions. Its necessary tendency seems to be to destroy the idea of public action, indeed the idea of community itself. One reason for this is that its method tends to resolve all communities and organizations into the individual human actors who constitute them: for economics the whole—the family, the institution, the village, the nation—is never more than the sum of its parts. Another reason is that the commitment to the market system leads to the view that everything that can be made the subject of the market should be. The idea is that every economic actor should pay for what he wants and should not have to pay for what he doesn't want. But this tends to destroy our public institutions, all of which extend benefits far beyond those who would pay (if they were reduced to markets) or who do pay (when they are supported by taxes). Such institutions reflect a communal judgment that we need to educate ourselves and each other, that our "tastes" are not all of equal value but need to be formed, and formed well rather than badly. Public[29] universities, libraries, orchestras, museums, parks,—all these would fall before the ideology that denies the existence and reality of community and reduces all institutions, all human production, to the language of the market.

This at least is the tendency of the popularized version of this kind of economics. In its more sophisticated forms it seeks to describe and explain cooperation—this is what the literature on the institution of the firm is about, for example—but it does so in its familiar terms, those of individual actors pursuing individual interests. The force and reality and presence of institutions as entities in our lives is erased. And of course there is no way to judge them, except as they approximate the market.[30]

Think here of the way economists explain why people who will probably never visit, say, the Everglades or an art museum are happy to have their taxes used to maintain them. The economist says it is because the actor wants to maintain the option of visiting them some day, and calls this an "option demand." But may it not be that the voter simply takes pleasure in what other people have and in what other people can do, in belonging to a community which is good for all its members? Or that he respects their desires and wants a community based on that kind of mutual respect? This possibility is systematically denied by the assumption of economic talk that individuals and communities are on principle incapable of generosity, or more precisely, that "altruism" can adequately be talked about as a species of selfishness. The idea of community is reduced to "the insurance principle."

The language of self and self-interest not only fails to reflect the reality of community and of shared interests, it draws attention away from those aspects of life as well, and devalues them. To continue to talk on these assumptions, even hypothetically, is to encourage "self-interest" in an ethical sense and to erode the commitments we have to each other which underlie such essential practices of citizenship as the willingness to pay taxes, to work for the local school, or to serve in the army, upon which everything depends. To adopt the economic view would in fact threaten the very existence of community, for on these premises no one would conceivably die or risk her life for her community: at the point of danger, one's self-interest in survival would outweigh all other self interests. And to speak of all "tastes" as if they were equivalent is to invite oneself and others to think that they are, and to confirm the premises of our culture, already drummed into the mind by the consumer economy, that the consumer is king, that whatever you happen to want is a good that you should seek to satisfy, that no distinction can be drawn between the beautiful and ugly, the wise and foolish, and so on. It is to confirm a vulgar view of democracy that makes the preference or will supreme, as if we functioned by instant referendum. It erases the sense that a democracy is a mode of communal self-constitution and self-educa-tion that may have higher ends than the satisfaction of wants, namely the creation of a community of a certain sort, at once based upon a set of responsibilities and offering us a set of opportunities for civic and social action.

THE JUDICIAL OPINION
AS A FORM OF LIFE

4

Judicial Criticism

In the preceding chapters I have examined two rather closely related tendencies that are powerfully at work in our culture and hence, of necessity, in our own minds: to think of language in what I call "conceptual" terms and to think of social life in "economic" ones. Each tendency has particularly sharp versions—the first in the modes of thought typical of analytic philosophy, scientific linguistics, and most empirical social science, the second in those of neoclassical microeconomics—but each also has versions that are far more widespread and diffuse (though by no means for this reason necessarily less pronounced in their effects). At one level of intensity or another these two attitudes towards language and the world dominate a great deal of both academic and popular thought. While there are of course people who work on a different set of understandings—in certain branches of anthropology, in humanistic linguistics and psychology, in much literary criticism, and so on—they remain exceptions, and some of the more extreme of these exceptions provide little help to the lawyer, for they posit individuals hopelessly entrapped in language, incapable of the kind of independent action that any internal view of law requires.

In this and the following chapters I mean to resist these tendencies of mind by invoking a literary view of language, a lawyer's view of the world. In doing this I turn particularly to the form of language and of life that we call the judicial opinion. This (as lawyers of course know but others may not) is the text in which a judge seeks to explain what questions a case presents, how she resolves them, and why she resolves them as she does. For far more than other legal actors, judges are, under our arrangements, expected to explain their decisions and, they must hope, to justify them, and the opinion is the form in which they do so. Today's opinion, making law, is tomorrow's precedent; taken as a whole, a string of opinions represent a collective effort to come to terms with a problem of legal judgment in varying contexts.

The study of the judicial opinion has traditionally been placed at the center of a legal education, and I think properly so, for this is a moment at which the law is made real, a moment when the welter of statutes and precedents and maxims and other materials of the past are brought to bear with force and clarity upon an actual dispute. Law schools are sometimes criticized for focusing too much on the opinion, especially in an age of statutes, and of course students should study statutes and regulations (and contracts too), as well as opinions, and think about how to read and draft them. But both the reading and the drafting of such texts are best done by imagining the cases in which a lawyer might turn to them. The nature of human imagination and language being what they are, many of these cases will lie at the borders of the text, or present conflicts within its discourse or between it and other legal texts, conflicts that no one thought about ahead of time. This is part of what makes the actual legal case so interesting and challenging, both for the lawyer and for the judge: it is not simply an item to be placed into a preexisting grid but an occasion for thought and argument of a kind that throws into question the assumption that the statute—or regulation, or contract, or constitutional provision—in any simple way disposes of the case. It may of course at first glance seem to do so; but whether it should be held to do so, and if so how far, and why, are questions the lawyers and the court must address. The modes of thought and argument by which they do so are the center of the law.

The opinion is the main model of thought for the lawyer as well as the student, for nearly everything he does—drafting, negotiating, reading contracts and statutes—is done, as it were, under the shadow of the judicial proceeding that might come. He naturally thinks, all the time, of the terms in which a case or question might be argued to a judge, terms that are for the most part established in the opinions by which the judges speak to us. The judicial opinion is in this sense the representative legal text, the document that catches and freezes for a moment the legal mind at work.

* * *

I begin this series of chapters with a double quotation, which can serve as a theme for the whole. It comes from the linguist Alton Becker, who once began a lecture on language and culture by saying that one universal aspect of cultural life is the keeping alive of old texts, a reiteration of what was said before in a new context where it can have a life that is at once old and new. (The Javanese even have a word for it.) The text that Becker chose to keep alive in his own lecture was a remark made by John Dewey when, towards the end of his long life, he summed up what he had learned from it all. Dewey said: "Democracy begins in conversation."[1] In this chapter and those that follow I shall try to give that same sentence a continued life, by locating it in a new context.

The process of giving life to old texts by placing them in new ways and in new relations is of course familiar to us as lawyers. It is how the law lives and grows and transforms itself, for the law is nothing if it is not a way of paying attention and respect to what is outside of ourselves: to texts made by others in the past, which we regard as authoritative, and to texts made in the present by our fellow citizens, to which we listen. We try to place texts of both sorts in patterns of what has been and what will be, and these patterns are themselves compositions. The law is thus at its heart an interpretive and compositional—and in this sense a radically literary—activity.

Such at least is my view: for others the law is policy, nothing but policy, and the only question, what results we prefer; or power, nothing but power, and the only question, who has it; or perhaps it is morality, and the only question, what is "right" or "wrong." So in this and the following chapters I will be making a claim for the character of law itself, as a way of reading, comparing, and criticizing authoritative texts, and, in so doing, as a way of constituting, through conversation, a community and a culture of a certain kind. In doing this I shall try to give a series of old legal texts renewed life too, beginning (later in this chapter) with the opinion of Justice Frankfurter in *Rochin v. California*.[2]

Opinion and Result

In speaking of the criticism of judicial opinions I mean to accept, though only for the moment, the rather common separation of the opinion from the result, the form from the content, and to focus upon the former: the text in which the judge explains or justifies or otherwise talks about the decision that he, and his court, have reached in the particular case.

It is, after all, to a large degree in the opinion, not the decision, that the great judge manifests her greatness: anyone can vote her intuitions or biases or feelings—for or against the plaintiff, the poor, the rich, the government—and in the nature of things all our decisions of that kind are ultimately mysterious, even to ourselves. The great contribution of the judicial mind is not the vote but the judicial opinion, which gives meaning to the vote. This is the text in which—at least in its ideal form—the case is characterized and located with respect to a series of prior, authoritative texts, assimilated to one line, distinguished from another; in which competing lines of argument are developed, with the object of exposing to view what is most deeply problematic both in our resources of legal meaning and in the case upon which they bear; in which the power of generality is brought to bear upon a case presented in its full particularity; and in which the speaker shows sensitivity to the imperatives and limits of his or her institutional situation. The opinions we were as students taught to admire were formed by such aspirations, and they taught us much of what there was to admire in the law and in the legal process. Of course results matter too; but most cases that reach the Supreme Court, at least, are hard—decent and intelligent people could vote either way and in fact have usually done so—and in an important sense what distinguishes the work of a good judge is not the vote but the achievement of mind, essentially literary in character, by which the results are given meaning in the context of the rest of law, the rest of life.

I do not mean to express indifference to the results in particular cases. The result is always important to the parties and in a series of results a court defines itself, the law, and us, in important ways. But what are those "results?" At the most rudimentary level they are a series of judgments of affirmance or reversal, or perhaps refusals to review, each of which may of course be of great significance to the parties involved and perhaps of some interest to others. But beyond this simple act of approval or disapproval the meaning of the case—of the "result"—must lie in the language and opinion of the court, in what it is made to mean in the first instance by the judges, and in the second instance by us. The "result" is not just an act, but always an act for which meaning is claimed.

The distinction between result and opinion with which I began thus itself breaks down, and we can see that the most important "result" is often the opinion itself. This line is blurred in another way as well, for part of our faith as lawyers is that the process of judgment and explanation that writing a series of opinions requires, or makes possible, is itself deeply educative, a training of the mind and sensibility of the individual judge—and of the collectivity of judges, of the lawyers and the public—of such a kind that over time the decisions in the cruder sense, the votes, as well as the opinions, will be more sound, more intelligent, and more just.

Another way to suggest the line of thought I am taking is to invoke (as I did in the Introduction) a feeling that is familiar to all lawyers and law professors, that there is often something to admire in an opinion with the result of which we disagree (in the simple sense that we would have voted the other way) and often something to deplore in opinions that "come out" the way we would vote if we had the responsibility of judging. There is for all of us, that is, a standard of judicial excellence that is different from the standard by which we determine how we would have voted on the question of affirmance or reversal. My question is, What is that standard of judicial excellence? What should it be?

Our present language for talking about these matters is not very satisfactory, a fact that is revealed with special sharpness by the difficulty many of us have in explaining our strong but inarticulate feeling that the art form of the judicial opinion has in recent years fallen on very hard times indeed. "Judicial opinions are becoming worse and worse," we find ourselves saying with increasing frequency. But when we are asked to explain what we mean, we tend to fall into an embarrassed silence: We perhaps claim that the "level of analysis" is "lower" than it used to be, or the "quality of mind" less "acute," or some such thing, but beyond that kind of conclusory remark we have very little to say.[3] Some people have tried to explain the deterioration in quality as resulting from the bureaucratization of law, from the writing of opinions by law clerks for example, and there is a great deal of force in that line of thought, though I think there are other causes too (including an increased acceptance of economic language). But at the moment I am interested less in why the discourse of the law has deteriorated than in what that deterioration itself consists of: What do we mean—or what can we mean—when we say that judicial opinions are worse than they used to be? Does this deterioration really matter much, and if so, why?

These are large questions, to say the least, and in this chapter I can at most make a beginning on them. My hope here and in the following chapters is to start to work out a language of judicial criticism, a language in which the various possibilities of this form, for good and ill, can be identified and judged.

Methods of Criticism

It may be surprising to suggest that those of us who are lawyers, at least, do not know how to criticize judicial opinions well, for in law school, both as students and as teachers, we seem to do little else. The judicial opinion is the core of a legal education. Learning to analyze and judge opinions is what we do and we have traditionally believed that this is a good thing. To learn to read judicial opinions is the best possible way to learn to "think like a lawyer," we say, and thus the best possible way to prepare to engage not only in judicial argument but in all the activities that make up a lawyer's life, including such apparently different activities as negotiation and drafting. Nearly everything that lawyers do takes place on the understanding that our ultimate forum is likely to be judicial, and this means that some kind of judicial criticism is necessarily present in all that we do.

But what kind of judicial criticism do we actually practice and teach? What is the language in which we describe how opinions are made, in which we admire and condemn what we see? What, that is, is the equivalent in law and law schools of historiography, of the philosophy of science, or of literary criticism in the fields to which those disciplines relate?

The Craft Tradition and "Legal Realism"

The established tradition of judicial criticism, like the legal tradition more generally, has been a craft tradition, in which we all too often speak as if all "good lawyers" (and sensible people) will automatically see what is to be admired in a judicial opinion, and what condemned, as soon as it is pointed out to them. This form of judicial criticism is in structure similar to the old-fashioned kind of literary criticism that consisted of pointing out "beauties" and "defects." Thus in class law teachers will work over a judicial opinion, testing its "reasoning," looking for omissions or weak arguments and the like, and leave the class with a sense, usually, of defectiveness. The students learn to critize by imitating and pleasing a master, and all too often the kind of criticism they learn is fundamentally destructive in nature. (One is sometimes reminded of Swift's definition of the *"True Critick"*: "he is *a Discoverer and Collector of Writers Faults."*)[4] But the students are to imagine themselves doing it better and it is in this imagined compositional process that the center of a legal education can be found.

I believe that there is much to be said for this kind of teaching, both intellectually and ethically,[5] but it requires a shared sense of what we admire and what we deplore, or at least a language in which to talk about our different views of these things. The craft tradition does not supply this need, both because that tradition by its nature provides almost nothing to serve as a language of criticism and because the consensus of taste or value underlying it has for some time been breaking down, leaving little or nothing to take its place. We are left with the question, how can we make what we do the subject of conscious and critical thought of a respectable kind?

One common tendency has been to disregard the opinion itself and to focus solely on the result, piercing the felt artificiality of the words to reach the "reality" that lies behind the facade. Such was the effort of the "legal realism" that sought to penetrate the seemingly deceptive, or self-deceptive, formulations of traditional legal discourse. This of course did not wholly avoid the problem of criticism, for one had still to ask how the results were to be explained and criticized; but it did relocate it, by directing attention away from the composition the judge makes towards the holding and its consequences. And it suggested a method too, at least for minds inclined to think in terms of social science. Surely one social science or another would be adequate to the job—at the beginning, and on the left, sociology and psychology; latterly, and on the right, economics. The idea of all of them is that we can "see through" the opinion (which is, after all, only words) to the reality that lies behind it, which can best be talked about not in legal but in social, psychological, or economic terms. About that kind of reality we all have a lot to say and a lot of languages to say it in.[6] The extreme step in this direction is to declare that there is, or ought to be, no discourse that is distinctively legal, no distinctively legal questions, methods, or institutions. All is reduced to the level of policy or politics.

But important as the "results" of opinions are, and necessary as it is that we be able to talk about them in many ways, in my view these efforts have failed badly, in large part because they have denied another reality, that of the opinion itself, which gives the "results" their most important definition and meaning or, to put it another way, in which the most important "results" can actually be found. In doing so, they erase what is distinctive about legal judgments: that they are not simply policy or political judgments, made by actors with assumed despotic powers, but judgments made by actors with limited authority, an authority that is governed by texts external to themselves to which they must look to determine both the proper scope of their power and the standards by which it is to be exercised. Every lawyer, after all, must ground every legal argument she makes in an interpretation of a text external to her and to her audience alike, a text from the past, remote or recent, that it is her task to keep alive. The statute, the opinion, the contract, the constitution, the regulation— these give her the terms with which her issues are stated, they define the topics she and her audience must address. The activity of law is the interpretation and composition of authoritative texts, a fact that is simply ignored or denied by those who would "look through" the text to something else.

The pure policymaker—whether he speaks in the classroom, on

the pages of journals, in the legislature, or in the courts—assumes for the purposes of his present speech that he has despotic powers to create "the best results" for the parties and for society as a whole, whether this is defined in terms of solving a problem, of maximizing utility, or of defending rights or liberties. The only question is, What is the best result? This question can be asked in general terms or particular ones, it can exclude or include questions of institutional competence, expected rates of voluntary compliance, and so forth. It can be a complex investigation that includes an abstract inquiry as to the standards by which the "best" should be determined. But in all such cases, unlike the law, this kind of conversation takes place on a plane removed from the processes of institutional life, without any sense of obligation to texts or choices made by others, among a "we" who are defined only by our commitment to this sort of talk.

In the law, by contrast, every speaker is particularly located, both rhetorically and socially. He or she is a lawyer or a judge, a judge of a state or federal court, a lawyer arguing to a jury or making a motion to a judge, and in every instance is situated as well with reference to a set of prior and arguably authoritative texts: constitutions, statutes, earlier cases, and the like. This is the context in which "policy" questions are discussed in law, and these conversations receive their proper shape from that context. The authority of the legal actor is never self-established, but always rests, at least in argument, upon prior texts, which provide the standards that govern the authority they establish. This means, among other things, that the legal speaker must always look outside himself for his source of authority; that his every action rests upon a claimed interpretation of those sources of authority; and that these interpretations, of necessity, are compositions to which he asks that authority be given.

One of the central characteristics of law, then, is that it works on the principle of the separation of powers: Each actor, private or public, inhabits a world in which some issues, some questions, are reserved for him, at least in the first instance, while others are remitted to others. To live sensibly and effectively in this world requires constant attention to the limits of one's own authority and a habit of respect for the choices made by others within their respective spheres of competence. The question for the lawyer is *always* more than what the best result or rule would be, for it includes as well the question: Who should have the power to decide what the best result or rule is, under what standards, and subject to what review? The activities of the law create a social universe in which power is allocated or distributed among many, and every act of the lawyer or judge must reflect a judgment about how this allocation works, or should work. This is an important way in which the law undercuts the tendencies towards tyranny that exist whenever one person has power over another.

This means that the question, who should have the power to decide, and why, is present whenever lawyers talk. To say this does not mean of course that this question is answered satisfactorily, either in general or in a particular case. But in keeping such a question constantly before us the law takes a step of a kind that the policymaker, who thinks in terms of "results" on a large scale, cannot contemplate. Another way to put this is to say that while the economist or other policy scientist can offer us ways of characterizing the world as it is, or as it ought to be (all on certain assumptions), such analyses are always addressed to those who make social choices as if they made them in the abstract, unconstrained by external authorities. To the extent that these analyses do acknowledge an institutional constraint, say in the form of a constitutional or statutory prohibition, this must be acknowledgment merely: they cannot interpret that constraint, or give it meaning, for that is the task of law. As soon as someone begins to interpret such a constraint, explaining how a particular actor is limited or empowered by them or predicting how others will interpret them, he is no longer engaging in his own discipline, whatever it is, but in law.

Law and Literary Criticism

The general perception that law is interpretive, and with it an associated suggestion that literary criticism may provide a model for judicial criticism, have considerable currency at the moment. Indeed, to judge by the amount of writing one finds in the law journals about hermeneutics or literary theory and the law, it is something of a fad. Much of this work, however, argues at an abstract plane about questions that are so theoretically stated as to be virtually false—for example, whether meaning resides "in the text," or in the "interpretive community," or whether "original intention" should bind absolutely or not at all.[7] Some of this work has a related weakness, namely that it is not actually grounded in the intellectual or literary disciplines out of which the theoretical debates arose in the first place, and this tends to render the discussion empty. Sometimes lawyers reach for what they call literary theory, not to learn how to think better about the process of reading, but to support predetermined legal positions of their own, thus carrying over the shell of one conversation to a new context without much attention to the particulars that gave the original conversation life and significance, much as poor translations might carry over to a new language the forms of an original text, whether poem or law, without adequate sensitivity to the context that gave the original its meaning. What is most needed in law and literature alike is not abstract theoretical argument but a more fully informed and argumentative critical practice, from which generalizations of a different sort might emerge. Practice—not theory—is the level at which comparison is likely to be most helpful, at which the work of one community can best illuminate that of another.

But critical practice of what kind? In particular, how helpful to the law can the practices of contemporary literary criticism be?

Here I have to say that contemporary literary criticism, natural an ally as it seems to be, is in something of a crisis of its own that renders it much less useful as a model or analogy than one might have hoped. For one thing, literary criticism—like legal criticism—has in my view been rather too obsessed with questions of theory, rather too abstractly and conceptually put, and has accordingly tended to neglect the more difficult and interesting engagements, practical in kind, that the great texts with which literary criticism is concerned naturally afford. I think it has perhaps unwittingly been driven by a desire to attain the purportedly higher status of science, which has led not only to a focus on theory but to a method of analysis and explanation that tends to avoid critical judgment of individual works. It is now thought to be old-fashioned, for example, to ask whether a novel or poem is great, or greater than some other, or to suggest that there may be proper standards of literary excellence. The modern critic will often engage instead in a process of explanation that connects the configuration of a particular text with its literary, political, psychological, or economic context, asserting a causal connection, a thematic or generic parallel, or a new relation to another field of literature, and then stop.

But as "legal realism" in all of its forms tends to deny what is distinctively legal in our thought and expression as lawyers, this kind of literary criticism tends to deny what is distinctively literary in our reading of literature and in our writing about it, to reduce the processes by which we have engaged with these great texts to another mode entirely, that of explanation in nonliterary terms. At its most extreme, this method reduces all texts to the same level and abandons the central function of criticism, namely the formation of taste and judgment. And in reducing the text to an object it assumes that the critic and his audience have nothing to learn from this text or others like it. Thus even a critic of the reader-response school may outline, as a kind of engineer, the kinds of responses the text seems designed to elicit but without ever himself seeming actually to respond, in this or any other way, to the text. He is an analyst, not a reader. Too little attention seems to be given to the possibility that we have something to learn, as individuals, as communities, and as cultures, from the texts we study, and from the minds who composed them, as if they spoke to us. This is a kind of criticism, in short, that seeks to become a science which can explain phenomena rather than an art of understanding, response, and judgment. At its most extreme, it results in the destruction of an entire cultural inheritance.

All this means that in literature and in law alike there is often a perceptible want of love for the subject matter, for the texts and what they mean, and for what can be learned from them. The driving emotion often seems not to be love but a desire to dissect, to dominate, to conquer, both the past and one's contemporary peers. The erotics of this kind of criticism is not reciprocal or mutually recognizing, but competitive and dominating. One way to put our question could be: What should be the erotics of legal criticism?

If I am right in all this—that what is needed in law is not more theory, but more practical criticism; that legal criticism of the craft variety is insufficient; and that literary criticism of the sort generally practiced today is defective in the respects I have described—then what kind of criticism can we engage in?

In the chapters that follow I shall define my response to that question by bringing to a series of judicial opinions a version of the way of reading worked out in *When Words Lose Their Meaning*. This, as I said in chapter 1, focuses upon three interrelated points of attention: the language and culture within which the writer works; the art by which he reconstitutes it in his use of it; and—my particular concern at the outset—the kind of community he establishes with his readers in the experience he offers them. To some it may be surprising to think of a text as creating a community. At least one distinguished modern critic, Stanley Fish, likes to look at it the other way round and see the text as created by community of interpreters,[8] and others look right past the social and ethical significance of the text to what they see as its intellectual or aesthetic "substance." But every text constitutes a community and is in this sense political and ethical in nature.*

---

*I use the word "community" here (and elsewhere) as a way of drawing attention to the political and ethical dimensions of a literary performance, and not to suggest that the community a particular writer establishes meets any criteria we might have for a good community, or that all textual communities are intimate, trusting, or cozy. The

The kind of community a text creates can range from the relationship of two that is implied in the making of any text to a set of relationships that create a whole world: Burke's attempt to create a constitution in his *Reflections on the French Revolution* that will be a constitution for Great Britain—a way of talking that defines a community and its relation to nature—is one example, as is Paine's response to Burke in *The Rights of Man*; our own Constitution and certain public and legal texts made under it are others. The verbs we apply to the conduct of people in ordinary life, when we say that they patronize or seek to dominate us, or when we say that they recognize or seek to respect us—when in Plato's terms they seek a dialectical rather than a rhetorical relation with us—can be applied to written texts too (and not just to advertisements and political slogans); likewise the terms we apply to human and political relations—equality, friendship, power—can be used to describe the form of the relations we find enacted in our forms of language. The achievement of great art is ethical and political as well as aesthetic in character, and the same is true of great judicial opinions.

One way to think of the relation a text establishes with its reader—and a way that connects the textual community constituted in the text with the process of reading it—is to think of the text as creating an Ideal Reader, the version of himself or herself that it asks each of its readers to become. Thus the Ideal Reader of a call to arms will grab the musket from the mantle and head for the training grounds; the Ideal Reader of an advertisement for men's cologne will buy and use, and buy again, the particular brand and no other; the Ideal Reader of a great work of literature, on the other hand, may feel that her whole language, and the motives it expresses and stimulates, are thrown into question, or she may find her sympathies extended in ways she could not have imagined, or she may discover herself holding for a moment contrasting perceptions in her mind, both of them true despite their incompatibility. This is one way to describe the way texts teach.

Not all Ideal Readers, even of books supposed to be great, are people we would want to be. In reading a complex and serious text we thus engage in a perpetual negotiation: we find ourselves becoming, in response to the text, some of the things it is possible for us to

---

authoritarian writer creates an authoritarian community, the sadist a sadistic community, and so on.

Similarly, by "conversation" I do not mean to suggest face-to-face, informal talk but any form of responsive discourse.

be, then we check that movement against the rest of what we are, or wish we were, knowing all the time that our resistances are sometimes pathological, sometimes valid, and can therefore be neither blindly followed nor discounted absolutely. Reading is in this sense an ethical activity, a way of becoming someone in relation to another, and writing is too, for in our writing we invite from our reader one kind of response or another, as we call upon different capacities of mind or feeling.[9] I am thus suggesting a way of reading a text as rhetorically constitutive: as an act of expression that reconstitutes its own resources of language and in doing so constitutes a community, directly with its reader and indirectly with those others in the world about whom it speaks (or towards whom it invites its reader to take one attitude or another).

What happens when we read legal texts in such a way? Who, we can ask, is the Ideal Reader defined by the Constitution or by this statute or contract? This is a question that every judicial opinion can be said to address, whether its author knows it or not; and a question that every opinion invites of itself, for it too claims to speak with authority. Of the opinion and statute alike, then, we can ask what relation it establishes with its reader: Is this an authoritarian text, one that demands simple and total obedience of its reader, or does it define the reader as a person with a mind, with a heart—as a free agent—who in reading the text is encouraged to activate these capacities in certain ways? These are large questions, especially in the law, for it is essential to the existence of law that we think of ourselves as in some ways and on some occasions bound by the judgments of others; yet it is also essential to any legal system worthy of respect that it invite the use of mind and judgment in its readers, that it create an occasion for a certain sort of wholeness of thought that does not otherwise exist. To put the question in terms of the sentence taken as the theme for this series of chapters, we can say that the legal text, like every text, is a stage in a conversation and ask of it: Is this conversation one in which "democracy begins?" If not, the consequences are serious indeed; if so, it remains to be shown how.

* * *

In every opinion a court not only resolves a particular dispute one way or another, it validates or authorizes one form of life—one kind of reasoning, one kind of response to argument, one way of looking at the world and at its own authority—or another. Whether or not the process is conscious, the judge seeks to persuade her reader not only to the rightness of the result reached and the propriety of the analysis used, but to her understanding of what the judge—and the law, the lawyer, and the citizen—are and should be, in short, to her conception of the kind of conversation that does and should constitute us. In rhetorical terms, the court gives itself an ethos, or character, and does the same both for the parties to a case and for the larger audience it addresses—the lawyers, the public, and the other agencies in government. It creates by performance its own character and role and establishes a community with others. I think this is in fact the most important part of the meaning of what a court does: what it actually becomes, independently and in relation to others.

The life of the law is in large part a life of response to these judicial texts. They invite some kinds of response and preclude others; as we deal with these invitations, both as individuals and as a community, we define our own characters, our own minds and values, not by abstract elaboration but in performance and action. Much of the life and meaning of an opinion (or a set of opinions) thus lies in the activities it invites or makes possible for judges, for lawyers, and for citizens; in the way it seeks to constitute the citizen, the lawyer, and the judge, and the relations among them; and in the kind of discoursing community it helps to create.

When we turn to a judicial opinion, then, we can ask not only how we evaluate its "result" but, more importantly, how and what it makes that result mean, not only for the parties in that case, and for the contemporary public, but for the future: for each case is an invitation to lawyers and judges to talk one way rather than another, to constitute themselves in language one way rather than another, to give one kind of meaning rather than another to what they do, and this invitation can itself be analyzed and judged. Is this an invitation to a conversation in which democracy begins (or flourishes)? Or to one in which it ends?

Rochin v. California

I shall start with Justice Frankfurter's opinion in *Rochin v. California*.[10] I choose this opinion partly for the extraordinary clarity with which it presents the dimension of meaning upon which I want to focus first, namely, the way the judge defines himself in his writing, both as a mind and as a judge; the way he defines his audience—other judges, lawyers, citizens—and his own relationship with them as well as their relations with each other; and the way he defines the legal and constitutional conversation to which he contributes. This opinion provides a striking example of judicial self-definition, indeed of self-creation. But the way it does so is of independent interest, for what Frankfurter achieves here is deeply flawed—one could not really imagine what we call a legal system working in such a way—and this will leave us with a sense of deficiency that may carry us forward to the other opinions we shall read.

"Shock the Conscience"

The question the Supreme Court faced in *Rochin* was whether a state conviction based upon evidence seized in the rather extraordinary circumstances to be described below violated that part of the fourteenth amendment which reads "No state shall . . . deprive any person of life, liberty, or property without due process of law." But before we examine the way Justice Frankfurter spoke to this question, a word is required on the legal context in which he worked.

As most readers will know, the original Constitution was amended in 1791 by the addition of the Bill of Rights, a set of amendments protecting freedom of speech and religion, guaranteeing jury trial, prohibiting self-incrimination and unreasonable searches, and the like. These amendments were early held to apply only to the relation between the individual and the federal government; the relation between the individual and his state government was for the most part left to state law. (How else could slavery have flourished?) The effect of the fourteenth amendment, passed after the Civil War, was to bring those relations too under federal constitutional regulation. The question was, how was the language that did this, especially the due process clause quoted above, to be read?

Rochin was decided at a time when some commentators, lawyers, and Justices thought that the vague term "due process" should be given more particular meaning by construing it as having "incorporated" the Bill of Rights (or some of them). This would at once give content to a nearly empty clause, they thought, and limit the power of the Court, for on this view nothing beyond the Bill of Rights would be included in the fourteenth amendment. Others resisted that view, on the grounds that it was mechanistic, unsupported by history, and evasive of the responsibility of judgment. As time went on the Court was in fact to adopt a compromise, by which certain provisions of the Bill of Rights, such as the first amendment, were "incorporated" while others, such as the grand-jury guarantee of the fifth amendment, were not. *Rochin* was a significant stage in this process.

In *Wolf v. Colorado*,[11] a few years before *Rochin*, the Supreme

Court, also speaking through Justice Frankfurter, addressed the specific question whether the fourth amendment (which protects against "unreasonable searches and seizures") should be regarded as "incorporated" in the fourteenth. *Wolf's* answer was a complicated one: It held that the "core" of the fourth amendment, namely, protection against "arbitrary invasion of personal security," applied to the states under the fourteenth amendment, but that the "exclusionary rule," under which evidence seized in violation of the fourth amendment is excluded from a criminal proceeding, did not. The idea was that the exclusionary rule was a nonconstitutional, judicially fashioned remedy, just one among many possible remedies—including criminal sanctions, damages, injunctive relief, and internal police discipline—all of which had strengths and weaknesses and among which it was wrong to think of the Constitution as choosing. The states were thus bound by the "core" of the fourth amendment but were free to fashion "remedies" of their own.

Rochin tested this formula rather severely. The facts were these. The police broke into Mr. Rochin's house without probable cause and without a warrant (both normally required for a valid search), then went into his bedroom, where he was lying in bed. When he saw them, he hastily swallowed some pills; after a struggle, they took him to the hospital where he was given an emetic. The vomited pills were retrieved and used against him in his trial for possession of prohibited substances. All of this was done without judicial supervision of any sort, and was conceded to be plainly illegal under existing constitutional standards.

Justice Frankfurter, the author of *Wolf*, wrote the majority opinion in *Rochin*, which reversed the conviction. But on what grounds could he possibly do this, other than by applying the exclusionary rule to the states, contrary to his opinion in *Wolf*? His answer was that *Rochin* was not an ordinary exclusion case, to be governed by *Wolf*, but an extreme and shocking abuse of fundamental rights of a kind that required reversal under the due process clause. The famous central language of the opinion is this: ". . . [W]e are compelled to conclude that the proceedings by which this conviction was obtained do more than offend some fastidious squeamishness or private sentimentalism about combatting crime too energetically. This is conduct that shocks the conscience."

This language implies an extraordinary set of claims about the nature of the United States Constitution, federalism, and the role of the Supreme Court. Stripped to its essentials it is that the United States Supreme Court should function as the "conscience" of the nation, or of the legal part of the nation, which will reverse convictions obtained by otherwise sovereign states whenever it is sufficiently "shocked." To many people this claim was itself shocking, a kind of judicial usurpation. Who is Frankfurter to set himself up that way? What are the restraints upon the power that he claims? To claim to be the conscience of the nation is to claim to have a superior ethical or moral sense, and upon what can that claim rest? This sounds, to some people at least, not like law but like a kind of moral, almost aesthetic, elitism, the simple arrogation of power to the sensibility of the judge. What kind of regard for sources of law external to the judge himself does it make possible? None, it seems. If we ask John Dewey's question of this opinion, it is difficult indeed to see how this could be the kind of conversation in which democracy begins.

Justification by Performance

How, in the face of such obvious arguments, can Justice Frankfurter's opinion be explained or defended? His answer to this question lies in the part of the text that precedes the language quoted above, which, standing alone, seems such a bald and indefensible arrogation of power. The first part of the opinion, that is, is Frankfurter's attempt to earn the right to talk the way he does in the language I quoted. It is here that he tries to establish the conditions upon which the reader can regard him as authorized and entitled to speak as he does there.

He begins with a statement of the facts, in which the invasion of Rochin's rights are, not surprisingly, detailed with some fullness (including the statement made by the California District Court of Appeal that the officers were guilty of criminal assault and battery). Next he complicates our sense of the meaning of California's act in affirming the conviction by telling us that the decision of the California Supreme Court to affirm was made without opinion and over the dissent of two justices, who took the view that this extortion of incriminating objects from the defendant violated the privilege against self-incrimination. This conviction somehow has less than the whole weight of the state's authority behind it, or so Frankfurter is implicitly asking us to believe.

He then describes the federal system, and his role within it, in the following way. He acknowledges that the administration of criminal justice is predominantly committed to the states and that Congress may create crimes only when appropriate to the execution of its limited grants of power. The bearing of the Constitution is for the most part not upon the power of the state to define crime, but upon the manner in which the states may enforce their penal codes. The effect of these remarks is to narrow the scope of the claim Frankfurter is about to make, and to define its character: he will not concern himself (except in extraordinary or limited circumstances) with the "substance" of state concerns, but only with the "manner" in which the states choose to proceed. He thus at once confines his claim of authority and characterizes it as concerned with "manner"—method, style, or manners themselves.

To define the appropriate attitude with which this task should be undertaken Frankfurter quotes language from *Malinski v. New York*: "We must be deeply mindful of the responsibilities of the States for the enforcement of criminal laws, and exercise with due humility our merely negative function in subjecting convictions from state courts to the very narrow scrutiny" of the due process clause. This means that his own conduct has an essential moral quality, and this in turn defines him as a moral actor: he must be "mindful," full of "humility." Since he represents this as the language of an authority external to the present moment, in quoting it he seems to perform the very kind of mindful humility, of reasoned subordination, that he says is required of the Court.[12] In this way he seeks to demonstrate by performance that he has the attributes he designates as necessary for judgment.

But he has his "responsibilities" too: as a moral actor with a role in our system he is obliged to make judgments and to act upon them in certain circumstances. As for the standards by which the court must exercise its judgment, Frankfurter quotes again from *Malinski*: They are "those canons of decency and fairness which express the notions of justice of English-speaking people even toward those charged with the most heinous offenses." By their nature these standards require in the judge who applies them a degree of moral and aesthetic cultivation: a sense of what is decent and fair, a capacity, as he puts it elsewhere, to show "respect" for those personal immunities which are, in Justice Cardozo's famous phrase, "so rooted in the traditions and conscience of our people as to be ranked as fundamental."

But can such vague language as this possibly function as law, to guide and control the judge who exercises power under it? Frankfurter's next step is to address that question. Certain words present no problem of vagueness, he says, for they are adequately defined by context or history. He gives as an example the meaning of the word "jury." On the other hand, the terms in the Constitution that are not so clearly fixed do "exact a continuing process of application." This does mean that the judgment will "fall differently at different times and differently at the same time through different judges." But even here the judges are not left "at large": "We may not draw on our merely personal and private notions and disregard the limits that bind judges in their judicial function. Even though the concept of due process of law is not final and fixed, these limits are derived from considerations that are fused in the whole nature of our judicial process," considerations "deeply rooted in reason and in the compelling traditions of the legal profession."

Due process is thus an invitation for the judge to read, with sensitivity and intelligence, the traditions that "bind" him in order to determine what is required in a particular case; the standards are necessarily vague rather than formulaic, owing to the nature of the judgment that must, given appropriate respect for the states, be made. The guides are not inadequate for "us," however, but only because "we" have the capacity to make correct judgments on questions so refined that they cannot be reduced to rules or standards.

Listen now to the kinds of claims Frankfurter implicitly makes for himself in the way he describes what the art of judgment requires: "[T]o practice the requisite detachment and to achieve sufficient objectivity no doubt demands of judges the habit of self-discipline and self-criticism, incertitude that one's own views are incontestable and alert tolerance toward views not shared." But these "are precisely the qualities society has a right to expect from those entrusted with ultimate judicial power." These are, he is saying, the qualities that he claims to have, and to exhibit in his writing, not least in the sentence that he just composed. And if that is not enough, listen to this: "In each case 'due process of law' requires an evaluation based on a disinterested inquiry pursued in the spirit of science, on a balanced order of facts exactly and fairly stated, on the detached consideration of conflicting claims, see Hutchins County Water Co. v. McCarter, 209 U.S. 349, 355, on a judgment not ad hoc and episodic but duly mindful of reconciling the need both of continuity and of change in a progressive society." That peroration directly precedes the language quoted earlier: "Applying these general considerations to the circumstances of the present case, we are compelled to conclude that the proceedings by which this conviction was obtained do more than offend some fastidious squeamishness or some private sentimentalism about combatting crime too energetically. This is conduct that shocks the conscience."

It has been Frankfurter's aim to establish his right to talk this way by the way he has constituted himself in what has preceded it.

He represents himself as one who is respectful of the state's power to make substantive law, who is conscious that his jurisdiction is limited to questions of "manner," who is full of the sense of "humility" and "mindfulness" that his "responsibility" requires, and who is aware of the vagueness of the standard and its moral character—"canons of decency and fairness"—as well as of the essential indeterminacy of the constitutional process, which creates an empty space that he is obliged by his office to fill; to do this he should be, as he is, scornful of legalistic formulas, able to distinguish between words that can be given meaning by reference to their original context and those which require a continuing process of judgment, suppressive of "the private" or "merely personal," and willing to affirm both his cultural role and his capacity to perform as the exemplar of a definable and comprehensible tradition.

Looked at rhetorically rather than logically, then, his first claim is that the Constitution has quite properly used vague and indeterminate language to create a vacuum that the judge must fill; his next claim is that he is the kind of judge who can fill that vacuum, and who is in fact doing it in an appropriate way. The Constitution calls for a judge who is an ideal intellectual and moral actor, an ideal interpreter not only of texts, but of society and tradition, and a mind that can apply the touchstones of civilization to new and in principle unpredictable cases. In this opinion Frankfurter's claim is to define himself as exactly that person. "I can read the Constitution, with an eye both to its language and to its structure; I can read its words, by glossing them in their original context; I can tolerate uncertainty and ambiguity, and can use the word 'incertitude' to express that fact; I can draw fine and sound distinctions; I can hold opposing things in the mind at once. The Constitution creates a space or vacuum which it is my duty to fill and I can fill it, today and in the future."

The very absence of logic in his opinion supports this reading: when he comes to the critical passage, he gives no "reasons" why this behavior "shocks the conscience." Instead, he simply establishes his conscience as the ultimate standard, then reports that it is "shocked." This means that he is saying not only, "I can do what the Constitution calls upon me to do" (namely, to make a net judgment applying all the standards of the relevant part of our civilization) but also, "You can trust me to do it without further explication or justification: the Constitution is right to give me this job and to recognize my independence from the necessity of trying to explain what can not be explained." Instead of "explaining" in a usual lawyerly way, that is, Frankfurter exemplifies his meaning, and the persuasive power of his opinion depends entirely upon the persuasive power of his exemplification.

The rest of his opinion is consistent in aim. First he refutes the legalistic argument, based on the law of evidence, that the Constitution is blind to the means by which otherwise relevant evidence is obtained. He relies upon the recent cases that excluded statements obtained from a suspect by coercion. For him the confession cases do not stand alone; they are certainly "not sports in our constitutional law" but applications of the "general requirement that States in their prosecutions respect certain decencies of civilized conduct." He similarly rejects as a false legalistic distinction the claim that "real evidence" (i.e., physical objects) should be distinguished from "verbal evidence." Here Frankfurter resists the use of the categories of standard legal analysis, saying that the real issue is to be couched not in terms of such rules but in terms like those used in *Rochin* itself, namely, fairness, decency, and the like. "We are not unmindful that hypothetical situations can be conjured up, shading imperceptibly from the circumstances of this case and by gradation producing practical differences despite seemly logical extensions." But, he implicitly says, "Don't trouble us with hypotheticals. We will not descend to logic chopping; we are judges, not the kind of lawyers who think that their categories are fixed and self-authoritative."

In these paragraphs there is an assertion of the power of the moral, aesthetic, and civilized actor over the language and categories of the law. This is itself a performance and exemplification of the ground upon which his decision ultimately rests, namely, his own capacity to judge well. The world created by this opinion is a world of morals, manners, civilization, relations, decency, fairness, and, by implication, of the reverse of these. Reasoning in the usual sense of the term—but by no means its only sense—is missing from this opinion. He speaks as if the issue were aesthetic: in the bulk of the opinion he demonstrates his capacities for making the judgment required; he then reports the judgment he has made; he then expands upon that judgment by making others, which are related to the primary one. By all of this, he means to define the Constitution in a certain way, and to hold it out—with its judiciary—for veneration and respect.

How Does This Work as Law?

But what kind of conversation does Justice Frankfurter establish here, and with what relation to "democracy?" What kinds of argument does he invite in future cases, and what political and ethical world will that argument create? How, for example, is the lawyer to speak to this sensibility, other than simply by offering him the case for his final and authoritative judgment? Frankfurter requires us to locate a case strictly within his jurisdiction and invites us to invoke his modesty and humility on that point in cases of doubt. But on the merits, does he leave us (as he says the Constitution does *not* leave him) "at large," or does he suggest ways in which our conversation might proceed? One might think of this opinion as establishing a writing assignment: How should you write to this judge? How could you stir this sensibility to act?

Frankfurter plainly seeks to discourage arguments of some kinds, most notably of the mechanically "legal" variety, and to encourage others. To argue to the mind defined here the lawyers themselves will have to become their own versions of what Frankfurter makes himself: they will have to have a sense of what fairness and decency require and to be able to make that sense visible in their writing and their tones of voice, in the way they address the court, talk about the parties, and conceive of the past and the future. In all of this, following Frankfurter's lead, they will be enacting one, rather than another, understanding of the Constitution and human values, an understanding that is deeply aesthetic in character.

The claims to "democracy" here rest on the fact that this conversation is open to all who can qualify to participate in it; since the capacities of mind and sensibility that serve as qualifications are themselves good things to have, the principle of the opinion is meritocratic, for it assumes a standard of excellence and the freedom of opportunity to attain it.[13] Among those who qualify to talk this way there is deep equality, for there are no rules by which results can be compelled.[14] There is very little openness, however, to those who lie beyond this circle of qualified speakers. Another way to put this point is to say that the Ideal Reader created by this text is one who will have the kind of education and sensibility required to judge Frankfurter's claim to excellence. Even if one does qualify, the opinion suggests no way in which it can defend itself against a negative judgment, since it does so little by way of argument; the question of personal qualification becomes the only question, for the reader as well as for the judge. Except insofar as the opinion offers him something of an education along the requisite lines, the ordinary reader, indeed the ordinary lawyer, is left out.

Even when it is looked at in the most favorable light, then, the opinion establishes a conversation that slides right over the central judicial activity, namely, reasoning about the meaning of an authoritative text in such a way as to create another text that is also entitled to authority and likely to be of use in future stages of the conversation. Here the decision purports to be that simply of a wise judge, entitled to act as the "conscience" of the community—a kind of autocracy earned, it at all, by the display of certain qualities of mind and character. But law is a system by which the power to decide questions is distributed among official and private actors in intelligible ways, and subject to intelligible standards; one's obligation as a judge is not only to establish one's right or qualifications to decide the question, but to reveal how, by what process of thought and feeling, one did so, for in that act of revelation one at once gives guidance to others and exposes oneself to the kind of criticism that can work as a form of control. If all opinions were written with *Rochin* as a model, we would have a system of discourse that hardly deserved the name of law.

Of course Frankfurter does not propose to work this way in every case, only where the language of the Constitution itself is so vague as seemingly to invite this sort of judgment. In other words, one might argue, *Rochin* is an exception to usual standards, and a justified one. There is something in this; how much it is not now necessary to inquire, since for our purposes it suffices to see how clearly, and in one sense successfully, Frankfurter takes on the task of defining himself as a judge; and how inadequate (even if justified in this case) this method would be if it were adopted as the general method of judicial work.[15] *Rochin* thus defines a topic we can bring to the other opinions we shall read in the chapters that follow, asking of them what possibilities for judicial self-definition they realize.

* * *

My object here has not been to say that Frankfurter has succeeded in his effort to show that he is qualified for the office he describes, or that the office is properly to be regarded as he implicitly suggests far from it—but rather to observe how clearly this case identifies a key aspect of judicial opinions more generally, which may enable us to look at other opinions with a clearer eye. The feature that this opinion makes so prominent is that of the judicial persona or ethos: In every judicial opinion the judge gives himself a character or personality, demonstrating by performance certain intellectual and ethical qualities which he of necessity asserts to be appropriate to his role. This performance may be in harmony with the larger views of the Constitution and the judicial role that the opinion expresses— such is the case I believe in *Rochin*—or it may be in disharmony with them. If the former, we have a clear ground upon which the opinion can be evaluated; if the latter, the opinion criticizes itself.

Can we learn from this experience of reading *Rochin* to look, in our reading of other opinions, away from the "result" to the opinion itself and to see it as an ethical and political act—as a way of defining the judge himself, the court of which he is a part, the Constitution upon which his power depends, and the conversation that is the law? Can we learn to ask of a particular opinion how it creates its own authority, and what kind of conversation it establishes, with what relation to democracy?

5

"Original Intention" in the Slave Cases

The first set of opinions I wish to examine with this set of questions in mind are those of Justice Story in *Prigg v. Pennsylvania*[1] and of Chief Justice Taney in the Dred Scott case.[2] These are of special interest for both of them emphasize, in different ways, what many would regard as the simplest and most obvious method of constitutional adjudication, and one that seems to be full of deference to one's political (and democratic) superiors: that of resolving cases by referring to the "original intention" of the framers of the Constitution (or, in a statutory case, to the intention of the legislature).

Much can be said about the difficulty of this method as a general matter. Whose intention counts: those who drafted the provision, those who voted for it, those who have refrained from amending it? What intention counts: one's conscious hopes for the particular provision, one's subconscious desires, one's sense of what the language meant? I shall speak to such matters briefly below, but my present interest is of a somewhat different kind: What happens to the judge, to the Court, to the law—to the conversation that is the law—when one tries to decide cases in this way?

As I said in chapter 4, I shall focus especially on the ethical and political significance of the text, on its meaning as a performance of character and value. We shall examine the language of the opinion, that is, as we did with *Rochin*, with a view to asking who the judge makes himself, and his readers, in his writing: who he is as judge, and how he addresses us as citizens and lawyers; how his way of talking to us, and of inviting us in our turn to talk, defines the law in general and the Constitution in particular; and how the conversation it seeks to start, or to continue, defines those relations among individuals and institutions that make up our public world. Is this a conversation in which "democracy begins"?

In examining these opinions in the light of such questions we shall be working out the consequences of at least one version of the view that the Constitution should be interpreted by reference to the intention of the framers.

Prigg v. Pennsylvania

Let us begin with the facts of the case, as found by a jury in a special verdict. Margaret Morgan was a slave, held by Margaret Ashmore under the laws of Maryland. She escaped to Pennsylvania in 1832. Five years later, Prigg, a slave-catcher from Maryland working for Ashmore, went to Pennsylvania and obtained a warrant from a Pennsylvania magistrate authorizing Margaret Morgan's arrest by a state constable as a "fugitive from labor." She was then brought before the magistrate, who, for reasons we can only surmise, refused to have anything further to do with the case. Thereupon Prigg took Margaret Morgan, together with her children, out of Pennsylvania into Maryland and delivered them to Margaret Ashmore. At least one of Margaret Morgan's children was born in Pennsylvania, more than a year after she started residing there; others had been born in Maryland.

Pennsylvania successfully prosecuted Prigg under a Pennsylvania statute making it a crime to take away any "negro or mulatto" by force, fraud, or seduction with the design of carrying him or her into slavery. One question before the Supreme Court is whether this Pennsylvania statute is constitutional.

There are three main arguments that it is not: that it directly conflicts with what is usually called the fugitive slave clause of the Constitution;[3] that it conflicts with a federal statute, the Fugitive Slave Act of 1793;[4] and that it is in any event an impermissible exercise of state power, given either the existence of the federal statute, whether or not the state statute conflicts with it, or (more strongly) the mere existence of congressional power to act in the field, whether or not it is exercised. On the other side, it can be argued that the Pennsylvania statute does not conflict but actually harmonizes both with the constitutional provision and with the Fugitive Slave Act; that the Fugitive Slave Act itself is of dubious constitutionality; and that in any event the existence of congressional power in this field, or even the exercise of such power, ought not to invalidate state legislation unless there is an actual conflict between the provisions of state and federal law.

Legal Argument

As a way of working into this case, I would like us to imagine that we are modern lawyers thinking about how we would argue it on each side.

Let us begin with the constitutional provision, which reads as follows:

> No Person held to Service or Labour in one State, under the Laws thereof, escaping into another, shall, in Consequence of any Law or Regulation therein, be discharged from such Service or Labour, but shall be delivered up on Claim of the Party to whom such Service or Labour may be due.

Is the Pennsylvania statute that prohibits the removal of a "negro or mulatto" by force, fraud, or seduction inconsistent with this language? There are at least two rather obvious arguments that it is not.

The first is that the aim of the clause is simply to make it plain that the free states cannot constitutionally adopt a rule of law that automatically frees the escaped slave the moment he or she sets foot on their soil. This was in fact the rule of *Somerset's Case*,[5] decided in England not long before the adoption of the Constitution, which held that the presence of a slave on English soil released him instantly and automatically from the status of slavery. It would make sense that the southern states would insist upon a repudiation of this part of the common law. But Pennsylvania in this statute is not attempting to free all slaves who enter the state, and the statute should therefore be held constitutional, or so the state would argue.

Such a reading makes good enough sense of the first section of the provision, but the Constitution goes on to say that the slave shall "be delivered up on Claim of the Party to whom such Service or Labour may be due." This seems to go well beyond a repudiation of *Somerset's Case* and to impose on the state an affirmative obligation of return.

How is this language to be read? It is not clear upon whom the "claim" is to be made, or by whom the fugitive is to be "delivered up," or, even more importantly, how the essential facts upon which the duty arises shall be established, namely that the person whose liberty is in issue was in fact "held to Service or Labour" in another state, that he "escaped" into the state where he is found, and that the party claiming him is one "to whom such Service or Labour" is due. But unless all Blacks in the free states, whether themselves free or not, are to be subject to kidnapping by slave-catchers, there has to be some regular process to determine whether or not the duties that the Constitution creates actually exist in the particular case. From the structure of the provision, then, reinforced by its use of the procedural words "claim" and "delivery," it can easily be argued that this provision contemplates a judicial or quasi-judicial proceeding at which the essential facts shall be adjudicated.

What does this mean for the Pennsylvania statute? This statute prohibits kidnapping and does so as part of a scheme requiring the adjudication of such claims. It can be seen, therefore, not to conflict but to harmonize with the constitutional provision. This is the second, and far more powerful, argument for the statute's constitutional validity.

But would such an interpretation leave the southern states completely at the mercy of the free states, and therefore be an intolerable reading of the language both as a practical and as a theoretical matter? Would it, in other words, effectively permit the northern states to adopt the rule of *Somerset's Case*, against which the provision explicitly seems to be aimed? The answer I think is no, and for two reasons: first, it may well be that Congress could pass effectuating legislation, including provision for the use of the federal judiciary to try such cases; second, even in the absence of such legislation, or of the capacity to pass it, the failure of the state judiciary to enforce the rights of the out-of-state owner, upon claim being made, could, by legislation if necessary, be made grounds for federal question jurisdiction on appeal and thus for direct federal judicial protection of those rights.

Let us turn next to the Fugitive Slave Act of 1793. It provided in essence that when a slave escaped to another state the owner or agent might seize or arrest the slave, wherever found, and take him before a federal or state court. Upon proof to the satisfaction of the judge that the person so arrested was in fact the slave of the person claiming him, it would be the duty of the court to give a certificate to that effect, which would constitute sufficient warrant for returning the slave to the state from which he had escaped.

How does this statute bear upon the *Prigg* case? In the first place, it is not plain that the Constitution authorizes any federal legislation of this character at all, and if the federal statute is unconstitutional, it obviously leaves the state statute untouched. The Constitution does not in explicit terms authorize any such legislation nor is the fugitive slave clause one of those provisions to which the "necessary and proper" clause applies. On the other hand, it makes sense to assume that there should be some federal protection of the rights established here, and the route of appeal to the federal courts, suggested above, is cumbersome and somewhat inept. I think it is not unreasonable, on balance, to read the provision as authorizing legislation on the subject;[6] and the statute the Congress enacted seems to effectuate the purposes we have attributed to the clause, namely the protection both of southern masters and of free northern Blacks.

But even if the statute is valid, the Pennsylvania statute seems once again to harmonize rather than conflict with it. The federal statute requires the owner or the owner's agent to go to court, as the Pennsylvania statute does too, and it delegates the method of proof to the judge, leaving it open to state determination, and thus seems to contemplate ancillary state legislation. The Pennsylvania statute that prohibits kidnapping and requires adjudication can thus be seen to supplement the Act, not to frustrate it. Therefore there is no conflict between the Pennsylvania statute and any federal law, and no need for the doctrines of preemption or preclusion either, for the state law directly furthers federal policy.

* * *

Something like this is, in outline, the kind of argument that a modern constitutional lawyer might generate from these materials. I offer it not as a complete analysis of these questions, by any means, but as a definition by performance, however sketchy, of our own sense of how legal argument proceeds, and what it entails. This is how we lawyers think, or so I claim; and I want to use this definition of our own expectations as a way of looking at what we see when we read the opinion by Justice Story.

Judging by "Intention"

What is most striking about the opinion of Justice Story is that in it there is a deep tension between the sort of argument I have sketched out above and argument of a very different kind indeed. The topics I discuss are mentioned, and one or two of them—the constitutionality of the Fugitive Slave Act, for example—are developed at length. But upon close reading they are erased or short-circuited by the force of another mode of thought entirely, which it will be my next object to define.

After a brief statement of the facts—itself of interest because it is so clotted with legalisms as to distance both judge and reader from the human reality of which it speaks—Story moves directly to the fugitive slave clause of the Constitution. How is it to be interpreted? In a single sentence he pierces to a single ground of judgment:

> Historically, it is well known, that the object of this clause was to secure to the citizens of the slave-holding states the complete right and title of ownership in their slaves, as property, in every state in the Union into which they might escape from the state where they were held in servitude.

It cannot be doubted, he says, that this provision, so interpreted, "constituted a fundamental article, without the adoption of which the Union could not have been formed." The right of the owner, Story says, must be exactly the same in the state to which the slave escapes as in the owner's home state. If this be so, then all the incidents to that right must attach also; the owner must in particular have, as a matter of constitutional law, the rights to seize and to repossess the slave which the local laws of the owner's state provide.

Out of this language in the Constitution, Story thus creates an affirmative right in every slaveholder to recapture, with force if necessary, the owner's runaway slave in any state of the Union. This is a constitutional right with which no state may in any respect interfere. Story explains:

> Upon this ground we have not the slightest hesitation in holding, that, under and in virtue of the Constitution, the owner of a slave is clothed with entire authority, in every state in the Union, to seize and recapture his slave, whenever he can do it without any breach of the peace, or any illegal violence. In this sense, and to this extent this clause of the Constitution may properly be said to execute itself; and to require no aid from legislation, state or national.

It follows that the Pennsylvania statute flatly prohibiting such seizures is unconstitutional. Although much else is said in the opinion, none of it is essential to the holding. This is the heart of the case.

What is Story's method of constitutional interpretation here? Instead of looking to the language of the text, as I have suggested we would do, and seeing what range of meanings can be given to its terms, and how they fit with the general aims of that text, and with other related ones, Story pierces the text for the intention that he says underlies it and declares that this intention is its meaning. For him language is not the source of meaning, nor does it give it shape; meaning lies in the wish or aim or motive of the author.

In this instance Story finds that intention in entities called the southern states, who, he says, would not have entered the Union had this provision not been included and had it not meant what he now claims it to mean, namely, the creation of a right of recaption, guaranteed by the United States Constitution, running through all the states, free and slave. Story thus interprets the text not according to its language but according to what he thought the motives and desires of its signatories were. Of course, he may be entirely right that "the southern states"—assuming that it makes sense to talk about such an entity, or set of entities, as if they had motives and wishes—would not have acquiesced in the Constitution had this language not been included, and that they would be pleased by the construction he gives it. But that is not to say that this construction of this language is correct.[7]

It may help us to think about what Story's method means if we ask how his position could in its own terms possibly be met: by a competing analysis of the actual (or probable) wishes and opinions of the southern representatives at the constitutional convention, or those of the southern spokesmen for—or against—the Constitution in their ratification debates, or those of ordinary white southerners? By similar inquiry into the thoughts and desires of the northerners? The inquiry in every case would be into the motives, desires, and expectations of those who are gone, into internal phenomena regarded as historical facts, not into the meaning of the words they uttered as their way of saying what they meant. The argument would be purely factual in form; it could not contain the kind of attention to language, to public purpose and balance and harmony, that the sort of argument sketched out above—a legal argument—naturally entails. In this sense the effect of Story's method is to destroy even the possibility of the kind of reasoning we think of as legal.

Consider, for example, what happens in Story's opinion to the word "discharge" in the constitutional provision that says that no fugitive shall be "discharged" by any state law or regulation from service or labor. Story reads it this way: "any state law or state regulation, which interrupts, limits, delays or postpones the right of the owner to the immediate possession of the slave, and the immediate command of his service and labor, operates, pro tanto, a discharge of the slave therefrom." The Pennsylvania statute requiring adjudication of the claim is therefore, in Story's view, a "discharge" of it.

But this is an impossible diction, in which the distinctions between "interrupt," "limit," "delay," "postpone," and "discharge" are all erased. The meaning of language is destroyed, and with it the authority of those practices of argument—of interpretation and composition—that are the center of the law. Instead of a testamentary trust, as Marshall defined it, to be construed as an instrument meant to constitute a national community,[8] the Constitution according to Story is the expression or, perhaps more accurately, an act simply of the will.

"Intention" and the Idea of Law

Why did Story think this way in this case? In many respects, after all, he was a most sophisticated legal interpreter, capable of thinking about interpretation in complex and general ways.[9] Among his views, however, was the doctrine that constitutional powers granted the federal government should be construed not so much by careful reading of the language but by reference to the basic "ends" for which the powers were given. And in many cases, as in the present one, he was eager to reach out on behalf of the federal government to claim that its powers were exclusive, invalidating state lawmaking even of a kind that was harmonious with national policies, whether these were expressed in the Constitution itself or in congressional legislation.[10] One way to read *Prigg*, then, is to say that Story is applying to the fugitive slave clause the kind of reading that he elsewhere recommends for interpreting the powers granted the federal government, that is to say, a most generous reading in light of the main end of the provision.

But what is that end? To say that the end was the universalization of the slaveowners' rights is to beg the question. There were northerners, and white southerners too, who deeply opposed slavery; the document was obviously a compromise, and an uncertain one. But the reading Story gives the language denies the character of the provision as a compromise and seems to threaten the North with universal slavery: If the Constitution protects the owner's rights to the runaway slave, why does it not protect the owner's rights to the slave whom the owner carries into the free state as well? If so, of course, there would in practice no longer be such a thing as a free state.

Story's method of interpreting the fugitive slave clause of the Constitution is to look through its language for the intention that lies behind it, an intention he sees on the one side as insistence that maximum protection be given to southern slaveowning interests, and on the other as acquiescence in this claim. For him it seems that there has to be an intention lying behind the words and a single, dominating intention at that. His is a universe in which claims to power are absolute and unyielding. Thus in his interpretation of national powers he normally sees the existence of a federal power, whether exercised or not, as inconsistent with the existence of a simultaneous state power. There cannot be harmony; there must be mastery. In the relation between the national and the state governments, the mastery lies in the former; in the relation between the southern and northern states, as expressed in the fugitive slave clause, mastery lies with the South.

This way of reading legal texts is inconsistent with the fundamental idea of law on at least two counts: first, as we think of it, law is a way of creating a world that accommodates opposing interests and claims, a world in which distinct voices can be heard. The fugitive slave clause seems in fact to be framed upon exactly that principle, offering neither the South nor the North everything they might want, but creating a text tolerable to both, with the open questions to be resolved by future interpretation. Story's method of reading is incompatible with this conception of law, for it erases the language of the text and with it all attempts to build a more coherent and complex world upon that basis. This means that the arts of legal interpretation and composition that would naturally be employed in the way I suggested in the beginning of this chapter—in this case with the most likely result of finding the Pennsylvania statute constitutional—are erased too. If you think of the law as in large measure what we do as lawyers, there is no room in Story's universe for the law, for the arts of construction and argument by which and in which we live.

Second, Story's method eliminates the aspirational or idealizing element that is essential to what we think of as law: it reduces talk about what "ought to be" to talk about what "is," or what "was," thus reducing aspiration to mere will. The ultimate question for him is not what result makes best sense of the instrument as that document was originally composed, but what the South wanted. This is to destroy the ground of authority upon which law rests: the authority that derives not from the power of the person who makes the law but from the character of the law that is made, from the kind of conversation by which it is to become real in the world. Instead of participating in an argumentative or discoursing community that struggles with the questions, what kind of world we ought to have, what the authoritative language ought to mean, we are offered a world in which the only question is what someone wanted. The vice of this opinion is worse than authoritarianism: it is to destroy authority.

* * *

All this shows up in the kind of argument Story himself engages in and thus allows to lawyers in the future. His opinion has the surface form of legal argument—as I said, the appropriate topics are mentioned—but, in fact, it turns upon a simple judgment, unde-fended and represented as factual, about what the framers, in this case the South, wanted. How are we to read this opinion as a set of directions to future argument, then? It seems to tell us to engage in the appearance of legal argument, interpretive and institutional in character, but to expect to win or lose on the basis of unarticulated or barely articulated assumptions of fact (or value); that is, to engage in a kind of hypocrisy ourselves and to expect it from our judges.

This has a modern ring, for in our own era many people have wanted to say that legal argument about precedent and doctrine, about policy and institutions, is epiphenomenal, that what really counts is unexpressed in this discourse, and that law, as we think of it, is therefore a sham or a charade. But the consequence of this view, popular though it may be, is nothing less than the destruction of law itself, for on such terms what we think of as legal conversation is impossible.

Let me illustrate this point with a further comment about *Prigg*. Suppose we think of its meaning not in the terms I have suggested but solely in terms of its practical effects on the freedom of fugitive slaves. While the interpretation of the fugitive slave clause given above is drastically one-sided, Story went on to hold that the mere existence of congressional power to legislate on the matter invalidated any state statute in the field, whether or not there was a conflict be-tween it and any federal provision. This, as I have said, is an appli-cation of Story's own developed view in favor of the powers of the centralized government. But the consequence here is surprisingly antislavery, for Story's view would invalidate not only statutes such as that in Pennsylvania, which aim to protect the slave, but also stat-utes in aid of the owner and the owner's agent. Under this opinion it seems that the entire burden of pursuing fugitive slaves would fall upon the federal government, whose resources, especially judicial resources, were then extremely limited. Despite its powerfully pro-slavery surface, then, Story's opinion could be read as having, or even as intended to have, a powerful antislavery effect. Both Justice Story and his son in later years spoke of the opinion rather proudly in such terms, and recent scholarship has to some extent borne out this view of its consequences.[11]

But what are we to think of this kind of claim on behalf of this opinion? It is really just the other side of Justice Story's "legal real-ism": as in the interpretation of the Constitution the only thing that matters is the wishes of the signatories (or some of them), and not their language, so in drafting, reading, or judging a judicial opinion, our concern should not be with what it says, or what the language means, but with what we estimate the practical effects of the document to be. In both respects, the method of Story, and of Story's heirs, is antilegal, destroying the whole world of meaning created by legal interpretation and composition.

Finally, there is in *Prigg* a paradox that we shall see emerge again in *Dred Scott*, that as the judge tries to turn away from the language to the "reality" that lies behind it, he finds himself attending not to a reality at all but to a fictive creation of his own mind, of his own time; in this case the image of the united southern states insisting upon this language, meaning it to be read as Story has read it, while the united northern states acquiesce. This is an impossibly simplistic view of the process by which this provision became law, and of its language too; but the apparent desire for the "real" is all too often in fact a desire for one's own image of things, not for the complex and uncertain body of evidence that actually exists.

Dred Scott

In turning now to the enormously rich text presented by the *Dred Scott* case, I shall focus only on the opinion of Chief Justice Taney and of that indeed on only one aspect, the method by which the Constitution is interpreted in light of the intention of the framers.

This case made two explosive holdings, the first of them that no descendant of African slaves could, as a matter of constitutional law, ever be a citizen of the United States. The particular consequence of this ruling here was that the plaintiff, Dred Scott, could not invoke the diversity jurisdiction of the courts of the United States, which Taney interpreted as a privilege of national, not state, citizenship. The second holding—the first invalidation of a federal statute since *Marbury v. Madison*—was that the Missouri Compromise of 1820, by which slavery was excluded from the territories to the north of 36° 30', was unconstitutional.[12]

Our attention will be given to the Court's treatment of the first question, whether former African slaves or their descendants can become citizens of the United States. In reaching a negative answer, Taney's opinion rests almost entirely upon a construction of the "intention of the framers"; it has to, for there is no language in the Constitution itself upon which such an argument can readily rest. My question of Taney, as of Story, is how, in making this construction, Taney defines himself as a judge; the Supreme Court as an institution;

his audience as lawyers; the public as citizens; and the kind of conversation among these various actors that is the law.

Legal Argument

Just as Story's opinion was split between two forms of thought and argument, which I have called the "legal" and the "intentional," so is Taney's opinion in *Dred Scott* split by an analogous tension. One difference between the opinions, however, is the way in which what I have called the "legal" mode of argument is presented. In *Prigg* the legal topics are presented but simultaneously undercut by the true ground of decision, which is Story's conclusory attribution of an "intention" to the framers. In *Dred Scott* this kind of legal argument is rendered explicit in quite an impressive way, at the outset, then undercut, not simultaneously, but after the fact.

His version of "legal argument" is developed in the first three-and-a-half pages of the opinion. It is important for the impression it gives of his mind and attitudes and for the kind of claim it correspondingly makes for his authority, and ultimately for the meaning of the opinion as a whole. These pages analyze what Taney presents as a technical lawyer's issue, whether the question of jurisdiction over the subject matter, upon which the defendant relies, is properly before the Supreme Court.

This case was a suit by Scott for his freedom and that of his wife and children, brought in the federal court in Missouri against their putative owner. The defendant answered the complaint with a plea in abatement, claiming that owing to his African ancestry the plaintiff was not a citizen of the state of Missouri and that, therefore, there was no diversity of citizenship as required for federal jurisdiction. The plaintiff's response to this plea was to demur, thus putting it in issue. The trial court ruled for the plaintiff, holding that he was a citizen and that diversity jurisdiction existed. At that stage the defendant elected not to suffer judgment and appeal but to make further pleadings in bar, that is, on the merits of the case. Issue was joined on these questions, resulting in verdict and judgment for the defendant, from which the plaintiff has appealed. In the Supreme Court the defendant seeks to support the judgment in his favor not only on the merits but also on the earlier-asserted jurisdictional ground. Dred Scott argues that the defendant waived this jurisdictional point by his further pleadings: if the defendant wished to preserve it, he should have accepted the judgment on that ground and appealed.

Scott's argument lacks immediate attraction for us—it seems awfully technical, and this is not how modern pleading works—but this was the era of common-law pleading, a system that worked by a series of binding elections made on one side or the other until issue was joined on a single matter of fact or law that would determine the case. Waivers of the sort that Scott alleged were built into the system. Since the federal courts in this era applied state procedural law, the question was presumably one of Missouri law, and there would at first seem to be little ground for argument with the lower court's judgment that the jurisdictional claim was out of the case.

Taney holds, however, that jurisdiction is still in issue. His reason is not that the trial court misread Missouri law, or that such elections are normally not binding in federal courts, but that the special character of the courts of the United States, as courts of limited jurisdiction, requires this result at least with respect to jurisdictional claims. His reasoning is this: In an ordinary state court of general jurisdiction no jurisdictional averment is necessary on the part of the plaintiff. If the defendant objects to jurisdiction, he must plead specially to that effect, and unless the facts upon which he relies are found by the jury or admitted by the plaintiff, the jurisdiction cannot be attacked on appeal. But federal courts have limited jurisdiction: the plaintiff must affirmatively allege in his pleadings that the action he brings is within the jurisdiction of the court, and if he fails to do so, he is subject to demurrer. In the present case, therefore, the plaintiff must aver and show that he is a citizen of Missouri. The jurisdictional defect, if there is one, cannot be waived by one of the parties, because the court has its own interest in not exceeding its proper authority. Here the defendant expressly raised the question of jurisdiction; by demurring, the plaintiff conceded the facts upon which the defendant's argument rests, which are not otherwise contradicted in the record. The question whether the lower court had subject-matter jurisdiction is thus not lost by the defendant's alleged waiver but is properly before the Supreme Court.

This is an argument of a familiar and appealing kind. Sensitive to the peculiar character of federal courts, and to procedural issues more generally, these pages could almost serve as a model of the kind of legal reasoning taught at good American law schools a generation ago. We are comfortable with, and can readily admire, this kind of thought. Here is an American constitutional lawyer talking, we feel, with all that means.

But what does that mean? How do these pages define Chief Justice Taney, the Court of which he is a part, the litigants before him, and the various audiences, popular and legal, to which the text is addressed? How, that is, do they work rhetorically?

The essential claim performed by this sort of argument is that this Court is a court of reason, one that will proceed by the canons of logic and clarity, even those of elegance. Its judgment will be shaped by institutional and lawyerly understandings. The claim that the Court's power will be shaped by reason, and reason of a complex and neutral kind, has a political meaning too: it is at once a recognition of external authority—of the larger world in which the Court occupies its defined place—and a promise of equality, for both of the litigants will have their interests determined by the same intellectual process. The Court has power, but power shaped by reason and limited by it; the litigants and the public stand before the court as parties equally entitled to have their cases adjudicated by neutral standards.

This part of the opinion establishes a respectful relationship with its reader, for the commitment to reason is necessarily a commitment as well to the process of argument and discussion by which the reasoning can be tested, a process in which the reader is a participant. The opinion rests not only on the political authority of the Chief Justice but on the propriety and coherence of his reasoning as well. The audience is thus addressed as a fellow reasoner, as one who can check the intellectual processes by which the Court reaches its result, and as one who can approve or disapprove them. In these ways the voice of this opinion recognizes the limits of its own authority.

The fundamental promise made here, then, is that this is a government of laws, not of men, and law is defined as reason—as the reasoned interpretation of the relevant texts in light of circumstances, both of their promulgation and of their application—with the evenhandedness and equality not only among litigants, but between the Court and its audience, that implies. As for Dred Scott, he is a litigant in this system, one whose claims will be considered, and accepted or rejected, on the merits.

The Language of Race

The promise of these opening pages is immediately betrayed by what follows. To read Taney's statement of the question before him, in the context he has established, is a stunning shock:

> Can a negro, whose ancestors were imported into this country, and sold as slaves, become a member of the political community formed and brought into existence by the Constitution of the United States, and as such become entitled to all the rights and privileges, and immunities, guaranteed by that instrument to the citizen? One of which rights is the privilege of suing in a court of the United States in the cases specified in the Constitution.

The first and most obvious source of shock is Taney's use of racial terms. Where does this language come from and how is its use justified or explained? Who, in the world of legal reasoning he has just created, would ever think this way? Here Taney speaks not in constitutional categories, but in social ones, and by what warrant does he do this? To put it slightly differently, how is the question he states a constitutional one at all, since it is not cast in constitutional terms? For nowhere in the Constitution is race mentioned, nor does it list other categories of human beings, some who can become citizens, others who cannot, to which racial categories might be assimilated. There is, in fact, no language in the Constitution (as it then existed) that suggests that any constitutional question could be cast in racial terms at all.

Formally speaking, of course, this language has its origin in the plea made by the defendant at trial, when he claimed that African-Americans could not become citizens. But the normal practice when a party makes a claim cast in extra-legal terms is either to disregard it or to recast it, so far as possible, in legal terms. (Suppose, for example, that the defendant had argued that a short person or a blind person could not become a citizen. Would the Supreme Court have accepted that as its question?) To accept the terms of the defendant's question is by that very act to make the categories it uses legal ones. Thus for Taney to state the question as he does is to go a very long way indeed towards answering it. And the fact that it is an extra-constitutional question makes it less surprising than otherwise might be the case that it will receive, as it does, an extra-constitutional answer.

The second defect with Taney's statement of the question is its lumping all rights of "citizenship" together, as if they were necessarily indivisible. While Dred Scott would doubtless have liked to have all the rights of white male citizens, he was arguing for only one, the right to sue in federal court on diversity grounds, and one could imagine that right as not necessarily entailing all others. But, without discussion, Taney claims otherwise, not by accident but, as I shall show below, as part of an argumentative strategy close to the center of his opinion.

In the next paragraph of the opinion Taney meets the needs created by his use of racial language, and his unitary view of citizenship, by developing the ideology of race upon which the case will ultimately turn. He explains his racial terminology by saying that he is talking about "that class of persons only whose ancestors were negroes of the African race, and imported into this country, and sold and held as slaves." He will later tell us that this means all members of what he calls the "African race," because, he explains, none of them emigrated voluntarily (a matter as to which he cannot possibly know the truth). Even more significantly, he here assumes—indeed he makes it a matter of constitutional law—that any "descendant" of a member of the African "race" is himself or herself to be regarded as a member of that "race," irrespective of the fact that the person may of course be "descended from" members of other "races" as well.

This premise—perhaps in some form it is central to all racism—is worth special attention because it is one that the racism of our present society shares. Why is the child born of a "Black" mother and a "white" father, or vice versa, to be considered "Black" rather than "white?" Every child in America must have wondered about this simple question. The answer does not lie in the nature of things but in our culture and our feelings, in the patterns of fear and desire that find expression in our ideologies of race. After all, "race" is not a natural but a cultural category.[13] "Race" may seem natural to one raised in a racist culture, to be as obvious a "fact" as exists in the world, but in truth—as Malcolm X discovered on his pilgrimage to Mecca, and as others have learned elsewhere—it is created and maintained solely by social and cultural conventions.

These conventions of racial categorization purport to rest on "factual" judgments of "difference" and "superiority"—superior looks, intelligence, wisdom—but are in fact ultimately rooted in desire, the desire to be a member of one group that dominates another. That is where the satisfaction comes: I may be ugly, but I belong to the beautiful race; I may be stupid, but members of my clan are smarter than members of your clan; and so on. "I have power because we have power." But the use of racial categories is attended by a fear as well, a sense of weakness deriving from the recognition that the lines between the "races," so seemingly fixed, are in fact permeable. This is the recognition, to them unbearable, that William Faulkner brings his white characters to face again and again.[14]

The determination that one characteristic shall outweigh all others is essential to all racist ideologies, to all sense of racial superiority, yet its effect is to empower the Other. The racial fiction must be maintained at all costs; otherwise the simple truth, that we are all people, all one species, and that "race" itself is not a natural category—that the only sense it makes is intolerable—would be revealed, and the whole edifice tumble to the ground. Taney's paragraph commits him and his reader to the wholly false (but deeply American) view that Blacks are all one thing, whites all another, a view that leads naturally to his other position that "all" the rights of citizenship must belong to one group, none to the other. In this Taney claims all legal power for the "whites," but in doing so grants enormous natural power to the "Blacks," whom he fears so greatly.

The next paragraph continues the development of this ideology in a rather odd way. Taney makes a special point of saying that he is *not* talking about American Indians.

> These Indian Governments were regarded and treated as foreign Governments, as much so as if an ocean had separated the red man from the white; and their freedom has constantly been acknowledged, from the time of the first emigration to the English colonies to the present day, by the different governments which succeeded each other. . . . [But it] has been found necessary, for their sake as well as our own, to regard them as in a state of pupilage, and to legislate to a certain extent over them and the territory they occupy.

Why is this paragraph here? The answer is that Taney is engaged in the construction of a mythical world out of which will flow the imperatives that will decide the case. The primary actors in this world are not individuals, or nations, or cities, or institutions, but "races," and "races" fictively constituted, as they always are, to deny biological facts. For Taney the world—of the framers, of his own world—consists of the white man, the red man, and the Black man, three actors arrayed in hierarchical order, with all power residing in white hands.

This means, as a rhetorical matter, that the "we" constituted in the community of discourse of which Taney and his audience are members, the community of law and constitution, has already been defined as purely white. To talk this way he must be white and speaking exclusively to whites. This is just another way of saying that citizenship in the world created by this kind of talk is necessarily white too, and that Dred Scott must therefore lose on his claim to speak with "us," both as a social and as a legal matter. The result of the case is determined by the mythical world in which Taney encloses it.

"Original Intention"

But Taney does not rest solely on the creation of this mythical universe, in which he has located his reader as among the fortunate few. He appeals to "history" as well—to the intentions of the framers—and to develop this appeal is the purpose of the next, quite long, section of his opinion.

As Taney puts it, the question is whether the "people of the

United States" or the "citizens" thereof, which in his view amount to the same thing, can include persons of African descent. He holds no, on the ground that at the time of the framing of the Constitution persons of African descent were

> considered as a subordinate and inferior class of beings, who had been subjugated by the dominant race, and, whether emancipated or not, yet remained subject to their authority, and had no rights or privileges but such as those who held the power and the government might grant to them.

There is of course nothing to this effect in the language of the Constitution itself, but for Taney the question is not what the document says but what its "true intent" is, its "meaning when it was adopted." He finds this meaning not in what it says but in the context in which it was composed, the most salient feature of which was the social fact, which he claims was universal, that Blacks were degraded by whites. It is upon this that he bases his claim as to what the framers intended.

This is a developed form of Story's method of interpretation: it pierces the text itself and looks to the context in which it was composed and published, giving to that context a standing equal to, perhaps superior to, that of the language itself. The implicit reason is that the text is purposive or intentional: the object of reading words in a text is only to gain access to the intention of the writer; surely if there are other routes to that intention, they should have equal validity; "history" affords such access by revealing the unexpressed, but universally held, views of the authors. The question is not what they said but what they meant. While Story looks to those who negotiated the instrument, Taney looks beyond them to what he calls the polity as a whole. In his view what the "white" polity "meant," as demonstrated by the consistent pattern of racial degradation, was to be forever dominant over "Blacks."[15] The thrust of his method is to claim that the fact of past discriminatory and abusive behavior is authority for future discrimination and abuse. At its heart this is the argument so familiar to students of fascism: the results of past degradation are used to justify its present perpetuation.

The degradation upon which Taney relies, he says, was universal and tied to race, not legal status: "No one of that race had ever migrated to the United States voluntarily; all of them had been brought here as articles of merchandise." The number that had been emancipated "at that time were but few in comparison with those held in slavery; and they were identified in the public mind with the race to which they belonged, and regarded as part of the slave population rather than the free." The extinction of slavery in the North was not "produced by any change of opinion in relation to this race" but caused by the unsuitability of slave labor to the "climate and productions" of these states. Northern states, and before them the colonies, had anti-miscegenation laws[16] and provided for the apprehension of wandering Blacks or Indians as vagrants. In New Hampshire the militia was limited to "free white citizens," and "in no part of the country except Maine, did the African race, in point of fact, participate equally with the whites in the exercise of civil and political rights." If this is the case in the North, how much more clear it must be in the South. Indeed, it is obvious that the southern states would never have entered into the Constitution if it were conceivable that Africans could become citizens, because—on Taney's view of the matter—if they could, they would be entitled to all the privileges and immunities of citizenship in all the states.[17]

What about the language in the Declaration of Independence that "all men are created equal"? This cannot possibly be extended to include the enslaved African race, says Taney, for so many of the signatories were slaveholders, and as men of honor cannot have been guilty of such a discrepancy between principle and conduct. As for the Constitution, it explicitly permitted the slave trade until the year 1808 and protected the owner's rights in fugitive slaves thereafter.

* * *

What has Taney done in this section of his opinion? He has first cast the question in racist terms, whether a "negro" can become a citizen; there being no language in the Constitution to support his position on that point, he has then purported to pierce the Constitution to discover the understandings that lay behind it. These unarticulated assumptions, if universal, are in his view as much part of the Constitution as if they were written into the text. After all, if it is what everybody thought, why should it matter whether it was written down or just assumed?

Taney's evidence establishes what no one could have doubted, that Blacks were systematically abused and degraded in the colonies and in the early years of the national government, as well in as the heyday of slavery. What is striking is the inference that Taney wishes to draw from this fact: he wishes to say that the fact of general, though certainly not universal, social degradation becomes a value, and a constitutional one at that. If the framers in fact treated Black people viciously, they must have intended their Constitution to validate such viciousness. This is to destroy, even more dramatically than Story's opinion in *Prigg*, the essential character of law as aspirational or idealizing. Taney tells us that we can be no better than the worst of what we are. The idea that a community marked by a particular kind of viciousness might wish to constitute itself in such a way as to transform itself is unimaginable to Taney, and in his opinion he tries to make it unimaginable in the world.

The "Intentional" Method

My hope in examining these cases has been that we could learn something from them about the implications of the method of constitutional interpretation that they both use, the method used by Story and developed by Taney. Actually, as we have seen, these Justices do not employ one method, but two, and each opinion is marked by a tension between them. The two methods are what I have called "legal"—by which I mean a traditional examination of the meaning of the language of the authoritative text in the context in which it was issued—and what I have called "intentional," by which I mean piercing the language of the instrument in order to look to the supposed sentiments, motives, wishes, or aims of those who composed it. In each opinion, however, the "intentional" method is plainly dominant, and it is that which I now wish to explore further.

Theory and Performance

I would like to begin by asking how far the actual performance of the writer of each opinion comports with his theory of the constitution and of judging. As we have seen, Story's opinion can be seen to follow rather closely the implications of its fundamental theory for, at least on one reading, it asks to be judged not by what it says, which is a powerfully proslavery, but by what it does, which is to impair the apprehension of slaves. Thus it is "really" an antislavery decision. Taney's opinion too can seem to comport with its fundamental method, for just as he reduces the Constitution to an act of racist will, his own opinion is just such an act. Consider, for example, his claim that all descendants of Africans must be treated as the degraded descendants of slaves, for none of them immigrated voluntarily. He cannot possibly know whether that is true or false. It is perfectly possible that some Blacks escaped from the Caribbean colonies and found their way to America. His statement is really a way of saying that it doesn't matter if one, or a hundred, or a thousand, people of African origin do not fit his description; he is going to treat them all as if they did. This is an insistence upon a racist generalization, made for the purpose of maintaining domination in the face of what may be the facts, a performance in the text that directly parallels the performance he purports to see in the Constitution itself.

Think here of what happens to Dred Scott in the course of the opinion: he begins as a litigant, objecting on procedural grounds to the Court's consideration of a jurisdictional question; as such, he is heard and responded to, in a gesture that necessarily accords him dignity and respect. By the end of the opinion, however, he, along with every other slave, has been reduced to a piece of property; the function of the law, and of the Constitution, is to protect someone else's rights in him, in this case to the extent of guaranteeing his owner the right to carry him into any territory of the United States without molestation from local regulations. Dred Scott is converted before our eyes from a person into an object. This is a performance of what Taney sees the framers of the Constitution to desire.*

But what does this add up to as a general matter? Of course these cases are terrible cases, you may say, but what relationship is there between the method they employ and whatever it is that makes them terrible? Is the "result" a consequence of the use of the "intentional" method? Or is their use of the method perhaps a sign that something else is wrong? Or is there no relationship between method and consequence at all? Have I been guilty, that is, of attacking the "intentional" method by finding uses of it that are independently dreadful?

I would like to propose at least the outline of an answer to that question. In my view there is a connection, though not an obvious one, between the "intentional" method and the rest of what is wrong with these cases. I have said that this method pretends to reduce questions of law to those of "fact" and in doing so to make impossible the fundamental process of law itself: the process by which we establish authoritative texts and interpret them in compositions of our own, and in so doing create a new world of talk and action of a certain kind that in turn affects the other world, the world of motive and

---

*Story foreshadowed this gesture in his extraordinary treatment of Mrs. Morgan's freeborn child: under any view, there is at least a substantial question whether that child is not legally free from recapture by the slave catcher, whether as a matter of Maryland law, Pennsylvania law (which might well be constitutionally held to supersede Maryland law), or of the Constitution itself. While Story mentions the existence of this child in his statement of facts, he does not address the child's fate at all. The child is simply lumped with the others. 41 U.S. (16 Pet.) at 608.

social fact, out of which we emerge. To pierce the language for the "intention" that lies behind it is a kind of reductionism that strikes at the heart of what we mean by law.

But how and why is the appeal to intention reductionist? One might think that it was the opposite of that, a way of going behind the surface of mere words to the rich and complex reality that underlies them. This method does not reduce the composer to the text, but honors his or her full complexity, one might say. And it is true that attention to the context of an utterance can enrich and complicate our reading of it; in some sense indeed it may be essential to understanding it at all. But this is not what this method proposes: not an enrichment or complication of the text but its erasure, the substitution of "intention" for "meaning." This is to eliminate one level of experience entirely—the textual, the legal—and to do so in favor of a language and a view of life that is for many reasons in other respects inherently simplifying.

The intentional method necessarily assumes, for example, the existence of an actor capable of forming a single intention. This is unrealistic in any case—none of us is in a simple sense "one" person, nor do we ever have "one" intention. We are complex beings with simultaneously diverging impulses and wishes—some conscious, others not; some immediate, others distant—all at varying levels of intensity. The composition of a text, and its publication as authoritative, is an act of resolution whose meaning is to be found in the language we use, in the context we modify, not in some conscious or unconscious desire. To pierce the language for the intention lying behind it, as if that intention could be discovered, is to deny the complexity and uncertainty of human motivation as well as the reality of the text itself.

To assume the existence of a masterful and coherent human actor who knows everything about both his own wishes and the possible circumstances in which these wishes will be significant is especially unrealistic in interpreting the Constitution, for, as many have observed, it is not even clear who the relevant actors are: Are they the people who drafted the Constitution; those who voted or argued for it in the ratification conventions; those who spoke against it; those who, decades later, have refrained from amending it; or who? And the instrument is by its nature meant to reach circumstances that are not known, and cannot be fully imagined, with respect to which "intent" must be used in a highly attenuated or fictionalized way, if at all. What is more, in actually doing "intentional" reading it is nearly inescapable that the "intention" will in fact be construed in light of the present case, as though the writers had in mind this case, and others like it, and were committed to a particular view of it, which cannot be the case. This kind of interpretation thus tends to create not only a single actor, but a single intention, and one falsely directed at a particular, future question.

To put this point a slightly different way, I have so far assumed that the "intentional" reading of a text really is not, as it is claimed to be, an interpretation of the text at all, but something else, a reading of the motives or wishes of a designated framer of the text, which are claimed to have greater authority than the text itself. I think, however, as I have claimed elsewhere,[18] that this kind of reading can never be a substitute for interpretation, but is always an act of interpretation; what is more, it is a mode of interpretation that is invariably invoked in order to evade the difficulties presented by the language that the drafters have given us. In this sense it is inherently simplifying, reductionist, or simply evasive.

Of course, I am not denying that the adoption of a Constitution, or the passage of legislation, is in some sense an intentional act. Like almost all human behavior it asks to be interpreted not as random, accidental, or coerced, but as seriously meant. The question is *how* it should be interpreted. The law's answer is by reading the text in the context of its making.

To hope to pierce the text for an intention underlying it, which can then substitute for it, seems to be wrong-headed on several grounds, one of them "intentional": the framers chose to express their "intention" not in the words in which the modern interpreter would do it for them, but in their own words. To seek for "intentions" in this way is to substitute one text, of our own composition, for the real and authorized text actually made by the framers. In this sense the method of "original intention" always erases the one intention we do know about, the intention to publish this language as authoritative. The substituted text will always be of our own imagining, for (except for simple mistakes) it is simply not the case that behind a written text lies another in the minds and hearts of the people, which represents the published text in purer or more complete form. If there were such a text, we could not read it. We cannot avoid the difficulties of reading by looking up from the text for a "truer version" of it, because in doing so we will invariably reduce the text to our own vision of reality. To search for an "intention" that is wholly restatable in terms other than those the authors chose to employ is to search for what could never be found. It is to substitute psychological speculation of an inherently contradictory kind—if that is what they "intended," why didn't they say so?—for the interpretive process of law. And we still are faced with the problem of reading, for even the version we substitute for the original will itself require interpretation, and how is that to be done? Instead of an impossible search for "intention," then, we should treat the text as seriously meant: as if those who wrote it meant it to be read as their statement on the question it addresses.

We cannot simply look past the language to something else—to "what they meant"—but must engage in the arts of construction and composition that are the center of law. What we have before us is a text made in one context, a gesture whose meaning at the time it was made was shaped in part by that context, by the prior gestures against which it is a performance; we now wish to give it meaning in another context, at another stage of the dance; this meaning will have to be somewhat different from the original just as a translation will have to have a meaning different from the original, if only by virtue of the fact that it is a translation.

The claim of the "intentional" reading is a claim of greater realism, a claim to go behind the words for what "really" lies behind them. But the effect is quite the reverse, to create a fiction even greater than the fiction of the "wise legislator": a kind of mythical history the very description of which is claimed to answer our contemporary questions with automatic and perfect force. This is, in turn, to destroy the only premise upon which the text can operate as a text, namely, that we are reasoning people reading language. Argument of this kind will always purport to be factual, about what somebody else intended; in fact, it will be about value, through the disguised creation of ideology.

In what I have called legal argument about the meaning of texts, justice is always our fundamental topic. It opens the talk up to every consideration legitimately bearing on what ought to happen. To attempt to reduce this conversation about what we ought to do (in the light of our authoritative texts) to one about "what they intended" is in its way as dead as the old attempt to claim that we simply discover what the law "is," as though that could be divorced from what it "ought to be." Closing off conversation in this way, in the name of a deliberately created fictional reality, is a radically authoritarian, not a democratic, act.

The claim of the "realist," then and now—I think of the economist who wishes to reduce us to economic utility-maximizers, of the political radical who sees law simply as the expression of class interest, or the psychological realist who sees it as the expression of subconscious needs—is never in favor of a truer grasp of reality, but always in favor of a reductive fiction. This is true because all such views wish to erase the complex reality of the text, and the intellectual, ethical, and political relations embodied in it.

Text and Context

There is another, perhaps more troubling, question about what I have said. This relates not so much to the reconstruction of intention as to the relevance of the context in which a text is produced. Even if we do not think of ourselves as trying to read, in place of the text, some "intention" of its author, but, as I think lawyers typically do, to arrive at some judgment as to the meaning of the text, is it not true that widely shared understandings that lie behind the text—in these cases understandings about racial relations—properly become relevant to that meaning? After all, in our normal communications we understand that the context is as much a part of the meaning of the text as what is said in it. As a theoretical matter, indeed, the text can be said to derive all of its meaning from its various contexts, into which it can be seen as a kind of intrusion; it says only what needs to be said, leaving the rest untouched.[19] On this view, whether the authors of the Constitution included some specific reference to the African-American people is of no real significance. Meaning can be found as readily in context as in text; the effort of Story and Taney is to establish that context.

However sensible this view may be of ordinary communications—where I leave a shopping list on the refrigerator door, for example, which you rightly read in light of your knowledge of my feelings about rutabagas, say, or Bermuda onions—it has a serious defect in principle as applied to a legal or constitutional text. It denies the possibility that a people might wish to use a text to change their context, to constitute an idealized version of themselves in their laws that would alter who they were. This is, in turn, to deny a fundamental characteristic of the law, at least among us, for law is often, and perhaps always, a way of saying that although we are one thing, and our context reflects it, we would like to make ourselves something else. The law is by its nature not merely the expression of a command or a desire, it is a tentative and idealized reconstitution of the community. It is inherently aspirational.*

---

*When I speak of "aspirations" I do not mean to suggest that all legal texts have aspirations that we would share. A particular aspiration might be horrible—to perpetuate racial subjugation, for example—but it would still be in the sense I mean it an aspiration, a way of trying to make the world and oneself different through the creation of a text, which is to be read as the expression not merely of will or feeling but of ideals.

Think here of the way the *Federalist Papers* constantly talk about provisions of the Constitution that were arrived at by compromise as if they were based on principle (for example: representation by states in the Senate, by population in the House). This is not in my view evasive or dishonest, but a practice essential to what we mean by law. The proper question is not in what principle a provision has its origins—for the framers chose not to rest upon that principle, or upon a statement of it, but to make a text of another kind—but in what principle it can have its life. The place to look for coherence is not in the welter of motives and expectations that lie behind the making of the text, but in the text itself, as it is made and published in a certain context.

On this view, the absence in the Constitution of any talk about race, and the oblique references to slavery, could be read very differently from the way Taney suggests: not as pointing to views so deeply and obviously held that they need not be expressed, but as a deliberate attempt to escape from those views. The enormous gap between the race-free language of the Constitution and the kinds of social facts to which Taney points would then have a shouting significance. Of course Blacks, slave or free, were systematically degraded, and in ways we could not or would not change overnight; but this fact was inconsistent with our ideals for ourselves, and in writing the Constitution as we did, we chose not to perpetuate or confirm those aspects of our lives, but to disapprove them.

Of course, meaning lies partly in context; normally we only say what needs to be said in light of what is already understood. But the law is a special form of speech, a way of constituting ourselves in light of what we think we ought to be. It can be a way of removing ourselves from our context, or at least from a part of it; the method of construction employed by Story and Taney denies that possibility.

* * *

In one of his *Rambler* essays, Number 14, Samuel Johnson addresses the question whether it is right to tax a person with hypocrisy who fails to practice the virtues that he preaches. Johnson denies it: it is the very nature of our experience to be unable to live up to our own conceptions of what we ought to be. The fact that we struggle and fail does not mean that our ideals and our values are empty or hypocritical. It seems to me that the law is founded upon exactly the understanding Johnson offers us, for it is a way of establishing a conversation about who we ought to become that acknowledges from the outset that we are not that already, and cannot make ourselves that simply by an act of will. What we can do is make law.

There are legal thinkers—let us call them "pure realists"—who reject this view and regard all legal texts as mere verbiage, epiphenomena: what matters is what is "real," namely, what economic and power relations exist in the world, what different actors want, and what the economic and political effects of various decisions are. The only way to understand the law is to see what its effects are. For such people law talk is essentially empty. The gap between the ideals of the legal system and the realities of the social and political system are naturally pointed to as demonstrating the validity of this approach.

I think that gap can be read differently, for it is essential to the operation of law that the community be able to establish aspirations that are belied by its present condition. The law is at its heart a way of carrying on a conversation about our desires and feelings and wishes in other terms, a way of translating or converting them into the subject of a different kind of discourse altogether. Thus it is in the ordinary lawyer's life that the client comes in the door, full of rage or a sense of injury, of greed or fear, and the lawyer goes to work, converting these primitive feelings into the material for argument and thought of quite a different kind. That conversion establishes a plane at which we exist collectively, and which becomes, by our acquiescence and participation in the conversation that constitutes it, a reality we inhabit. To look through the language to what lies behind it destroys this reality, which is the law itself.

* * *

But suppose I am right, you say, how would it work out in the Slave Cases? Suppose Story and Taney had been "real lawyers," that they had not subverted the processes of law in the ways that they did, how would the results in these cases have been different? If not different, doesn't that prove that it doesn't matter what they say?

This is a difficult question, partly speculative, to which I do not pretend any omniscient answer, but you can gather that I think the proper result in *Prigg* would be to uphold the Pennsylvania kidnapping statute, in *Dred Scott* to find the plaintiff a citizen of the United States. In addition I think that the reading of the Constitution in a more lawyerly way would have led to substantial difficulties, emotional and intellectual, with the results reached in these cases—difficulties which the formulations actually employed by the Justices enabled them, and their readers, to avoid. To focus, for example, upon the circumstances of Mrs. Morgan's freeborn child in a way that recognized that he was a person, entitled to freedom but needing his family, would have been to realize that Mrs. Morgan and indeed her unfree children were people too; a realization, which, if articulated with sufficient clarity, would have tended to erode, not the discourse of law, which it would have exemplified, but that part of it which maintained slavery.

Today we have no slavery, but we do have people suffering greatly, victimized greatly, who in the law and elsewhere are talked about in highly distancing and objectifying ways. Real attention to the fundamental character and commitments of legal discourse, by lawyers and judges and others, might help us bring to our collective attention, however reluctantly, the circumstances of the successors of Margaret Morgan and her children—of all races—and prepare us to address them with more responsiveness and responsibility alike.

6

"Plain Meaning" and Translation: The *Olmstead* Opinions

In the cases discussed above, both Justice Story and Chief Justice Taney sought to avoid the difficulties of reading the text before them by looking to the "original intention" of the framers, with the consequences I have described. Another common interpretive method, similarly evasive of difficulty, is to read the language as if its meaning is plain, unproblematic, simply authoritative as composed. This is the method used by Chief Justice Taft in his opinion for the majority in *Olmstead v. United States*,[1] and resisted by Justice Brandeis in his celebrated dissent.

We now turn to these two opinions, asking of each our familiar questions: How does it define the Constitution it is interpreting; the process of constitutional interpretation in which it is engaged; the meaning of the particular provision at issue (in this instance the fourth amendment); the place and character of the individual citizen in our country, and that of the judge, the law, and the lawyer? What conversation does it establish, with what relation to "democracy?" What community does it call into being, constituted by what practices and enacting what values?

Chief Justice Taft

Since *Olmstead* is the first of a series of cases we shall examine that interpret the fourth amendment, we should perhaps begin with the language of that provision:

The right of the people to be secure in their persons, houses, papers, and effects, against unreasonable searches and seizures

141

shall not be violated; and no Warrant shall issue but upon probable cause, supported by Oath or affirmation and particularly describing the place to be searched and the persons or things to be seized.

Many questions are suggested by that language, some of which will be considered in the following chapters, but here we shall focus on only one: the meaning of the words "search" and "seizure." They define the scope of the amendment, for if there is no "search" or "seizure" it does not apply at all. How, in what kind of text, informed by what ways of reading and speaking, are those words to be given meaning?

We can start with the facts of *Olmstead*: federal officials, with some state police assistance, systematically tapped the telephone wires of persons they suspected to be involved in a large-scale bootlegging operation. They did so without probable cause or a warrant, normally required for valid searches, and in direct violation of state laws that made wiretapping a crime. Upon the basis of evidence obtained as a result of this activity, the defendant was convicted of a federal offense and appealed. The only question is whether the wiretapping violated the defendant's fourth amendment rights, for if it did, the government concedes that the "exclusionary rule" applies to prohibit the admission of that evidence.

It is important to emphasize that the question is not whether the intrusion could be justified—by reason of the degree of probable cause, by the presence of a judicial warrant, or on some other ground—but whether what the officers did counts as an intrusion, as a "search" or "seizure," to which the Constitution speaks at all. If it does not, then the police may tap the wires not only of suspected criminals but of everyone, without constitutional consequence. In this respect *Olmstead* is one of a series of cases that mark out what we are now likely to call the "privacy interests" protected by the fourth amendment, the invasion of which requires prior or after-the-fact judicial approval. Subsequent cases have involved such things as affixing a beeper to a car in order to trace its movements, scraping paint from a car in order to make a chemical analysis, taking finger prints, blood samples, or hair clippings, stopping and frisking people, examining bank records or employment files, and using marijuana-sniffing dogs and undercover agents.[2] The Court's view on these questions does much to define what it means to be a citizen in our country, for these cases tell us what actions by officials will count as invasions or intrusions to which the Constitution speaks.

"Plain Meaning"

In his opinion for the majority, Chief Justice Taft makes short work of the defendant's claim that this was a "search":

> The Amendment itself shows that the search is to be of material things—the person, the house, his papers or his effects. The description of the warrant necessary to make the proceeding lawful, is that it must specify the place to be searched and the persons or *things* to be seized . . .
>
> The Amendment does not forbid what was done here. There was no searching. There was no seizure. The evidence was secured by the sense of hearing and that only. There was no entry of the houses or offices of the defendants.

The fourth amendment does not apply, he says, because there was no "search" and there was no "seizure," defining these words in terms of trespass and materiality. This definition is itself of course arguable—in his dissent, for example, Justice Brandeis will argue that the fourth amendment should be conceived of as protecting privacy rather than property. But in our effort to understand the meaning of Taft's opinion, let us suppose for the moment that we are not to go so far as that, and that we accept Taft's view that the fourth amendment requires a trespassory invasion of an individual's right. Let us also put aside the argument that the illegality of the conduct itself should require exclusion. Accepting Taft's property-trespass theory, then, is the result in *Olmstead* as self-evidently clear and correct as the opinion makes it seem?

I think not. Even on Taft's view of the law the defendant has much to say. After all, the officials undoubtedly trespassed against the telephone company in inserting tapping wires into its lines, and the defendant might well be given standing to protect that interest, especially since in this case the telephone company entered an appearance to argue on his behalf. Or, if a "property" or "possessory" interest on the part of the defendant himself is required, one might argue that he had a leasehold or easement in the wires, created by contract with the telephone company, or an interest created by the operation of trust law—the telephone company holding the wires beneficially for the defendant—or even by the penal law of Washington that made the tapping of the wires a crime. Or the company could be seen as the custodian of the defendant's interests by contract, just as the bank that holds papers in a safe deposit box, the lawyer who holds papers in a file, the United Parcel Service which contracts to deliver a package, can be said to be custodians of someone else's interest. There was certainly a trespass, notwithstanding Chief Justice Taft's claim; and there are at least colorable arguments either that the trespass was upon an interest of the defendant, or that, owing to his relation to the holder of the primary right, the defendant ought to have standing to raise the question. But in the Taft opinion no response whatever is made to these lines of argument.

Taft makes another conclusory claim that is also based on what appears to him the plain language of the fourth amendment. The amendment protects "persons, houses, papers, and effects," and requires a warrant "particularly describing" the "persons or things to be seized." Taft reads this language as saying that intangibles are not protected by it. This is of course one possible reading, but even if it is accepted, it does not necessarily follow that the officer's testimony as to the overheard words should not be excluded. Even if the words themselves are not seizable objects under the fourth amendment their exclusion could be required, for example because the proffered testimony is the fruit of the admittedly unlawful trespassory invasion. Moreover, a different reading of the language of the amendment on this point is itself also possible, namely, that the seizure of words, oral words, is not "covered" by the amendment in another sense: not that they are unprotected by the amendment, but that under its provisions they are in practice immune from seizure, at least whenever there is a prior trespass. This immunity, it would be argued, arises from the fact that no warrant could properly issue for them, since it would never be possible to meet the particularity requirements of the warrant clause. Finally, and most significantly, it is simply conclusory to say that words cannot be seized—in fact, what took place in this case could fairly be described without any violence to the term as the "seizure" of words. Analogies from property law can be employed to support this result, for, under federal law today and under state and federal law then, words can be made the object of property under copyright laws. The right to say or to write them can be bought and sold. And if the state may create a property right directly through its copyright laws, why can it not do so indirectly through its penal law, prohibiting the seizure of some words in some circumstances?

The point of these remarks is not to argue that words are seizable objects, or that a trespass against the defendant occurred, or any of the other matters suggested above, but merely to make plain that colorable arguments along these lines can be developed, none of which was addressed by Taft himself. If Taft did not meet such obvious arguments in his opinion, upon what did he rely to make the conclusory language quoted above persuasive to his readers? One will read his opinion in vain for an explicit justification of those characterizations. He does discuss cases, but only in the most conclusory way, summarizing their facts and sometimes their holdings, but never attempting to draw an analytic connection between those cases and the case before him. (He says, for example, of *Gouled v. United States*,[3] which dealt with a surreptitious filching of papers, that it "carried the inhibition against unreasonable searches and seizures to the extreme limit." But he says nothing to explain or validate that characterization.)

Upon what, then, does Taft rely in his effort to make his conclusions persuasive to his reader? I think that he relies more than anything else upon the very power of characterization that he has exemplified throughout his opinion, upon the voice of authority with which he has been speaking. His ultimate ground is literary and ethical in nature: who he has made himself, and his readers, in his writing. For he repeatedly characterizes both the facts and the law with a kind of blunt and unquestioning finality, as if everything were obviously and unarguably as he sees them; in doing this he prepares us for the conclusory and unreasoned characterizations upon which the case ultimately turns. Rather like Justice Frankfurter in *Rochin*, he makes a character for himself in his writing and then relies upon that created self as the ground upon which his opinion rests. This character is not that of Frankfurter's man of educated sensibility, but, as I will suggest more fully below, that of a simple, even simple-minded, authoritarian.

There is a kind of self-evident circularity about the logic of Taft's opinion, of course, but here as elsewhere arguments from self-evidence have a remarkable power, at least to those disposed to share the basic premises. And the method works: if we accept his lesser characterizations of fact and law, for whatever reason we do so, we find ourselves increasingly ready to submit to the final and conclusive characterization, that there is no "search."

What Kind of Conversation?

What is the view of the Constitution, the law, the citizen, and the reader that is enacted in this writing? For Taft the Constitution is a document that is in its own terms authoritative, telling the rest of us what to do. It has, so far as can be gleaned from this opinion, no higher purposes, no discernible values, no aims or context; it is simply an authoritative document, the ultimate boss giving ultimate orders. The task of the judge is to be an intermediate boss, producing a text that has a similar structure: not reasoned, not explained, not creating in the reader the power that reason and explanation do—for if you are unpersuaded by an opinion that purports to rest upon reason, you may reject the authority of the opinion itself—but an act of power resting upon power, pure and simple. The Constitution is a document written in plain English making plain commands: if you think they are not plain, wait till I have spoken and I will make them plain.

If one were to read this opinion as a literary text and ask what it is that Taft really values and thinks is important, the first answer would be his own voice and his own power; the second, rather surprisingly, would be the criminal enterprise itself. He describes this at great length and in glowing terms:

> The evidence in the records discloses a conspiracy of amazing magnitude to import, possess and sell liquor unlawfully. It involved the employment of not less than fifty persons, of two sea-going vessels for the transportation of liquor to British Columbia, of smaller vessels for coast-wise transportation to the State of Washington, the purchase and use of a ranch beyond the suburban limits of Seattle, with a large underground cache for storage and a number of smaller caches in that city, the maintenance of a central office manned with operators, the employment of executives, salesmen, deliverymen, dispatchers, scouts, bookkeepers, collectors and an attorney. In a bad month sales amounted to $176,000; the aggregate for a year must have exceeded two millions of dollars.

Taft then describes with similar, but perhaps somewhat less intense, feeling the attempts of law enforcement agencies to bring this conspiracy to its knees: "The gathering of evidence continued for many months. Conversations of the conspirators of which refreshing stenographic notes were concurrently made, were testified to by government witnesses. They revealed the large business transactions of the partners and their subordinates." That is what this voice admires: organization, scale, enterprise, and success. It would be possible to imagine someone else saying: "The Constitution of the United States is an achievement of amazing magnitude." But no sentiment of that kind appears in Taft's writing: his enthusiasm and admiration, as expressed in this text at least, lie elsewhere.

Not that he makes no reference to the Constitution: at the end of this long statement of the facts Taft abruptly interposes the language of the fourth amendment, flopped before us like a pancake.

The reader cannot help wondering what this language can possibly have to do with the detective story we have just read, with this thrilling world of organized scale and competition, for Taft—in this sense a "realist"—the real world. This is of course exactly the feeling that Taft's opinion is designed to elicit in us, the sense that the fourth amendment has nothing to do with what is really at stake in the case. The narrative thus implicitly supports the constitutional ideology he has been enacting, for it invites us to see power and force as real, language as simple, and government as about the struggle between the forces of good and the forces of evil. Nothing more than that and nothing less. And law is simply the will of good authority.[4]

To sum up: Taft has, and exemplifies in this opinion, a view of the process in which he is engaged which goes something like this. "My job is to decide this case in light of the Constitution. Here are the facts. They are as plain as can be. Here is the text. It is as plain as can be. It speaks of searches and seizures and here there is neither." This is a commitment by Taft to a particular text and to a particular way of reading it: for him it is composed in simple English—therefore plainly readable—and it is to be read "literally." But since there is in fact no such thing as a "literal" reading of words, that repudiation of ambiguity and complexity itself works as an unexposed, unexplained, and unjustified claim to authority, including the authority to reduce difficulty to simplicity—a claim that is in fact implicit in every claim to read language "literally." And the claim that one is simply reading plain language in a plain way not only creates a false pretense of submission to external authority, it also creates a false pretense of a democratic alliance with the ordinary reader against the obscurantist lawyers. But behind these pretenses, power is taken both from the text and from the reader.

The function of the Court as Taft enacts it is thus not to reason, not to argue, not to explain, but to declare the meaning of an authoritative text. The judge is qualified for this function primarily by his position as judge; but also self-qualified, in the opinion itself, by the skill and force with which the facts and law are stated, and by the very force of his voice: in this instance a no-nonsense voice, businesslike, a bit like that of a crusty old boss from a 1930's movie. And the congruence or harmony between Taft's view of the Constitution and his view of his own role under it, between his voice and his sense of the Constitution's voice, gives his performance the great rhetorical force that arises when different dimensions of meaning coincide.

What kind of argument does this opinion invite in future cases? What kind of conversation does it establish? The answer is, "Make any argument you want and I'll tell you what the result is." The opinion invites a conversation of countering characterizations, conclusory in form, between which the judge will choose, or which he will resolve by making characterizations of his own.

The education required to perform the function Taft defines, or to argue to him, or to be a lawyer or judge in our system as he sees it, is very reduced indeed. You must of course know the legal categories in which the conclusions will be stated, and be able to relate them to each other. But the only question contemplated in this opinion is whether the person speaking has the authority to make his characterizations, not whether something is right or wrong. Legal training, if it were guided by this opinion, would not be an education of the mind and sensibility, surely not an introduction to our tradition and the way it has grappled with questions justice and injustice, but simply the memorization of legal categories and the development of the capacity to make one's voice authoritative, unquestioning and unquestionable.[5]

To judge from this opinion, what is the Constitution in general, the fourth amendment in particular, really about? What values do these texts establish, what values do we serve in our reading of them? For Taft, as he writes here, neither the Constitution nor the fourth amendment is about anything very important or valuable; it is simply a set of words that tell us what to do. Real value is to be found in the fact of authority, in the reduction to simplicity, in the "no-nonsense" voice, in the very control, acquiesced in by his reader, that he exercises over the facts and the language of the case.

This performance works as well as it does, I think, because it appeals to our desires for simplicity, for authority of a certain kind, and for a boss who will tell us what things mean and how they are. Some of these desires show up again, with quite a different quality, in the work of Justice Black, who struggled valiantly to see in the Bill of Rights a certain and clear body of law by which "due process of law" could be defined.[6] We often see a similar authoritarian claim, acquiesced in for similar reasons, in the interpretation of sacred texts: a person, or a group, claim the authority to declare the meaning of the sacred language, with which it is in fact the individual's responsibility to engage as an autonomous and present person, and we yield to the claimed authority. We do so because it relieves us of the task and responsibility of facing what is difficult, complex, and uncertain, of making judgments of our own, of responding as ourselves. To yield in either context is to destroy the life the text makes possible; yet we do it. When we do so, we participate in a conversation that is not the beginning but the end of democracy.

Justice Brandeis

The opinion of Justice Brandeis, justly famous, is different in almost every respect. To begin with the statement of the facts, Justice Brandeis (not surprisingly) describes not the "conspiracy of amazing magnitude" of the defendants but the behavior of the federal officials who arranged to tap the defendant's telephone wires: "To this end, a lineman of long experience in wiretapping was employed, on behalf of the Government and at its expense. . . . Their operations extended over a period of nearly 5 months. The typewritten record of the notes of conversations overheard occupy 775 typewritten pages." This is to focus the reader's attention not on the criminal enterprise engaged in by the defendant but upon the government's concededly improper conduct. Brandeis concludes this statement by saying that the government "makes no attempt to defend the methods employed by its officers," but instead "relies on the language of the Amendment; and it claims that the protection given thereby cannot properly be held to include a telephone conversation."

This is to put directly in issue the question how that language should be read. Instead of simply asserting a conclusion, or implying as Taft did when he quoted the language that one answer was obviously right, Brandeis focuses our attention on the general question of interpretation and puts the burden of advancing its particular reading on the government. He thus poses a question never explicitly addressed by Taft: How are we to think about our reading of this text?

Expounding the Constitution

His first step in responding to that question is to begin his next paragraph with the famous remark of Chief Justice Marshall: "We must never forget that it is *a constitution* that we are expounding." This is to assert, against Taft, that the question, how the Constitution ought to be read, or expounded, deserves explicit thought of a special kind. Brandeis next defines what "expounding" has meant in the past by summarizing cases in which the Court sustained the exercise of powers by Congress over "objects of which the Fathers could not have dreamed." This is a way of showing that the kind of "non-literalist" reading he favors, which he calls "expounding," has been part of our tradition not only on behalf of the individual in his struggles with the government, but on behalf of Congress itself. The next series of examples shows that the Court has adopted a similar view of the Constitution in its approval of state regulations which, quoting *Euclid v. Ambler Realty Co.*, "a century ago, or even half a century ago, probably would have been rejected as arbitrary and oppressive."[7] Only then does Brandeis move to clauses protecting the individual and claim that they must be read in the way he has now established as traditional and neutral, to allow adaptation to a changing world.

But exactly what is this way of reading? If a "literalist" reading of the Constitution will not do, what will? Brandeis has given examples of flexibility but no general principle, and the principle of "adaptation" alone will not do, for it is a principle of change for its own sake. To meet the need he has created, he now quotes from *Weems v. United States*:[8]

> Legislation, both statutory and constitutional, is enacted, it is true, from an experience of evils, but its general language should not, therefore, be necessarily confined to the form that evil had theretofore taken. Time works changes, brings into existence new conditions and purposes. Therefore a principle to be vital must be capable of wider application than the mischief which gave it birth. This is particularly true of constitutions. . . . [O]ur contemplation cannot be only of what has been but of what may be. Under any other rule a constitution would indeed be as easy of application as it would be deficient in efficacy and power.

Brandeis uses this language to define his own fundamental attitude: that the interpretation of the general language of the Constitution, though naturally to be informed by the nature of the evils or mischiefs which gave rise to the language in the first place, must not be limited by those configurations but should be guided by an understanding of the general evils, or goods, of which these are local examples. This view of what the Constitution is and how it is made is altogether different from Taft's, and it is ultimately based on a different vision of human life: that we have limited intelligence, limited imagination, limited grasp of facts; that our thinking is naturally shaped by our immediate experience; that we live in time, through which our experience and every aspect of our culture changes; that one central object of collective life is at once to maintain a central identity while undergoing this process of change and to learn from that process, and that all this was as true of the framers of the Constitution as it is of us today.

On the view implied in Brandeis's opinion the Constitution in fact addresses these very limitations, for it provides us at once with a collective experience and with institutions by which we can to some degree transcend our circumstances. The very point of the Constitution is to enable us to bring into our minds at once both our own experience and that of our predecessors, and to think about that experience as a whole in a disciplined way. It is in principle a mode of education and self-creation over time.

The framers, that is, sought at once to establish and to limit their government, basing their effort on views of the individual, of democracy, and of republican government that made sense to them and that were partly—but like all views, only partly—susceptible to definition and expression in their own language. They spoke that language directly and with confidence. But they also wished this text to be authoritative in other contexts, in other configurations of social reality, in conjunction with other languages. They therefore must have meant it to be read in a way that would permit it to be relocated in a new, and in principle to them unknowable, context, that is, "non-literally."[9] What is required in interpreting the Constitution, therefore, is a kind of translation, a bringing into the present a text of the past. But we all know that perfect translation is impossible—no one thinks that Chapman's Homer is Homer, or Lattimore's either—and this in turn requires us to recognize that our own formulations of the meaning of the text to which our primary fidelity extends must be made in the knowledge that they are in part our own creation.

This view of constitutional interpretation requires of the reader not merely the explication of plain English, as Taft's method does, but the capacity to penetrate the surface of language, and of social and cultural reality as well, in order to reach an understanding of the deepest questions that arise in social life, forever changing their particular forms. It requires, as all translation does, an attempt to be perfectly at home in two worlds, an attempt that must always fail. Our compositions should therefore reflect an awareness of the silence, the ignorance, that surrounds them. What Brandeis asks of the judge, and therefore of the lawyer, is not merely the ability to characterize facts and language as meaning one thing or another, but the capacity to find out what has been, what is, and what shall be, and to conceive of the Constitution as trying to provide, through its language, and through the general principles that it expresses, a way of constituting ourselves in relation to our self-transforming world.

But how is all this to be done? Brandeis has implicitly committed himself to exemplifying the process that he recommends, and he proceeds to do that. He says, "When the fourth and fifth amendments were adopted, 'the form that evil had theretofore taken,' had been necessarily simple. Force and violence were then the only means known to man by which a government could directly effect self-incrimination." But circumstances have since changed—"time works changes"—and the government has already discovered other means for achieving its primary objective, "to obtain disclosure in court of what is whispered in the closet." And since we are to think about "what may be," it also becomes important for Brandeis to say that "the progress of science in furnishing the Government with means of espionage is not likely to stop with wire-tapping." One can scarcely imagine what may be possible in the future. He concludes by asking: "Can it be that the Constitution affords no protection against such invasions of individual security?"

Notice that Brandeis here defines in his own writing the word "security," which he implies, is plainly violated by wiretapping; then he uses "security" to define "search" and "seizure." He is thus making a supplementary language for the analysis of the authoritative text, and doing so by using and transforming one of its own central terms ("The right of the people to be secure . . .). This is just what Taft did not do; yet something like this is an essential step in doing what we think of as law, for it is only by making such a language that we can begin to think as lawyers about that text and its context.

We can therefore put the question slightly differently and ask whether we are we able to think about this question in any terms other than those actually used by the framers. If we cannot, the Constitution in the nature of things cannot endure, for its continued life requires its constant translation into new circumstances and new terms, a translation to which the Constitution itself offers guides, through what Brandeis calls its "principles." The text must be removed from the web of associations that once gave particular meaning to its terms and relocated in a new set of such associations. The text remains the same, but its translation—its being carried over—to our own time locates it in a new context of particularities which will, and should, give it a transformed meaning.

But how is this to be done in practical terms? Here Brandeis shows what is peculiar to the lawyer's way of facing these questions, by turning to precedent. He begins with *Boyd v. United States*,[10] defined now not merely as an invoice-discovery case, as Taft read it, but as establishing the right to personal security, personal liberty, and private property. For Brandeis, *Boyd* is about the relation between the individual and the government on the most fundamental level, establishing zones into which the government may not enter. Ex parte *Jackson*,[11] which held that a sealed letter in the mails was entitled to fourth and fifth amendment protection, is for him not distinguishable from *Olmstead*, as it is for Taft, who said that *Jackson* was different from

Olmstead because the government had created the monopoly involved in that case. Brandeis denies the distinction: "The mail is a public service furnished by the government. The telephone is a public service furnished by its authority. There is, in essence, no difference between the sealed letter and the private telephone message." It is true that one is tangible and the other not, but the evil—the invasion of privacy—of wiretapping is actually far greater than that involved in tampering with the mails. That is, when you look at judicial precedent in the way that Brandeis's conception of the Constitution and of law more generally requires us to do, with an eye to the general principles of the texts in question, the distinctions upon which Taft relies disappear. Conceived of as a case about privacy, as Brandeis says it should be, *Jackson* actually establishes the principle for which the defendants argue.

Brandeis then turns again to the general question of constitutional construction, arguing that "an unduly literal" method of construction ought to be rejected in this case as it has been in others. The nature of the Constitution requires an examination not merely of its words but its "underlying purposes." In this spirit he then summarizes the holdings of the cases since *Boyd*, which have, he says, settled the following things:

> Unjustified search and seizure violates the Fourth Amendment, whatever the character of the paper; whether the paper when taken by the federal officers was in the home, in an office, or elsewhere; whether the taking was effected by force, by fraud, or in the orderly process of a court's procedure. From these decisions, it follows necessarily that the Amendment is violated by the officer's reading the paper without a physical seizure, without his even touching it; and that use, in any criminal proceeding, of the contents of the paper so examined—as where they are testified to by a federal officer who thus saw the document or where, through knowledge so obtained, a copy has been procured elsewhere—any such use constitutes a violation of the Fifth Amendment.

This is an argument from a series of holdings to a general conclusion (which he will shortly state in terms of "privacy") that determines the result in the particular case. Brandeis here exemplifies the process by which the Constitution, according to him, should be read—that is, the method of "expounding" that is required by the temporal and shifting nature of our experience and by the central aim of the Constitution, which is to provide a matrix of relations between the individual and the government that can endure throughout the changes of social and intellectual forms. In making the translation from one context to another, in pushing the old text into current life, Brandeis shows that the lawyer and judge are not lost at sea but have the assistance of precedent, the set of prior translations, that themselves form a way of moving from one world to the other.

In perhaps his most famous passage, Justice Brandeis states as fully as he can the general principle which he perceives lying behind the constitutional language.

> The makers of our Constitution undertook to secure conditions favorable to the pursuit of happiness. They recognized the significance of man's spiritual nature, of his feelings and of his intellect. They knew that only a part of the pain, pleasure and satisfactions of life are to be found in material things. They sought to protect Americans in their beliefs, their thoughts, their emotions and their sensations. They conferred, as against the Government, the right to be let alone—the most comprehensive of rights and the right most valued by civilized men.

This is a translation not only into contemporary legal language but beyond it, into contemporary ordinary language, into the vernacular. It thus invites a conversation not only among lawyers but among citizens, a conversation in that sense democratic. But this language does not supplant the law—the last thing Brandeis would argue for is the elimination of our cultural past in favor of the uninformed view of the moment. It is in fact his work with the legal language preceding this passage that has both made possible and justified this return of the Constitution to the people.[12]

As a second ground of reversal, Brandeis says that the crime committed by the federal officers renders the evidence seized inadmissible. "Here, the evidence obtained by crime was obtained at the Government's expense, by its officers, while acting on its behalf." For Brandeis the admission of the evidence constitutes a ratification of the lawbreaking. "When these unlawful acts were committed, they were crimes only of the officers individually. The Government was innocent, in legal contemplation; for no federal official is authorized to commit a crime on its behalf." But the admission of evidence constitutes a deliberate ratification of the illegal conduct, and this is violation of the deepest principles of self-government. He also invokes the settled principle that a court will "not redress a wrong when he who invokes its aid has unclean hands," and applies it to the present case.

What is significant here, especially after his earlier invocation of the vernacular, is his confidence in traditional legal language and categories—"ratification," "clean hands"—as his language of judgment. This embeds his opinion in the legal context as his earlier paragraph embedded it in the vernacular.

In his final paragraph he establishes himself, and his voice in the following terms:

> Decency, security and liberty alike demand that government officials shall be subjected to the same rules of conduct that are commands to the citizen. In a government of laws, existence of the government will be imperilled if it fails to observe the law scrupulously. Our Government is the potent, the omnipresent teacher. For good or for ill, it teaches the whole people by its example. Crime is contagious. If the Government becomes a lawbreaker, it breeds contempt for law; it invites every man to become a law unto himself; it invites anarchy. To declare that in the administration of the criminal law the end justifies the means—to declare that the Government may commit crimes in order to secure the conviction of a private criminal—would bring terrible retribution. Against that pernicious doctrine this Court should resolutely set its face.

It is not only the government that is the teacher: Brandeis himself establishes his own voice as that of a teacher, a teacher who must first learn, and who by having learned may teach. This is in turn to define the law, legal education, the Constitution, and all that is involved in thinking about a case such as this, as challenging every intellectual and moral capacity.

Translation

So what for Brandeis is a constitution? What is the judge's role? How is one to be qualified for the role that he defines? What is the meaning and importance of the enterprise in which he is engaged?

As for the Constitution, his view is that the framers, located in one cultural and social context, sought to create a document that would establish a government, limit that government, and protect individuals, all in the service of a larger understanding of the individual and his relation to his polity. The formulations employed by the framers were necessarily rooted in their experience and have a necessarily incomplete reach because the power of the human imagination to grasp the future is limited. For the most part they employ not archetypal examples or strict rules, but generalizations as their way of establishing a set of relations, a set of institutions, and a set of ways of thinking and talking that could structure our common life in the future. Certain language is broken out of its original context, set aside, and given special authority, so that it can be given a new range of significances, in new and in principle unknowable contexts, for it is meant to reach not only what is but what might be.

Since everything shifts, constantly, as time goes on, the Constitution can reach "what might be" only through the process by which we read it correctly and well. The Constitution is made, then, according to Brandeis, not merely by the framers but also by those who read the language of the framers well, who translate—"carry over"—its terms to the contemporary world, aided as they are by the earlier efforts at translation.

In this enterprise, as Brandeis defines it, everything is involved: the intellect, the capacity to read and express, the ability to penetrate surface forms to underlying truths, the sensitivity to shifts in social and intellectual forms, all in the service of the wise and just definition of the individual and his government. The reading of the Constitution is in fact a stage in the making of the Constitution, and everything that is present in that activity is present in this one: the definition of a civilized polity operating under the rule of law and protecting the deepest values of the culture. Accordingly, to become a good judge requires the greatest education imaginable, an education that will train us to see what the framers saw, to hear their language and to penetrate it, to see by analogy what fits and what does not, to see through the surface to the underlying truth—almost as Plato says one sees through the surfaces to permanent ideas and ideals—and to translate an old text into the current world.

But more even than this is required, for the opinion, in Brandeis's view, is constitutive in another way: it becomes part of the Constitution itself, and this means that the judge must be able to create a constitution, with his readers, of a kind that fits with, and carries forward into the future, the earlier constitution out of which he speaks. This requires Brandeis to become a maker and remaker of language. He makes a formulation, "the right to be let alone," that connects our own vernacular with the language of the Constitution and our past. A proper legal education, for lawyer as well as for judge, will be an education into the past as well as the present, an education of the vision and the imagination, and will ultimately require all of us to be, as Brandeis demonstrates himself to be, a teacher. For as judges, as well as in our other capacities, we teach our values by what we do, whether we know it or not. In the world defined by Brandeis, who would not be a lawyer?

The heart of Brandeis's opinion lies in a vision of human culture working over time, in a sense that we have something to learn from the past as well as something to give to the future. Nothing could be farther from our contemporary economic and political idea of the individual as sovereign consumer, implementing his tastes in competition with others. For Brandeis the individual and the community alike are engaged in a continual process of education, of intellectual and moral self-improvement; the law in general and the Constitution in particular provide a central and essential means to this process. The community makes and remakes itself in a conversation over time—a translation and retranslation—that is deeply democratic not in the sense that it reflects, as a market or referendum might, the momentary concatenation of individual wills, but in the sense that in it we can build, over time, a community that will enable us to acquire knowledge and to hold values of a sort that would otherwise be impossible. The conversation is democratic in its ultimate subjection to popular determination, in its openness to all who learn its terms, in its continuity with ordinary speech, but most of all in its recognition that the essential conditions of human life that it takes as its premises are shared by all of us.

* * *

One final point remains. The reader will have noticed that in this case it is the law-and-order man who is authoritarian in his voice and style, and the defender of individual rights who speaks as an individual himself and to us as individuals. Could this pattern be reversed?

I certainly think it would be possible to write an opinion that was as authoritarian as Taft's but came out the other way, say by simply declaring that this is a search or that the amendment protects privacy and stop. (Some of Justice Douglas's opinions have that flavor,[13] as indeed does Justice Stewart's opinion in *Katz v. United States*, the case that finally overruled *Olmstead*: "The Fourth Amendment protects people, not places."[14]) It is also true that I would not subscribe to every aspect of Brandeis's opinion: his prose is sometimes too heavy-handed for me, and I would have preferred to expand the meaning of "search" and "seizure" rather than leaping to "the right to be let alone" language, which in fact has authoritarian elements of its own.[15]

But how about an opinion "coming out" the way Taft's opinion does: can one imagine a good opinion doing that? It is certainly possible to imagine a better opinion doing so: one, for example, that spoke of the dangers that a new technology presented in the hands of law-breakers, of the national crisis of law enforcement presented by bootlegging, of the respect to be accorded the judgment made by the executive (which is, after all, democratically accountable), of the reasons why the states should not be able to interfere with a national solution to a national problem, of the need for adaptation in constitutional interpretation, and so on, or perhaps one explaining by reference to history why a strictly material conception of "search" or "seizure" is appropriate. As you can tell from this summary, I think it would be hard to do this very persuasively, but we cannot know that until someone has earnestly tried it.

To return now to my earlier claim that the distinction between opinion and result, form and content, ultimately disappears, all this means that the standards of excellence by which I have been suggesting we measure the literary work of the judge—his definition of himself, of us, and the conversation that constitutes us—are not merely technical, or verbal, but deeply value-laden and substantive. If we can arrive at shared standards of excellence in the domain that is the main concern of this book—the nature and quality of judicial thought, the ethics and politics of the judicial text—this will greatly limit the range of substantively permissible, or reachable, decisions, even in "hard" cases. You cannot write a great novel in support of anti-semitism, says Sartre, and I think you cannot write a great opinion that denies that sense of the ultimate value of the individual person that is necessarily enacted in any sincerely other-recognizing expression.

Will the range of permissible or good decisions ever narrow to "one correct result" in every case? Not while we are human beings, living in the world Brandeis defines—full of ignorance, with disturbed and feeble imaginations, caught by motives of which we are incompletely aware. We will always have much to disagree about. But if we focus real attention on the aspects of meaning I have tried to identify above, and ask ourselves and each other what excellences we demand there, I believe we shall be engaging in a conversation that will move us in the direction of enlightenment and justice in our votes, as well as our expressions.

* * *

I have offered you one reading of these opinions. There is of course much more to say about them, for example, that it is in some sense "unfair" to abstract Taft's opinion from the larger context of his work as a whole, or, more accurately, to draw sweeping conclusions about his work as a whole from this one text; that a part of the meaning of both opinions, untraced here, lies in their interactions with each other, with the other opinions in the same case—especially the striking opinion by Holmes[16]—and with those from earlier cases as well; and that the soundness of Brandeis's claims about "privacy" and the intentions of the "framers" is open to question. It is certainly true that Brandeis's image of the framers is romantic and itself unargued; that his talk about "principles" is a bit simple-minded and his application of them more than a bit authoritarian; and that he may be thought inadequately respectful of the language actually used in the constitutional text.

I also want to make explicit, what the reader has no doubt felt, that I myself give, by construction, Brandeis's opinion some of the meaning I claim for it, just as he gives the fourth amendment some of the meaning he claims for it. This, I think, is inevitable. The reader of this chapter will in turn give it much of whatever meaning she claims for it. The text at once creates and constrains a liberty (or a power) in its reader, and in doing so defines for the reader a particular kind of responsibility. It is indeed in that combination—liberty, constraint, and responsibility for the reader and maker of texts—that the ethical and intellectual life of the law can be found.

7

THE READING OF PRECEDENT:
UNITED STATES V. WHITE

In the cases we have discussed so far the Court's primary concern has been with the language of the Constitution itself and only secondarily, if at all, with the meaning and authority of other Supreme Court cases interpreting that language. In the slave cases and *Rochin* the reason seems to be that there is no clear line of authoritative and relevant cases; in *Olmstead* there are some cases—especially *Ex parte Jackson*, the mail search case—but both opinions focus their energies elsewhere, perhaps out of the realization that this case can be read to cut both ways, perhaps out of an eagerness to reach the large questions of interpretive method discussed above. It is more usual, however, for the Court to look to judicial precedent at least as much as to the language of the Constitution, for, under our understandings, the cases interpreting the Constitution are themselves entitled to considerable, if not conclusive, authority on the question of its meaning. It is in fact one of the objects of the Court to create over time a chain of such cases, elaborating in a consistent way a particular reading of the text. Normally, then, the question for the Court is not only what the Constitution means, standing alone, but what it should be taken to mean given its interpretive history, which has an authority of its own. The Court thus establishes a relation not only with the constitutional text but with the discourse, and the other texts, by which it is interpreted. What kind of relation should this be?

To address this question we turn now to *United States v. White*,[1] which, like *Olmstead* and *Rochin*, arose under the fourth amendment. This is a much less famous case than the others, but for our purposes of deep interest, for it provides us with three opinions that define with extraordinary clarity three distinct ways of reading relevant precedent. They thus present us, more sharply than *Olmstead* does, with the question of the way prior judicial opinions should be read: how they should be interpreted as single texts, and even more importantly, how a set of opinions, decided across time, should be interpreted, with particular attention to the conflicts among them. Sometimes, as here, the question has an especially dramatic focus: When—if ever—should a case be overruled, or be regarded as having already been overruled, and upon what authority?

Background

The holding in *Olmstead* was the subject of immediate and continuing criticism. Congress quickly passed a statute making wiretapping a federal crime. This statute was later read to require the exclusion from any criminal trial of any evidence obtained in violation of it.[2] But outside the wiretapping field *Olmstead* still had force until 1967, when it was finally overruled by *Katz v. United States*.[3]

The facts of *Katz* were these. Officers wanting to overhear a particular person's conversations attached an electronic listening device to the outside of a public telephone booth he regularly used, and did so both without a warrant and without any excuse for failing to obtain one. For fourth amendment purposes, then, the question was the same as that in *Olmstead*, namely whether this conduct was a "search." If it was, the evidence obtained by the eavesdrop must be excluded, because the warrant requirement of the fourth amendment had so obviously been violated. If not, this kind of conduct would be entirely unregulated by the fourth amendment.

In holding for the defendant, that the intrusion was a "search," the Court said that the right question was not whether the telephone booth was a "constitutionally protected area," as the defendant's lawyers had urged: "[T]he Fourth Amendment protects people, not places." The opinion went on: "What a person knowingly exposes to the public, even in his own home or office, is not a subject of Fourth Amendment protection . . . But what he seeks to preserve as private, even in an area accessible to the public, may be constitutionally protected." This opinion was widely heralded as establishing the fourth amendment on a new basis, protecting "privacy" rather than "property."[4]

This case brings to the surface certain difficulties with Justice Brandeis's opinion in *Olmstead*, for what is this vague term "privacy" to mean? In his opinion for the Court, Justice Stewart suggested that the "privacy" of the fourth amendment extended to anything that the individual sought to preserve in secret. But Justice Harlan, in concurrence, said that the case should be construed to protect only those expectations of privacy that are found by the Court to be "reasonable." This means that it is not just the individual's purposes or impressions that count but the Court's judgment as to whether those expectations should be protected. Justice Harlan's language has since been taken as the central holding of *Katz*; the Court has accordingly faced in a sequence of decisions the question what is, or is not, a reasonable expectation of privacy.

One such case was *United States v. White*, the facts of which were these. Government agents, suspecting the defendant of various narcotics violations, investigated him with the aid of an undercover informant armed with a radio transmitter. The informant engaged White in several conversations, which were broadcast by the concealed transmitter to agents waiting elsewhere. On four occasions the conversations took place in the informant's home; other conversations took place in his car, in a restaurant, and in the defendant's home. The prosecution did not produce the informant at trial and offered instead the testimony of the agents who had overheard the conversation through the radio signals. The Court of Appeals read *Katz* as forbidding the introduction of the agent's testimony in this case. The Supreme Court reversed on two grounds: first, that *Katz* should not apply to the events in this case because they took place before that case was decided; second, that *Katz*, properly read, would not require the exclusion of this evidence in any event. I shall be concerned only with what the Court said about the second question.

Justice White

The majority opinion was written by Justice White. For him this case is governed by a series of cases, decided before *Katz*, which held that when a person confides in another he runs the risk that this person will, contrary to his expectations, offer this evidence to the government, either by prior arrangement with the government or on his own present initiative. Thus when the government arranged with Edward Partin, an old associate of Jimmy Hoffa's, to report certain conversations with him, Partin's testimony about those conversations was admissible in Hoffa's trial. The Court said that the fourth amendment affords no protection "to a wrongdoer's misplaced belief that a person to whom he voluntarily confides his wrongdoing will not reveal it."[5] Since this is not an invasion of a fourth amendment interest—not a "search"—no warrant is required before engaging in it. The Court reached a similar result in the companion case of *Lewis v. United States*,[6] where the government sent an undercover agent to the defendant's home to make a purchase of narcotics, and in an earlier case, *Lopez v. United States*,[7] where an agent carried electronic equipment that recorded the defendant's words.

The intermediate appellate court in *White* conceded all of this but held that *Katz* nonetheless required a different result. The court focused on the early case of *On Lee v. United States*.[8] Here the informer entered the defendant's premises and not only heard the conversations, as in *Hoffa* and *Lewis*, and recorded them, as in *Lopez*, but, as in the *White* case, carried a transmitter that sent the conversations out to other agents equipped with receivers. In the court's view *Katz*, which in its own context of course regarded "bugging" as a search, implicitly overruled *On Lee*.

Justice White disagreed that *Katz* should be so read: while it is true that *On Lee* was based partly on the grounds that there was no trespass, a ground that indeed "cannot survive *Katz*," it had a "second and independent ground for its decision," namely, that the defendant had made a decision to trust the agent, and that the violation of this trust presents no fourth amendment issue, whether or not electronic transmission is involved. Justice White sees "no indication in *Katz* that the Court meant to disturb that understanding of the fourth amendment or to disturb the result reached in the *On Lee* case."

The ultimate reason, for Justice White, is that the fourth amendment does not protect a person against misplacing his confidence in another. It does not matter whether the other person testifies directly, writes down what he has heard and testifies from those notes, records what he hears on a tape, or broadcasts what he hears to agents waiting outside. "If the conduct and revelations of an agent operating without electronic equipment do not invade the defendant's constitutionally justifiable expectations of privacy, neither does the simultaneous recording of the same conversations made by the agent or by others from transmissions received from the agent to whom the agent is talking and whose trustworthiness the defendant necessarily risks."

Think of it in terms of expectations, Justice White says: we cannot believe that a suspect "would distinguish between probable informers on the one hand and probable informers with transmitters on the other." If a person thinks he is talking to an undercover agent, he will not reveal damaging information in either case; if he does not, he will, and it will not matter to him, from the point of view of his privacy, whether these conversations are simply remembered or broadcast. The fact that the informer has disappeared and is unavailable at trial should not affect this result.

* * *

This is in its own terms a highly persuasive opinion, and I shall have more to say about it below. For present purposes I want only to note that a large part of its force arises from a commitment to a certain way of reading precedent that is itself not explained or defended. It works this way: each case stands for a proposition, or a set of propositions, which are good law until the moment arrives at which they are overruled. Thus the cases can be laid out before the reader like cards on a table, in patterns of significance; the critical question is which case this one is most like. In this instance that question is first answered by pointing to *On Lee*, which on its facts is very close to this case and would presumably govern it; the next question is whether *Katz* overruled *On Lee*. This is to be determined by asking what the bases of *On Lee* are: for Justice White one of the bases is removed, the other untouched, by the rationale of *Katz*. It therefore remains good law.

This is almost a caricature of old-fashioned common-law adjudication. The cases all are authoritative, and until overruled equally so. They stand for propositions; the sole task of the court is to arrange those propositions in logical patterns of non-contradiction and to fit the present case within them. All authority is in the past, in the earlier cases. The function of the Supreme Court, including in the present opinion, is to produce a series of tags that tell you how future cases should be decided.

But this is to take an external view of a process to which Justice White and the reader are in fact internal. He speaks about the Court that overruled *Olmstead* without any sense of why it did so, with no sense of the feelings and attitudes that underlay that movement in the law. According to what he says in this opinion the task of the Court is simply to declare results: to decide particular cases and to publish the decisions in forms that will translate into rules that can be followed. The task of the later adjudicator is simply to try to obey these rules and harmonize them when necessary to keep them in coherent order. Perhaps one should be lopped or clipped when it does not fit with the others, but that is all. It is not easy to see how the person Justice White defines himself as being in this opinion could ever overrule a precedent; yet that is part of what the Court does and part of what it has done in the present series of cases. Virtually the only value asserted or performed here is the value of logical coherence, and with it legal stability.

If we ask what kind of conversation this opinion establishes, and with what relation to democracy, we see that there is reasoning here, and to that extent a sharing of power with the audience, but reasoning of a most limited kind. The sort of argument it invites from lawyers in future cases is also limited, a parsing of precedent to produce patterns of consistency, with none of the sense of uncertainty and responsibility that Brandeis's opinion begins to make vivid. The only questions the opinion contemplates are: what the earlier cases held, upon what principles, and how those principles bear on the present case. It is true that this is an essential part of lawyering and the law—and Justice White seems to do it very well—but it is not all of it. Suppose you ask of this opinion: What is the purpose of the guarantee of the fourth amendment that individuals shall be free from unreasonable searches and seizures? Why do we have a Supreme Court to define and protect these rights? By what processes of reasoning is the authority of the Supreme Court defined and established? To these questions this opinion gives no answer at all.

Justice Douglas

The dissent of Justice Douglas responds directly to what he regards as the hyperlegalistic quality of Justice White's opinion: "The issue in this case is clouded and concealed by the very discussion of it in legalistic terms." He then proceeds to talk not like a lawyer at all but almost like a newspaper reporter, in conclusory terms about general social phenomena:

> What the ancients knew as "eavesdropping," we now call "electronic surveillance"; but to equate the two is to treat man's first gunpowder on the same level as the nuclear bomb. Electronic surveillance is the greatest leveler of human privacy ever known. How most forms of it can be held "reasonable" within the meaning of the Fourth Amendment is a mystery.

This is the voice not of a lawyer, but of a citizen or as I say perhaps a journalist, and it is a central part of Douglas's point to speak that way. His object is to resist White's legal talk by insisting on the presence of an ordinary voice.

Not that he is without "precedents" of his own: he quotes, for example, a message by Franklin Roosevelt, dated May 21, 1940, which authorized wiretapping in the cases of spies and sabotage and went on to say that under ordinary circumstances "wiretapping by government agents should not be carried on for the excellent reason that it is almost bound to lead to abuse of civil rights." Or: "Today no one perhaps notices because only a small, obscure criminal is the victim. But every person is the victim, for the technology we exalt today is every man's master. Any doubters should read Arthur R.

Miller's *The Assault On Privacy* (1971)." He closes this section of his opinion by citing an article in *The Progressive* magazine. This is a kind of parody of the case-bound reasoning of Justice White.

We have here the assertion or display of a mentality that is as far from Justice White's as could well be imagined: Justice Douglas focuses upon the social phenomena of "surveillance," not the legal text—not the constitutional text, not the cases explicating it—and he opposes surveillance of any kind, on any grounds, without bothering to discriminate between one kind and the other. In particular he fails even to allude to the distinction that for Justice White is crucial, between the case in which the government intrudes upon a conversation which both parties wish private and the case in which one of the parties is himself an agent or wishes to disclose what is said to the government. This, added to his use of mock precedents, can be read as a kind of serious teasing of Justice White, the solemn and rigid lawyer who is bound by his sense of logic and nothing else.

In the second half of his opinion Justice Douglas does turn to the law, but in a very different way indeed from Justice White. For Douglas the precedents represent not static and equal authorities, like cards on a table, but a progressive movement in time, from less enlightened to more enlightened positions. He focuses especially on *Berger v. New York*,[9] which invalidated a comprehensive New York wiretapping statute on fourth amendment grounds, and *Katz*, which held that nonconsensual bugging was a "search" subject to fourth amendment regulation, and regards them as holding simply that all forms of electronic surveillance "are now covered by the Fourth Amendment." But once more he fails to make the fundamental distinction that is essential to the majority opinion in *White*, between surveillance that is consented to by one of the parties and surveillance that is not. It would flunk a law school exam.

Surely Justice Douglas, one of the smartest people ever to sit on the Supreme Court, knew this. Why then does he insist on talking this way? Simply to frustrate the lawyer-judge for whom such distinctions are the stuff of life? To express disdain for all reasoning of that kind in favor of the plain assertions of plain rights? Here Douglas is working rather like Taft, for he too seeks to shortcut the processes of legal thought by the use of common-sense language and ordinary talk. There is much to be said for the use of the vernacular in law, but to speak only in such terms, at least in such a conclusory way as Douglas and Taft do, is to eliminate the processes of law altogether.

When Douglas turns to prior law, he divides the cases into two classes, those that come after *Berger* and those that precede it. He discounts all the decisions decided before Berger as representing an "opposed view." Thus for him *On Lee* is really based upon the "idea, discredited by *Katz*, that there was no violation of the Fourth Amendment because there was no trespass." *Lopez*, where the government agent carried a pocket wire recorder, "was also pre-*Berger* and pre-*Katz*." He says: "We have moved far away from the rationale of *On Lee* and *Lopez* and only a retrogressive step of large dimensions would bring us back to it." He lives in a world of moral progress, in which the old is outmoded because it is unenlightened. Unlike Justice White, for whom all precedent is of equal authority, Justice Douglas creates a scale of authority, crediting one group of cases, discrediting others, according to the era they represent.

* * *

It would be easy to mock his opinion, but it is important to see that Douglas in fact focuses on a real element that White leaves out, namely, the way in which the law changes and the reasons for which it does so. Justice Douglas's statement of those reasons is crude— "for" or "against" electronic surveillance and wiretapping—and his attributions of motives to the Court is equally simplistic, for in his view the Justices are either high-minded protectors of civil rights or craven apologists for a tyrannical government. But he does see something that Justice White misses, and something central to the law. It is thus fair to say that each of these opinions has real merits as well as real defects; neither is adequate but they expose each other's deficiencies rather well.

Justice Harlan

Justice Harlan, normally a "conservative" who resisted the transformation of the law of criminal procedure worked by the Warren Court, here writes in dissent. Usually he and Douglas were deep antagonists; here in one sense—their "results"—they are on the same side, but in another—their sense of the law and the Court—they remain divided.

Justice Harlan begins by defining the question, much as Justice White did, in terms of the binding force of precedent: "The uncontested facts of this case squarely challenge the continuing viability of *On Lee v. United States*." But for Justice Harlan this is not merely a technical question about the holding of a prior case, as it is for Justice White, but an important social and political question; the prior case is accordingly to be read not as simply a declaration of a rule but as an attempt to find a meaningful resolution of an issue difficult on the merits, a matter that has "provoked sharp differences of opinion both within and without the judiciary." The "factors that must be reckoned with in reaching constitutional conclusions . . . are exceedingly subtle and complex." This is all a way of saying that this is a large and serious question, not to be reduced to a merely technical or easy one.

His next move is to reexamine the sequence of cases. This section of the opinion is a lesson in the reading of precedent, directed both to Justice White and to Justice Douglas, as well as to those who might be persuaded by them. First, as to *On Lee* itself, upon which the majority relies so strongly: this was a five-four judgment, Harlan reminds us, based solidly on the trespass rationale that *Katz* was later to overrule and which in fact three members of the Court disapproved of at the time. It is true "that the opinion in *On Lee* drew some support from a brief additional assertion that 'eavesdropping on a conversation, with the connivance of one of the parties' raises no Fourth Amendment problem. But surely it is a misreading of that opinion to view this unelaborated assertion as a wholly independent ground for decision." This "misreading" is of course essential to Justice White's opinion; Justice Harlan's remark thus challenges the central link in Justice White's chain of authority and challenges as well his methodological commitments to a reading of prior cases as propounding with equal weight a series of equally valid propositions.

Eleven years later the Court decided *Lopez v. United States*, the tape recording case. *Lopez* is cited by White as reaffirming *On Lee*, but Harlan, who was in fact the author of the majority opinion there, says it can hardly be thought to have done so. While the Court did not then take the step of overruling *Olmstead*, he says, it was careful to base its judgment on two premises: the fact that the tape recordings were used only to corroborate the evidence of the government informer and the fact that there was no risk here not fairly assumed by the defendant. "To the discerning lawyer"—unlike Justice White, Harlan is necessarily implying—"*Lopez* could give only pause, not comfort."

Harlan next turns to *Osborn v. United States*,[10] a companion to the *Hoffa* and *Lewis* cases, but to which White made no reference at all. In *Osborn* agents investigating the attempted subornation of a juror were equipped with tape recording devices, the contents of which were sought to be used in evidence against the defendants. In this it was like *Lopez* and similar to *On Lee* and *White*. But there was a dramatic difference as well, for here the police had sought and obtained judicial authorization for what they did. They had, that is, a form of the judicial "warrant" required by the fourth amendment. The Supreme Court opinion upholding the police conduct in *Osborn* praised the government in the warmest terms and approved most strongly of what it had done. While this did not entail an explicit holding that there was a "search"—for the government had done what was required of them if there were—some sense that the fourth amendment spoke to this situation was certainly implicit in the Court's pleased approval.[11]

Justice Harlan thus challenges Justice White in two related ways. First, he rejects the implicit theory that cases are to be read simply as rules to be followed until overruled. Rather they are complex struggles to come to terms with real difficulty, to be read in light of the Court's perception of that difficulty and to be given weight reflecting both the Court's confidence in its judgment at the time and our own sense of its wisdom. Second, he insists that one take all the judicial evidence into account, which Justice White cannot do, for his reading cannot explain the enthusiasm with which the Court approved of the result in *Osborne*. It can of course explain the narrow holding, for his theory would also have led to affirmance, but to reduce a case to its result in that way is to destroy its character as a communicative act, as an expression of mind to mind.

Justice Harlan, then, sees the law as developing, as Justice White did not, but developing in a complex and reasoned way, not in the simple fashion that Justice Douglas describes. For him, indeed, the ultimate overruling of *Olmstead* by *Katz* was deeply foreshadowed by other developments: "Viewed in perspective, then, *Katz* added no new dimension to the law. At most it was a formal dispatch of *Olmstead* and the notion that such problems may usefully be resolved in the light of the trespass doctrine, and, of course, it freed for speculation what was already evident, that *On Lee* was completely open to question."[12]

So far all of Justice Harlan's reading of precedent has merely established this last point: that *On Lee* is open to question. How is the matter of its continued force to be decided? This is a version of the central question that faces every judge examining any case that bears upon the one before her: Is this a case to which she should submit her own judgment, or is it properly to be regarded as no longer having effect? How is this decision to be made: by the strength of one's own agreement or disagreement with the case? Or by something external to the self, in the law, and if so, what?

Justice Harlan makes no claim that he is entitled to oppose his will or preference to that of a prior court. But as a reader of the legal context in which he acts, as an interpreter of the cases which define it, he attempts to find an authority outside the self—though in part established by his skill and understanding—upon which to rest. He reads the decisions of the Court since *On Lee* and finds in them "sound general principles for the application of the Fourth Amendment" of a kind that were either "dimly perceived or not fully worked out" at the time of *On Lee* itself, and which, therefore, have a higher standing than the holding of that case. These general principles, Harlan says, include the following: "That verbal communications are protected by the Fourth Amendment, that the reasonableness of a search does not depend on the presence or absence of a trespass, and that the Fourth Amendment is principally concerned with protecting interests of privacy, rather than property rights."

How do these principles bear upon the *Lewis* and *Hoffa* cases? Do they suggest, for example, that a warrant should be required whenever anyone acts as an undercover agent? Justice Harlan says no, asserting as a crucial difference that "in each of these cases the risk the general populace faced was different from that surfaced by the instant case. No surreptitious third ear was present, and in each opinion that fact was carefully noted." It will not do, as Justice White will have it, simply to assert that there is "no difference" between a case in which an individual talks to a government informer and the case in which that conversation is recorded or transmitted. While the "risk analysis" approach represents "an advance over the unsophisticated trespass analysis of the common law," it too has its "limitations and can, ultimately, lead to the substitution of words for analysis." In particular, Harlan says, we must "transcend the search for subjective expectations or legal attribution of assumptions of risk. Our expectations, and the risks we assume, are in large part reflections of laws that translate into rules the customs and values of the past and the present."

The real question, then, is whether the risk that is imposed on the public by saying that the use of such bugging devices presents no fourth amendment issue is a proper one. This question should be answered, he says, "by assessing the nature of a particular practice and the likely extent of its impact on the individual's sense of security balanced against the utility of the conduct as a technique of law enforcement."

The issue for Justice Harlan, then, is not what risks wrongdoers must have to contemplate, but what risks every person in the country must have to contemplate. If the use of electronic surveillance of this kind is not regulated by the fourth amendment, it means that the police may do it to any person at any time, without any controls whatsoever. "The interest *On Lee* fails to protect is the expectation of the ordinary citizen, who has never engaged in illegal conduct in his life, that he may carry on his private discourse freely, openly, and spontaneously without measuring his every word against the connotations it might carry when instantaneously heard by others unknown to him and unfamiliar with his situation or analyzed in a cold, formal record played days, months, or years after the conversation." Interposition of a warrant requirement is designed not to shield "wrongdoers" but to secure a measure of privacy and a sense of personal security throughout our society.

At the end, then, Harlan must choose, and choose upon the basis of his own construction of the fourth amendment, of the values it protects, and of the social effects of the practice of consensual bugging. But this act of choice is not the raw exercise of power, or the imposition of his values on the law, or the simple assertion of a "cost-benefit" method of reasoning, for it takes place in the context created by the rest of his opinion, in which he defines himself as faithful to the law, as a responsible and intelligent reader of the cases that give it meaning—far better than the literalist White or the simplistic Douglas—and as one whose values, and hence whose choice, are inspired in large measure by the law to which he is paying such careful attention. When he makes his choice it is to fill a gap left by the law, a gap that requires a choice; and he grounds his choice in an educative process—in which his reader may share—by which it is not he alone, as an atomized bearer of tastes and preferences, who acts, but he as one who is formed by the very tradition to which he contributes in this opinion. When this case is read in the context of his work as a whole—in which he repeatedly argues for judicial restraint, on the grounds that the residual power of the Court should be reserved for great matters on which the tradition is inconclusive—we can see it as the fulfillment of an implied promise, that when such a case arose he would act, and here he did.

* * *

When we put these opinions together with those in *Olmstead*, certain parallels emerge. Justice White's opinion, like Taft's, purports to locate all authority externally to itself, in the authoritative declarations of others. For Taft this declaration was the fourth amendment, for White, the series of cases construing it. His texts are more complex than Taft's, and harder to read—they require an understanding of the reasons why the cases were decided as they were and the construction of the distinctions that organize them—but for White as for Taft there is nothing in principle problematic about the process of reading them, at least for the legally trained mind. But this is an important qualification: the authority he rests upon is not just the text plus "common sense," as with Taft; it is the text plus a certain form of disciplined reading.

Justice Douglas finds his authority not in the specific language of the Constitution—one remembers his famous opinion in *Griswold v. Connecticut*,[13] outlawing state-imposed contraceptive bans upon married couples, in which he spoke of the "penumbras" of the various amendments—nor in the specific holdings of prior cases, but in the providential history of which he is an observer and in which he is an actor. "Once we thought this, but we were wrong; gradually we have come to see the truth." This movement is its own authority, at least as it is reported by a mind correctly attuned to it. To compare for a moment legal with biblical interpretation, one is reminded of those Protestants—among whom Douglas was in fact raised—who focused like all Protestants upon the sacred text rather than the tradition, but who read the text with an eye not to its letter but to its spirit.[14] This is a kind of reading that it is easy to mock—one thinks of the famous pages in Hooker and Swift where this is done—but for us perhaps too easy. There is much to the view that what is required to read a text is not mere "reason," as if that could be segmented off from the rest of experience and the self, but attunement, or right orientation: the effort to make oneself its ideal reader.

Harlan sees authority not simply in the cases, certainly not in the spirit of change, but in the tradition out of which he speaks; this tradition must be read, and we are responsible for the way we choose to read it, and hence to construct it. The right way of reading is not legalistic, as White's is, but as a "discerning lawyer," that is, with a kind of thoughtfulness and attention that go beyond the local holdings to what Harlan calls the "principles" that the cases can be seen gradually to create. Authority thus lies in a kind of respectful interaction between mind and material, past and present, in which each has its proper contribution to make: not simply in the tradition, then, but in the tradition as it is reconstituted in the present text. The central excellence of the judicial mind is an excellence in the art of composition by which this is achieved.

With his reader Justice Harlan establishes a double relation: in one sense he educates us—he trains us in the art of "discerning," of seeing through the holdings to the deeper patterns—but at the same time he holds up his own efforts of that kind to our own scrutiny and criticism, thus establishing a kind of fundamental equality with us too. In this sense the conversation he establishes, despite its traditional cast, is deeply democratic.

The past is there and he treats it seriously, as Douglas does not; but he knows, as White in this opinion seems not to have known, that it is impossible simply to set over the meaning of this past, without gain or loss or modification, into a series of declaratory propositions. Like Brandeis, he sees that the past must be translated and that this necessarily involves making it mean something new, something it does not already mean. The present mind creates out of the materials of the past the meanings upon which its own authority rests, but always acting under an obligation of fidelity to what is external to the present self, the present moment.

* * *

In all of this there are many paradoxes and ironies. It is, for example, Brandeis's opinion, in many ways so admirable, that provides the ground used in *Katz* to overrule *Olmstead*, but the opinion in *Katz* has some of the conclusory and authoritarian characteristics of Taft's opinion, in many ways so objectionable. And the fourth amendment is here converted from a text regulating "search and seizure" into a "right of privacy against the government," leaving us with the kind of question the due process clause itself presents, how such vague language is to be given meaning, but without the history that might help us do this. Does *Katz* mean that judges will have to become, like Frankfurter, authoritative sensibilities? Or can the processes of legal thought still find a way to work?

White provides three responses to this question, of which the first, that of Justice White, can perhaps be explained by this history. He insists upon reading the prior constitutional cases as a set of authoritative holdings, in a rigid adherence to a very old-fashioned model of a common-law thought. This method can easily be criticized, as I have done, but perhaps in fairness one should also say that this choice may be self-consciously motivated by Justice White's sense of the current state of constitutional law, and in particular the law of the fourth amendment, namely, that we are in danger of losing all sense of obligation to the past. After all, *White* was decided at the end of the Warren Court era, when, in a burst of judicial energy, case after case had been overruled; the style of White's opinion here can be thus taken as an argument by performance that the Court should look at prior cases as constraining it far more than it had come to do. This caricatured form of thought, that is, can itself be read as a kind of corrective argument about the way we ought to think.

Much can also be said in defense of Douglas's opinion, which at once mocks White's and introduces important ways of thinking which that opinion excludes. The deep question Douglas brings to the surface is the proper role of *stare decisis*, the doctrine that gives opinions their authority. White pretends to see no problem of this sort, and seems simply to regard all opinions as of equal weight. But to do this he must treat the opinions in a rather reduced way, as each promulgating a rule or a set of rules resting on wholly restatable reasons rather than seeing them as parts of a process in self-education and self-constitution. Equally important, his method has no place for the kind of change this sort of law requires, namely, by overruling.

Our reading of Douglas's opinion thus suggests the general question: What kind of respect should be paid to the opinions of the past and why? One might think, for example, that the only text that matters is the Constitution (or, in a statutory case, the statute): whatever other judges have said is only their opinion, to be given no more weight than their reasons seem to us to warrant. On this view all real authority would reside in the primary text; the opinion of the court would be entitled to no more consideration than an academic or even journalistic commentary. (This is roughly the way in which civil-law systems treat statutory adjudication.) This is a difficult position for our Supreme Court in practice to accept, for it would change the meaning of what it is doing in the case before it. The Justices do not feel that they are just commentators but that they are acting as lawmakers, and they no doubt want their own opinions to receive the kind of attention that law commands. For that to happen they must accord other opinions equal respect, or their own claims to authority will be undermined.

But the question can be put more generally, whether the Court should seek to have its decisions regarded as law in the first place. What would be lost if they were not? How are judicial decisions different, for example, from the opinions of commentators? The difference lies not in the intelligence or virtue of judges as people but in the process and discipline by which they act. Their decisions are not abstract but contextualized in the demands of a particular case; they are not volunteered, but required of them, for they do not choose what comes before them; they are informed by argument both ways, both oral and written, and by argument that is itself informed and constrained by what has preceded it. The array of decisions a court makes over time in this way constitutes an enormous reservoir of intellectual and practical experience upon which future lawyers and judges may draw. In this sense the heart of the law is that it is a mode of communal self-education and self-constitution. This process can work as it does only if the cases we read are entitled to attention of a very high degree of intensity. This is indeed a function of their authority as law.

There are those who would argue with this view, wishing to reduce law to what I have called policy and to act as though our freedom to choose at any point were wholly unconstrained except by the nature of our resources. But it is the nature of the law to constitute a set of constraints; its art lies in living with and within them.

All this is not to say that all cases should be given equal weight. This is the point that Douglas sees and that White's opinion slides over. How are we to decide which cases are no longer "good law?" How are we to talk about the process by which we do so? But Douglas is less helpful than he might be, speaking as he does in terms of self-evident moral progress. Here Harlan's achievement is remarkable, for in his opinion he re-creates the past in such a way as to pay it the respect it is due and in two seemingly conflicting ways: he respects both the particular conclusions the cases have reached and the process of transformation by which certain of these cases lose their authority as law. For in his view the proper overruling of a case is not a simple act of will or judgment, a decision to overturn, but a gradual process by which the understandings that underlie the case are eroded or modified, over time, and by others as well as oneself. The law is a community in the process of its own transformation, and for him the transformation is entitled to the same kind of weight that the particular decisions have. The transformation that counts as authority is not to be found in one's preferences but in the world. It is not his will that decides but his sense of the meaning of the authoritative past. And what changes can include his own mind: Justice Harlan here reaches a judgment that would require a different result in *Lopez*, the case of which he was the author.

* * *

Much as I admire the spirit in which Harlan does all this, I should say that on the merits I myself am unconvinced that the line he draws between the agent without a transmitter and the agent with a transmitter is the important one. There is much to be said for Justice White's view that not a great deal hangs on this. I agree with much of Justice Harlan's sense of the meaning of the past but think that it is the use of the informer itself (at least in any case in which the initial contact is not criminal) that should count as a search requiring judicial approval.[15] In this sense my view on the "merits" is closest to that of Douglas, whose opinion is in my view much less admirable than Harlan's. I say all this not because my views on these matters have special importance, but to suggest by this example one way in which one's estimate of the quality of an opinion can differ from one's imagined vote.[16]

8

THE FOURTH AMENDMENT AS A
WAY OF TALKING ABOUT PEOPLE:
THE *ROBINSON* CASE

So far we have focused on the character the Court gives itself in its opinion, on the kind of community it creates with its reader, and on the sort of relation it establishes with the prior texts—constitutions, statutes, judicial precedents—to which it owes fidelity. But there is another dimension to the meaning of an opinion, one that can be found in the way it defines not the people it talks to but those it talks about—for example, in the cases we have read, Mr. Rochin and the officers who barged into his room; Mr. Olmstead and the zealous federal agents; Margaret Morgan—and her children—and Dred Scott (who are reduced to objects of property), and their "owners" and pursuers. How are these people defined in the text created by the Court? What relations does it establish between them (or any one of them) and the Court itself, or with other agencies of government? What relations does it establish among them? By asking such questions as these we can reach beyond the immediate participants in the rhetorical community to those who are spoken about in its terms—to those who are subject to the power of the law—and ask, from their point of view, what the meaning is of the conversation that the Court establishes in a particular opinion, or in a series of them.

In the present chapter we shall do this by examining a particular fourth amendment case, *United States v. Robinson*,[1] but I hope that what is said about it can be seen to have a more general resonance as well. As the recitation of facts to be given below will show in more detail, *Robinson* is a complex case about a very common and significant question, namely, how far, and for what reasons, the police may search (without a warrant) someone they have validly arrested for a crime. Obviously they may search for weapons, in order to protect themselves and others from violence and to guard against escape, and perhaps also they may search for evidence of crime, in order to prevent its destruction. But what of a case where there is no evidence of the crime in question—say, driving when one's license is revoked—and no reason to believe that the suspect is armed: May the person arrested be frisked for a weapon? If no weapon is found in a frisk, may her pockets and their contents be searched? What if a small package or envelope is found in her shirt pocket: May it be seized and brought before a court for permission to open it? May it be opened on the spot? May its contents be examined or read? Why? What does it mean, what do we make it mean, that we answer these questions as we do?

These are difficult questions, with much to be said on both sides. We shall approach them by way of two introductory sections, the first of which develops the perspective from which we shall look at the opinion in *Robinson* (that is, by seeing it as a stage in the creation of a discourse that constitutes a social and political world). The second consists of a brief survey, from this point of view, of the law of the fourth amendment as that body of law existed at the time of *Robinson* itself. For to understand that case we shall need to have some sense of the shape of the discourse of the fourth amendment as a whole, going well beyond the single question—is this a "search?"—that we have so far been pursuing.

The Constitution of a Social World

As you already know, the fourth amendment requires that "searches" and "seizures" (including arrests) be "reasonable" and at least in some cases subject to judicial warrant, which can issue only upon "probable cause."[2] More than any other single constitutional provision it stands between us and a police state, for its central premise is that police (or other governmental) conduct that interferes with a person's liberty, bodily integrity, or right to exclude others from what is hers shall be subject to judicial control, either before the event (through the warrant procedure) or afterwards, for example when she challenges that conduct by habeas corpus (a special action brought to challenge the legality of one's physical detention), by a motion to exclude evidence from a criminal or other proceeding, or by the initiation of a private or public suit.

In a series of cases beginning with *Boyd v. United States* in 1886,[3] and including *Olmstead, Rochin,* and *White,* the Supreme Court has sought to give content to this provision. In doing so it has created a language, a set of terms and assumptions and gestures in which it can talk about and dispose of the conflicts that repeatedly arise between members of police departments and investigative agencies on the one hand and those members of the public upon whom they intrude on the other. This language is itself a way of constituting and thinking about the world, a way of defining the citizen and the officer and the relation between them.

Imagine, for example, a typical fourth amendment case. A serious crime has occurred, such as robbery or rape; a policeman has stopped a suspect, and searched him and his car, perhaps finding evidence, perhaps not. In order to make a motion to suppress, or to bring a civil action against the officer, the person searched must talk about this event in a language of legal significance. The discourse of the fourth amendment—the conventional ways of characterizing facts, stating values, and articulating criteria of judgment—is the language he must use, and he will demand of it that it speak to the situation in a way that he can respect. On the other side, the representative of the state, speaking for the officer and the victim of the crime, must use the same language, and he will likewise demand that it respect what he regards as the important concerns he stands for. One way to conceive of the task of the Court in this field, then, is to say that it is to define and regulate the relationship between policeman and citizen, through the thousands of different forms and factual situations in which conflicts can arise between them, by affording a language in which their representatives can carry on intelligible argument about the transaction that they share, and in which, so far as possible, justice is done to the legitimate claims and expectations of both sides. The making of such a language of adjudication, setting the terms in which conversation will proceed, is one way in which the Court contributes to the definition and the education of a national community.

This language is artificial, in the sense that it is made by the Court, not the parties: its terms are not those in which either the officer or the citizen would naturally talk, say to their friends or family. But it is possible that the officer, the suspect, and those who readily identify with either, can find in that language an expression or recognition of what they regard as their important and legitimate concerns. To the extent this is so, the discourse functions as an important force of social definition and cohesion, placing the individual or the official in a comprehensible public world in ways that she can respect. But to the extent that the individual or the official faces a public world defined by a language she cannot speak, in which she cannot locate herself, which does not deal in intelligible ways with claims she regards as important, the discourse becomes exclusive and authoritarian in character, denying the significance of her experience and silencing her attempts to express its meaning.

It is worth emphasizing that this language is compulsory, and this in a very practical way. Anyone who wishes to employ the machinery of the law to assert a right or to protect an interest must speak it. He need not mean what he says, of course, but he is nevertheless forced to participate in a rhetorical process designed to express certain more or less clearly articulated values, whether or not he agrees with them. One of the functions of the law is indeed to provide a rhetorical coherence to public life by compelling those who disagree about one thing to speak a language which expresses their actual or pretended agreement about everything else. In this way the law makes the disagreement both intelligible and amenable to resolution, it establishes in the real world an idealized conversation. This compulsion is not a bad thing—indeed it seems essential unless every case is to raise as a wholly new question how our society and its members are to be talked about—but it is important to recognize its force, and that it has both highly creative and highly fictional aspects.

How will the officer want the law to talk about him and his situation? His claim will be that the law ought to recognize the difficulty and uncertainty of his job by giving the greatest possible weight to his expert judgment both as to when a search or arrest ought to be made and as to what ought to be done next. To the extent that the courts require that these judgments ultimately be judicial ones, or judicially reviewable, his claim may shift slightly, to an insistence that, if the courts are to decide these matters, they should promulgate clear and specific rules that the police can reasonably follow. Judicial attempts to frame such rules, however, have foundered on several stubborn realities: the complexity of the factual experiences with which they are concerned; the discovery that rules employing clear and general categories, or making highly specific directions, will sacrifice legitimate concerns of one side or the other; and the great diversity of attitude on substantive questions among the members of the Supreme Court. The result has been an uncertain and confusing body of cases and principles which fail to provide the sort of respect and guidance the police understandably demand. It is not surprising that the police, and those who readily identify with them, feel unfairly treated.

The Court has not been much more successful in talking about the citizen who complains of his treatment by the police. At one time, property law was conceived of as drawing a bright line around the individual, defining in relatively clear and certain terms a zone of autonomy and privacy. On this view, as we know from *Olmstead*, there was no search if there was no trespass, and the fourth amendment normally did not apply to such things as wiretapping and eavesdropping. But this position had its protective side too, for under it no search whatever was permitted except for items in which the state or another had a superior property interest, such as stolen goods or contraband. (This was in fact the original basis of the "exclusionary rule," as chapter 9 will explain in greater detail.) Understandably enough, the Court has found the "property" view insufficiently protective of individual privacy, especially in an era of sophisticated electronic devices, and at the same time excessively restrictive of legitimate state interests in searching for and seizing evidence. But, as perhaps our reading of *White* has suggested, attempts to produce a body of "privacy" law to supplement or supplant the use of property concepts have not been eminently successful.

* * *

The decision of a fourth amendment case is thus a point at which a judgment is made as to how people will be talked about in our public world. In deciding a case, and in explaining its decision, the Court makes an example of a certain set of people and the transaction in which they have participated; it writes a drama, as it were, of public significance. The language in which this is done is much more than a technical or professional language, to be evaluated by its clarity, precision, and efficiency. It is a social and intellectual force of enormous significance, an expression of value and attitude that is in some ways far more important to the quality of the community it defines than the particular decisions taken under it.

Our questions are these: How does the discourse of adjudication that the Court has made under the fourth amendment define its principal actors, the citizen and the officer, and what relation does it establish between them? What does it give each of them to say, and to whom—to what kind of court, engaged in what kind of conversational and political life—can they say it? How does this language define this part of our civilization? Then: What contribution does the *Robinson* case make to that discourse, that civilization?

The Structure of Fourth Amendment Discourse

The language of the fourth amendment, you may remember, reads as follows:

> The right of the people to be secure in their persons, houses, papers, and effects, against unreasonable searches and seizures, shall not be violated, and no Warrants shall issue, but upon probable cause, supported by Oath or affirmation, and particularly describing the place to be searched, and the persons or things to be seized.

Two things are immediately apparent even from an initial reading. First, like all texts, this one is incomplete; such key terms as "search," "seizure," and "probable cause" must be given meaning through a process of reading. Second, the relationship between the two clauses is unclear.[4]

I take up the second point first. One syntactically possible reading is that the primary prohibition is against "unreasonable searches and seizures" under standards of reasonableness to be evolved by the Court; the "probable cause" and other specific requirements of the second clause would then be taken as constitutional definitions of reasonableness only in that class of cases where warrants happen to be obtained. But as a practical matter this reading makes almost no sense, for under it an officer would never be required to obtain a warrant, and the warrant clause would be pointless if it could be evaded at the officer's will.[5] This suggests that the heart of the amendment lies in the warrant clause and requires that a judicial warrant be obtained for any search or seizure, unless for good reason excused, and, wherever a warrant is so excused, that the same standards of probable cause and specificity, so far as possible, be applied. Under this reading "reasonableness" would be defined by the criteria of the warrant clause—probable cause, specificity, and the implicit warrant requirement—which are presumed to apply to every search. When the direct application of the warrant clause is excused, on grounds of emergency, its criteria still operate as standards or guides for the evaluation of searches.

Although there has been some argument both as to its historical basis and as to its wisdom, it is pretty much this reading the Court adopted when, upon the passage of far-reaching federal criminal laws—especially prohibition laws—it began to work out a meaning for the fourth amendment.[6]

What Is a Search?

In *Olmstead v. United States*, as you know, the Court defined a fourth amendment "search" as a kind of trespass, and accordingly held that wiretapping was not a "search." But it never explicitly said how this term was to be further defined, apparently on the assumption that it was obvious. Is this to depend upon state property law, federal common law, or some combination of the two? Property rights are thought to be established by the state, after all, not the federal government; yet the rights established by the Constitution ought not be subject to revision by state courts and legislatures.[7]

When *Olmstead* was abandoned in the series of cases culminating in *Katz v. United States* (discussed in chapter 7), the problem of definition was compounded. Who is to determine what is a "privacy" interest for the purposes of the fourth amendment, and under what criteria? To what extent, if any, is this to be at least initially a question of state law? If there is to be a federal law of privacy, what shall be its bases, its terms, and its contours?

What is an Arrest? What is a Seizure?

Perhaps more surprising has been the Court's failure over the years to tell us what constitutes a "seizure" (or arrest) of the person of the sort requiring probable cause, and what should be done with detentions short of these: Are they to be permitted freely, subject to no fourth amendment regulation; prohibited entirely, unless probable cause exists; or subjected to intermediate regulation, and if so under what authority? In an early case[8] the Court seemed to assume that any interference with liberty was an "arrest" requiring probable cause. But the Court later backed away from this view and held that when an "arrest" occurred, and by implication whether one did, were to be regarded as matters of "fact."[9] But it gave the trier of fact no criteria by which to approach, let alone resolve, the question.

This uncertainty was in part resolved by the famous case of *Terry v. Ohio*,[10] which held that some interferences with liberty—in this case a frisk for weapons and the detention necessary to complete that frisk—would be regarded as "seizures" distinct from "arrests," and therefore not requiring "probable cause" but nonetheless subject to fourth amendment regulation under its first clause, prohibiting "unreasonable searches and seizures." The idea apparently was that out of the universe of "seizures" some were "arrests," regulated by the probable cause requirement, while others were "less than arrests," regulated by the first clause.[11] What justified the "frisk" in *Terry* was an officer's reasonable apprehension that a man he suspected of planning a robbery—but whom he had no probable cause to arrest—was armed. In investigating this possibility he approached the suspect to ask him questions about what he was doing. The Court held that in this situation he could protect himself by a frisk, if he could articulate reasonable grounds for his suspicion that the suspect was armed.

Terry suggests that at least in "frisk" cases both the specificity requirement (limiting the frisk to an external pat-down of the sort that would reveal a weapon) and a depreciated version of the probable cause requirement (requiring "articulable suspicion" that the person is armed) should apply. But this does not tell us what to do with other cases. And it reaches a result inconsistent with the Court's earlier reading of the relationship between the two clauses, for here an officer alone can do what a judge could not, under the probable cause language of the amendment, authorize her to do.

How is "Probable Cause" to be Measured?

There is an enormous body of law giving a complicated and somewhat uncertain content to the "probable cause" language,[12] varying especially in the methods by which the requisite probability is to be measured and established. Virtually all these cases, however, agree on one thing: probable cause sufficient to permit a search or arrest requires a good basis for believing it probable or likely that the particular search contemplated will produce the items legitimately sought, or that the particular person arrested has in fact committed a crime for which arrest is permissible. In making and reviewing determinations of probable cause a court functions as a sort of trier of fact, asking a particular question about a particular case: Does the evidence properly before it support, to the requisite degree, the inference of "probability?" This is the approach used even in *Terry v. Ohio* to determine whether the particular facts of the case justified the frisk engaged in there.

In *Camara v. Municipal Court*[13] a different conception of the "probable cause" judgment was employed for the first time. On first reading, that case may seem to add to the protections of the fourth amendment, for it overruled an earlier case[14] holding that an "administrative inspection" of a residence to determine whether it complied with housing code requirements was for fourth amendment purposes not a "search." For the *Camara* Court the fact that this was a "civil" search carried out as part of an administrative scheme rather than as part of a criminal investigation did not remove it from the reach of the fourth amendment, including the warrant requirement.

But in requiring a warrant the Court faced a new difficulty, for in the normal housing-inspection case there will be no specific reason to believe that a particular house is substandard. Indeed, the purpose of such schemes is to inspect whole neighborhoods or even cities to uncover dangers of which even the occupants may be unaware. The Court thus had to choose between invalidating these obviously valuable inspections or interpreting "probable cause," for the first time, to require evidence not of a certain degree of probability with respect to the particular invasion but of the reasonableness of the scheme as a whole. The latter was the view adopted by the Court, which held that the standard for the issuance of a warrant in this kind of case is not the "probability" test articulated in the warrant clause but a general "reasonableness" standard. To put it somewhat differently, the Court here regulates the search by a principle of general, rather than particular, justification.

My point here is not to claim that *Terry* and *Camara* are diabolical cases—indeed it is difficult to see how they could properly have been decided differently on their facts—but to identify some of the impact they have had on the probable cause and warrant protections of the fourth amendment, removing some classes of search and seizure from those protections altogether and, at least in some cases, changing the fundamental nature of the probable cause inquiry.

When is a Warrant Required?

As I said above, the reading the Court has given the fourth amendment through most of its history has been that a search is valid only if made pursuant to a proper warrant, unless an emergency or "exigency" exists which excuses that requirement.[15] But in working out the implications of this formulation, the Court has met two problems of extreme difficulty.

The first is how the "exigent circumstances" which excuse a warrant are to be defined. In some opinions it seems implied that the categories of exigency are closed—the warrant is excused where the search is incident to an arrest, or of a movable vehicle, or of an object in plain view[16]—while others suggest that new categories can be added, perhaps indefinitely. In one case,[17] for example, it was held that an entry of a house by police in "hot pursuit" of a fleeing suspect whom they had probable cause to arrest was valid, notwithstanding the failure to obtain a warrant. In another—a blood-test case[18]—it was said that a warrant could be excused where there was a real possibility that evidence would be lost or destroyed. The danger is, of course, that the exception will eat up the rule. Is there not always a danger that what one is searching for may be moved or destroyed?

Attempts to employ sharp categories have not, however, been

wholly successful. An early case[19] established the proposition that the search of a car on the highway could be carried out without a warrant if there were probable cause, for the obvious reason that the car might be driven away while a warrant was applied for. But in *Chambers v. Maroney*[20] this principle was applied to permit the warrantless search of a car that had been impounded by the police, for the search of which there was obviously plenty of opportunity to get a warrant. Is the rule then to be an "exigency" rule, requiring a showing that the vehicle or other item to be searched is in fact in some danger of being moved? Or a "car" rule, simply permitting warrantless searches of cars, and, if so, on what grounds?[21] The major argument in support of *Chambers* is that where a car is involved, there will be an actual exigency in such a large percentage of the cases that the Court will not stop to inquire whether one exists in a particular case. But this raises a large question about fourth amendment adjudication. Is it proper for the Court to operate, for the sake of apparent clarity and efficiency, by such categorical rules, or is the Court not obliged rather to determine and judge the constitutionally relevant interests at stake in the particular case? This question will recur in our analysis of *United States v. Robinson*, below, which presents it in a particularly stark form.

The second problem in the administration of the "exigency" exception to the warrant requirement arises with respect to searches incident to arrest, with which *Robinson* itself is concerned. If the arrest creates an exigency excusing the warrant, how far does the exigency go and why? In *United States v. Rabinowitz*[22] the Court permitted an exhaustive search of the defendant's office incident to his arrest for possessing and selling stamps with a forged overprint. (The overprint makes them valuable to collectors.) In a famous dissent, Justice Frankfurter argued that the power to search without a warrant ought to go no further than the reasons for which it exists, namely, to search for evidence the defendant might try to grab and destroy and for weapons he might use against the officers. "To say that a search must be reasonable is to require some criterion of reason," said Justice Frankfurter, and he found these criteria in the traditional requirements that probable cause exist and that a warrant be obtained, except to the degree that the warrant is excused for the reasons stated. In *Chimel v. California*[23] the Court repudiated *Rabinowitz* and adopted Justice Frankfurter's reasoning: A warrant is not required for a search of the arrestee's person or the area in which he might grab to obtain a weapon or destroy evidence, but for any search beyond that area both probable cause and a warrant are required.

Justice White, speaking also for Justice Black, would have used a different rule in *Chimel*. The police should be free, incident to an arrest, to carry out a search of the whole premises—even beyond the "grabbing area"—without a warrant, but only insofar as they have probable cause. The argument is the same as that supporting his opinion in *Chambers*, namely, that it will so often be the case that there is a warrant-excusing exigency in such circumstances that we ought to permit such searches without a warrant. But this is not to permit a search "without criterion of reason," for the police are still subject to the restrictions imposed by the probable cause and specificity requirements, which determine the direction and intensity of the permissible search. The "categorical rule" argued for by Justice White would thus excuse (as to the search beyond the person, at least) only the warrant requirement, not the substantive criteria of that clause.

What *Rabinowitz* or *Chimel* left wholly open is the question whether the search within the "grabbing area"—which everyone agrees requires no warrant—is limited by a probable cause requirement, as even Mr. Justice White would limit the search beyond it. Or is the authority to search an arrested defendant an "automatic" or "per se" authority, not controlled even by the probable cause standard of the fourth amendment? This is the question to which *Robinson* is addressed.

* * *

Before turning to that case let me briefly note that the discourse I have sketched out above, while not perfectly coherent, nonetheless defines certain deep and consistent commitments. These include the premise that the action of the officer is to be evaluated by a court, preferably before the intrusion takes place, but in any event afterwards; that every intrusion must be justified by reasons that support it; and that whim and discrimination are alike improper grounds for official action. The heart of it is that the citizen does not belong to the state but remains always a juridical actor, entitled to judicial review of any invasion of his interests, in the course of which the government must ground its conduct in reason.

What is more, as *Terry* and *Camara* make plain, his fourth amendment interests include any interference with liberty, not just arrests, and any invasion of his house or premises, not just searches for evidence of crime. In such cases the justification to which the citizen is entitled is somewhat different—*Terry* depends upon the officer's apprehension of danger, *Camara* upon the reasonableness of an inspection program—but he remains entitled to a justification. At the most fundamental level, then, this discourse of rights and reasoned justifications establishes a conversation that strives to reflect the needs both of the citizen and of the state.

United States v. Robinson

"I just searched him. I didn't think about what I was looking for. I just searched him."[24]

The Facts

On 19 April 1968, Officer Jenks of the District of Columbia police department made what he called a "routine spot check"[25] of an automobile. He asked for and examined the driver's registration and his license, which proved to be a temporary operator's permit in the name of Willie Robinson. He also examined the driver's draft card, apparently having requested it.[26] He noticed that the operator's permit gave a birth date of "1938," and the draft card one of "1927." He made notes of the cards and permitted the driver to depart. A later check of license records showed that one Willie Robinson, Jr., born in 1927 had his license revoked; and that a temporary permit had subsequently been issued to one Willie Robinson, born in 1938. The pictures on the revoked license and the application for the temporary license were both of the man Jenks had stopped.[27]

Four days later, while on duty, Jenks saw Robinson driving the same car, stopped him and asked to see his license and registration. Upon being shown the same cards as before, he placed Robinson under arrest (a) for driving while his license was revoked and (b) for obtaining a license by misrepresentation. These offenses carry substantial penalties, including the possibility of imprisonment. The arrest was what the Supreme Court called a "full custody arrest," by which they mean that Officer Jenks had decided to take the suspect to the station for booking. It is significant for reasons to be explained below that under District of Columbia law the offenses were automatically bailable, that is, that the defendant had the right to be released, after booking, if he could post bond.

It is not clear from the record whether Jenks had been looking for Robinson, or whether he just happened to see him. The court of appeals proceeded on the assumption, however, that Jenks's purpose was to make an arrest for the license offenses described and not for some other improper purpose, such as searching him or his car for drugs.[28] All the opinions agree that Jenks had probable cause to make the arrest for the reasons stated.

The dispute is about the propriety of the subsequent search. Jenks engaged in what his departmental regulations call a "full field type search," in which the officer examines the contents of all the pockets, removing every item, even one "that he believes is not a weapon." According to Sergeant Donaldson, a police training instructor: "Basically it is a thorough search of the individual. We would expect that in a field search that the officer completely search the individual and inspect areas such as behind the collar, underneath the collar, the waistband of the trousers, the cuffs, the socks and shoes." [29] Of the search carried out in this case, Jenks said, "I just searched him. I didn't think about what I was looking for. I just searched him." [30] He found in Robinson's jacket pocket a crumpled-up cigarette packet, which seemed to have some objects other than cigarettes inside it. Jenks opened the packet and found fourteen gelatin capsules of heroin, for the possession of which Robinson was ultimately convicted.

The question is whether the capsules were properly admitted at trial, or whether they should have been excluded as the fruit of a search improper under the standards of the fourth amendment. This question can be broken down into two others (both on the assumption that the arrest itself was legal): (1) Were the initial search of Robinson and the seizure of the packet within the scope of a permissible search incident to arrest? (2) If so, was the opening of the packet, once it had been seized, permissible?

Both of these questions were left open, you will remember, by *Chimel*, which required probable cause and a warrant for a search beyond the arrestee's "grabbing area," but which was rather opaque as to the character of the search it permitted of the suspect himself and of the area he could easily reach.

Justice Rehnquist's Opinion for the Court

Justice Rehnquist (as he then was, now Chief Justice) wrote for the majority, speaking at first as though this were a simple case that could be disposed of by reference to a well-established rule. "The validity of the search of a person incident to a lawful arrest has been regarded as settled from its first enunciation, and has remained virtually unchallenged until the present case." The question that has troubled the Court in the past, how far beyond the person such a search may go, is not at issue, he said, and the limitations of *Terry v. Ohio* do not apply where a "full custody arrest" has occurred. He pointed to many cases, state and federal, which establish in general terms the right to search the person of one who is arrested, a principle that has been stated over and over again.

But the statements establishing this right are cast in extremely general terms, without any consideration at all of the question before the Court in this case, namely whether that right is absolute or in some way conditional or restricted. In fact, they are usually accompanied by statements of the reasons supporting the search, namely, the need to discover weapons the person arrested might use against the officer and evidence of the crime which he might try to destroy, and these reasons suggest that the right is not absolute. Implicit in the justifications, that is, may be principles of limitation: if the reasons aren't present, the right to search disappears.

In Robinson's case—unlike many others, in which the general rule would properly apply—it was conceded by the government that there was no possible evidence of the crime which the defendant might have tried to destroy, so that basis for the search falls away.[31] With respect to the protection of the officer, the court of appeals found that the factual record supported the conclusion that a *Terry* "frisk" was adequate to uncover virtually any weapons the defendant might seek to employ. Both the seizure of the cigarette packet and its opening exceeded the limits of such a frisk and were accordingly found improper by the court of appeals.

Justice Rehnquist speaks to these objections in a critically important paragraph:

> [O]ur more fundamental disagreement with the Court of Appeals arises from its suggestion that there must be litigated in each case the issue of whether or not there was present one of the reasons supporting the authority for a search of the person incident to a lawful arrest. We do not think the long line of authorities of this Court dating back to *Weeks*, or what we can glean from the history of practice in this country and in England, requires such a case-by-case adjudication. A police officer's determination as to how and where to search the person of a suspect whom he has arrested is necessarily a quick *ad hoc* judgment which the fourth amendment does not require to be broken down in each instance into an analysis of each step in the search. The authority to search the person incident to a lawful custodial arrest, while based upon the need to disarm and to discover evidence, does not depend on what a court may later decide was the probability in a particular arrest situation that weapons or evidence would in fact be found upon the person of the suspect. A custodial arrest of a suspect based on probable cause is a reasonable intrusion under the

> fourth amendment; that intrusion being lawful, a search incident to the arrest requires no additional justification. It is the fact of the lawful arrest which establishes the authority to search, and we hold that in the case of a lawful custodial arrest a full search of the person is not only an exception to the warrant requirement of the fourth amendment, but is also a "reasonable" search under that amendment.[32]

Justice Rehnquist here says that the Court will simply not listen to the claim that a particular search incident to an arrest was not in fact supported by the reasons that underlie the practice generally. The right to search rests simply on the authority of the arrest itself and is absolute, not regulated by any other principle of justification.

When this opinion authorizes the search for weapons and the seizure of the packet without requiring any showing of a basis to suspect that the defendant might be armed, it dispenses with the principle—a version of which was employed even in *Terry*—that a search be based upon probabilities reasonably assessed with respect to the facts of the particular case. When it validates the opening and examination of the packet, it departs from tradition even more markedly. It was impossible that the packet could contain any evidence of the crime for which Robinson was arrested, and any weapons it might contain could be rendered harmless by simply retaining the packet, unexamined, until the defendant was released. To permit the opening and examination of the packet in these circumstances is inconsistent with the basic principle underlying all the cases in the fourth amendment field, including *Camara*, that each intrusion must be justified in some way by reasoned reference to the legitimate interests of the state. When this opinion departs from this principle and validates the search as a matter simply of "authority," it propounds a doctrine that changes the structure of fourth amendment law in a fundamental way.

Yet there is considerable force in Justice Rehnquist's position that after-the-fact adjudication of the risks and necessities presented by each search incident to an arrest is impracticable in the highest degree. We have no videotape of the event. On what basis can these factual judgments be made? And great latitude should be given to the officer's judgment of what his safety requires. The process of arrest can be extremely dangerous, and the claim of the officer that he is entitled to take whatever steps seem reasonable to him to protect himself is understandable and urgent. Indeed, any limiting rule is likely to have little effect in practice upon conduct genuinely thought necessary to self-protection. And the blanket authority of the *Robin-*

son rule seems to provide a simple rule that the police and lower courts can follow, and, to this extent, to introduce a measure of order into what is otherwise a confusing sea of adjudication.

Prior Law

Faced with these tensions, how should argument over their resolution proceed? With an ambiguity of attitude that has become traditional in such cases, Justice Rehnquist suggested history as a starting place and claimed to find widespread, indeed practically universal, support for his position in the statements of state and federal courts and the views of commentators. But, also typically, he ultimately conceded that the question had not been authoritatively settled and regarded the Court as free to decide the matter either way in light of fourth amendment principles and practical realities.

Justice Rehnquist relies on a vast number of general statements to the effect that there is a "right to search incident to arrest." But in that form no one would deny the correctness of the rule. The question is whether this power is limited by its purposes, and, as I suggested above, many of the statements upon which the Court relies do contain references to the justifications for the rule, seemingly implying limitations on its scope. For example, in the important case of *Weeks v. United States*, the Court said:

> What then is the present case? Before answering that inquiry specifically, it may be well by a process of exclusion to state what it is not. It is not an assertion of the right on the part of the Government, always recognized under English and American law, to search the person of the accused when legally arrested *to discover and seize the fruits or evidences of crime.* This right has been uniformly maintained in many cases. (Emphasis added.) [232 U.S. 383, 392 (1914).][33]

Justice Rehnquist approvingly quotes an extensive passage from the early New Hampshire case of Closson v. Morrison, 47 N.H. 482, 485 (1867), which concludes this way:

> We think the officer arresting a man for crime, not only may, but frequently should, make such searches and seizures; that in many cases they might be reasonable and proper, and courts would hold him harmless for so doing, when he acts in good faith, and from a regard to his own or the public safety, or the security of his prisoner.

But the next sentence in the New Hampshire opinion makes the qualification express: "It must, we think, in a case like this, be a question of fact for the jury, whether the taking of the property from the prisoner were *bona fide*, for any purpose indicated above as reasonable and proper, and, of course, justifiable, or whether it were *mala fide*, unreasonable, and for an improper and unjustifiable purpose." And there is at least some evidence that the practice was not wholly uniform. In Illinois, for example, it was said that "[a]n officer has no right to search a prisoner unless he has a warrant authorizing him to make the search."[34]

It thus seems plain not only that the Supreme Court had never explicitly addressed the question presented by *Robinson* but that there was no widespread and explicit understanding on the point. What we do have is, on the one hand, nearly unanimous general statements of the right to search incident to arrest and the absence of any Supreme Court holdings expressly limiting that right; on the other, statements of justification seeming to imply limitations, and a general understanding, running very deeply through the fourth amendment cases, that intrusions must be justified in some rational way by reference to the interests of the state they are meant to serve.

There is another difficulty, not mentioned in *Robinson*, in making sense of what evidence there is. Many of the statements in support of the right to search seem to assume that the suspect is to be placed in jail, which provides a whole new set of justifications for a search: to prevent the introduction of weapons and contraband to the jail, and to protect the police (by making an inventory of the defendant's possessions) against charges of theft, neglect, and the like. These factors are not present in the *Robinson* case—although they would be in a large number of arrest cases—because under District of Columbia law Robinson had a right to be released on payment of a bond, without being incarcerated.

The Merits

I begin with a reminder of three important factual peculiarities of this case. (1) It is agreed that there existed no evidence of crime for which Jenks could have been searching. (2) The arrest was a "full custody" arrest, after which the defendant was to be taken to the station and booked; but (3) incarceration could legally follow only if the defendant did not make bail. In these circumstances and in the light of the fourth amendment tradition described above, are the frisk, the seizure of the cigarette packet, and the opening of the packet to be regarded as permissible?

Terry v. Ohio

One possibility is to regard the case as governed by *Terry v. Ohio*. If an officer can point to particular facts leading him to believe that the person he is arresting may be armed, under that case he may carry on a "frisk" of the sort described in *Terry* to discover any weapons the arrestee might use. Where, as in *Robinson*, there is no claim that the search can be justified as a search for evidence, under this analysis no search beyond such a frisk would be permitted incident to arrest. This would limit the intrusion by the justifications that support it as determined with respect to the facts of the particular case.

But as the Court points out, there are substantial differences between the facts of *Terry* and the facts of custodial arrest cases that might make one hesitate to apply the *Terry* rule without change. As a matter of psychology, the person subjected to full arrest is more likely to use a weapon, if he has one, than is one who is simply being talked to by the police, as in *Terry*. He presumably has more to lose from what the police seek to do to him and is more likely to make a determined resistance. The physical circumstances of a custodial arrest are also different from those of a stop and frisk, especially when the officer is alone and must take the arrestee to the station in his car. Because the officer's attention must be given to other matters, it will be easier for the suspect to employ a weapon, if he has one, without interference by the officer, and it is less likely that an attempt to reach a weapon will give risk to "articulable suspicion" permitting a *Terry* frisk. For similar reasons, smaller and more carefully hidden weapons—razor blades, small knives, and the like—may present a greater danger in the arrest than the stop-and-frisk situation. Handcuffing may limit the danger, but a court naturally hesitates to turn such probabilities into rules of constitutional law. And, as the Court recognized in *Terry* itself, when we deal with the steps taken by an officer to protect himself because he genuinely feels endangered, we have to face the fact that rules may have very little effect on his conduct. Finally, *Terry* requires the existence of particular suspicion based upon articulable facts,[35] and this requires the Court to make post hoc judgments about the degree of risk, or the probability of weapons, of a sort it cannot confidently or competently make.

For all these reasons the officer may legitimately feel that *Terry* does not speak fairly to the hazards and uncertainties of his task. He has no clear guides. His judgment must be made fast and on the basis of incomplete information. The requirement, if followed, puts him at risk of his life whenever he cannot justify his sense of danger by pointing to reportable facts. Yet he knows and we know that his sense of danger may be both real and accurate. We have all seen people so hard or mean in appearance that they make us feel uncomfortable, perhaps to the point of crossing the street or moving our seat on the subway. We have confidence in such judgments, and act on them ourselves, yet how could we explain them in a court of law? How can we ask an officer to do so?[36]

The lower court in Robinson recognized the force of these arguments to the extent of holding that whenever a custodial arrest is made a *Terry* frisk may be carried out, whether or not there are particular facts giving rise to articulable suspicion that the suspect is armed. In holding the frisk a sufficiently protective measure the court relied heavily upon the fact that Sergeant Donaldson admitted on cross-examination that a "properly conducted *Terry*-type frisk could uncover virtually every weapon he had ever encountered in the course of in-custody searches."[37] And the government arms expert, who appeared on the stand with twenty-five deadly weapons secreted on his person, admitted that "virtually all of these weapons could be detected in the course of a properly conducted frisk." But as the court's footnote makes plain, there was some confusion as to what he meant by the term "frisk," and to rest a constitutional holding upon such a factual basis makes one uneasy. Suppose in the next case more knowledge or skill on the part of the expert or the prosecuting attorney leads to testimony that contradicts these admissions? And it is admitted by the court of appeals that some weapons could not be discovered by a frisk. In a world of violence, why should the officer not be able to take whatever steps are necessary to satisfy himself that he is not in danger from a person he has arrested?

All this is a way of saying that this is a genuinely hard case. In thinking about the way Justice Rehnquist dealt with it, it is important to bear in mind that it presents two distinct issues: (1) Is a full search of an arrestee's person for weapons (or evidence) automatically permissible, notwithstanding the inconsistency of such a rule with the principle of particular justification? Or is the officer limited to a frisk, and perhaps to a frisk only upon reasonable suspicion? (2) If such a search is automatically permissible—under what I have called the principle of general justification—is the Court right in validating the additional intrusion entailed in the opening and examination of the packet, and, if so, on what grounds?

Opening the Packet: A Rule of Lawlessness?

I take up the second question first and assume for the moment that the automatic search for weapons is permissible as a reasonable response to the dangers typically present in arrest situations. Can the opening of the packet be justified? By hypothesis there was no evidence to discover, and the officer could presumably have protected himself against the use of any weapon it might have contained by simply retaining it until the suspect was released. Since the Court made no inquiry into this factual question, it seems to permit this intrusion without requiring that it be justified in any fashion, even by reference to the needs of the situation stated in the most general way.

It is one thing to say that the emergency situation, and the legitimate claims of the officer to protect himself, justify a shift from the requirement of particular justification to a rule, permitting an arms search, that is based upon general or categorical probabilities and necessities. But it is quite another to permit the opening of the packet, for this seems to abandon the very idea that the intrusion need be justified at all. This would disregard not only the standards of both halves of the fourth amendment but perhaps the most fundamental notion of legality, that the government is bound to justify, by reference to its legitimate interests and concerns, any intrusions on the liberty and bodily integrity of its citizens.[38]

Imagine a situation in which an arrested person is being searched. He asks the officer, "Why are you searching me? Why are you taking away from me the things that I am carrying?" The officer may answer, "Because I am taking you to the station and I want to be sure that there is no weapon you may use against me." That response may or may not be sufficient under the standards of the fourth amendment but it is an exercise in reasoned justification. Contrast: "Why are you opening that packet [or wallet, or envelope] and examining what is in it?" The officer responds, in a paraphrase of Officer Jenks's words: "I'm just searching. I don't think about what I'm searching for. I'm just searching."

A rule permitting a search on this basis says, for the first time, that the citizen whose rights are invaded is not entitled to insist that the invasion be limited by a stated justification. Instead of being regarded as a person, whose interests clash with those of the police, the suspect is here told that in some important way he belongs to the police and not to himself. One is reminded of the *Dred Scott* case, which converted Scott from a litigant into a voiceless piece of property, and of the Fugitive Slave Act of 1850, which prohibited a court that was determining the status of a person alleged to be a slave from hearing the testimony of that person herself.

I suggested earlier that the task of the Court under the fourth amendment is to find a way to talk about an irreconcilable clash of interests that does some real justice to the claims on both sides, that is, to find a language in which the opposing sides could both talk, expressing their claims and defining their disagreement. The idea is not that either or both sides should be compelled to accept as right a decision reached, but that both should recognize that they have an opportunity to put their cases as rational people and have them heard. In this part of the *Robinson* opinion, Justice Rehnquist talks about the officer and citizen in radically different ways, not as opposing litigants with equal standing, but of one as an agent who simply has power to use as he wills, and of the other as one who is simply subject to it. If a citizen asked how this part of *Robinson* defined his place in a public world, he would find that he is given no right to insist that the officer explain or justify what he does; his role is simply to submit. And since the power to which he is subject need not be justified or explained, there is no rational way to determine its scope. If the officer may look in the packet, may he open an envelope and read a letter? May he open a briefcase and read the files? Why not search the entire car, the home, the office? If the grant of authority is not based upon reasons, it cannot be limited by them either.*

Despite the claim that *Robinson* affords the officer a clear-cut rule, a plain guide to conduct, the actual impact of the case is one not of clarification but incoherence, for clarity is a function of intelligibility. And the effects run deep. *Robinson* stands as a permanent rhetorical resource, a case that can be called upon in the widest range of cases by anyone who wishes to argue that the police should have one blanket power or another as a matter simply of "authority." If I read *Robinson* accurately in this way, it introduces into our constitutional law a principle of moral and intellectual brutality that is inconsistent with the deepest values of our legal tradition.

Can the case be read any other way? As I understand the opinion of Justice Rehnquist, it cannot.[39] Indeed, it seems to be a primary purpose of this opinion to establish the radically new way of talking about the relationship between the suspect and the officer described above. The potential consequences of this rule are enormous, for it

---

*Compare here the famous case of *Miranda v. Arizona*, 384 U.S. 435 (1966), which explicitly works by regulating the rhetorical relation between the police officer and the citizen. By reading the suspect the well-known warnings the officer acknowledges that he himself is subject to the law. (The more evidently he is doing this against his will, the more evident is the reality of his acknowledgment.) By this conduct he defines the suspect as a person with a right—the right to remain silent—and with the power to choose to exercise that right if he wishes; and he offers him the assistance of another person, a lawyer, if he feels he needs it. The relation established here is in fact like that established in a court; the police interrogation has in these respects become assimilated to a preliminary examination by a magistrate.

exposes to a substantial, arbitrary, and unreviewable exercise of police power every person who violates a substantial traffic rule, which is in practice virtually everyone. To the extent that not all of us are in fact arrested and searched, our wallets and purses opened and ransacked, when we make a left turn without signaling or when we go through a stop light, the evil of the rule shifts from the breadth and multiplicity of the incursions it authorizes to their discriminatory character. This aspect of *Robinson* does more than legitimate demands of the police for security and their claims of expertise; it removes this part of their conduct from regulation by law.

In this opinion Rehnquist reduces the arrested citizen to an object and the law to the bare grant of power. The opinion in fact treats the citizen as it invites the officer to do, with a kind of brutality; and it treats the intellectual and rhetorical processes of the law with contempt. This is the most significant "result" of the opinion, but it is related to the "result" in another sense as well, for an attitude of respect towards the suspect and the law would have required a different outcome, at least with respect to the issue presented by the opening of the packet, and would have given it a different meaning.

The Initial Search: Justice as Relations

What I have said so far deals only with the opening of the cigarette packet. While this is the most disturbing part of the Court's holding, it is not the most difficult to think about. What of the body search itself (and the subsequent seizure of the lumpy object that turned out to be a cigarette packet)? Is this kind of intrusion to be validated on an automatic basis, so that it is permissible on every full-custody arrest, whether or not there is reasonable apprehension of danger from the suspect and whether or not there is likely to be evidence of the crime that he may try to destroy or conceal? The question here is not, as it is with respect to the packet, whether an intrusion will be permitted without any justification at all, but whether the justification must be particular, rooted in the likelihoods suggested by the facts of the case, or can be general in character, rooted in the kinds of dangers, risks, and opportunities that arrests present as a general matter. Here, unlike the other portion of the opinion, there is much to be said on both sides.

One possibility, as I said above, is to apply the *Terry* "frisk-on-suspicion-of-danger" rule. But this will not satisfy the legitimate concerns of the officers, both because it requires that the grounds for suspicion be "articulable" which they may not be, and because it limits the intrusion to a frisk, which may be inadequately protective where there is a full arrest. Yet to permit a full search on an automatic basis (or even to permit a frisk without requiring articulable suspicion, as the court of appeals did) seems to be inconsistent with the fundamental principle of the fourth amendment tradition, which requires particular justifications for particular searches, especially of a criminal suspect.

But perhaps that tradition can be seen to speak more usefully than we have yet imagined. Remember that *Terry* itself was a rule based on the need for the officer to protect his safety and that *Camara* permitted housing-code searches, without a particularized showing of the probability of violation, on the grounds that the inspections were necessary to protect the health and safety of the public. These searches, that is, are conceived of not as criminal searches, aimed at the discovery of evidence to be used against the person searched, but as civil searches, intrusions rationally imposed for reasons of safety. They rest upon different motives, and have been held to call for a different form of justification, general rather than particular in kind. Despite its apparently "criminal" context, then, *Robinson* might be seen to belong to this category, rather than the true criminal search, because the proper reason for permitting the search is not to uncover evidence of crime, or to prevent its destruction, but to protect the officer against harm.

To generalize: The fourth amendment could be read to regulate civil searches, as *Camara* held, but to do so in a different way from criminal searches. Criminal searches would be regulated by the requirement of particular justification: to validate such a search one would have to show that the probabilities assessed on the facts of the individual case supported the search—this is what would be meant by "probable cause"—and the search itself would be limited in scope and intensity by the justifications asserted. Civil searches, on the other hand, would be regulated by the principle of general justification: to support such a search one need only show that the intrusion is rationally supported by a legitimate need to protect people from serious harm, and that the intrusion is tailored narrowly to that end.

Of course there is the obvious danger that police officers might abuse the opportunity to carry on civil searches, regulated by the "reasonableness" clause, in order to acquire evidence of crime. One way to limit that possibility would be to hold the officers to the ground on which the intrusion is justified in the first place and prohibit them from using any item found in a civil search in a criminal proceeding. This would permit inspection of premises where fires had occurred (to discover the causes), compulsory medical tests and treatments when there was a danger of epidemic, the inspection of luggage and the person as a condition upon the right to fly, the stopping of automobiles for license and registration checks, and so on, but without the risk that this power, granted for one set of purposes, would be abusively used to pursue another.[40]

Of course, even if this principle were adopted the power to search an arrested person would sometimes be exercised improperly, and what should happen then? What should be done, for example, about opening and reading letters; examination of the contents of wallets and billfolds; body-cavity searches; opening crumpled cigarette packages? The answer is that in addition to the rule of exclusion there should be the right to bring a civil proceeding: if the citizen can satisfy the trier of fact that an intrusion took place that was not honestly intended as a protective search, he should be entitled to recover damages for a violation of his constitutional rights.[41] The burden should be on him, of course, and great latitude should be afforded the officer's judgment, as no doubt it would be. But the reading of documents, the examination of pictures, and searches beyond the area into which the suspect could reach would plainly be bad.

This is how the proposed reading of the fourth amendment, and the cases decided under it, would work out in the *Robinson* case. The officer would have the right to make a full search for arms incident to a custodial arrest, but nothing found in the course of such a search would be admissible in the trial of the person arrested. The premise is that the officer's safety requires this much, and that no other rule is workable: post hoc review of his grounds of suspicion is not likely to be satisfactory, and deterrent rules are not going to work—and probably should not work—where there is genuine fear. As a matter of fourth amendment theory, such a search could be justified, not as Justice Rehnquist does, as a matter of "authority," but on the grounds that it is a civil search to be regulated by the principle of general justification.

But without more, this rule—which is in essence the rule of *Robinson* itself—exposes every person arrested to the arbitrary power of the officer to search him, for any reason or no reason, and whether or not he is in fear of danger or searching for weapons. The proposed rule that nothing found during a search for weapons could be used as evidence in a criminal proceeding against the person searched is meant to limit the power to search to the reasons that justify it.

This reading of the amendment proceeds on an assumption about its meaning that could be put this way: at its heart it is not simply about the preservation of privacy or property, defined as circles into which no one may step, but about the kind of relationship that exists between an individual and his government. It accordingly has different meanings where the state is rationally imposing a civil obligation on the citizen in order to protect people against harm and where it is proceeding against him as a possible criminal.

Each of us has her field of property and privacy, secure against official intrusion; the necessities of public safety require that some invasions upon that field occur on the basis of general probabilities, and speaking as a group of ideal citizens, we agree that such intrusions should be permitted for those reasons and we submit to that civil obligation. But to allow the police to use what they discover in such a search as evidence in a criminal case against the ideally acquiescing citizen involves an unfair shift of role. It is as if one had lent one's car to the police to drive an injured person to the hospital and were later charged with possession of the marijuana seen on the seat by the officer, or with failure to have a proper inspection sticker. As a matter of ordinary expectation, the claim of an emergency implies a simplicity and consistency of relation, a fidelity to premises, which is betrayed by a conversion to a criminal proceeding. Where the right of the citizen to exclude officials is overridden because of some pressing necessity—to put out fires, stop airplane bombings, halt the spread of disease, and the like—the officers should be able to do only what the necessity authorizes.

Another way to put this point is to say that when the search for or seizure of evidence takes place, the criminal process has begun. It has always been accepted that the citizen in that situation has special safeguards against the power the state proposes to use against her, set forth in several of the original amendments to the Constitution. It is not that these amendments protect criminals more than honest people, but that they are meant to regulate the criminal process, not the rational imposition of obligations of citizenship. The paradigmatic injury with which the amendment is concerned is not the search or seizure alone, but the use of that power as a part of the criminal process.

Fourth amendment privacy ought not to be regarded as a kind of virginity that is preserved intact or, by definition, utterly gone. It is a way of regulating a relationship between a citizen and his government. This is one sense, as the Court in *Boyd v. United States* [42] said, in which the fourth and fifth amendments "run almost into each other."

* * *

There are no doubt difficulties with this proposed reading of the amendment, and of the cases, but it does seem to me that it speaks to the officer in a way that does justice to the dangers and complexities of his job, respects his claims to expertise, and provides him with a rule he can follow, namely, that he may carry on a search reasonably and honestly calculated to produce weapons or to prevent the destruction of evidence. To the arrested citizen it speaks with a very different voice from *Robinson*. It does require that he be subjected to intrusions of a kind the general or categorical necessity for which should be plain enough. Yet it protects him, so far as the law can do so, against searches designed for other purposes and against deceit and abuse, both by removing the incentive for improper searches and by providing a remedy for abuse of power if it occurs. The officer is told that he must be prepared to explain what he has done in light of the purposes of the authority he has been granted, but that is no less than he should be expected to do. The citizen is told that he may recover damages if he can show that the authority has been exceeded, which he should be entitled to do. It is true that successful civil actions will not be numerous, since they will be inhibited by the cost of suing, by the occasional unattractiveness of a plaintiff to the jury, and by the probable low amount of damages in the usual case. But that is often true of civil suits now, against policemen and others, and perhaps ought to be true: if the intrusion is not the beginning of the criminal process, the first step in the exercise of the power of the state to try and convict, it seems appropriate that it should be regarded as an ordinary tort, subject to the usual restrictions on such actions.

To think of it in the terms suggested at the beginning of the chapter, as *Robinson* now stands it defines the arrested citizen as a voiceless object who belongs to the officer to search as he will, whether or not he has any legitimate reason for doing what he does. It gives the suspect nothing to say. If the case had been decided more fully in accordance with the basic principles of the fourth amendment, as I have tried to summarize and explicate them here, it would have gone far towards giving both the officer and the suspect the opportunity to say what they should be able to say. The function of the discourse of the fourth amendment, so defined, would be to create a world in which officer and suspect could both speak as people, both have their legitimate needs recognized and responded to.

Of course this does not mean that either person would be able to say all that he thinks or feels or wants. Far from it; as I said at the outset this is an artificial language that at most allows each party to say what the Court, or the community, thinks it right that he should be able to say. The law speaks neither the language of the officer nor that of the suspect, nor should it do so: part of its function is to insist that each recognize the validity of the claims of the other, and this requires the creation of another language, different from either.[43] The law in this way constructs a discourse and a community even for those who resist it. The law works by an act of coercion, requiring argument to proceed in certain terms; but it is an act of coercion that creates something new, a place and mode of discourse, a set of relations, that form a central part of our civilization. And it can itself be judged on political and ethical terms; at its best it can work as a way of respecting the human beings on both sides of a controversy by giving each something to say that is appropriate to their legitimate needs and to the character of the relation that exists between them. The insistence upon reasoned justification is a principle of rhetorical equality which implies an equality more generously defined. In all of this it works by a process of composition and transformation: creating texts that transform what may seem at first to be trivial events into narratives with meanings that touch our largest concerns as a people engaged in self-government under law.

9

The Constitutive Character of the Exclusionary Rule

As *Rochin*, *Olmstead*, *White*, and *Robinson* all make clear, the requirements of the fourth amendment have been enforced largely by what is known as the "exclusionary rule," under which evidence seized in violation of a person's fourth amendment rights cannot be admitted in evidence against him in a criminal trial. The propriety of this rule is a topic of the greatest controversy, and the Supreme Court has in recent years cut it back severely.

My question in this chapter is what this rule means, or can mean, as part of a discourse that creates a community; here, that is, I am suggesting that a rule of law can be looked at much as I have suggested opinions can be, namely, by asking how it defines the various actors it addresses—the citizen, the officer, the court—and the relations it establishes among them. What kind of conversation does it invite, with what relation to democracy? In suggesting that the extended search for arms authorized by *Robinson* should be accompanied by an extension of the exclusionary rule, I have proposed one way to give the rule a certain ethical and political meaning, at least in that particular situation. But what has its meaning traditionally been, or, more accurately, what range of views as to its meaning have we had, and what is at stake in the choice among them? To examine this question will require us not only to look at the rule itself but also to examine and compare the different ways it is talked about; in exploring it we return to the subject of *Rochin*, which was, as you remember, the use of improperly seized evidence.

Historical Origins

Most contemporary discussions assume or assert that the exclusionary rule is not part of the fourth amendment, nor required by its terms, but is rather a judicial "remedy" that was fashioned to protect those rights against unreasonable search and seizure that actually are granted by the fourth amendment.[1] The rule is normally said to work by "deterring" official violations, although this is an odd use of the word: the rule does not punish violations but merely deprives the government of some of the benefits that might ensue from them, namely, the use in a criminal case of evidence so obtained.

The deterrent view of the "exclusionary rule" receives support from—perhaps it has its origins in—*Wolf v. Colorado*[2] which, as we saw in chapter 4, addressed the question whether the fourth amendment should be regarded as "incorporated" in the fourteenth, and hence applicable to the states. Here, the reader may remember, Justice Frankfurter (writing for the Court) purported to apply to the states the "security of one's privacy against arbitrary intrusion," which is "at the core of the fourth amendment," but to withhold the "remedy" of exclusion on the ground that principles of federalism should allow the states freedom to make remedial choices of their own. When the Court overruled *Wolf* in *Mapp v. Ohio*,[3] the plurality opinion explicitly said that the deterrent theory was the basis of the exclusionary remedy. This belief continues,[4] accompanied by occasional talk about the "imperative of judicial integrity."[5]

But the origins of what we now call the exclusionary rule were in fact very different from what is suggested above. Far from being a secondary rule designed to enforce other standards, the right to exclusion was, at least in some cases, an essential part of the fourth amendment's protection. It was indeed more fully "substantive" than those procedural protections—probable cause, warrant, specificity— that have since been regarded as the heart of the fourth amendment.

Property

The historical roots of exclusion lie in a conception of property which holds that even where a search is procedurally reasonable, the government simply has no right to seize the property of the citizen for use against him in a criminal proceeding. This is so whether the government uses the warrant mechanism or proceeds without warrant to forcible seizure, and even where milder forms of coercion are employed. In *Boyd v. United States*,[6] where the Court first excluded evidence on fourth amendment grounds, the lower court ordered the production of an invoice for 29 cases of plate glass which were thought to have been imported without payment of duty. The sanction for refusing to comply with the production order was that the propositions the government sought to establish by the admission of the invoice would be taken as established. This was enough, in the Court's view, to constitute a search and seizure, and an impermissible one, for the invoice was unquestionably the property of the litigant and thus beyond the reach of the government.

Although this view is first articulated in *Boyd*, it finds consistent and powerful expression running back through *Entick v. Carrington*,[7] to Hale's *Pleas of the Crown*, to Coke, and even earlier. At the time of Hale, for example, evidently the only form of search warrant known to the law was the warrant for stolen goods.[8] Coke doubted even this, but Hale supported it on the ground of social necessity; *Entick* supported it on the true owner's higher right to possession. The same kind of reasoning was used in America after *Boyd* to limit the power of search. *Gouled v. United States* said the government could seize property only where "a primary right to such search and seizure may be found in the interest which the public or the complainant may have in the property to be seized, or in the right to the possession of it, or when a valid exercise of the police power renders possession of the property by the accused unlawful and provides that it may be taken."[9] Stolen goods are obviously subject to seizure in this view, as both contraband and "instrumentalities of crime" are as well: the defendant can have no right to possess the former, and by his use of the latter has lost his right to possess them and they become a kind of deodand.[10] This rule was explicitly reaffirmed ten years later,[11] and remained the law until *Warden v. Hayden*.[12]

That case overruled *Gouled* on the ground that it depended on outmoded property distinctions that were rationally related neither to the right to privacy the Court found in the fourth amendment nor to the countervailing governmental interest in investigating crime. But in so doing, the opinion slid over the fact that the property-immunity rule of *Boyd* and *Gouled* had significant consequences for both the probable cause and the specificity requirements of the fourth amendment.

Where an item meets the *Boyd-Gouled* requirements, for example, the police are entitled to its possession; the only question that remains is whether they have sufficient reason to believe that it is in the place they wish to search. The warrant, if obtained, can name the item, or class of item, and if other items are found in the course of the search, the only question the officer must ask is whether they also meet the *Boyd-Gouled* requirement; if so they may be seized under the "plain view" rule. But when this requirement is abandoned, an additional question must now be asked: whether the government's interest in possessing the item is sufficiently great to justify its seizure.

This is a complex and highly conjectural question to which the Court in *Warden* gives no guidance. Is all "admissible" evidence seizable, as Federal Rule 41 declares? This requires the court asked to issue a warrant, or the officer contemplating the seizure of items in plain view, to make a legal judgment of a new and difficult kind. In many cases it will be of an impossible kind, for the ultimate admissibility of a particular item will depend upon the way the issues have developed at trial, the duplicative nature of the evidence, and so forth.[13]

The immunity established in *Boyd* and *Gouled* derives from a conception of property that is larger and deeper than our own. In England, property law was directly continuous with constitutional law: the property of a landholder gave him a kind of jurisdiction over it, with which others could not interfere except through the Parliamentary process. Often, indeed, land-owning entailed rights that seem to us even more obviously jurisdictional or political in kind: the right to hold a certain court or to present a clerical living, for example, or the right to a seat in the House of Lords. These rights were themselves inheritable, and inheritable in connection with a landed estate. Liberty was conceived of in a similar way, as a kind of property in the arrangements and traditions of the law itself. In his *Reflections on the French Revolution*, for example, Burke said: "You will observe, that, from Magna Charta to the Declaration of Right, it has been the uniform policy of our constitution to claim and assert our liberties as an entailed inheritance derived to us from our forefathers, and to be transmitted to our posterity. . . ."[14]

In America, the Constitution became written and explicit, and property came to have different overtones, but it remained jurisdictional in character: property was not what one held against a sovereign who had notionally granted it (and whom one supported in return), but was what one had not yielded to the governments one had created by the process of social contract.[15] In both England and America property and liberty were thus readily overlapping terms; both were ways of conceiving of rights not as grants of power or capacity, to be justified by their contribution to the general welfare, but as true entitlements. You can "exclude the universe" from your property, in Blackstone's phrase, not because it is wise or good that you should be able to do so, but because your property is yours, to dispose of as you wish.[16] Property was an extension of the person, indeed in some ways a definition of the person, for the relations defined by property holdings were political and social as well as economic. This is perhaps why the use of one's property in a criminal proceeding was felt to violate the fifth amendment prohibition of compulsory self-incrimination, as well as the fourth amendment prohibition of unreasonable seizures. "The fourth and fifth amendments run almost into each other," said the Court in *Boyd*.[17]

The connection between this view of property and the exclusionary rule is plain enough. Where a seizure is unreasonable for the substantive reason that a person's property has been taken, the defendant is constitutionally entitled not only to its "exclusion" but to its return. Its continued possession is a continuing wrong, and he is entitled to get it back. In such a case the exclusionary rule is thus required by the fourth amendment itself. Accordingly, *Boyd* —not, as usually said, *Weeks v. United States*[18]—was in fact the first exclusion case.[19]

Procedural Wrongs

Weeks was, however, the first case to apply the exclusionary rule to procedural defects—in this case the seizure of goods without a warrant—and it is plain that the *Weeks* Court saw the rule not as a deterrent meant to protect others against improper invasions in the future, but as a rule designed to make the original prohibition meaningful to the person whose rights were violated:

> If letters and private documents can thus be seized and held and used in evidence against a citizen accused of an offense, the protection of the Fourth Amendment declaring *his* right to be secure against such searches and seizures is of no value, and, *as far as those thus placed are concerned*, might as well be stricken from the Constitution . . . . To sanction such proceedings would be to affirm by judicial decision a manifest neglect if not an open defiance of the prohibitions of the Constitution, intended for the protection of the people against such unauthorized action.[20]

When the rule was extended in *Silverthorne Lumber Co. v. United States*[21] to include the derivative use of improperly seized property—in this case improperly seized papers were copied—this was a natural outgrowth of the primary prohibition.

The most natural and complete remedy is to place the parties so far as possible in the situation that would have existed had the wrong never occurred, and the exclusionary rule does much to achieve this.[22] At private law there is often a preference for a damage remedy over specific relief of this kind, but the reasons supporting that preference do not apply with the same force where one party is the government, the other an individual who holds constitutional rights of liberty and property against it. Damages are a kind of forced exchange, and however appropriate that may be in a commercial context where all things are thought to be exchangeable, such compulsion would be incompatible with the idea of a right against the government, and with the reasons why such rights exist. This is especially so when the right is in large part a political, and in this sense truly a constitutional, right. The right to be free from arbitrary and oppressive governmental interference with one's freedom of person and of place is an essential precondition to the exercise of all the other rights, including those of expression and association, upon which our democratic system of self-government rests. And even at private law specific relief is often available where the wrong-doing party has a continuing advantage of a kind for which the victim cannot readily be compensated, as is the case with improperly seized evidence.

What of the interference with one's rights to property that is routinely imposed by the obligation to produce papers and other objects for discovery purposes in civil litigation? The *Boyd* Court discussed that question, noting that the Congress that passed the original judiciary act provided for discovery orders in cases and circumstances permitted by chancery practice, and that chancery practice has always prohibited the production of papers that would incriminate the party producing them. One's property rights are absolute in the *Boyd-Gouled* sense, that is, when they are performing the jurisdictional and political function described above, and especially where the state is proceeding against the individual in a criminal action. The situation is obviously different where the government imposes obligations even-handedly upon all its citizens for their mutual benefit. Here, as I suggested in chapter 8 may more generally be the case, it is appropriate for the government to authorize an interference with property or liberty that would otherwise be prohibited; but only so long as the interference remains truly civil, and not criminal, in character.[23]

The power of the government to take "private property" for "public use" upon payment of "just compensation," established by the fifth amendment, is not incompatible with *Boyd*: the requisite "public purposes" obviously cannot include the purpose of convicting the possessor or owner of the property; but rather must involve a relationship that is essentially civil, in every sense of the term, between government and citizen. The main idea of eminent domain, after all, is to prevent the individual from holding up the government to obtain more than the fair market value of the property and thus from appropriating to himself the portion of the value of his property that is in fact created by the public use to which the government intends to put it. To apply this reasoning to non-economic rights the individual has against the government, such as rights of liberty, choice, and freedom from harassment, would be inconsistent with the whole idea of such rights, whether they are found in the first, the fourth, or the fifth amendments.

The exclusion of contraband, in which the defendant has no rightful possessory interest, rested on a different but related basis. The main idea here was that of a remedy for trespassory wrong, not a means of regulating police in future cases.[24] One major case is *Agnello v. United States*,[25] where contraband seized during an unreasonable search of the defendant's home was excluded. Before this case, the practice had been for the defendant to petition for the return of his property, but where the item is contraband, and its possession criminal, one can understand why defendants were reluctant to do this. *Agnello* held that fourth amendment questions could be raised at trial in a motion to exclude, as well as upon pretrial petition for return, and proceeded to exclude the contraband. The primary reason for this decision was not to deter police in other cases, but to make the original procedural protections—probable cause and the warrant requirement—meaningful in the present case.

History thus reveals not one exclusionary rule but several, each resting on a different basis and having a somewhat different scope. The original rule was simply an automatic consequence of the *Boyd* and *Gouled* view that one's property was immune from seizure; on this understanding exclusion is built into the fourth amendment itself. The derivative evidence and contraband cases are natural extensions of the rule, designed to offer meaningful remedies for violations and to deprive the wrongdoing government of a continuing benefit from its wrong. The idea that due process may require exclusion in certain cases of criminal or highly objectionable police conduct, as seen in *Rochin* and discussed briefly below, has still a different basis: that the state must obey the law in enforcing the law. "Deterrence," now claimed to be the primary ground for exclusion, had no substantial place in any of these conceptions of the practice.

"Deterrence"

It was in *Wolf* and *Mapp* that the "right" and the "remedy" were first separated, then rejoined, and it is true that one part of the theory of the *Mapp* majority was deterrence. But the vote of Justice Black, essential to the result in *Mapp*, rested on a view derived from *Boyd* that the exclusionary rule was constitutionally required because the use of improperly seized evidence involved testimonial compulsion. And in

Wolf the Court was led into the error of splitting the "right" from the "remedy" by accepting the formulation of the issue before it as the "incorporation" of the fourth amendment into the fourteenth. The question thus framed, it was natural for the federalist Frankfurter to "incorporate" the substantive "core" but not the "remedial"—and presumably less important—fringe.

Actually, of course, the fourteenth amendment itself, without reference to the fourth, speaks directly to every case in which a state officer interferes with the liberty or property of an individual, and does so whether the alleged interference takes the form of a search or seizure made by a police officer or a fine or imprisonment imposed by a judge after criminal trial. It thus explicitly requires the Court to make a body of constitutional law governing state searches and seizures, a law that might in principle have been no less protective of the individual than the fourth amendment (especially in its incorporated form) has proved to be. When Frankfurter in *Wolf* holds that the "security . . . against arbitrary intrusion,"[26] which is at the "core" of the fourth amendment, applies to the states, he thus really holds very little indeed; when he holds that the "remedy" does *not* apply to the states, he evades the major thrust of the "due process of law" standard by which he is plainly bound, for this standard is more obviously concerned with remedy and procedure than with "substantive" rules. It would indeed have been more consistent with his stated federalist values to reverse the holding in *Wolf*: to provide that the states are free to set widely varying standards of police conduct, but to hold that due process—if it is to mean anything at all—means that the state must comply with its own law when it seeks to prosecute the citizen. This is not the kind of discretionary skirt-cleaning that is usually meant by talk about "judicial integrity"; it is an insistence upon a fundamental element of due process of law itself.[27] Frankfurter himself was compelled to recognize in *Rochin* that the only appropriate response to the blatant brutality and illegality of the case was to hold that due process was violated when the evidence obtained by an emetic was admitted in a criminal trial. The role of exclusion in *Rochin* was not to deter police from behaving badly in other cases but to insist upon the right of the individual to be treated by officers and the courts in a way that accords with the rule of law, which means in a fundamentally decent way.[28]

* * *

The "deterrence" feature of the exclusionary rule discourse has at least three unfortunate consequences. First, it is a difficult rule for the courts to apply or administer, for it requires judgments as to the probable effects of particular decisions, or of the rule in general, that are beyond its competence to make. How is a court to know whether, or how far, a particular act of exclusion, or the existence of the possibility of exclusion, will in fact deter officers from violating individual rights? Second, when deterrence—rather than the protection of the defendant's right to due process at the hand of the state that seeks to convict him—becomes the basis for exclusion, that shift generates an enormous pressure for reduction of the scope of the rule: for in each case the real cost of the possible release of a guilty defendant is weighed against the merely contingent advantage of the marginal deterrent impact of exclusion in a diffuse and unknown future, and it is easy to see how that will come out. The decisions cutting back on the rule in a wide variety of situations thus flow directly from the Court's ideology of deterrence; that fact may indeed go far to explain the Court's resistance to taking any other view of the matter. Here, for example, is Justice Powell in *United States v. Calandra*:

> Any incremental deterrent effect which might be achieved by extending the rule to grand jury proceedings is uncertain at best. Whatever deterrence of police misconduct may result from the exclusion of illegally seized evidence from criminal trials, it is unrealistic to assume that application of the rule to grand jury proceedings would significantly further that goal. Such an extension would deter only police investigation consciously directed toward the discovery of evidence solely for use in a grand jury investigation. The incentive to disregard the requirement of the Fourth Amendment solely to obtain an indictment from a grand jury is substantially negated by the inadmissibility of the illegally seized evidence in a subsequent criminal prosecution of the search victim. For the most part, a prosecutor would be unlikely to request an indictment where a conviction could not be obtained. We therefore decline to embrace a view that would achieve a speculative and undoubtedly minimal advance in the deterrence of police misconduct at the expense of substantially impeding the role of the grand jury.[29]

Another view would of course be possible: that the deterrent rationale requires exclusion of improperly seized evidence in all cases, under all circumstances, for the police must be deprived of every possible benefit of their wrong if the deterrence is to work. How is a responsible choice to be made between these views? The fact that the choice between them cannot really be reasoned, but must remain attitudinal, itself reflects the institutional defectiveness of the deterrence ideology itself, the fact that it rests on purportedly empirical judgments that themselves have no adequate basis.

Third, and perhaps most important, in so conceiving of the rule, the Court is operating not on the idea that its task is to be faithful to judgments that the Constitution has authoritatively expressed in more or less intelligible language, which the Court must interpret against the twin backgrounds of historical context and present life, but on the notion that the Constitution is a general warrant for the judicial determination of the "reasonableness" of government action in the light of the costs and benefits of alternative classifications and programs, the notion, that is, that the Constitution invites its judges not to be judges in the usual sense at all—not readers of an authoritative past and culture—but economists, makers of social policy. This at a blow destroys the ethical basis upon which judicial authority rests, that is, fidelity to the authoritative judgments of others; its intellectual basis, that is, that this authority is to be defined and exercised by informed inquiry into the legal traditions that underlie the Constitution and our own past;[30] and its political basis, for the Court can no longer be regarded as the servant of our Constitution, but as an agency whose task is to determine risks and calculate probabilities. The rhetoric of "deterrence" actually ensures that the class of cases governed by unarticulated assumptions and attitudes will be very large indeed, for while the apparent structure of that rhetoric is scientific—it is an inquiry into those facts that define the costs and benefits that determine the result—the inquiry can never be performed in an adequate way. The reality thus is that the decision must rest not upon those grounds, but upon prior dispositions or intuitions that are never explained or justified.[31]

Another way to put this point is to say that reasoning by cost-benefit analysis, of which the deterrence theory of the exclusionary rule is one example, involves a pretense, that the relevant facts can all be known, and, when known, that they dictate the result. This is an attempt to locate authority not in the text or in the past, not in processes by which text and past are read, but in the "facts"; it is similar in structure to the attempt to locate authority in "original intention," for it too leads to a kind of fantasy of perfect knowledge that at once releases the judge from the responsibility for the decision he makes, and obscures, even from him, the true grounds of that judgment. Like the language of "original intent," then, the language of "deterrence" and social planning denies the responsibility of the individual judge for the decision he or she is making in the case (by

giving it a false scientific form); this, in turn, denies all of us the benefits of a judicial process in which judges acknowledge their ultimately
personal responsibility for their decision, which they are obliged to
justify in their opinions and for which it is their duty to educate their
minds by the experience of argument and thought.

The historical point made here may be thought by some to be
irrelevant, especially since *Boyd* in all its aspects has been overruled,[32]
and since it is now commonly said that the fourth amendment is concerned not with "property" but with "privacy." But if this history is
to be disregarded, the decision ought at least to be knowingly made.
As for the other point—that the language of deterrence involves the
Court in a set of judgments that it is incompetent to make and avoids
those more particular judgments that it is its duty to make—the difficulty, of course, extends far beyond the exclusionary rule, for this is
just one instance of a modern judicial tendency that has become so
deeply settled in the contemporary mind as to determine the very
structure, for some people, of what is meant by the judicial function,
the legal process, and rationality itself.

* * *

A final point. It may not have escaped the reader that the cases
we have talked about shift their meanings as they are seen in varying
relation with each other. Think of *Rochin*, for example: at first it may
have seemed a valiant if unsuccessful struggle with a kind of vacuum
left by the Constitution, but when put together with the other cases
that give shape and meaning to the exclusionary rule, we can see that
its major premise, that exclusion is remedial and not substantive, is
open to serious challenge. And the remedy of exclusion itself means
something different when it is used in different ways, for different
purposes: for example, when it is used to validate a property right
and where it is used (as I suggest in chapter 8 it should be) to enforce
the relations implied in a claim to carry out a "civil" search.

The opinions in *Olmstead* shift their meaning too: Brandeis's
dissent, as I suggested above, is perhaps too little respectful of the
language of property used in the fourth amendment, too eager to
employ a new language of privacy. This language has certainly not
provided a magic key to judgment, and, as *Katz* makes plain, it can
be used in just as conclusory a way as Taft used the language of property. Similarly, the talk about "principles" that is so important to both
Brandeis and Harlan is no automatic guarantee of excellence, but can
collapse into conclusory cliché.

From one point of view these shifts of significance may be paradoxical or distressing; from another, however, they are just what is to be expected, and heartening rather than the reverse. For what they show is that the most important significance of an opinion is not propositional or doctrinal—not the simple choice of "property" or "privacy" as one's language, for example—but lies in the dimension we have been examining in this book: in the character the opinion gives the court, in the kind of relations it establishes with those it talks to (and about), and in the kind of conversation it establishes for the future. Judicial excellence lies less in the choice of doctrine than in what the doctrine chosen is made to mean.

Of course judicial opinions acquire different meanings as they are placed in new arrangements and patterns, in new contexts, for that is true of every text, every action. Meaning and identity lie not in the object itself but in its relations with others. The art of the lawyer, like that of the judge, is to put together the prior texts that are the material of law in new compositions, which, while respecting the nature of each item, so order them as to create a new arrangement with a meaning of its own. The art of law is the art of integration.

10

THE JUDICIAL OPINION AS
A FORM OF LIFE

In the last several chapters we have examined a set of judicial opinions, reading them as intellectual and ethical and political texts—as exemplifications of "constitutive rhetoric"—with the idea of learning something about the possibilities of this form of language and life. Obviously our set of opinions is a small one, and the range of subject-matter is small too: all the cases are constitutional ones, and all but one deals with the same constitutional amendment. Many important judicial voices from our own era have been left out or barely touched on, including Holmes, Cardozo, Black, and Jackson, to mention only the great, and we have not addressed at all the wonderful difficulties of thinking about the ways in which judges in different eras and cultures are situated differently. But perhaps even from such an experience something can be learned.

As I said at the outset, this book is written out of the sense that our languages, and acts of languaging, are not transparencies through which thoughts or objects are to be seen, but ways of being and acting and living in the world. Forms of language are forms of life. This means that our performances with language are ethical and political performances, whether we know it or not, and that they can be analyzed as such. Thus to speak and act "like a lawyer," as one learns to do in law school, is to commit oneself to a certain community and discourse, to enact a view of language and the world that entails an ethics and politics of its own, even to give oneself a certain character, and these things can be studied and judged.

Of course different lawyers and judges present different versions of their common language, for their life is one of art, not bureaucracy: they act on their resources in different ways, reconstitute them differently, and in the process create somewhat different characters for themselves and different communities with others. It is not

215

just the language that can be studied, then, but the reconstitution of it achieved in an act of art; and this reconstitution always and necessarily has an ethical and political meaning. For in his writing the judge always establishes a relation directly with his reader, as a partner in the conversation that is the life of the law, and a relation as well with those other people that he talks about. In both cases we can ask what political and ethical character these relations have.

For me the law in all these dimensions has great possibilities, seldom enough realized in the event though they may be, for it is a way of living and thinking that is, or can become, self-conscious of its own implications. Its ethical and intellectual center is the set of argumentative and discursive practices in which the lawyer learns to engage as his way of speaking to another lawyer, to his client, and to the judge. All of these practices are premised upon the view that each person is entitled to make his own case, his own argument, out of the materials of our common past. What happens today is not thought to be identical to what happened yesterday, as a bureaucracy would conceive it: you are entitled to show what is new or different about your case. Of course the language of the past, and the decisions of the past too, have authority, but this authority is always qualified by the practices of legal argument. The authority of the past does not simply exist, that is, but must be re-created, just as it can be eroded, in our present talk. The law in this sense is structurally tentative, a mode of transformation as well as preservation. It is a method of exposition that is, in principle at least, also a method to self-criticism; at its best it can recognize what and who it leaves out.

But in the series of opinions we have read from *Prigg* to *Robinson*, and in the development of the exclusionary rule as well, we have seen instance after instance in which a Justice has found ways to avoid the difficulties of judging by turning to false grounds of authority. Thus Story and Taney seek to base their judgments on the "original intention" of the framers, Taft on the "plain meaning" of language, White on the clear commands of "precedent," the *Mapp* and *Calandra* Courts, both in extending and in cutting back the exclusionary rule, on what might be called "the facts." All of these movements—and this is no exhaustive list—seem, as I say, to be ways of avoiding the true responsibilities of judging, including that of establishing a suitable character for oneself and an appropriate relation both with the prior texts that define one's role and with other people: the responsibility of creating a character and a set of relations that will make possible a conversation "in which democracy begins."

These are difficulties that in their rather different ways Frankfurter, Brandeis, and Harlan all address. The heart of their achievement lies in the recognition that their authority must be created rhetorically, in the opinion itself; that it depends upon the informed understanding of the reader and upon his acquiescence, not in the "result" or even the "reasoning" by which the result is reached, but in the set of relations and activities created in the opinion itself. This is part of an even larger point, that what we mean by justice is a matter not so much of consequences as of characters and relations: who we are to each other in our talk and in our lives.

In doing this work the judge is performing acts of language and of life that cannot be reduced to rule or system, but this is true for others too. Compare the historian: no one would say that there is one ideal history of the Battle of Gettysburg, for instance, to which all accounts should aspire and by which they will all be judged. The question is rather how the historian comes to terms with the limits of her knowledge, with the intractability and uncertainty of the facts, with the desire to make meaning where there is none, with the knowledge that there is meaning of some kind there after all, and so on. History inherently involves the expression and enactment of what is individual in the historian herself. Her work, like that of the judge, necessarily establishes a triadic relation between material, the mind of the historian, and the reader, and this is where its excellence lies. Or think of the teacher or parent: what we admire here is not expressible in terms of rule or outcome—the 7:30 bedtime or the high SAT scores—but in the kind of engagement one person offers another, the sort of relation and community one person establishes with others. And so too with judging: its excellence is definable in terms of character and relations, in the kind of conversation it establishes, not in the "result" or "rule" or "reason" abstracted from the text in which they are given meaning.

In all of this the law can be seen as an enterprise of self-creation. There is no ground in nature, in the facts, or in uninterpreted texts, upon which the law and its authority can rest. Both law and authority are made, and largely made in the process of writing the opinions by which the decisions reached by courts are given their meaning. In this sense the law can teach all of us how to live in a world in which each culture is its own ground, made out of itself, as a language or a human life is made out of its own beginnings.

The critical study of the judicial opinion in this way leads to the acknowledgment of the contingency of language and the self, and of community too—for we are made by the very language that we use—and beyond that to a sense of the art by which life on such terms is possible. This is the art by which one text is made in response to another. Not on the assumption that it can replicate it—as if the fourth amendment or the precedents explicating it spoke in plain terms that we could simply follow, or as if a language could be made in which both officers and suspects would feel that all their views were expressed—but in the acknowledgment that each text is a new act, resting in part upon the ground of its own creation, yet faithful to the old one too. In both respects the law works as a form of translation. Here, in the tension between the requirement that we read the texts of others, to which fidelity is due, and the knowledge that our reading is partly our own, lies the ethical and intellectual heart of the law.

* * *

As a way of giving content to these reflections it might be useful to think briefly not of a completed opinion but of a case for which an opinion has, in our imagination at least, yet to be written, so that we can see something of what is involved in making of such a text and in reaching the judgment it expresses. For these purposes, let us now turn to *United Steelworkers of America v. Weber*,[1] a case that involves, as *Prigg* and *Dred Scott* of course also did, the question how the law should deal with the fact of race in our society.

This case turned on the interpretation of a federal statute making it an unfair labor practice for any employee or union "to discriminate against any individual because of his race. . . ."[2] The question was whether the terms of this statute were violated by an affirmative action program that was adopted as part of a collective bargaining agreement entered into by the Steelworkers and the Kaiser company. This program was meant to redress the great racial imbalance that had existed in Kaiser's craft work force, which was at that time almost entirely white, by reserving 50 percent of the openings in the plant's craft training programs for Black employees, until the percentage of Black craftworkers was the same as the percentage of Blacks in the particular plant.

For present purposes I am interested less in evaluating the opinions the Court actually produced than in identifying the kinds of questions that our shared reading of the opinions in this book suggests that we can bring to them. One place to begin is with the statutory language, which in this case seems to present a real paradox: its language prohibits all racial "discrimination," which could easily be read to include such "discrimination" as is necessary to an affirmative action program, yet its larger purposes are to advance the cause of racial equality as a general matter, which the affirmative action plan surely seems to do. We can see the case setting up, that is, as an argument between those who see the meaning of the statute as "plain" in its terms (and as prohibiting the program) and those who want to look through the words to something else, namely, to the "intention" of the legislature or "purpose" of the statute, which would presumably support the program. It is indeed along these lines that the Court divides.

But is the formulation of the issue as "plain language" versus "intention" one that should be accepted in the first place? We have seen the Supreme Court founder on one course in *Olmstead*, on the other in the *Prigg* and *Dred Scott* cases. One might start by asking here, as always when the plainness of meaning is asserted, whether this language is in fact so very plain. That I think depends on how one reads the meaning of the central verb "discriminate": it might indeed be read as meaning "draw any lines based on race," as both majority and minority opinions affirm, but it might also be read as "draw any lines based on race with the intention (or effect) of perpetuating our existing racial inequalities." Like other verbs of action, that is, "discriminate" could be read as implying a requirement of intention or motive.

Which reading is to be preferred and why? This cannot be a matter of determining legislative "intent," as if one could simply reach out and see what that intent was. The one intent that we securely know was the intent to publish this language as effective. Anything else is not only for a host of familiar reasons conjectural, it is, as chapter 5 suggested, actually anti-intentional, for it undermines the one intentional act that is indeed the legislature's own. Yet to think that the meaning is "plain" is often to simplify beyond reason and to do so on the basis either of misunderstandings of the nature of language itself and one's role as a reader,[3] or, more likely, of unarticulated commitments of one's own on the merits. (Will it surprise you to be told that Rehnquist found this language "plain," or that Brennan found its meaning in its "purposes?")

No one can escape the force of unarticulated commitments, including you and me, and this means that the real question is how we deal with our double uncertainties, about the text we are reading and about ourselves as readers. In a case like *Weber* there may be no right answer, not only in the sense that we cannot all agree but in the even more problematic sense that no result you can imagine is wholly satisfactory even to you as a judge. But there may still be more or less satisfactory responses to this very circumstance, the first essential ingredient of which would be the recognition of the force of what can be said on the other side, or what might be called judicial "openness." The best we may be able to do, that is, is to specify the elements of the paradox coupled with frank responsibility for the choice taken.

* * *

So far I have spoken of the relation between Court and statute and the kind of conversation internal to the law that an opinion begins. But what of the people the opinion speaks about, in this case the Black and white workers in the Kaiser plants? It is deep in our culture—part of what makes us "economists" in fact—to think of these people as individuals in competition with each other for a limited "good," in this case a job (in the famous *Bakke*[4] case admission to medical school), and to assume that racial justice requires us all to pretend that we are color blind. On this view, no discrimination should be made on racial lines in distributing the good, which should instead go to the "best qualified."

But this construction of a social universe erases the significance of the past in creating our present. Even if we accept the image of the actors as atoms, they do not have a race-neutral common starting-point, not at all: one person bears the burden of slavery and Jim Crow and endures the psychic and economic wounds that have injured him and his family—and still do; the other enjoys a comparative advantage created by the artificial depression of the capacities of his minority competitors.

Think of this from the point of view of the white child who complains that by reason of affirmative action programs many of the Blacks in his high school can get into good colleges with only medium grades, while he has to have high grades to do so. He might go on in this vein to say that he never owned or transported slaves, and neither did his ancestors—who, perhaps, like Bakke's, came to America after slavery was abolished—and that he has never profited personally from the wrongs done to Blacks, so why should he suffer this deprivation? In his own life he has never discriminated against others, he says, but now he has been discriminated against, on the ground of race. One can of course see the logic by which this seems unfair: but if Blacks had for the past 200 years had equal opportunities with whites, entry to good colleges might be even more competitive than it now is. There is a sense, then, in which all whites as competitors with Blacks have benefited from racist discrimination. One might thus understandably see the setting aside of places for Blacks in medical school or in plant training programs at least partly as a way of attempting to reduce harms inflicted upon them or their families by the white race, from which they are still suffering and from which all whites are still in some sense continuing to benefit.

But even this is to accept the idea that all is reducible to atomistic or group competition, and the facts of the *Weber* case itself show that this is not so. Here there was a political process in which the Union, representing many more whites than Blacks, agreed to the plan in question; here is acceptance of communal responsibility, an ethical and political act that transforms the meaning of the agreement reached. The idea is no longer that the white applicant for the training program must pay today for what someone of his race did a hundred years ago or that he must give up something to this Black competitor because of prior crimes. There is, after all, another possibility. Think for a moment of the relationship we can imagine existing between an ideal white Union soldier and the slave he fought to free: the soldier was not paying a debt for his past transgressions, but risking, perhaps losing, his life and wealth in order to live in a national community in which no people would be slaves, and in which the effects of slavery would be destroyed. The relation he would in this way have established with the imagined slave would have been not that of a competitor, but of a friend.

What the Kaiser-Steelworkers agreement says to the modern white applicant for job training is that he too is a member of a community that is seeking to rid itself of the residual and terrible evils of slavery, and that he should look upon what it costs him as a burden of that improvement, a burden like the soldier's burden which is in some sense a privilege to bear, even when imposed upon a draftee, then or now. This case rests upon his imagined identity not with the white slave owner, but with the white liberator, and asks that he share and act upon those values. As applied to the *Weber* statute, this is a way of reading it as permitting unions and employers to insist upon a community of value between ourselves and those who won that war and established the Constitution of the country on a new basis. As applied to the *Bakke* case, where there is no agreement, and which turns not on a statute but the equal protection clause, this is a way of reading the Constitution to permit a state to make such an insistence. And such a community is what an inherited constitution is, a cultural legacy: not a penalty paid for the crimes of one's ancestors, but an opportunity for meaningful action.

* * *

As you think about *Weber*, you will no doubt discover that you have, as everyone does, prior commitments that dispose you to approve or disapprove affirmative action programs in general, and this side of you will applaud or condemn the opinion of the Court by its result measured in those terms. But we also know that this is a difficult case, with much to be said on both sides, and one can imagine oneself approving or condemning the opinions not on the basis of their results, but on the basis of something else, namely their qualities as acts of mind and character. Even if you favored affirmative action programs, for example, you still might find yourself, as I have in this book repeatedly suggested, dismayed by an opinion supporting the program, yet having real admiration for an opinion that argued the other way. Of course the bare result of the case matters, and matters a lot, to Blacks and whites, to employers and workers, and it is important and right to talk about it. But when we do so, we learn that the result is never "bare," for it derives much of its meaning from the way it is conceived and talked about, and from the kinds of relations that this talking makes. While we talk about it, then, we should think as well about how we do so, and in the long run what matters most is that we do that thinking and talking well. If the opinion establishes an appropriate relation with the prior texts to which it owes fidelity, with the reader, and with those other people that it talks about, this is of greater ultimate value than reaching the result that one happens to approve in the case at hand.

The judge's responsibility for the particular result, though real and often denied, is never total, for the case is always decided in light of other texts reflecting other decisions made by other people, to which all agree some kind and degree of fidelity is due. These texts will sometimes dictate a result, in the sense that no serious argument can be made for a contrary interpretation,* and they should always affect the way the result is reached. Here, in the process of mind and character by which a judge addresses the texts of the past and relates them to the present, and by which he establishes or modifies a discursive and political community with his readers—and among those beyond his readership as well—is where his work and art lie; and it is ultimately by how well he does these things that he should be judged.

* * *

To judge opinions by the standards I suggest is not to aspire to a kind of ultimate neutrality on important questions, but to make sub-

---

*Even one committed to affirmative action as a general matter, for example, should recognize that it would be linguistically possible for Congress to pass a statute which would properly be interpreted the way Justice Rehnquist interpreted the statute in *Weber*, i.e., as prohibiting the use of racial classifications entirely.

stantive judgments about the most important questions that a court actually faces, namely, those implied in Dewey's great question, whether the conversation the opinion seeks to establish is one in which "democracy begins." This is the center of the political and ethical meaning of judicial work. It is not political in our usual terms, which imagine a spectrum running from right to left (and hence from good to bad or vice versa), but political in a deeper and more structural sense.

To think about the law as a conversational process does not mean that we have to focus our attention only on those who directly participate in it; indeed, this kind of thinking provides a way of talking about those who are left out or objectified, and a way of criticizing the law on that basis. Reading legal texts as exemplifications of constitutive rhetoric can thus lead not only to understanding but to judgment as well, and on political and ethical, as well as intellectual, grounds.

From the point of view worked out in this book, the law is now in peril of losing its essential character. Our tradition has embodied a sense of law as a way of respecting that which is external to the present moment and to the present will, namely, the judgments and experiences of others as these are recorded or reported in authoritative texts. The law thus creates a political world characterized by the separation of powers, a world in which there is no despot but in which each of us must live with judgments with which we disagree, when made by those authorized to make them. Of course this authority is not absolute, but depends upon its perpetual reconstitution by the people of the law. Each legal actor must constantly ask himself what respect must be paid to the decisions and wishes of others, as these are expressed in a series of texts from the past and in the statements of living people in the present. The reading of the former establishes connections across generations, the reading of the latter connections across the lines that separate groups and individuals. It is all done on the premise that we have something to learn from others. The law at once calls upon us to educate ourselves and at the same time offers us a way of doing that. Since it is from those situated differently that we are to learn, to whose worlds we are to pay respect, this is an education in learning how to see and understand things from a different point of view. This leads us in the direction of seeing our own language, our own assumptions, as cultural and not natural—as the proper object of criticism.

But all this is threatened by intellectual and political movements, epitomized in the practices of much political philosophy on the one hand and much modern economics on the other, that reduce language to a transparent code, deny the political and ethical meanings of our intellectual practices, and assume that justice means a certain distribution of goods, not a set of relations, not a self and community with a certain character. Thus it is that, at the popular level, democracy can be equated with capitalism, or, in other circles, justice with equal distribution of goods. And thus it is that we see in the work of judges a shift from the sense of obligation to give meaning to the texts that make up our world to the simple analysis of costs and benefits, a mode of thought that has no way to imagine a community of difference and respect.

* * *

One of the virtues of good judicial writing to which I have perhaps not as yet given sufficient attention is what I have called its openness. A common view of the judicial opinion is that it is a kind of brief, a mobilization of all the arguments that can colorably be made on behalf of the result chosen, with somewhat less superficial acknowledgment of what can be said on the other side than one finds in a lawyer's brief. But it might be thought that the task of the judge in writing an opinion is to expose to the reader the grounds upon which her judgment actually rests, with as full and fair a statement of her doubts and uncertainties as she can manage. Such an opinion would establish a relation of fundamental equality with the reader, who might follow the whole argument, consider himself enlightened by it, but come to the opposite conclusion. I think no Justice has consistently written out of such an understanding; Harlan comes closest, but one can see instances of such authenticity of mind in the work of others as well, including Holmes, Jackson, Black, and Douglas.

This kind of openness, if it could be achieved, would not only establish an admirable relation with the reader, it would enact an important intellectual virtue, perhaps the central virtue for the lawyer, namely, the suspension of judgment. If the lawyer knows anything at all, he knows that when he has heard one party's story he has heard only half the case; that when he feels a reaction or response leading him in one way, it is likely to be matched by one tugging in the opposite direction as well; and that the art of law is not that of linear reasoning to a secure conclusion, but an art, fundamentally literary and rhetorical in kind, of comprehension and integration: the art of creating a text—a mind and a community—which can comprise two things at once, and two things pulling in different directions. In speaking for one side as a lawyer, or for one result as a judge, that is, the legal mind should recognize (implicitly in the lawyer's case, explicitly in the judge's) what can be said for the other, thus by an art of integration creating a world in which differences can coexist.

* * *

The movement of the present chapter has been towards closure and conclusion. In Part Three I wish to open things out again and to talk in a somewhat different way about what is at stake in our readings of each other and in our own compositions, not only in judicial opinions but in the law more generally, and beyond the law in the rest of life, indeed whenever we seek to understand and respond to each other. In this book I have brought to legal texts a version of a way of reading that was worked out in large part by interaction with texts of rather a different kind; now I wish to move from the law outwards again, and ask in what ways this experience of reading judicial opinions, which are explicitly about justice, can help us to read other kinds of texts as well, and to see them too as ethical and political performances, as texts about justice. I shall do this by focusing on the activity of translation, to which this book has so frequently turned as a way of thinking about what we do when we read each other's texts and respond to them.

I have suggested above, for example, that translation offers a way of thinking about the relations we can establish among different discourse systems, and among the different communities they embody; that reflection about and the practice of translation will naturally lead one to an understanding of what language is, what languages are, that is far more accurate and comprehensive than the understanding implied in conceptual discourse of the modern academic kind; that translation is a model of social life that is far more responsive to the realities of our experience than those used by the social sciences, especially economics; and that the excellence we hope for in a judicial opinion can best be understood and spoken of as an excellence in translation.

But in each instance I make the point largely by suggestion, and I define translation itself mainly by contrast to something else. In the following chapter I wish to pull together these threads and ask at some length what translation is, or can be, and how it can serve as a model of thought and life, especially in the law.

THE ACTIVITY OF
TRANSLATION

11

TRANSLATION, INTERPRETATION, AND LAW

Starting to Talk

Imagine for the moment that I am speaking to you not in writing but face-to-face, and that, in an effort to make a new start, I say: "I want to talk to you next about justice and translation."

So I want to begin. But what kind of sentence is that? It makes "justice" and "translation" nouns, or nomens, as if there were entities in the world that could be named—pointed out and referred to—by these words, which of course there are not. And I say I want to talk "about" them as if "talking" were one kind of thing, "justice" and "translation" another, and as though the first took the second in some sense as its object. "There is the world of talk, and the world beyond talk," I seem to say; the relation between them is that the first is "about" the other. But translation is a form of talk, as perhaps justice is too, and there may be important continuities among these three practices that the formula "talk about" obscures or denies.

And I say "I" and "you" with great assurance, as though there were one "me," who "wants to talk," and one "you," who is expected to—to do what? "listen?" "receive?" "understand?" Or simply do nothing, not to be there in the discourse at all? (Does my talking imply no correlative activity on your part?) Certainly there is no suggestion in my opening sentence that you "want" anything, that you have a will or a set of desires; and no suggestion either that each of us is actually a set of multiple selves, speaking and acting sometimes in discord, sometimes in harmony.

If the words "justice" and "translation" do not point to nameable entities in the world, intellectual or social objects—like "concepts," say—observable by us independently of our talk about them, what do they do? Perhaps we can say this: that they are what the rhetoricians call topics. These terms invoke the prior experiences we have had with them, experiences that will of necessity be to some degree different for all of us and in many ways incoherent or confused; and they define a commitment on my part to expand and elaborate them, to make a text that will give them meaning in relation to each other. "Justice" and "translation" are not labels but words, and they must receive much of their meaning from the text I make in talking to you, and in your response to it. They are references to the past and a promise for the future.

* * *

In this chapter and the next I want to say: (1) that translation is an art of recognition and response, both to another person and to another language; (2) that it carries the translator to a point between languages, between people (and between peoples), where the differences between them can be more fully seen and more nearly comprehended—differences that enable us to see in a new way what each one is, or, perhaps more properly, differences in which the meaning and identity of each resides; (3) that it involves an assertion of the self, and of one's language too, that is simultaneously a limiting of both; and (4) that in all these respects it is a model of law and justice, for these two are at their heart also ways of establishing right relations, both between one person and another and between a mind and the languages it confronts.

But what can it mean for me to try to "say" such things? For example, will I simply trace out a mechanical analogy between two sets of practices, translation and the law, observing correspondences and differences, as if the whole world could be described in terms of interacting parts, as a kind of machine, in a language that mirrors such a reality—as if language were simply a system for naming? When I come to talk about the art of recognizing another and respecting difference, which is my true subject, will I find a language adequate to the task or will I reduce myself to clichés about "empathy" or "diversity?"

* * *

In this chapter I have been speaking as it were dialectically, saying one thing and then responding to myself in a somewhat different voice, and I shall continue to do this. In talking in this odd and double way, I am trying to direct your attention to a central expectation that we all have about a disquisition of this sort: namely, that in it I will try to "say" something, either in direct propositional form or in the kind of extended analogy that is a set of propositions in another guise. "I will try to utter propositions that are clear: you will try to apprehend them, so that you may test their validity in your own way."

But all that is to presuppose a view of language and of conversation I wish to resist, with which indeed my views of "translation" and "justice" are inconsistent. So I write and speak against the very force of the language I am using, against the occasion of my writing, against the expectations that bring us for this moment together. The question for me and for you is, then: Can I make a text that will embody or enact the view of language—of "translation" and "justice"—out of which I function and do so in a way that will be of use to you?

So I want to say: Do not look for propositions here, for conceptual elaborations and extended analogies, for anything stated, but for movement, for shifts in the meanings of words. Listen to the voices: my voices and your own, as you hear yourself respond in different ways to what I say. There, in the music the voices make, whether beautiful and harmonious or raw and ugly, is where the meaning lies; it is to that music that our attention and judgment should above all be directed.

* * *

My friend the translator lives on the margins of his world, spun out to them as if by centrifugal force: on the margins of his natal family, otherwise full of business people and sportsmen; on the margins of his academic department, full of those who aspire to make the study of language a science; on the margins of his midwestern and American culture, for who else here knows or thinks about Bali and its people (as he does); on the margins of the world created by our English language and its literatures, for he sees them in part from that cone-like mountain, covered in mist, rising out of the flat gray eastern sea; but on the margins of Bali too, for who is he there but a large and hairy Westerner who can understand so little?

Who is the translator, then? I don't mean the practicing bureaucrat, moving from one technical language to another, but the person who wishes to connect two worlds, two ways of being and seeing, in his own mind, in his own perceptions and feelings. Can the translator in fact be a person at all in the usual sense, with a place, a world to name and respond to, or is that kind of identity lost for such a one, or split irremediably in two? Think of it this way: With what voices can the translator possibly speak? In what sense can any voice ever be his own?

And what can I possibly mean when I suggest that the translator, who suffers this apparent loss (by duplication) of self and voice, can become a model for the rest of us, especially for lawyers and judges? The translator by circumstance inhabits the margins of culture, the lawyer the center, or so it may seem. And, more generally, does not the practice of translation, fully imagined and felt, lead to pure relativism: to the localization of all value, all identity, to the loss of all standards of judgment; perhaps even to the moral chaos from which those who insist upon the primacy of our own culture (or a part of it), and upon the discoverability of universal truth, promise to save us?

* * *

Some years ago I was leading my usual domestic and professional life in a small midwestern city with my wife and two young children when my oldest son arrived, bringing with him the entire family with whom he had spent a high school year abroad in Honduras. There were five in this family: the father, who spoke no English at all; the mother, who spoke very broken English; and three late-teenaged children, each of whom spoke English fairly well. Full of a desire to know each other and to affirm a common bond, we tried to talk. But I knew no Spanish at all. What happened? The part of my brain that is activated by social necessity, deep in the sub-cortex, turned on and I tried to learn the language: listening to every phrase, every word, intently hoping that I could understand the fragments, as I gradually came to do; dreaming at night, not in Spanish, not even in broken Spanish, but in words and phrases that sounded, to me at least, somewhat like Spanish. Of course the same thing was going on the other side as well: the Spanish speakers were trying to learn English, and to do so not as an intellectual exercise but out of a deep desire to understand, and to be understood by, people they did not know but who were already important to them. Small increases in comprehension were greeted as major triumphs, with laughter and applause; continued blankness and failure and frustration were cheerfully tolerated. The whole thing was at once exhausting and exhilarating.

What was the understanding that we sought? Was it simply the capacity to "express our ideas" in Spanish or English, as the case might be? To be able to say "I like these pancakes" or "your son was a great pleasure to us when he stayed with us in Honduras?" No: what I wanted to be able to do, and I think the others did too, was to inhabit the world of the other, to speak Spanish, or English, with the right intonation, cadence, texture, with the right position of the body and timbre of the voice, to respond and be responded to in a whole way. That sense of human reciprocity, of shared movements, is where the deepest meaning lies.

For language has its roots not in ideas but in social relations, and its deepest motives and meaning are social still. Think of the baby in his mother's arms: learning the language of her body, of her tones of voice and touch and gesture, and teaching her his, as together they learn to move in recognition and response. The words and phrases he gradually learns—in English or Chinese or Turkish, as the case may be—are late and relatively minor stages in the development of his capacity to understand and respond to another person. These words float as it were on a deep sea of competence without which they would be nothing at all, the mind nothing but a computer. To put it slightly differently, our language is at the deepest level the expression of a set of motives and gestures we share with all mammals; its radical meaning is social and relational. "Who are we to each other?" This is the question two dogs ask when they meet on the street, or two boys at the corner; and, whether they know it or not, the lawyer and her client, or two negotiating heads of state, ask this question too when they meet in an office or a conference room.

This is the radical question of justice, too: not, "How much do I get?" but "Who are we to each other?" What place is there for me in your universe, or for you in mine? Upon what understandings, giving rise to what expectations, do we talk? What world, what relations do we make together? These are the questions we ask our law to answer.

Translation and justice first meet at the point where we recognize that they are both ways of talking about right relations, and of two kinds simultaneously: relations with languages, relations with people.

* * *

Whenever we speak of "translation" we use a metaphor, that of "carrying something over" from one place to another, for the word itself comes from the Latin *trans* (across) and *latus* (past participle of *fero, ferre, tuli, latus*: carry).[1] It thus comes from the same Latin verb as "transfer" and has much the same meaning, suggesting that one might carry something over from one language to another as one carries something over from one side of the river to another, or from one tax year to another (as in "tax-loss carryover"). This idea of translation as transportation commits us implicitly to a certain view of meaning, namely, that it is like an object that can be picked up out of the place where it is found and dropped into another place; or, to put it another way, that the meaning of a sentence can be separated from its words—from its language, from its cultural context—and reproduced in another.

One of the miracles of our talk is that sometimes this actually makes a kind of sense. Think, for example, of directions for travel or directions for use: we can use a Serbo-Croatian phrasebook to ask our way to the beach, or we can translate French directions for building a bridge (whether made out of tinker toys or concrete), and do so largely without loss. One reason is that in these cases our immediate motives can be represented in material or instrumental terms—getting to the beach, building a bridge. In this sense both speakers have agreed to speak as if their utterances worked by naming or pointing, and in such a case the reduction of their uses of language to "translatable" meanings does little violence to their practical motives or wishes. For the purposes of the conversation, that is, both assume that one party wants only to get to the beach, or build the bridge, and that the task of the other is to point the way. Both speakers inhabit the same context, or pretend that they do, and they agree to use language to point out certain features of that context, such as "hospital," "hotel," or "restaurant." Neither for the moment takes any interest in a larger relationship with the other person or with either language, both of which are by agreement treated as purely indexical systems.

But the minute the context changes, the indexical function must be expanded to include something else, a teaching of the language to the one who does not know it. Think, for example, about how easily Americans get confused by continental terms for "school," "college," and "university": "In Germany the Gymnasium . . . . " And there are many situations in which this view of meaning and translation makes no sense at all: think of translating a poem, for example, or a political speech, or an expression of love, from one language to another. In such cases the very attempt to translate brings us again and again to face that which is particular or unique to the language and its context, to the speaker himself, and therefore cannot be translated, cannot be "set over."

How far does the impossibility of "translation" go? The Spanish linguist Ortega y Gasset tells us that it reaches all acts of translation, for in every representation of a text in another language there are necessarily modifications of the original, and modifications of two kinds: what he calls "deficiencies," by which he means aspects of the meaning of the original that are not replicated in the translation, and what he calls "exuberances," by which he means aspects of meaning that appear in the translation but are not part of the original.[2]

Exuberances and deficiencies arise from many sources: from the fact that the words we use have different histories in the two cultures, hence necessarily different and unreproducible meanings; from the very structures of the two languages, each of which will require that we specify something—gender, tense, aspect, number—as to which the other is silent; and from the differing social, cultural, and physical contexts into which each utterance is an intrusion. (The German "Wald" is different from the English "forest," or the American "woods," not only linguistically but physically: the trees are different.) In addition, a very large "exuberance" arises from the fact that the new text is a translation in the first place, and thus bears a relation to a prior text, in another language, of a kind that the original does not. Even in the simplest case, then, there is a sense in which translation is necessarily imperfect; as speech becomes more complex, the imperfections increase until we wonder what connections can exist at all between the original text and its purported replication.[3]

The translator must perpetually inhabit the uncertain space between two truths, that it is possible to make a text in one language that to some degree mirrors or reproduces the text made in another, and that this enterprise, so conceived, is always in a fuller sense utterly doomed. How then are we to conceive of and talk about the "meanings" of the texts we translate, and about the process of "translation" itself?

The word "metaphor," in its Greek root, is a direct parallel to "translate"—*meta* means "across" and *phor* means carry; indeed *-phor* and *-fer* (in "transfer") are different versions of the same word. Both are creations, neither mechanical: a translation is a metaphor.

* * *

I want now to turn from "translation" to what we call "interpretation" and say: "Interpretation is directly continuous with translation, for one who seeks to make a text in response to a text in his own language must inhabit his own version of the translator's uncertain space, knowing that it is impossible fully to reproduce the meaning of the prior text except in the words of the prior text, in its context, yet knowing as well that conversations can take place about such texts in which they are for some purposes, and in some ways, usefully represented in other terms. This is true not only in literary criticism, where the critic must create his own sense of the text he talks about, but true in law as well, where we are forever reducing a case to what we call its 'holding,' and where the meaning of one case is shifted by subsequent cases that depend upon it."

We can think of an expression, then, not as a way of conveying a message or idea, as a "vehicle" with a "content," but as a gesture the meaning of which is indissolubly tied to its immediate and unique context: to its language and culture, to the social relations out of which it emerges and upon which it acts, to the prior texts that its author and audience use to establish and understand its terms, to its location in a particular place in the physical world, and so on. Our responses to such expressions, whether "interpretations" or "translations," are not to be thought of as replicating the originals or conveying their "content" but as gestures themselves; as if the first expression were a piece of a dance, an invitation to make a dance together, and as if our responses to it were answering movements.* There is to such a gesture no single right response but an infinite number of possible responses, many of them good ones, many not so good; in evaluating them we should not speak of accuracy so much as appropriateness.[4]

* * *

---

*Translation and interpretation have in common that they invite their reader to hold in his head the prior text or to refer to it, or at least to acknowledge that it is there, if only as a ghost behind the form; and both establish a relation of fidelity to that text, though in somewhat different ways. In both cases the meaning of the second text depends upon its relation to the first.

The difference is that the translation offers itself as a kind of substitute for the original and undertakes to have an analogous form, as the interpretation does not. (I owe this observation to Kenneth DeWoskin). Is there otherwise a difference in principle between translation and interpretation? I think not: one could imagine, for example, a

I now write down the following words:

Andra moi ennepe, Mousa, polytropon . . . .

Some readers will recognize this as the first clause of the *Odyssey*, but for most I assume this will be a set of unintelligible marks and sounds. I want to ask: What actually happens as I start to give it further meaning?

This process has in fact already begun, and the passage has acquired a kind of meaning it lacked when you first read it, for I have identified it as coming from the *Odyssey*. This means that you will attend to it differently, with a different attitude and a different part of the mind, from the way you would if I told you, say, that this was a Finnish phrase meaning, "Please leave the washroom clean for the next passenger."

Now I say that this Greek phrase means: "Speak, Muse, of the man of many turnings." Have I actually replicated the meaning of the Greek in that phrase, and if not, what have I done? What attitude should you have towards these English words? What else do you need to learn in order to feel that you understand this line of Greek?

Consider the phrase "Speak, Muse . . ." (*ennepe Mousa*), and think of the questions you could ask of it. What is this "Muse" invoked here, why is she invoked this way, and what is the "speaking" she is asked to do? How is this line to be read, for example, against the first line of the *Iliad*, which asks the "goddess" (*thea*) (not the Muse) to "sing" (*aoide*) (not speak)? What is the role of the poet supposed to be? (Here you need to be told that the poet here appears as a dative pronoun—*moi*, suppressed in my translation—that means "to me" or "through me" or "for me" or something like that.) And "man" (*andra*): does this just mean "person," or is it emphatically male? Does it express or suggest a set of values about men, and by implication women, in this world? These are questions of real difficulty, each of which could be pursued at considerable length.

Beyond them there is the way the words fit together in the two languages: the Greek poet can begin with *andra* (accusative of *aner*) for Greek is an inflected language that does not depend as English does primarily on order or sequence to establish relations among its

---

translation that was "looser," more "free," than a particular interpretation which tied itself as closely as possible to the verbal forms of the original.

The heart of both is the same: the presence of two texts, two voices, and the making of a relation between them.

words. Here the noun is put in a case that implies an action and an actor affecting it. The next word—*moi*—defines the poet's role, suggesting, by the dative, that something is being done to or for the speaker. The "speak" verb—*ennepe*—comes next, defining this activity, and "*Mousa*"—the Muse—provides the nominative agent. (A name, in the vocative, that implies the existence of a person; but there is no such person, so how is this gesture to be read? As the formal marker that tells us we are beginning a certain sort of poem? As a statement of "religious belief"? But what could such a phrase mean in this unretrievable context?) The last word, *polytropon*, in the accusative masculine singular, goes with the first—inflection permits it to be placed at the end of the clause, for shape and emphasis—and combines elements meaning "many" or "much" and "turn," ambiguous as to whether objective or subjective, so at once: "man suffering many turns" and "man capable of many turns." We thus end our translation this way:

Andra moi ennepe, Mousa, polytropon

This sketch is only the merest beginning: even if you were to spend your life on it, this text would always be imperfectly before you, the questions we have just raised serious and open ones, for we can never fully know what needs to be known about the prior texts and social facts that defined the context into which it was an intrusion, in which it was a performance. Any interpretation we give it, like any translation of it, will be full of exuberances and deficiencies.

* * *

Suppose we were to discover, in China or among the American Indians, a community in which a bird dance was periodically performed. What would it mean to tell the story, or draw the picture, of this dance? Suppose, for example, that in this dance a man otherwise clad normally carries a stick with three great feathers hanging from it. When I draw a picture of that, do I do so most accurately by drawing a man with three feathers on a stick or by drawing a bird the size of a man? Similarly, when I tell the story of the bird dance, should I refer to the man acting as a bird, or to the bird itself? Often in Han Dynasty descriptions, I am told, the narrative begins by referring to the man and ends by referring to the bird. I think here of the rule in African life, described in one of the novels of Chinua Achebe, that the children must pretend on pain of death not to know that the masked dancers are their fathers. This is a way of insisting that the man is not a man but a bird, not a man but a god; in each case the language has ways of creating realities that can exist only in its terms. This is what we do when we insist that a man or woman is not that but a judge, or a priest. It is the creation of social identity and meaning.

Law as Translation

One of the speeches of the Greek orator Lysias is conventionally entitled "Against Theomnestus, on a Charge of Slander." Lysias wrote this speech on behalf of an unnamed speaker who is suing Theomnestus for having said that the plaintiff "killed" his own father. (The word I translate as "kill" is *apokteinein*.) Athenian law had no general cause of action for defamation, as we do, couched in terms of injury to reputation, but instead by legislation made actionable certain specific utterances, including charges of murder, of throwing away one's shield, and of beating a parent. In the part of the speech that is for present purposes of greatest interest, the speaker responds to an anticipated defense by Theomnestus, namely, that he is charged only with having said that the plaintiff "killed" his father (*apokteinein*) not, what the law prohibits, that he "murdered" him (*androphonein*). The question is whether this difference should matter.[5]

Lysias argues that it should not, on the grounds that it would be impossible for the lawgiver to write down all the words that have the same force. In saying one he makes clear his meaning with respect to all the others that are like it. Lysias then gives examples. It is actionable to call someone a "father-beater" or "mother-beater"; should someone escape liability who says that a person had beaten his "male" or "female parent"? The law makes it actionable to say that someone "threw" (*apoballasthai*) away his shield; should someone be able to avoid liability by saying instead that he "flung" (*riptein*) away his shield? Similarly, it is a statutory offense to steal "clothes"; should someone be able to escape liability by saying that he had only stolen a "cloak" or "chiton?"

He then reads a series of old laws, each one of which uses an archaic term that means something different in the ordinary language of his day from what it meant when it was used. One such law, for example, authorizes certain people to be placed in the stocks (*podokakai*); it would certainly not be a valid complaint against the official who did this that he otherwise properly placed an offender instead "in the wood" (*xulos*), which is the modern name for stocks. Similarly the law uses a word for "swearing" that in contemporary Greek means "false swearing," but it should obviously be taken in the former sense. Antique words used in legislation that prohibited "shutting the door" to protect a thief, "placing out" money for interest, "street-walking," and the like have also changed their meaning in ordinary discourse, but in all these cases the original meaning of the word, not the current one, should prevail.

This argument for the maintenance of old meanings, and old words, is in effect—though Lysias may not have known it—an argument that the law should be regarded as creating a distinct discourse of its own, in which words are given their meanings by reference to the purposes and contexts of the law, not to the shifting usages of ordinary speech. To us this seems obvious, for we have long lived with a technical legal language; to the Athenian, who tried cases without lawyers, without precedent, without legal scholars, before juries that sometimes included as many as one-tenth of the entire body of the citizens (who were of course also the legislators), the idea of a distinct legal discourse was a foreign one. (By what special speakers, in what special conversations, was it to be maintained? You can see how the Athenian democrat would resist it.)

But beyond that, Lysias is here arguing that interpretation is a kind of translation: one cannot simply use the old words as if they meant what they do in today's ordinary Greek; one must recognize their different meanings and try to give them life in the present moment. And what Lysias claims for the Greeks is also true for us as well, that the law written at one time must be interpreted in another, when not only social and cultural circumstances but even more explicitly the language itself has undergone a change. We often say that the words are to be given the meaning that they had in their original context, so far as this is possible; this necessarily requires both the maintenance of that language as a distinct one and a kind of glossing that is really a form of translation, a recasting of the old text to state its meaning in new terms. But this activity is far more complex and uncertain than Lysias makes it seem, for, as we know from our reading of Supreme Court cases, one cannot simply look to the original meaning of the words and carry that meaning without loss into the present. The act of setting over—of interpretation or translation—will always involve "exuberances" and "deficiencies"; indeed it should also involve an acknowledgment on our part that our sense of the meaning both of the past expression and of our own version of it (by a comparison of which the exuberances and deficiencies might be measured) is itself incomplete and uncertain.

The reading of legal texts requires a kind of judgment that is in fact of form of lawmaking, entailed in the very act of interpretation itself. Think, for example, of common-law adjudication, where one typically asks of a set of cases: "What general principle can be found here that will explain them all?" and "How does that principle bear on the present one?" This kind of common-law interpretation is explicitly a form of lawmaking, and legitimately so. Lysias shows that statutory interpretation is too, and for the same reason, namely, that the original text must be "translated" to present circumstances and contemporary language; what we can see more clearly than he acknowledges is that in this process of translation there is always gain and always loss, always transformation; that the "original meaning" of the text cannot be our meaning, for in restating it in our terms, in our world, no matter how faithfully or literally, we produce something new and different.

The central activity of law is the reading of texts—cases, statutes, regulations—and their imperfect reproduction and arrangement, in compositions of our making, in contexts to some degree distinct from those in which they were made. It is in fact a kind of translation, and this knowledge should shape both the way we engage in it ourselves and the way we judge the productions of others.

* * *

Some years ago the Canadian Royal Commission on Bilingualism and Biculturalism published a series of Studies on the problems of life in a two-language culture, one of which (prepared by Claude-Armand Sheppard) was entitled *The Law of Languages in Canada* (1971). In Canada both French and English are official languages: languages of the law, of theoretically equal status. But how does this work out in practice? Think, for example, of the process by which laws are made: Are they to be "drafted" in one language, then "translated" into another, or are they to be drafted simultaneously in both languages? In either case how will this to be done?

In fact at the time of the Study the practice of the Canadian federal government had been the former, to draft all national legislation in English, then translate it into French. The achievement of the Study is to show that this practice operates on a set of false assumptions not only about translation but also about the process of statutory drafting, activities that the Report sees not as discrete but as continuous and of deeply similar structure. Think of the way legislation is drafted, for example: the draftsman starts with a rather general statement by the legislature, or more properly by a ministerial department or committee, which it is his job to convert into the language of the law. This requires continuing thought and reflection both about the proposed legislation and about the legal context into which it is an intrusion; the task of the draftsman, like that of the translator, is to create a text that is different from, yet faithful to, a text composed by another.

Here is what the Study says:

> The draftsman of a statute must first of all understand the legislative policy which the statute is intended to express. He must examine critically, as a lawyer, the policy which he is to draft into a legislative enactment. He may have to round out that policy and supply a multitude of details since the legislative proposal he receives is in the form of a broad statement. Some of these details and refinements of policy appear only while the statute is actually being drafted. In drafting the statute the draftsman must consider it in relation to other statutes and the law generally. Where it happens that more than one government department may be interested in a proposed piece of legislation, the draftsman brings together officials from these various departments, and the initial decisions as to the policy of the act may be altered as a result. Sometimes the legislative proposal has not been properly prepared by the departments concerned and the draftsman must join with the departments in policy discussions. He sometimes has to elicit opinions on policy or to prepare alternative drafts. In order to understand the legislative proposal fully, he must familiarize himself with its subject matter, with the legislative problems involved, and with the proposed solutions. Conferences with the sponsoring department may become necessary for this purpose. Once he truly understands what is expected, he must then plan the kinds of provisions the statute will have to include. This will entail further discussions with the sponsoring department, as a result of which further changes may be made. Finally he is ready to draft. Once he has completed his draft, it must be revised, examined for imperfections, commented upon, and considered and discussed with the sponsoring department until both the sponsors and the draftsmen are satisfied with the statute's form and content. It is then submitted to the deputy minister or minister and further conferences take place, after which further change may also be required. In the process the draftsman, having participated in all the deliberations culminating in the production of a statute, will have become somewhat imbued with the spirit in which the original policy and its subsequent modifications were conceived, and should therefore be more thoroughly acquainted with it than would someone who merely reads his finished product. (Pp. 111–12.)

The reason for the present practice, the Commission was told, is that "statutes can be drafted only in one language," and that language has to be English, for it is the majority language. Only after they are drafted in English are the statutes translated,[6] and this by officers of the Bureau for Translation, who have no particular legal expertise. The result is this:

> Anyone who has examined the French text of any federal statute, even in the most perfunctory manner, has become painfully aware not so much of grammatical errors as of the totally non-Latin and non-idiomatic use of language. In fact, the French text is frequently almost incomprehensible to a French lawyer. The reason was best explained by [Adjutor] Rivard:
> "The way an Englishman likes to develop an idea bears scarcely any resemblance to the way a Frenchman would do it. The mentality, turn of mind, and method are different. One may thoroughly grasp the idea of a law as expressed in one language, and yet be unable to translate it properly into the other. Unless the two languages have a common genius and the intellectual processes of both peoples are identical, any attempt at translation is vain if it is not preceded by a complete dissimilation of the legal idea to be transplanted. And that will necessarily involve fundamental modifications, the development of new insights, the organization of both the whole and the parts along different lines—in fact a new concept of the law with all the changes necessary to conform to a different way of thinking, doing and speaking. Any other method of borrowing will lead to deplorable consequences." (P. 114.)

In its quiet way the Study thus shows that the activities of "drafting" and "translating" cannot be separated from each other, as we normally think, or from "interpretation" either. These are not so much distinct practices as the same practice in different forms: in all three a person is seeking to elaborate the meaning of one text by composing another, of his or her own making. In each case fidelity to the prior text is the central ethical imperative, yet in none can that faithfulness be defined as a mindless literalism—which would be no fidelity at all—nor can the duty of fidelity be discharged in any other merely mechanical or technical way. There is in fact no one right way to discharge it; it requires a response of the individual mind and imagination, the kind of self-assertion implied in the making of any real text. It presents us with a genuine intellectual and ethical difficulty.[7]

How are we to talk about this difficulty and the art of language and of judgment by which it might be met? The Study talks about what the "draftsman" knows by virtue of his participation in the legislative process that the mere "translator" of the finished product does not by saying that he understands the "policy" of the legislation. But, it goes on, this is not just a matter of obedience to the will of another, or of simple cognition, for he must "examine the policy critically, as a lawyer." His task is to "round it out" and to "supply details," for what he receives is a "broad statement," what he produces is legislation. He must "consider it, in relation to other statutes and the law generally."

This is a welcome relief from simple-minded talk about "effectuating the legislative intention," for it is obvious that the drafter helps to create that "intention." But the Study speaks in largely conclusory terms, as though we all knew what it meant to examine a policy "critically as a lawyer," or to "consider" a statute "in relation to other statutes and the law generally." And the text shifts emphasis, between seeing the drafter as an active source of law and pretending that he is only the tool of the true lawmaker (whose "intention" he is to realize) in a way that is less than fully coherent:

> In the process, the draftsman, having participated in all the deliberations culminating in the production of a statute, will have become somewhat imbued with the spirit in which the original policy and its subsequent modifications were conceived, and should be therefore somewhat more acquainted with it than would someone who merely reads his finished product. (P. 112.)

What is the "it" in that sentence? the spirit? the policy? the statute?

Turn now to the remarks of Adjutor Rivard quoted above. He says that the difficulty is at heart what we would call cultural (or perhaps psychological): "the mentality, the turn of mind are different. Unless the two languages have a common genius, and the intellectual processes of both people are identical, any attempt at translation is vain if it is not preceded by complete dissimilation of the legal idea to be 'transplanted.'" This will in turn require the creation of a whole new idea of law, a culture in the space between cultures, resulting less in a "translation" from English to French than in the invention of a new language, a new world.

* * *

Think here of the problems that arise in international law when the terms of a treaty provide that it be authoritative in both (or all) the languages in which it is composed (or into which it is translated before signing). The effect of such a provision is not to give, by fiat, both versions the same meaning, for that is impossible; it is simply to postpone the problem of language difference and make it the subject of negotiation at some later date, when the two sides propose differing constructions of the treaty, each relying on its own version.[8]

For it is inevitable that the two texts will generate differences of meaning. These will be resolved, if at all, not by simple assertion, but by a process of conversation that draws upon the rest of the document, upon its evident aims, upon the prior texts defining the context upon which it acted, and so forth. Obviously in such a case the "interpreter" is not simply yielding obedience to a plain text but construing it, translating it, giving it meaning, and doing so in ways that cannot be reduced to rules or organized by them either. Here, as elsewhere, "reading" is an art, to be judged in its particular performances, not a "science" reducible to system.

Consider what "intention" means in the treaty context: two heads of state work out a rough agreement about arms reduction (or rather a pair of rough agreements), say in Russian and in English. What happens next? "Drafters" and "translators" go to work producing a pair of texts which are authenticated by the leaders. Do the leaders understand what they authenticate? In some sense certainly not: each is rather acting in confidence upon the advice of his subordinates and committing himself and his country to a set of rhetorical practices by which the future relations between the countries will to some degree be shaped. "We agree that this document can be invoked as authoritative; we know it is full of uncertainty, but we have confidence in our skill at managing the kind of argument by which its interpretation will go on." This is what they are saying, whether they know it or not.

Is this a foolish confidence? Not at all: it is full of uncertainty but it is the only kind of confidence it is open to us to have; it is certainly less foolish than thinking that your wishes have been clearly and immutably set down in writing in such a way as to govern any future dispute. In particular it is the only kind of confidence that the framer of a legal text can ever have—whether it is a contract, a statute, a constitution, or an opinion that he has written—for the meaning of his text will of necessity be given it in considerable part by others, engaged in practices of thought and argument which are only roughly predictable ahead of time. This does not mean, as some would say, that it is senseless to talk of the text having any meaning at all, on the theory that all the meaning is made by the "community of interpreters"—a view that is as wrong as its opposite, that the meaning of a text simply lies there in the text, for future generations to pick up. Meaning is always made by interaction between mind and text, and this is true in what we think of as interpretation and translation alike: the real question is, with what attitude and skill we engage in this process.

* * *

The law works by the translation of authoritative texts into the present moment, a kind of pushing forward of what was written in one context into another, where it has a necessarily somewhat different meaning. This is not a mechanical or technical process and its burdens and responsibilities cannot be cut short by any of the devices used to avoid them, such as resort to the "original intention" of the framers or the "plain words" of the text. It always requires an act of creation, a making of something new; yet the original text cannot be forgotten, for fidelity is always due to it. Indeed it is the upon prior text that our right to speak at all depends. One has no authority to disregard it and substitute for it texts of one's own composition, setting forth one's own view of proper policy, proper practice. One must inhabit the space of uncertainty, at once bound by fidelity to the texts of the law and burdened with the knowledge that these texts do not translate (or interpret) themselves and that any construction of them is an act of one's own for which one is oneself responsible.

At the center of law is the activity of translation.

Talking about Translation

I have spoken above of the impossibility of complete translation from one language, one text, to another. Here I wish to expand and complicate that theme, beginning with the implications of our ordinary talk about translation. In the translator's preface to the *New English Bible*,[9] for example, we find the following sentence about translation, which states rather well what many people—what all of us, sometimes—would be inclined to say: "We have conceived our task to be that of understanding the original as precisely as we could (using all available aids), and then saying again in our own native idiom what we believed the author to be saying in his."

What are we to think of this language? It is familiar—it is how we all talk—but to me it seems utterly wrong. Of course it is important to try to "understand" the original, but what does it mean to try to do that? As we know from our brief experience with the *Odyssey*, the process is problematic at its heart: we can never "understand" a text completely in the first place and what we do "understand" can really be said only in the original language and in the forms of the original text. The word "precisely" in the sentence above, and the talk about the use of "aids," seem to me to point in just the wrong direction: towards something called the "meaning" of the text that is imagined to exist above, or beyond, or behind its language, when in truth the meaning is in the words as they are uttered in their particular context and nowhere else. The rest of the sentence, which assumes that someone is "saying something" in his language that can be separated from it and "said again" in another, is a formula that is in its own way as misleading as talk about "concepts," or as misleading as the familiar nostrum in which one says that one is trying to translate the *Aeneid,* say, in such a way as "to produce the poem that Virgil would have written had he been alive today"—when "Virgil" could not be "alive" today, for he was in large part formed by the language and education in which he was raised, and, still more perplexingly, when the "today" in which we are to imagine him is in part shaped by the *Aeneid* itself.

But these ways of talking about translation run deep in our culture. To return for the moment to Lysias, he argues that in the instances he gives—of "stocks," "oaths," and the like—the things (*pragmatai*) are the same, but we sometimes use different names (*onoma*). With respect to the slander cases, he says that what counts is not the name (*onoma*) but the meaning (*dianoia*). He is here talking as if words were merely labels, either for realities (*pragmata*) or for meanings (*dianoia*). But this will hardly do. Circumstances and meanings change, as Lysias himself elaborates; there is in fact no stable nonlinguistic reality to which words can simply "refer" as "names."

Or think of the formulation, common in our own day, that words have "core" meanings, often called "denotative," that are readily translatable; it is their "associations" or "connotations" that cannot be set over. (Compare the idea of Justice Frankfurter in *Wolf* that the "core" of the fourth amendment should be applied to the states but not its "remedial" periphery.) But there is no translatable "core": all the meanings of words are established by connections either to other words (and other texts) or to our world of particular experiences. In the sense that is implicit in our usual ways of thinking and talking about it, "translation" is impossible: one cannot get the "ideas" or "concepts" or "information" contained in one text, composed in one language, "over" into another text, composed in another language, nor can one in other respects create the "equivalent" in one's own language of a text composed in another. What one can do is to create a text in response to an earlier text, a gesture answering a gesture.

Or so I have been saying. There are those who disagree. Roman Jacobsen, for example, asserts that "all cognitive experience and its classification is conveyable in any existing language."[10] But he goes on to say that "poetry" is not in this sense translatable, for in poetry "syntactic and morphological categories, roots, and affixes, phonemes and their components (distinctive features)—in short, any constituents of the verbal code—are confronted, juxtaposed, brought into contiguous relation according to the principle of similarity and contrast and carry their own autonomous signification." He is of course right about poetry but not only for these reasons—think, for example, of the music of a line, in French or English or Greek, and how obviously that cannot be reproduced elsewhere. But what he says about poetry is right about prose too: every element in the new text has different meanings from the old, for, like the old, the new one acquires its meanings from its context—from the expectations of its audience, against which it plays, by confirmation or surprise—and this context is always new. Think, to take an obvious example, of the translation of a funeral scene from Chinese, where "white" is the color of death: do you write "white" or "black?"[11] And, as we saw in reading the line from Homer, different languages create different kinds of relations among their words, and these cannot be replicated.

To take a more extended example, consider Sir Ernest Barker's introduction to his translation of Aristotle's *Politics*. As Barker says, it is not only in their poetry but also in their writings on political theory that the vocabulary of the Greeks had "overtones, echoes, and associations" of a kind we "can hardly recapture." "Their political terms were charged with the significance of their own political environment and their own political experience; and neither the environment nor the experience is ours."

He addresses this gap in part by giving his reader a kind of lexical introduction to the central terms of the Athenian political life, part of which is reproduced immediately below. He starts with the distinction between the Greek word *polis* and our word "state,"* often used

---

*"The word 'state' comes to us from the Latin *status*, in its sense of standing or position: it meant, when we adopted it in the sixteenth century, the standing or position of the person (or persons) in authority, so that Louis XIV was etymologically justified in saying *L'Etat, c'est moi!*; and though it has widened in the course of time to designate also the whole political community, it is still used today in its old sense (as when we speak of 'state interference'), and its overtones are still the overtones of authority." Ernest Barker, *The Politics of Aristotle*, p. xi (1948).

to translate it. One problem with "state," he says, is its Latin origins, and in this it is typical of much of our political vocabulary:

> We speak not only of the 'state', but also of 'constitution', 'government', 'administration', 'sovereignty', 'statute', 'justice',—and every word is derived from the Latin. The bulk of our political vocabulary is a Latin vocabulary. It is a useful, and indeed a majestic vocabulary: Latin has not only sonority, but it has also the gift of solemnity; and it adds precision to both. But the precision of Latin cannot do proper justice to the flexibility and nuances of the Greek. [p. xii.]

Barker then goes on to discuss a series of key terms, the first of which is *polis* itself.

> The word *polis*, as has already been implied at the beginning of this prefatory note, means a civic republic, or, more particularly and especially, the city which is its heart. But this is a general statement; and it instantly needs qualification. We must therefore add, speaking more precisely, that the Greeks had a special word for the city as a place of residence—the word *asty*—and that the word *polis* originally meant the citadel (or acropolis, as it was called at Athens) at the foot of which lay the *asty*. But if this was its original sense, the word *polis* came in time to mean the whole organized political community, including both the residents in the *asty* (with, of course, any magistrates or others resident in the citadel) and the country-dwellers around the *asty* who frequented it for business and politics. This transference and extension of the sense of the word *polis* is easy to understand. The citadel, to which alone the appellation of *polis* was originally given, was the natural centre of gravity and the focus of authority; and it was an easy matter to use the term which originally denoted the centre in order to denote the whole circle and its content.
>
> A further refinement may be added. It has been noted by scholars that the word *polis* was specially applied in Athenian documents to denote the circle of the organized community when it was acting externally (in the way of treaties or otherwise), and was thus engaged in relations with other organized communities. In other words, it was used as a term of the language of diplomacy; and it signified a 'power' engaged in relation with other 'powers'. Another term was employed, in the usage of Athenian documents, to designate the organized community when it was acting internally, and was thus engaged in the conduct of its own domestic

affairs. This was the term *demos*, the ancestor of the word 'democracy'. Here again we have to record a growth and a transference of the original sense of the term. The word *demos* was originally used to denote the country-side and the country-dwellers (the people of the *agros*, as distinct from the people of the *asty*); and we accordingly find the units of the country-side called, in general Athenian usage, by the name of *demoi*, and their inhabitants by the name of *demotai*. But by the fifth century a new use had supervened. The term *demos*, used in the singular as a general collective noun, had come to signify more particularly the whole Athenian community when assembled for its domestic affairs in an 'assembly of the summoned' or 'meeting of those called out for attendance'— which is the literal meaning of the word *ecclesia*. . . .

From this refinement (which, it will be noticed, relates specifically to Athens—but Attic speech and Athenian terminology set the general tone for all Greece) we may now return to the word *polis*. It had a large number of derivatives. There is the derivative *polites*, or, as we translate it by a Latin word, 'citizen'. There is the derivative *politikos*, which is better translated (though, even so, it is translated imperfectly) by the Latin word 'statesman' than by the word 'politician'. There is the derivative *politeia*, which we translate by the Latin terms 'constitution' or 'form of government', but which again is something different from either; for it means, as Aristotle explains, a way of life, or a system of social ethics, as well as a way of assigning political offices. Finally, there is the derivative *politeuma*, which is used by Aristotle to signify the concrete or personal side of the *politeia*, or, in other words, to mean the body of persons enjoying full civic rights under the *politeia*. [Pp. xiii–xv.]

Notice that despite the implications of his earlier talk about "associations," Barker does not here proceed on the assumption that the "core" meaning of *polis* and "state" are the same, and that his task is thus to inform us about the "overtones" of the term, but recognizes that the terms are completely different in their origin and significance. It is not their secondary meanings that are different but their primary meanings; they are different all the way through. His method is not that of the abstract philosopher who aims to produce a definition of a term by equation or description, merely seeking an equivalent term or phrase, but that of the philologist who gives you one word in relation to others. This is where their meanings lie.[12] He teaches his reader something of the language she does not know.

All this means that to talk about a transparent proposition (whether about the natural or intellectual world) that can be translated without gain or loss, without transformation, is to mislead. No sentence can be translated into another language without change.[13]

Suppose, for example, that instead of the first line of the *Odyssey* I had reproduced above the first sentence of Socrates' *Apology*, pure prose: the problems of comprehension would have been nearly the same, and would have begun with our ignorance about the social and rhetorical context in which he acted. Who are these "judges" or "men of Athens" he addresses, what kind of thing is this trial, what does this charge about impiety really mean, in short, against what expectations does this text play?[14] The words, in Barker's phrase, have their meaning in an "environment" and "experience" which we can only guess at, and which is itself partly linguistic in nature; and, as we saw in the *Odyssey* too, part of the experience of language is the experience of the way words connect with each other, which is different in the two languages and not translatable. Our attempt to translate the *Apology* would once more have ended, as Barker's translation itself does too, in a language lesson.

* * *

In his essay *On Translating Homer* Matthew Arnold says that the translator of Homer should try not to replicate the meaning of particular words, one at a time, or even whole sentences, but to produce on the reader who knows both languages a "general effect" that is similar to the effect of the original text. Word-for-word translation will obviously lose the literary meaning of the text; yet we cannot know the effect the text had on its original audience, and it is pointless to aim for that. Similarly we cannot describe the original with a precision adequate to establish impersonal criteria of meaning. Only the educated judgment of one who knows both languages will do. And it is similarity not in form or detail we look for, but in effect: the sentiments it arouses, the activities the text stimulates, in the reader.[15] The translation should thus aim to reproduce the qualities of Homer's poetry as these are experienced by the English reader who is at home in Homer's Greek.

The central quality of Homer's verse, Arnold goes on to say, is that it is "rapid," "plain and direct" (both in style and idea), and "noble." These terms of description give him his terms of judgment too: a translation of Homer should be rapid, plain and direct, and noble.

This way of talking about translation has the great merit of avoiding mechanistic and quantitative talk about "content" (or about "the core" and the "periphery" of meaning) in favor of the nature and quality of literary experience. But Arnold speaks on the assumption that his terms of description—rapidity, nobility, etc.—are transparent or cross-culturally valid. He rests on them, that is, as if they told a translatable truth. His more general point, that the translation should aim at the "same effect" as the original, has a similar difficulty, for he speaks as though texts were like experience-machines that affected the organism of the reader in certain programmed ways that could be fairly reproduced in different languages. His position is to this extent another version of the claim that the meaning is language-free.

Would Arnold make the same claim for translations of Homer into French or Chinese, which do not have our words "noble," "direct," etc.? Or does he recognize that the English person of the nineteenth century will in fact see something different in the original, be affected by it differently, from a person in a different culture, time, or place?

There is no position outside of culture from which the original can be experienced or described. It is read by one of us, translated by one of us speaking to the rest of us. The meaning and identity of the original are defined in the differences we perceive in it, in what makes it strange to us. To another it will present a different set of differences, and thus be a different text, with a different meaning.

For us it is almost impossible not to think and speak as if there were an objectifiable meaning out there, in Greek or Japanese, say, which it is our task to "set over" or "transfer" to English, in a process thought of as a kind of transportation. But we can come to recognize that what is out there is not a meaning but a text, and that the text cannot be set over into English; it is Greek or Japanese. Instead, what happens in what we call translation—and drafting and interpretation too—is that we make one text in response to another. The heart of the process is learning the language of another not as material for transposition but as a language of meaning in its own right,[16] then making a text of one's own in the full knowledge that it will have a meaning of its own, different from but related to that of the original, and that one is responsible for the meaning one makes. The translated poem is both a poem itself and an interpretation of the original,[17] and I think this doubleness is characteristic of all translation, and all interpretation too, indeed of all speech: one produces a text that is of value (good or bad) both in its own right and by virtue of its relation to another.

* * *

To translate at all thus requires that one learn the language of another, recognize the inadequacy of one's own language to that reality, yet make a text, nonetheless, in response to it. Should it accordingly be a constant and central aim of the translator to bring his own reader to a new consciousness of the limits of his language in relation to another? Not by changing English, say, into some foreign thing, but far more subtly, by reminding the reader that one is always at the edge of what can be done; that beyond it is something unknown and if only for that reason wonderful; that, like a grammar, a translation can never be more than a partial substitute for an education.[18]

Think here of the King James Version of the Bible. In his fine work on this translation,[19] Gerald Hammond points first to the *New English Bible*, which in his words attempted to produce a text that would "not tax its readers' linguistic and interpretive abilities one bit,"[20] then to the King James Version, which on the contrary deliberately presents its readers with problems of both kinds. These occur in many ways: in formulas that have become familiar to us but were strange to the original English audience (such as "And it came to pass"); in the use of a single English word across a text, in the Hebrew fashion, rather than making an array of supposedly more precise substitutions (a feature of style that accentuates the degree to which words can acquire their meanings from the texts that employ them, rather than from the prior texts in which they have been embedded); and in the use of what are in English syntactic irregularities, which in fact imitate Hebrew structures. The effect is not to produce a Bible that fits effortlessly into the stream of ordinary English, to which in our day, for example, one might turn without a break from the Reader's Digest or television news, but to make a language that is to some degree exotic and specialized, a language appropriate to a foreign and a sacred text.[21]

* * *

The common mistaken expectation about translation—that "what is said" in one language can be "said" in another—is itself I think the result of the defective view of language more generally against which I have been writing throughout this book, namely, that language is a "code" into which "messages" are encoded, or perhaps a system of "signifiers" that derives its ultimate meaning from the real or imaginary things "signified." In both cases language is conceived of as transparent; the speaker is assumed to engage, before speaking, in intellectual processes that in some way yield the content—the "message" or proposition or observation—that will ultimately be expressed in the utterance but have as yet no linguistic form. In its strongest version it assumes that we all live in a common nonlinguistic world of shapes, objects, animals, colors, ideas, concepts, and so forth, which different languages happen to label differently, with different sounds.[22]

But in fact our experience is linguistic at every stage: our languages shape what we say and what we mean, what we see and what we experience; we are always talking in inner or outer speech; there can be no "content" without language; and language is neither a "code" nor a system of signification that points to things external to it. To think of the nonlinguistic world as the same for all of us is to erase the whole plane of cultural and social reality that is constituted in language and that in turn gives meaning to the natural world. Who among us sees the sea and rocks as Odysseus did, or as the geologist does?

There is, then, no "translation," only transformation achieved in a process by which one seeks to attune oneself to another's text and language, to appropriate them yet to respect their difference and autonomy as well, in what Hugh Kenner calls "interchanges of voice and personality."[23] In making (and reading) translations we should think and speak, then, not about transportable "content," but about the relations—between texts, between languages, between people—that we establish in our own compositions; about the attitudes towards other people, other languages, that we embody in our expressions.

* * *

Thinking about translation thus brings us to face the facts, present in all reading and writing and talking, that perfect communication is impossible, that we always write and talk across our languages, as well as within them, and that there is no such thing as "understanding" in any simple sense of the word. Think, for example, of the definition of what we ordinarily mean by "a language": when I say I will try to translate this text from "French" to "English," the question can be asked, "What French and whose English?" We speak as if all French-speakers spoke the same language, but obviously that is not true. No two people speak exactly the same French; their vocabularies overlap imperfectly, the prior texts that make up their reservoir of resources and allusions vary, their life experiences and range of associations differ, and so on. In the real world all language is idiolect, and this is as true of English as of French.

What then can translation be? It cannot be the setting over of meaning from one non-existent linguistic abstraction into another; it must be the composition of a particular text by one individual mind in response to another text. Neither of these texts can be understood perfectly, let alone "translated." To try to "translate," in the sense of fully reproducing meaning, is to experience radical failure.

But failure of a most instructive kind, for it brings one to a sense of self and language that is very different from, and erosive of, those that guide our initial expectations. Much the same is true when one tries to "interpret" a text with the idea of reproducing its meaning, or when one seeks to be wholly "obedient" to a text, say by giving it a "literal" reading, or when one wishes to arrive at perfect "understanding" of a text. To attempt to translate puts you in a place between texts, between languages, where you must respect both; to attempt to interpret puts you between the text and the present, where again you must respect both. In either case the more fully you inhabit the original—the more familiar you make it—the stranger and more unsatisfactory your own language (or your own version of the text you are reading) becomes. You always reproduce less than you find in the original, but you always intrude upon it as well, and as you work, you become increasingly conscious of these things. The effect is to render your own language problematic: opaque, awkward, restrictive. You open a chamber of the mind that before was closed and bring under scrutiny that which had theretofore seemed invisible, natural, beyond any imagined contemplation, your language itself.

* * *

But there is another side to all this, for something we call translation takes place all the time, and so do the associated practices of drafting and interpretation. We cannot read a foreign text at all without translating it, at least until we have made the language our own (and it has made us its own). We must talk in our own words about the texts we read, in law and literature and ordinary life alike, and we can sometimes do this satisfactorily. Translation is a necessary part of life. It is the process by which human beings understand and respond to one another.

What is more, we can—indeed we must—judge our own performances of these kinds, and the performances of others, as being done well or badly, of value to us or the reverse. We must not forget that early in this chapter we talked about a Greek text—was that a translation?—and that the remarks of Adjutor Rivard in the Canadian Commission Report may or may not have been translated. (Does it matter whether they were?) Some success is possible, then, if not full and perfect "translation": What is it, and how is it to be talked about?

If we think that the proper measure of a "translation" is the degree to which it succeeds in "setting over" the meaning of an original, we shall indeed find translation to be impossible. But if we think of translation instead as the composition of one text in response to another, as a way of establishing relations by reciprocal gesture, to be judged by criteria of appropriateness, translation can of course "succeed" and do so in ways beyond number. There is no single appropriate response to the text of another, nor even a finite appropriate set of responses; what is called for is a kind of imaginative self-assertion in relation to another. It will be judged by its coherence, by the kinds of fidelity it establishes with the original, and by the ethical and cultural meaning it performs as a gesture of its own.

12

Justice as Translation

Translation as I am now defining it is thus the art of facing the impossible, of confronting unbridgeable discontinuities between texts, between languages, and between people. As such it has an ethical as well as an intellectual dimension. It recognizes the other—the composer of the original text—as a center of meaning apart from oneself. It requires one to discover both the value of the other's language and the limits of one's own. Good translation thus proceeds not by the motives of dominance or acquisition, but by respect. It is a word for a set of practices by which we learn to live with difference, with the fluidity of culture and with the instability of the self. It is not simply an operation of mind on material, but a way of being oneself in relation to another being.

This is the sense in which translation can be an image of thought, a model of social life, including in the law, for all of our life together requires the constant reading of one another's texts and the creation of texts in response to them. The activity of translation in fact offers an education in what is required for this interactive life, for, as I have suggested, to attempt to "translate" is to experience a failure at once radical and felicitous: radical, for it throws into question our sense of ourselves, our languages, of others; felicitous, for it releases us momentarily from the prison of our own ways of thinking and being.

* * *

I say that translation is a way of thinking not only about relations with languages and cultures—relations with "texts"—but about relations with individual people (and groups) as well. The reason is that our conversations with each other have the same structure as our conversations across languages and cultures, namely, this: that what you say to me is never wholly understood by me and is not reproducible in my terms; nonetheless I can, indeed I should and must, create

texts in response to yours about which I claim that they bear a relationship of fidelity to what you say and in this sense do them justice.
My hope is not that they imitate or replicate your text but that they
speak to it faithfully. The central truths of translation are the central
truths of human interaction.

To say this suggests an excellence of mind and character, that of
the good translator, to which we can aspire: an attempt to be oneself
in relation to an always imperfectly known and imperfectly knowable
other who is entitled to a respect equal to our own. It is ultimately a
question of understanding and attitude: recognizing, while we com-
pose our text, its inadequacy as the representation of another, and
finding a way to express that recognition in what we say. To put it
differently, it means the perpetual acknowledgment of the limits of
our minds and languages, the sense that they are bounded by the
minds and languages of others. It is in these ways that the activity I
call "translation"—making texts in response to others while recognizing the impossibility of full comprehension or reproduction—
becomes a set of practices that can serve as an ethical and political
model for the law and, beyond it, as a standard of justice.

* * *

By this I mean nothing out of our ordinary experience, for we
engage in this sort of translation—the creation of texts in response to
texts, meant to honor the other and assert the self—all the time.
Think of the way in which we respond to a painting or a work of
music: we do not just look and listen, we also talk, and write, about
our experience; in fact this "talking and writing," this work in language, is an essential part of the "looking and listening." But we
know perfectly well that our experience of response cannot be reproduced in our own texts, cannot in that sense be translated into words.
The artist painted, the composer thought of sounds, the performer
created sounds because these are the ways in which they could make
what they wanted to make. They wanted their works to be experienced directly, to live in the mind in their original form, not as interpreted or translated into words—to be remembered with the eye and
the ear, not through some interpretation or translation, like a trot or
crib in an art appreciation course. Thus when we talk about a work of
art we do not pretend to be able to produce a text that will substitute
for the original work, but try to find a way to talk about our experience of it that will be helpful to others, and ourselves, to start a conversation of a certain sort. This is largely a matter of drawing attention
to patterns, movements, or other features of the work that might oth-

erwise be out of focus, in this way making it more fully present to the mind; and at the same time asserting oneself with respect to it, locating it in one's own world and expressing a judgment about it from a place of one's own making.

Every conversation of this kind is tentative, suggestive, incomplete: I can never say all that could be said about this painting or sonata, or about who I am in relation to it, and neither can you. In good writing or conversation of this sort our attention is constantly drawn to that fact, to the limits of our own discourse and enterprise. The good critic is always reminding her reader that this is only part of what can be said, that the work of art lives in sound or painting, not these words; her reader is not to stop with the criticism but is to return to the work to make it more fully his own. This is true not only of the plastic arts but of poetry as well, which is a verbal art. Robert Frost first taught poetry (at Lawrence High School) as an art of reading aloud, believing that if the students could read the poems well, they would understand them the only way that poems ask to be understood.[1] Much of the effort of modern poetry is in fact directed towards establishing its nontranslatability, but I think it is true as well of all speech. It is an odd quirk of our own discourse that when we move from painting and music and architecture—and such "personal" experiences as religious belief or physical sensation—to what we think of as prose, or exposition, we suddenly talk as though full translation were possible, as though we could make a text that could substitute for the original.

This is especially a feature of modern academic discourse, which can be seen to proceed as a kind of competition in translation: the psychologist says that all of your experience can be reproduced on his grid, the economist that all transactions between people can be talked about as the "exchanges" they really are, and so on, as if everybody is trying to establish a universal language. It is in fact the radical intellectual vice of our day to insist that everything can be translated into one's own terms. This is the vice of economics, which has no way of seeing itself as one language among many, and of much modern philosophy too, which talks as if all intellectual texts, whatever their form, could be reproduced in a series of propositions cast in a discourse that itself cannot be questioned.

* * *

I am holding out the good translator as a model for us, as defining a set of intellectual and ethical possibilities from which we can learn, both as people and as lawyers. But, you may ask, if the translator lives in the space between two languages how can he act or speak in either? How can he ever have a voice or identity of his own? He is an inherently marginal figure. How can he possibly be a model for the rest of us, especially lawyers, who inhabit the central spaces of our culture? Or, to frame it in the terms just suggested, from what position can the lawyer prefer one language, one person, one set of possibilities over another? How can she make the choices for which she is responsible?

This question assumes that for the most part our voices, or our actions, really are "our own," but to what extent, as things now are for us, is that true? To the extent that we speak and act (however confidently) through inherited forms upon which we do not reflect, we may only seem to have identities or voices of our own, not actually have them. The confidence we feel may be in the culture, not in us. Is it perhaps only the person who opens his mind to two languages, two worlds—to the reality of another—that can have the faintest sense of his own identity in relation to his culture? Perhaps only in the kind of place made by the translator between two worlds is it possible to begin to have a voice of one's own.

And must the translator remain constantly on the margin, between worlds? Why cannot he enter one or another and act and speak with momentary, if qualified, confidence within it? Indeed he can do these things, I think, and do them well. I am saying, then, not that we should all zip to the edge of our cultures and live there forever, but that we should move from immersion in our world and its languages to a place critical of them, on the margin, and then return. There is, as I suggested earlier, a new chamber of the mind and self that we can learn to open and inhabit, the translator's chamber: if we can learn to do this the powers of humanity will be ours in a new way—if we can learn to be conscious at once (or in such quick alternations as to be almost at once) of the languages we use and the intentions we wish to realize through them. Our language would be at once opaque—strange, awkward, the object of thought and criticism—and transparent, invisible, the instrument of social life. Both chambers of our minds would be alive and active, together.

* * *

Think now of the life of the lawyer: in her conversations with her client, from the beginning, her task is to help him tell his story, both in his own language and in the languages into which she will translate it. This conversation proceeds in large part by her questioning, trying to get it straight, suggesting complexities and difficulties, as she tries to help her client understand things more fully both in his terms and so far as possible in the language of the law, in which to a large degree the matter will be negotiated and argued. The client is thus led to learn something of the language of the law; at the same time, the lawyer must learn something of the language of the client; between them they create a series of texts that are necessarily imperfect translations of the client's story into legal terms, and in doing so they also create something new, a discourse in which this story, and others, can have meaning and force of a different kind: the meaning and force of the law.*

The lawyer is thus constantly moving between languages, mediating between them; yet she must also be prepared to immerse herself in verbal action and argument, on one set of terms or another, at any time. She must be ready to speak the client's language as fully as she can, yet ready also to turn to the judge, or other lawyer, and speak in terms—about jurisdiction, say, or conflicts of laws—that will, initially at least, be wholly foreign to the client. Or think of the trial of a case involving technical expertise: here the lawyer must not simply "translate" the expert's "findings" into ordinary English, as if that were a nonproblematic enterprise; she must also learn the technical language herself, and do so well enough to prepare one witness and to cross-examine another, and well enough to teach some of it to the judge and jury as well, a bit as Barker, say, teaches us something of Aristotle's Greek. In this process she will constantly test the expert's language by other languages, to see how it can be challenged or broken down or perhaps remade, just as, indeed, she constantly tests the languages of the parties and of the law itself by putting them in competition with each other.

What is true for the lawyer is true for the law as well: it is a discourse that mediates among virtually all the discourses of our world, all ways of talking, and it does this not on the premise that meaning can be translated from one discourse directly into a different

---

*Think here of the series of conversations by which two people develop a friendship, which will really be a friendship only to the extent that they learn each other's language, and in doing so making a "third" language that they share; or of the conversations by which a good psychoanalysis proceeds, where the analyst learns the language of the analysand, its terms and images and movements, and seeks to integrate it with his own. Or think of the interpretation of painting: the ultimate goal is not to explain in words why this patch of textured crimson appears where it does, but to understand why it does in a different way, in the language of painting itself.

one, but by the creation of texts that are new compositions. In this sense the law (like the lawyer) is both central and marginal at once: it exists at the edge of our discourses, outside all of them, structurally supplementary; yet it is also the discourse of power in our official world. This doubleness is felt by the lawyer, too, who knows that her clients' real lives are elsewhere, that these people are only here in her office because they have to be, and so on, and that in this sense the law and the lawyer are marginal in the extreme. Yet she also knows that her clients have to be there, in her office or someone else's, for the law is the instrument of official power; in this sense it is central as nothing else is. It is crucial to its democratic character that in the end it make sense not only to those who speak the language of the law by profession but to the men and women of a jury: the ultimate translation is into the ordinary language of the citizen.

The existing practices at work in the law thus already call upon the two "chambers" of the mind of which I have spoken and require us to engage in these two sets of practices—the linguistically participatory and the linguistically self-conscious—that they entail. To think of the lawyer's or judge's life as a kind of "translation" brings to the surface, where they may be seen and felt, the tensions produced by this deep feature of our professional life, at once problematic and liberating, requiring an art of which we have only the dimmest awareness, but which at the same time promises us a new sense of ourselves and our possibilities. It is in what we already know how to do that we can find the ground upon which to make our selves and our world in new ways.

* * *

In the law, and to some degree in other translations as well, there is always conflict and always loss: the stories of the two parties conflict or compete (or there would not be a law suit), and do so not only in detail but in their shape and language, in their deepest meanings to the speaker and to others. Neither story, neither language, is the sole source of authority; at some points choices will have to be made that favor one over the other. And both must yield, in much if not in all, to a third force, the language of the law that governs the process as a whole. Something new is made—what Adjutor Rivard might call a new world, the world of the law, with new possibilities of meaning—but something is lost as well. The law builds itself, over time, by discarding possibilities for speech and thought as well as by making them; and what it discards is for some person or people a living language, a living truth. Such losses cannot be avoided, but should be faced directly by the law, and by those who speak its language, as losses for which it, and we, are responsible.

* * *

Think now of the judicial opinion. Properly written it would reflect the competing voices and languages that define the case before it (including those that it ultimately disregards or silences) and thus expose the ground upon which its own result, its own achievement, can be qualified and criticized. When we act, whether as judges or as people, in choosing one possibility over another, or in silencing a voice, it should be with the knowledge that we do so, and this knowledge should find expression in what we say. The art is that of simultaneous affirmation and negation, the art that lies at the center of poetry as well as law.

Translation is thus a species of what in the opening chapter I called "integration": putting two things together in such a way as to make a third, a new thing with a meaning of its own. The effect of the composition is not to merge the two elements, or to blur the distinction between them, but to sharpen the sense we have of each, and of the differences that play between them. Such a composition naturally dissolves in time, and must be remade afresh, in new forms; it is, as Frost said of the poem, "a momentary stay against confusion."

* * *

Is all this a recipe for pure relativism? Is there no truth, you may ask, that is permanent, cross-cultural, valid for both you and me? If communication and understanding and translation, as usually meant, are impossible, and each of us writes as a poet speaking to poets, making texts that cannot adequately be reproduced in other terms, what facts or propositions can count for all of us?

Perhaps only the facts that we all inhabit different languages, which cannot be reproduced in each other's terms, and that each of us is a distinct center of meaning and experience that cannot be reduced to the language of another. The one great human universal then, is that we all speak languages none of which can become a universal language; our universal question is how to relate to one another across this fact.

To conceive of each person as a center of meaning, a maker of a language that is in some respects different from any other, and to acknowledge that this language cannot be translated into other languages (or into some superlanguage) without real loss requires us to give up the dream of an Objective or Universal language of authority, one into which all others can be translated and in which the truth can be spoken plainly and clearly. It requires us to recognize that the insistence upon the adequacy of a single language is a kind of tyranny.

This image of human life asserts an essential and radical equality among us. For if we all speak differently, and there is no superlanguage in which these differences can be defined and adjudicated, what is necessarily called for is a kind of negotiation between us, I from my position—embedded in my language and culture—you from yours. We can and do make judgments, but we need to learn that they are limited and tentative; they can represent what we think, and can be in this sense quite firm, but they should also reflect the recognition that all this would look quite different from some other point of view.

But we should not feel that respect for the other obliges us to erase ourselves, or our culture, as if all value lay out there and none here. As the traditions of the other are entitled to respect, despite their oddness to us, and sometimes despite their inhumanities, so too our own tradition is entitled to respect as well. Our task is to be distinctively ourselves in a world of others: to create a frame that includes both self and other, neither dominant, in a image of fundamental equality. This is true of us as individuals in our relations with other, and true of us as a culture too, as we face the diversity of our world. It is analytically true of translation, which owes fidelity to the other language and text but requires the assertion of one's own as well. This is not the kind of relativism that asserts that nothing can be known, but is itself a way of knowing: a way of seeing one thing in terms of another. Similarly it does not assert that no judgments can be reached, but is itself a way of judging, and of doing so out of a sense of our position in a shifting world.

* * *

All this is to define life as a certain kind of art, an art of composition—of integration or translation—and to define our central communal task as an education in that art. For we are all artists, both in language and in the rest of life. We live on conditions of radical uncertainty and do so often with success, and sometimes with ease. Starting from our first movements in the arms of our parents, we make and manage our own social relations, as we learn about kindness and cruelty, truth and deception, recognition and objectification. As we construct, and reconstruct, the narratives of our lives from their beginnings we make stories or histories, and as these stories are shared—as we make collective stories with others in our families and elsewhere—we create and recreate communities and languages as well. Modern developmental psychology has taught us (if we needed to be taught it) that we do not so much learn our languages as invent them, partly out of the life of the texts we hear, as we try out new forms and see how they work, constantly experimenting. Invention is essential to all learning, from the very first moment of life, and it can remain a present and active part of the intellect to the very end. Ours is a life of language and of art.

But to claim for our lives the quality of art and invention is of course not to say that we are totally free and unconstrained. Quite the verse: art in every field is a way of addressing the limits as well as the resources of one's materials—the limits of one's social and cultural situation, of one's language, of one's mind. Between two nonexistent opposites—total freedom and total constraint—we inhabit a ground that we must fill up by our own activity.

To speak of art is to accept that we speak out of circumstances incompletely known and to others similarly situated. The artist knows that he or she will never have a perfect photograph of the relevant world with every detail in perfect focus, never the sort of representation science once dreamed of or aspired to. Instead, we always act in partial ignorance. In our makings we choose a subject, a direction, and a focus of attention; a starting point, a tone, and a set of terms; and we are responsible for what we choose. Some things and relations will be relatively clear, but always at the price of obscurity elsewhere. An important part of what we can teach each other is where to direct attention, how to focus it—and refocus it—in new ways.

Think of the way we work out our capacity to judge works of art. Not by inducing from the instances of certain masterpieces eternal laws of aesthetic excellence, which we can then turn around and apply to other objects, as if all art objects existed out of time and culture on an enamelled laboratory table, waiting to be classified by merit. Each work speaks to its own world, and is made out of the materials of that world: not only that musical instrument or this array of words, but materials in a purer sense cultural: one's knowledge of the prior works of music, or painting, or poetry, or law, that have formed the expectations of one's audience, that have formed the audience itself, and which one must therefore take as one's starting point. Music is made not only out of musical notes and silences, but out of earlier music. All art is about its culture, its context, and should be understood and judged that way.

As human beings we live on artistic and rhetorical, not scientific, terms. In our most important expressions we argue not from premise to conclusion, but by making whole ways of talking—ways of being and of acting in the language—which we offer each other for adoption, rejection, and modification. It is the modern habit to turn out texts into sets of propositions—of fact, value, or logic—that can be independently analyzed and judged. But little of our talk is propositional in that sense; far more often and deeply is it social and cultural. We persuade most fully by who we become in our practices of language, by who we invite others to become, by the languages we make and the experiences we offer: we persuade more by performance to whole languages, than by argument to propositions. ("Here is my way: what is yours?")

Our standards of judgment come not from a priori reasoning or from theories, but from our own experience of life and of other people. Of course, no one experience or work can stand as a perfect authority. We make sense of what we read as we make sense of life, by putting one tentative judgment together with another, one version of ourselves and our capacities together with another, seeing how it works out, trying it another way, and so on, continually growing and changing by progressive incorporations and discardings. We know how to do this, for we have always done it. These are the processes of reciprocal interaction with other people, with language, and with nature by which we have formed our own identities. We have no deeper knowledge.

* * *

We start by learning languages and social relations in our interactions with our families. Thereafter everything that makes sense to us does so only insofar as it makes sense in terms of what has gone before. A human life is thus made as a poetic or musical text is made, by unfolding out of itself; it is made out of its own origins and first growth, out of the opening line, the opening measures, against which everything that follows plays. The center of our being is the set of social and cultural practices we have been learning and modifying since birth.

The central image is that of autopoiesis, the organism making itself in interaction with its environment. In the process both organism and environment change. There is no one way the universe is constituted, no ultimate ontology upon which everything can be grounded. All species, all individuals, all languages and cultures and communities, are engaged alike in a process of reciprocal change. That is not to be feared but welcomed.

As for law, it too partakes of the radical uncertainty of the rest of life, the want of firm external standards. But it is also a special way of living on these conditions, a way of making standards internally, out of our experience, as we make ourselves in our talk. The law is in fact a method of cultural criticism and cultural transformation, as well as cultural preservation.

* * *

The practice of translation, and interpretation too, demands an excellence, fully attainable by no one, that is ethical as well as intellectual in character: that one be a certain sort of person, with a certain attitude, ready to act out of fidelity to the text in constantly new contexts; it calls for art and invention, for a quality of consciousness that can be heard in the voice; and in doing so it defines a set of opportunities for us both as lawyers and as people.[2]

In the law, the practical effect of such a consciousness, if we could attain it, would be the perpetual erosion of the force and authority of the merely bureaucratic, for the central vice of bureaucratic language—by which I mean the language of planning and the language of theory alike—is that it has no way to admit the value of any other way of talking, any other way of being. The translator, or the translator-lawyer, would thus perpetually resist the claim of bureaucratic language, and of its forms of life, that everything can be translated without loss into its terms; she would similarly challenge the formulations by which the power of one person (or a group) over the lives of another in the private sphere is justified or made to seem natural, by languages that assert their own unquestioned validity. It is the genius of the law to provide a place in which unheard voices can be heard and responded to; it is our task as lawyers to realize this possibility.

But as things now are, when bureaucratic and theoretical modes of thought have so nearly captured law, its future is in doubt: Shall the law be a force for multivocality, for the acknowledgment of the other—a species of translation working by an art that simultaneously asserts the self, and its language, and respects what is outside it—or shall it be reduced to an instrument of bureaucratic and theoretical power?

* * *

In Muslim law there is only one source of authority, the will of God. This is known to humanity only one way, through the words and acts of the Prophet. These in turn are known only through written texts, many of which were written as long as two hundred years after the events they record. Among them there are naturally certain inconsistencies; within them, ambiguities and uncertainties.

In a world driven by the need for certainty, how are these uncertainties to be addressed and tolerated? Mainly by the disciplined scholarly study of the texts and their words, we are told, by the interpretation of one phrase in light of the context created by all the other sacred texts. But different scholars, different schools, will necessarily disagree: How is this disagreement to be faced, by the judge applying the law, by the believer trying to follow it?

The traditional Muslim answer has been that all of the several readings of a text are valid, notwithstanding their inconsistency, if they are each reached by a mind diligently engaged, in good faith, in a search for its meaning.[3] The judge, or the believer, can follow any of them and still follow the law: but his choice too must arise from a good-faith search for meaning, within his capacities. A world of difference is thus created; it is kept from the prison-house of "single meanings"—of thinking that meanings translate directly from text to text—by honest attention to language, to particularity of phrase and context; it is kept from the chaos of indifferent relativism—of thinking that nothing can be known or understood, no common values held—by a principle of humility and sincerity, or what I would call the ethic of the translator.

* * *

At a time when British psychoanalysis was badly split between the camp of Melanie Klein (whose adherents apparently parroted her formulas in a way most irritating to others), and that of Anna Freud, the literal heir of the Master, David Winnicott, concerned for the health of the psychoanalytic community as a whole, wrote to Klein—who had been his own teacher—about this matter in the following terms:

> I personally think that it is very important that your work should be restated by people discovering in their own way and presenting what they discover in their own language. It is only in this way that the language will be kept alive. If you make the stipulation that in future only your language shall be used for the statement of other people's discoveries then the language becomes a dead language, as it has already become in the Society.[4]

What this suggests is that while "translation" is impossible—and we should school ourselves to speak in a way that recognizes that fact—the creation of our own texts in response to others is not only permissible and necessary, it is a good thing. It is the way culture is made, not only in the law and literature, but far more deeply than that, as we translate into the present the prior texts that define our collective memory and make us what we are.[5] Fidelity to the prior text itself requires that we "translate" it in the only way we can do so, by making texts of our own in response to it, composed not in its language but in our own. The poet is right to say that her poems cannot be translated; but they can be imitated, learned from, and talked about in the languages of others. The art by which this is done well is the art of recognizing the difference between two languages, two worlds, two people, yet speaking across it nonetheless. This is that point at which description and explanation exhaust themselves, and only performance can have meaning.

The proper object of human community is the recognition of the equal value of each person as a center of worth and meaning, as one who lives in a perpetual process of reciprocal interaction with nature, language, and other people, by which he is made and through which he makes himself. In this we are at once the same and different: the same in the essentials of our situation—in our dependence on culture and our need to remake it, in the creative center of our lives—but different in what we make, for each of us is ultimately unique. Our deepest obligation and highest hope is to create a world in which each person is fully recognized, in which each may achieve the realization of his or her capacities for life. That is easy to say and has often been said. The major difficulty is to give it meaning not at the level of concept or theory but in literary and intellectual practice, in our speech and conduct. This is the task of the art that unites justice and translation.

NOTES

Introduction

1. Thomas Hobbes, *Leviathan*, Pt. One, Chs. 4 and 5 (1651).

2. In philosophy this kind of thinking has been done most powerfully by the later Wittgenstein, though mention should also be made of Stanley Cavell, *Must We Mean What We Say? A Book of Essays* (1969) and *This New Yet Unapproachable America* (1989). Others who have taken a similar view of language include A. L. Becker in linguistics (esp. "Biography of a Sentence: A Burmese Proverb," in *Text, Play, and Story: The Construction and Reconstruction of Self and Society* [E. M. Bruner ed. 1984] and *Beyond Translation* [forthcoming]); Clifford Geertz in anthropology (esp. *Local Knowledge: Further Essays in Interpretive Anthropology* [1983] and *Works and Lives: The Anthropologist as Author* [1988]); Erving Goffman in sociology (esp. *Forms of Talk* [1981]); Richard Poirier in literary criticism (esp. *The Renewal of Literature: Emersonian Reflections* [1987] and *Robert Frost: The Work of Knowing* [1977]); Donald McCloskey in economics (esp. *The Rhetoric of Economics* [1985]); and Leston Havens in psychiatry (esp. *Making Contact: The Uses of Language in Psychotherapy* [1986]).

Chapter One

1. See, e.g., Washington v. United States, 390 F.2d 444 (D.C. Cir. 1967).

2. Edmund Wilson, "Books of Etiquette and Emily Post," in *A Literary Chronicle: 1920–1950*, p. 380 (Anchor ed. 1950).

3. What would happen if we took this seriously as a prescription for our own work?

One consequence would be that others would find what we wrote difficult to read. They would find it hard to understand what we wrote as history, or as law, or as literary theory; they would find that what we said did not fall neatly into focus given their present lenses, that parts were too near and parts were too far away; they would want to reduce or translate what we produced into other terms, to locate it in contexts not of our making, which they would feel would explain it. But if we wrote well our insights would not be portable, nor our texts readily outlined or skim-read. When people asked

us to be explicit in saying what we "mean," we would have to prepare ourselves, and them, for disappointment, since the language of explicit statement denies many of the ways we hope our texts would have meaning. We
would hope to speak in ways that could not readily be translated into the
propositional and assertive forms that are second nature to the academic
world; for instead of integrating diversity, such forms collapse the possibilities of speech to a single rather monotonous plane, in which it is indeed hard
to "tell the truth."

4. "The Figure a Poem Makes," in *Complete Poems of Robert Frost*,
p. v, vi (1965).

Chapter Two

1. Thucydides, *The Peloponnesian War*, pp. 189–91 (Crawley trans.
1951).

2. See *When Words Lose Their Meaning*, especially chapters 1 and 10
(1984). The title of that book was in fact suggested by the passage from Thucydides reproduced in the text.

3. See Milton Friedman, "The Methodology of Positive Economics," in
Essays in Positive Economics, pp. 3, 7 (1953).

4. Another danger, very widely realized in our own world, is that talk
about concepts tends to nominalize, and hence to reify, everything. The verb,
the adverb, the adjective all give way to the noun. The effect is to create a
universe of imagined intellectual objects arranged in quantitative or spatial
relations to each other but without the principle of life that is found in the
active verb. Imagine a language that emphasized the verb instead of the noun
and copula; our thought would be full of a sense of movement, life, and
change, of actors engaged in action.

For a fuller sense of this possibility, see the opening chapter of St. Augustine's *Confessions*, the whole point of which is to analyze not "concepts"
but practices—the practices of faith—as these are enacted in a series of verbs:
"praise," "invoke," "know," and "believe."

5. Of course one can talk about the "concepts" of others with an emphasis on the differences, in an effort to recognize and value another way of
thought and life, as Alasdair MacIntyre does in the book quoted above. But I
think that to use the term "concept" as a central part of one's vocabulary in
such an enterprise is to undercut the enterprise itself, to move oneself and
one's reader in the direction of thinking that the concepts exist apart from
language and that they can thus be seen by us directly and talked about in
our language without loss.

6. Consider especially the efforts of modern analytic philosophers to
translate into propositional and conceptual forms Wittgenstein's *Philosophical
Investigations*, a text that is meant to undermine those very forms. (For a good
discussion, see Stroud, "An End to Anxiety" [Book Review], London Review
of Books, July 18, 1985, p. 14.)

Wittgenstein said that the measure of understanding was whether one "knew how to go on," for example with a mathematical sequence. But most philosophers have tried to turn Wittgenstein into their kind of text rather than "going on" in the way he marked out.

Another way to put this is to say that while the rigid distinction between fact and value that characterized the kind of logical positivism that the later Wittgenstein opposed is no longer accepted as correct by most philosophers, the conception of reason that characterized that movement is still dominant. In this respect the work of Wittgenstein has yet to have its full effect. For promising beginnings in a new direction see Stanley Cavell, *This New Yet Unapproachable America* (1989) and Thomas Eisele, "Wittgenstein's Instructive Narratives: Leaving the Lessons Latent" (forthcoming).

For a work that explicitly recognizes the inadequacy of the kinds of assumptions at work in talk about concepts, see Owen Barfield, *Poetic Diction* (1928).

7. This is not to say that there is therefore no meaning, that language "doesn't work," or anything like that. Language has meaning, but not of the kind implied in most conceptual and analytic talk; it works and works well, but on its own terms, not those of scientific rationalism.

8. For an especially rich statement of the ways in which context gives meaning, see A. L. Becker, "Biography of a Sentence: A Burmese Proverb," in *Text, Play, and Story: The Construction and Reconstruction of Self and Society*, p. 136ff (E. M. Bruner ed. 1984) and *Beyond Translation* (forthcoming).

9. Consider here the different meanings of Robinson Crusoe's name "Master": (1) to the man Crusoe calls "Friday" as he learns it and (2) in the language he is learning, that is, the meaning to the reader. See note to page 31 above.

10. *The Federalist Papers*, p. 33 (C. Rossiter ed. 1961).

11. For a fine book on Jane Austen's language, see Stuart Tave, *Some Words of Jane Austen* (1973).

12. Think of your own first thoughts about learning a language: How different everything would be if you were to greet your neighbor, or your teacher, in French; or order a beer in German; or ask about the weather in Spanish. As sophisticated people we are likely to feel superior to such youthful and romantic expectations, but here, as often, the young and ingenuous have something we should pay attention to.

Or think of grammar: Is this the blueprint by which the language is built, the engineer's design document? Much language-teaching seems to assume so, but of course nothing could be further from the truth. Grammar is what we use when we do not have enough experience of a language to make it our own.

Chapter Three

1. The work that established law and economics as a generally visible field was Richard A. Posner, *Economic Analysis of Law* (1973). See also Robert Cooter and Thomas Ulen, *Law and Economics* (1988). For an introduction to

the methodology of microeconomics see Donald N. McCloskey, *The Applied Theory of Price* (2d ed. 1985). This is a particularly valuable book because the author is highly critical of the "scientific" claims of economics, but nonetheless devoted to it as a method. See also Donald N. McCloskey, *The Rhetoric of Economics* (1985).

A useful attempt to locate the way modern economists think and talk more globally, especially in their disagreements, is Arjo Klamer, *Conversations with Economists* (1983). For a recent book that locates economic analysis in the context of a particular kind of capitalist economy and subjects both to intelligent criticism, see Robert L. Heilbroner, *The Nature and Logic of Capitalism* (1985). An interesting attempt to apply the reasoning of economics to the "non-economic" use of one's time is S. B. Linder, *The Harried Leisure Class* (1970).

In addition, the reader may find the following books of some use: Isaac D. Balbus, *Marxism and Domination* (1982); Gary S. Becker, *The Economic Approach to Human Behavior* (1976); Mark Blaug, *The Methodology of Economics* (1980); Stephen Gudeman, *Economics As Culture* (1986); Richard A. Posner, *The Economics of Justice* (1981); Marshall Sahlins, *Culture and Practical Reason* (1976); E. F. Schumacher, *Small Is Beautiful: Economics As If People Mattered* (1975); T. Scitovsky, *The Joyless Economy* (1976); and the Symposium on Law and Economics that appeared in 85 *Columbia Law Review* 899 (1985).

Important articles include: Ackerman, "Law, Economics, and the Problem of Legal Culture," 1986 *Duke Law Journal* 929; Kelman, "Choice and Utility," 1979 *Wisconsin Law Review* 769; Kennedy, "Cost-Benefit Analysis of Entitlement Problems: A Critique," 33 *Stanford Law Review* 387 (1981); Leff, "Economic Analysis of Law: Some Realism about Nominalism," 60 *Virginia Law Review* 451 (1974); MacNeil, "Bureaucracy, Liberalism, and Community—American Style," 79 *Northwestern University Law Review* 900 (1985); Michelman, "Norms and Normativity in the Economic Theory of Law," 62 *Minnesota Law Review* 1015 (1978); Mishan, "The Folklore of the Market: An Inquiry into the Economic Doctrines of the Chicago School," 9 *Journal of Economic Issues* 681 (1975); Priest, "The New Scientism in Legal Scholarship: A Comment on Clark and Posner," 90 *Yale Law Journal* 1284 (1981); Reder, "Chicago Economics: Permanence and Change," 20 *Journal of Economic Literature* 1 (1982); Tribe, "Technology Assessment and the Fourth Discontinuity: The Limits of Instrumental Rationality," 46 *Southern California Law Review* 617 (1973); Williamson, "Intellectual Foundations: The Need for a Broader View," 33 *Journal of Legal Education* 210 (1983).

2. I speak here of total desire. Economics of course recognizes the declining marginal utility of particular items of consumption. And economics does not limit this desire to material goods, but includes whatever acquisitions will make the actor "happy." But in this system happiness is quantified on the assumption that every actor wants the "most" that he can get, which this is to speak of human life as acquisition or domination, not development or growth. For discussion of the consequences of this line of thought, see Linder, note 1 above, and Scitovsky, note 1 above.

3. Easterbrook, "Method, Result, and Authority: A Reply," 98 *Harvard Law Review* 622 (1985).

4. The economists' conception of the kind of reasoning that is at work in the world they describe or imagine is reinforced by the kind of reasoning they engage in themselves, which is logical and deductive in nature and in its own way equally narrow; or at least this is what they claim. For a different view of economic reasoning, see Donald N. McCloskey, *The Rhetoric of Economics* (1985).

5. See Milton Friedman, "The Methodology of Positive Economics," in *Essays in Positive Economics*, pp. 3, 7 (1953). For a response, see the Nutter Lecture delivered by Ronald Coase, "How Should Economists Choose?" (American Enterprise Institute [1982]).

6. On this point see Coase, note 5 above, pp. 6–7.

7. See generally Ian Robinson, *The Survival of English* (1973); George Orwell, "Politics and the English Language," in *Collected Essays*, p. 162 (1961).

8. It is hard to exaggerate the magnitude of the claims that have been made for economics. In *The Economic Approach to Human Behavior*, for example, Gary Becker says that in his view "the economic approach provides a united framework for understanding behavior that has long been sought by and eluded Bentham, Comte, Marx, and others." Becker, note 1 above, p. 12. Judge Easterbrook says that "economics is applied rationality." Easterbrook, note 3 above, p. 625. Or take this remark by George J. Stigler: "All of man's deliberative, forward-looking behavior follows the principles of economics." Convocation Address, *The University of Chicago Record*, p. 2 (June 1, 1981).

9. For differing views on this question see T. Scitovsky, note 1 above, and Stigler & Becker, "De Gustibus Non Est Disputandum," 67 *American Economic Review* 76 (1977).

10. My point here goes beyond the issue of constraint to the assumption of economics that all choices are comparable. In fact, choosing what to do with one's money is radically different from choosing what to do with one's body, one's time, or one's mind. To deny this assumes a commensurability that experience denies.

11. For a colloquy on this point between a critic and a friend of economics, see West, "Autonomy, and Choice: The Role of Consent in the Moral and Political Visions of Franz Kafka and Richard Posner," 99 *Harvard Law Review* 384 (1985); Posner, "The Ethical Significance of Free Choice: A Reply to Professor West," 99 *Harvard Law Review* 1431 (1986); and West, "Submission, Choice, and Ethics: A Rejoinder to Judge Posner," 99 *Harvard Law Review* 1449 (1986).

12. It is of course true that in talking about the relations among the entities it thus creates, economics speaks not in "either/or" terms but of continuous functions, but this does not change my point in the text.

13. The neutrality of economic discourse as to gender, race, class, and so on, which seems to make it an egalitarian system, works in practice simply a mask for the validation of whatever inequalities actually exist in the world, which it leaves untouched.

I would of course not want to deny that our democratic polity can itself exploit, oppress, and disempower, for it can and does. But it does so against its own ideals, against the pressure of its institutions and languages, not in accordance with them.

14. See generally Wendell Berry, *Home Economics* (1987); *The Gift of Good Land* (1981); *The Unsettling of America* (1977). See also "Farm Achieves Natural Balance," Washington Post, March 1, 1987, p. A3, col. 1.

15. See James Gustafson, *Ethics from a Theocentric Perspective* (1981).

16. It is of course true that one achievement of modern economics has been to think seriously about the ways in which an activity or enterprise exacts costs from others that are not reflected in the market price of the goods or services produced. The market ideology I have been discussing, at least in its welfare rather than its libertarian mode, naturally regards this, like any market imperfection, as a bad thing: people should pay for what they get, or the whole calculus of competing utilities is upset and we lose our confidence that market exchanges increase the total welfare. In this sense economics does make an attempt to think about what I call the social and natural matrix, and much of what has been done along these lines has been helpful, particularly, I suppose, in the environmental field. But when it does so, it thinks not in terms of the community or the natural world that may be injured or improved, but in terms of individuals suffering gains or losses. Its basic view of the relation between humankind and nature, its reduction of community to individuals, and its methods of valuation remain the same, and these tend to be skewed in the way I suggest in the text.

One way to frame this point is in terms of responsibility: the tendency of economic discourse is to deny responsibility for maintaining the natural and cultural base of wealth, just as it is to deny responsibility for the poor and incompetent. But, putting aside the question of morality, the assumption that one can safely do these things is hardly plausible. Compare Krier & Gillette, "The Uneasy Case for Technological Optimism," 84 *Michigan Law Review* 405 (1985).

17. Henry David Thoreau, *Walden*, p. 143 (Mod. Libr. ed. 1950). Elsewhere he says, "He is the richest who has most use for nature as raw material of tropes and symbols with which to describe his life." Thoreau, *Journal*, 5:203.

18. Joseph Conrad, *The Mirror of the Sea*, p. 30 (Dent Collected ed. 1946).

19. In this sense the modern economics of which I speak is radical, revolutionary really, rather than conservative. Compare the economics of Edmund Burke, for example, which included in its purview the need for the improvement and conservation of both the culture and the land as well as their productive uses. See generally, Edmund Burke, *Reflections on the Revolution in France* (1790).

20. See Isaac D. Balbus, note 1 above. On the other hand, Marx is always interested in the meaning of economic activity for the actors, in the power relations built into the forms of economic life, and with the problems of cultural criticism. For a helpful attempt to look at our economic ideology

from a point of view that might be described as eclectically Marxist, see Robert Heilbroner, note 1 above.

21. Schumacher, note 1 above, pp. 54–57. I owe this reference to Alton Becker. Compare Marshall Sahlins, *Stone Age Economics* (1972).

22. Economics has made real contributions to the law, in teaching us, as Ronald Coase has done, that we should focus our attention on the degree to which any arrangements we try to impose may be bargained away, (see Coase, "The Problem of Social Cost," 3 *Journal of Law and Economics*, 1 [1980]) or, as Judge Posner has done, that there can be new ways to think about "negligence" and "strict liability," (see Posner, note 1 above, pp. 160–65) or, more traditionally, that the actual burden of a tax may fall upon someone different from the one who pays it in the first instance. But the greatest contribution of this work has been to complicate our sense of our own language, and of the world, by showing us that other, often paradoxical, formulations are possible. It offers some of the mischievous pleasure of disturbing settled views. As one voice among many, one way of claiming meaning among many, it thus has a place in the legal process even outside the economic zone. It offers a way of arguing that should be met on the merits; one point of the present chapter is indeed to start to do that.

23. For a splendid analysis of mechanistic thought in the modern world, see Hugh Kenner, *The Counterfeiters: An Historical Comedy* (1968), or, even better, Jonathan Swift's *A Tale of a Tub* (1704).

24. Legal language has conceptual elements too, but the tendency of the law to become a purely conceptual system is systematically undercut by the pressures of the particular case, by the recognition that legal terms can (and will) be perpetually redefined, and by the knowledge that each case has two sides. The law is a system for the change of language as well as its application.

25. See Cooter and Rappoport, "Were the Ordinalists Wrong About Welfare Economics?," 22 *Journal of Economic Literature* 507 (1984) (discussing the difference between this kind of "agnostic" economics and an earlier one that saw certain needs, such as food, shelter, health, as primary).

26. The poor man, out of desperation, will often engage in other sorts of gambling, from numbers to slot machines. But poker, like the market, is a game not of luck but of skill on certain conditions, and the player with limited funds faces a worse fate than simply having numerical odds against him. How would you respond to an invitation to spend a pleasant evening playing Monopoly, on the understanding that one of the players started with three-quarters of the total wealth?

The shifting value of money can be suggested by a question of another kind: How would you like to be given one million dollars? Ten million? A billion or a hundred billion? At some point it would run, and ruin, your life. For all of us who are not insane—I think of Ferdinand Marcos here—the value of money ultimately becomes negative.

27. At this point, as I suggested above, some apologists for economics would concede the point and say that it is not our object to make people equal

but to maximize efficiency, "not to distribute wealth but to create it." If inequality promotes that, we are as a group by hypothesis better off. This move demonstrates one of the peculiarities of economic reasoning alluded to above, its necessary emptiness on philosophical and moral questions. Two economists may agree on the beauty of the market system, one grounding his belief in an unarticulated, or barely articulated, statement about the value of autonomy or liberty, the other on a similarly conclusory statement about the value of efficiency. But it is a consequence of the value-neutrality described above that the economists *as economists* have no way of talking about these important differences. These remain external to economic discourse, just as other values do. Economic discourse, though radically value-laden, is incapable of transforming itself into a discourse about value.

28. One response to this line of argument is to say that if the future is misvalued, it is only through the use of an inappropriate discount rate. But the difficulty cannot be solved by simply changing the discount rate, for, owing to the uncertainty as to the cultural and social base upon which economics ultimately depends, it is impossible to have any rate in which one can have confidence over an extended period of time. What is more, the value of money (or other medium of exchange) is itself completely dependent upon the larger social, natural, and cultural context of which economic exchange is only a part.

29. I include in the term "public" not only those facilities owned or managed by public agencies, but those that perform public functions, most of which are subsidized by our tax system.

30. The attempt to destroy the idea, and value, of institutions can extend even to governmental institutions. See e.g., Easterbrook, "The Supreme Court 1983 Term—Foreword: The Court and the Economic System," 98 *Harvard Law Review* 4 (1984). But see Macey, "Promoting Public-Regarding Legislation Through Statutory Interpretation: An Interest Group Model," 86 *Columbia Law Review* 223 (1986).

Chapter Four

1. *Dialogue on John Dewey*, p. 58 (Corliss Lamont ed. 1959).

2. 342 U.S. 165 (1952).

3. For more successful critiques, see, Aleinikoff, "Constitutional Law in the Age of Balancing," 96 *Yale Law Journal* 943 (1987); Nagel, "The Formulaic Constitution," 84 *Michigan Law Review* 165 (1985) and *Constitutive Cultures: The Mentality and Consequences of Judicial Review* (1988); and Joseph Vining, *The Authoritative and the Authoritarian* (1986).

4. Jonathan Swift, *A Tale of a Tub*, p. 95 (A. C. Guthkelch and D. N. Smith eds. 1920).

5. See, e.g., White, "Doctrine in a Vacuum: Reflections on What a Law School Ought (and Ought Not) To Be," 36 *Journal of Legal Education* 155 (1986).

6. There is a tendency in this tradition to avoid the problem of criticism by seeing one's task as scientific explanation alone. One shows how the result

was determined not by the law but by social, political, psychological, or economic forces external to it. In form this is not to judge but merely to explain. In such work the nonlegal reality examined is the antecedent, not the result, of the judicial case. But this exclusively backward-looking focus is hard to maintain, to say the least, and when such an analyst looks forward, and seeks to describe, and to judge, the future created by an opinion, he is likely to do so in whatever language he has used to describe, or create, past reality.

In its crudest form the tendency of this kind of realism is to reduce not only the opinion but all verbal activity (except its own) to an epiphenomenon at best, hypocrisy at worst, and all conduct to behaviorism. This kind of thinking obviously offers little assistance either to the judge faced with the tasks of deciding a case and writing an opinion or to the lawyer addressing him or her. And in all the forms that I know it, including the most sophisticated, "legal realism" suffers from the defect of being unaware that what we see as the larger social "reality" is itself in large measure the function of our language and our habits of mind, not simply and factually "there" to be observed. "Reality," that is—like the "law"—is not discovered but made; and we are responsible for the realities we make, including those by which we propose to test the law.

7. These questions are false, as I have elsewhere argued, because neither extreme can be adopted to the exclusion of the other—they are like asking whether you favor "form" over "content," for example, or "reason" over "emotion," or wish to follow the "letter" or the "spirit" of the law. See *Heracles' Bow*, pp. 79–81 (1985).

8. Stanley Fish, *Is There a Text in This Class? The Authority of Interpretive Communities* (1980).

9. To focus on this aspect of reading is sometimes called "ethical criticism." For a splendid book pursuing this line of thought, see Wayne C. Booth, *The Company We Keep: An Ethics of Fiction* (1988).

10. 342 U.S. 165 (1952).

11. 338 U.S. 25 (1949).

12. 324 U.S. 401, 412, 418 (1945). But Frankfurter here quotes from his own concurring opinion, not that of the Court, and this, to say the least, undercuts the appearance of respect for the authority of others that the quotation creates.

13. These are similar to the terms in which Frankfurter glowingly describes Harvard Law School and the Harvard Law Review. *Felix Frankfurter Reminisces*, pp. 26–29 (Harlan Philips ed. 1960).

14. Compare Henry Maine's views on the similarity of the education by which the Roman Praetor and the English Chancellor were prepared for their positions of great discretionary power, in *Ancient Law: Its Connection with the Early History of Society and its Relation to Modern Ideas*, pp. 61–65 (1861; Beacon Press ed. 1963).

15. One might usefully compare Frankfurter's opinion in *Rochin* with John Marshall's opinion in *McCulloch v. Maryland*. I discuss this opinion in Chapter 9 of *When Words Lose Their Meaning*, where I argue that Marshall

defines the Constitution in a striking way: as the act of a mythical figure, "The People of the United States," who existed at one time and for one purpose only, namely the creation of this document, after which they resolved themselves into the competing political and economic factions that we see around us. For Marshall the Constitution is thus a kind of testamentary trust, and he uses this conception of the Constitution to explain, and to justify, the extremely generous way in which he proposes to interpret the language of that instrument. Since the Author has departed forever from the world, the text is necessarily dependent upon a powerful interpreter for its effectuation, a role Marshall is happy to claim for himself.

But this is not just a claim of power. His image of the Constitution as a trust gives him a language for talking about—for both justifying and limiting—the kind of power he claims, namely that the document should be interpreted as a trust rather than as a legal code, by the principles of equity rather than those of law. That is his theory, and his actual performance can be tested against it; in this case it fits quite beautifully with it.

One effect is to claim that his role is, despite appearances, in an important sense democratic. The testator is none other than "The People of the United States," who existed as a unit at one moment in time only, when the Constitution was made and ratified, and have since resolved themselves into the constituent parts of that Constitution: into states, governors, citizens, congressman, parties, factions, economic interests, and the like. The implicit message is that the legislative process can be no more than the reflection of the competition of these various interest, inherently a kind of compromise. The Constitution, however, can be the ultimate and final statement by a unified people of its aims and values. Of course, the Constitution is not self-interpreting—it needs someone to read and to apply its terms—but the interpreter, if he reads rightly, is always serving the will of the people. Marshall's opinion thus creates the conditions under which the reader will feel the propriety, even the necessity, of the claim Marshall is making, to be the authorized interpreter of this authoritative, almost sacred document.

Chapter Five

1. 41 U.S. (16 Pet.) 539 (1842).
2. Dred Scott v. Sandford, 60 U.S. (19 How.) 393 (1857).
3. U.S. Const. art. IV, sec. 2, cl. 3. This clause, which is quoted in the text, is traditionally called the fugitive slave clause, but it makes no mention of slaves or slavery, and an argument can be made that it does not apply to slaves at all but only to indentured servants. *See* Douglass, "The Constitution of the United States: Is it Proslavery or Antislavery?" in, *The Life and Writings of Frederick Douglass*, vol. 2, p. 475 (P. Foner ed., 1950):

> [This clause] applies to a very large class of persons—namely redemptioners—persons who had come to America from Holland, from Ireland, and other quarters of the globe—like the Coolies to the West Indies—and had, for a consideration duly paid, become bound to "serve and labour" for the parties to whom their service

and labour was due. It applies to indentured apprentices and others who had become bound for a consideration, under contract duly made, to serve and labour. To such persons this provision applies, and only to such persons. The plain reading of this provision shows that it applies, and that it can only properly and legally apply, to persons "bound to service." Its object plainly is, to secure the fulfillment of contracts for "service and labour." It applies to indentured apprentices, and any other persons from whom service and labour may be due. The legal condition of the slave puts him beyond the operation of this provision. He is not described in it. He is a simple article of property. He does not owe and cannot owe service. He cannot even make a contract. It is impossible for him to do so. He can no more make such a contract than a horse or an ox can make one. This provision, then, only respects persons who owe service, and they only owe service who can receive an equivalent and make a bargain. The slave cannot do that, and is therefore exempted from the operation of this fugitive provision. In all matters where laws are taught to be made the means of oppression, cruelty, and wickedness, I am for strict construction. I will concede nothing. It must be shown that it is so nominated in the bond. The pound of flesh, but not one drop of blood. The very nature of law is opposed to all such wickedness, and makes it difficult to accomplish such objects under the forms of law.

(I owe this reference to Sanford Levinson.)

4. Fugitive Slave Act, ch. 7, sec. 3, 1 Stat. 302, 302–305 (1793) (repealed 1850).

5. 98 Eng. Rep. 499 (K.B. 1772).

6. Perhaps this is too strong. After all, sections 1 and 3 of article IV of the Constitution explicitly empower Congress to pass effectuating legislation. The absence of such provisions in sections 2 and 4 (guaranteeing a republican form of government) might well be read as significant omissions.

7. As I said above, I am for the moment putting aside the familiar argument that there can, in the nature of things, be no unitary intent of the framers to look to, both because it is unclear who should count as framers—the drafters? the voters? those who have refrained from amending?—and what should count as intent—one's motives for acquiescing in the language? One's hope or desire, or one's expectation, as to how the language will in fact be read?

Where, as here and as often, there is an element of compromise, the question of intent is muddied still further, for the "framers" have opposing motives and hopes, and perhaps opposing expectations too.

8. See p. 279 n. 15, above.

9. This is revealed especially in his "Rules of Interpretation of the Constitution," in *Commentaries on the Constitution of the United States*, vol. 3, pp. 397–457 (1858).

Compare the brief section of Blackstone's *Commentaries* that treats interpretation of legislation. The object is to discover the "intention" of the legislature through the "signs" the legislature has used: its words, read in the context of their enactment and in light of the wisdom or folly of their effect, given what we know of the general purposes of the act in question. The reader is to move in order from words to context to effect to reason, going on to the next step only when uncertainty forces him to do so. William Blackstone, 1 *Commentaries on the Laws of England*, p. 59 (W. Lewis ed. 1898). On the special meaning of the word "intention" in eighteenth-century legal discourse, see Powell, "The Original Understanding of Original Intent," 98 *Harvard Law Review* 885, 894–902 (1985).

10. Story did this on behalf of the national legislature through the doctrines of preemption and preclusion and on behalf of the judiciary directly. See, e.g., *Swift v. Tyson*, 41 U.S. (16 Pet.) 1 (1842). This is his version of judicial nationalism, built on Marshall's but going beyond it.

11. See Finkelman, "*Prigg v. Pennsylvania* and Northern State Courts: Anti-Slavery Use of a Pro-Slavery Decision," 25 *Civil War History* 5 (1979). This may be true in the short term, but in the longer run *Prigg* may have contributed to the passage of the Fugitive Slave Act of 1850, far harsher than the one at issue here. For example, a court determining the status of one alleged to be a slave was, under the terms of that Act, prohibited from hearing the testimony of that person herself.

12. Dred Scott v. Sandford, 60 U.S. (19 How.) 393, 452 (1857). Only slightly less dramatic were two other holdings: that territorial governments could not exclude slavery until the moment of statehood and that the effect of a slave's residence in a free state was to be determined by the law of the state to which the slave was returned. *Id.* On this case generally, see Don E. Fehrenbacher, *The Dred Scott Case: Its Significance in American Law and Politics* (1978).

13. On the relation between biological and sociological race, see *St. Francis College v. Al-Khazraji*, 481 U.S. 604 (1987) (summary of argument reported at 55 U.S. Law Week 3579 [1987]); Conrad Kottak, *Anthropology: The Exploration of Human Diversity*, ch. 3 (3d ed. 1982); Charles Wagley ed., *Race and Class in Rural Brazil* (2d ed. 1972); Marvin Harris, *Patterns of Race in the Americas* (1964). If you are doubtful, ask yourself this: For what purposes would a person wish to affirm that "races" exist as a matter of "natural fact"?

14. See, e.g., the story of the Sutpen family in William Faulkner, *Absalom! Absalom!* (1951).

15. There are only two ways in which one can become a citizen of the United States: "by naturalization, which is committed by the Constitution to the Congress; and by birth, but that right can attach only to the class and description of persons who were at the time of the adoption of the Constitution recognized as citizens in the several states." None of the states, Taney says, recognized persons of African descent as citizens at that time; therefore none can make them citizens now.

This line of reasoning assumes that the racial category employed by the defendant in his plea was universally accepted by all the framers of the Constitution and by all of the members of the body politic who adopted it, with the aim of excluding that class from membership in the polity. The idea is that all of the members of the founding community, who made the government for themselves and for their "posterity," desired to exclude from that community all members of the African "race," whether or not biologically part of that posterity. Nothing in the Constitution itself indicates this view or supports it. Taney's argument rests entirely upon a construction of the wishes and desires of those who framed and adopted the Constitution, or what he calls their original "intent."

16. The Court says:

"[Such statutes are a] faithful index to the state of feeling towards the class of persons of whom they speak, and of the position they occupied throughout the thirteen colonies, in the eyes and thoughts of the men who framed the Declaration of Independence and established the State Constitutions and Governments. They show that a perpetual and impassable barrier was intended to be erected between the white race and the one which they had reduced to slavery, and governed as subjects with absolute and despotic power, and which they then looked upon as so far below them in the scale of created beings, that intermarriages between white persons and negroes or mulattoes were regarded as unnatural and immoral, and punished as crimes, not only in the parties, but in the person who joined them in marriage. And no distinction in this respect was made between the free negro or mulatto and the slave, but this stigma, of the deepest degradation, was fixed upon the whole race." (60 U.S. at 409)

17. Here is the language:

"It would give to persons of the negro race, who were recognized as citizens in any one State of the Union, the right to enter every other State whenever they pleased, singly or in companies, without pass or passport, and without obstruction, to sojourn there as long as they pleased, to go where they pleased at every hour of the day or night without molestation, unless they committed some violation of law for which a white man would be punished; and it would give them the full liberty of speech in public and in private upon all subjects upon which its own citizens might speak; to hold public meetings upon political affairs, and to keep and carry arms wherever they went." (60 U.S. at 417)

Taney's remarks are offered as a *reductio ad absurdum*, appealing to the reader's own social instincts: any result such as this is utterly unthinkable. For a seriously different version of this history, see Justice MacLean's dissenting opinion.

18. For further discussion, see *Heracles' Bow*, ch. 5 (1985).

19. See, e.g., A. L. Becker, "Biography of a Sentence: A Burmese Proverb" in *Text, Play and Story: The Construction and Reconstruction of Self and Society*, p. 136 (E. Bruner ed. 1984) and *Beyond Translation* (forthcoming).

Chapter Six

1. 277 U.S. 438 (1928).

2. See, e.g., United States v. Knotts, 460 U.S. 276 (1983) (beeper signals); Cardwell v. Lewis, 417 U.S. 583 (1974) (paint scrapings); Davis v. Mississippi, 394 U.S. 721 (1969) (fingerprints); Schmerber v. California, 384 U.S.

757 (1966) (blood samples); Terry v. Ohio, 392 U.S. 1 (1968) ("stop and frisk"); United States v. Miller, 425 U.S. 435 (1976) (bank accounts); United States v. Place, 462 U.S. 696 (1983) (dogs sniffing luggage); United States v. White, 401 U.S. 745 (1971) (tape recording made by undercover agent). (*White* is discussed in Ch. 7 below.)

3. 255 U.S. 298 (1921).

4. Taft's summaries of the cases dealing with the fourth amendment since *Boyd v. United States*, 116 U.S. 616 (1886), are, as I said above, descriptive and conclusory. His apparent aim—as it is with respect to the language of the fourth amendment, too—is that the reader will instantly see that *this* has nothing to do with *that*.

His treatment of the defendant's claim that the criminality of the government's conduct requires exclusion of the evidence is of a piece with the rest. He simply subsumes it under a common-law rule of evidence, that admissibility is not affected by illegality. This move, the conclusory reduction of the constitutional to the merely evidentiary, is similar in structure to his definition of the Constitution and of his own role. He defines the common-law rule, then says "the common law rule must apply in the case at bar." Olmstead, 277 U.S. 438, at 468 (1928). But he gives no reason why it "must."

5. This could, of course, require considerable skill. Consider, for example, the comprehensiveness of Taft's summary of the statute at issue in *Boyd*:

> The fifth section of the Act of June 22, 1874, provided that in cases not criminal under the revenue laws, the United States Attorney, whenever he thought an invoice, belonging to the defendant, would tend to prove any allegation made by the United States, might by a written motion describing the invoice and setting forth the allegations which he expected to prove, secure a notice from the court to the defendant to produce the invoice, and if the defendant refuse to produce it, the allegation stated in the motion should be taken as confessed, but if produced, the United States Attorney should be permitted, under the direction of the court, to make an examination of the invoice, and might offer the same in evidence. [Olmstead, 227 U.S. at 458.]

6. See especially Adamson v. California, 332 U.S. 46, 68 (1947); Griswold v. Connecticut, 381 U.S. 479, 507 (1965).

7. 272 U.S. 365, 387 (1926).

8. 217 U.S. 349, 373 (1910).

9. Is Brandeis then resorting to original intention? Not in the sense in which the work of Taney and Story is criticized above, for Brandeis here looks not to an ulterior motive or wish, not to a supposed desire, unexpressed in the language, that the framers sought to achieve by it, but rather to the kind of "intention" that is enacted in the language itself, in the practice or form of life of which it is a part. This is the intention to make a constitution that will be read over generations: to intend that necessarily commits the writer to a process of interpretation (or translation); the relevant "intention" is not hidden, not to be guessed at, but manifest in the practice itself.

10. 116 U.S. 616 (1886).

11. 96 U.S. 727 (1877).

12. Compare here the way poets and other writers often give plain or ordinary speech a new freshness and power by locating it in a complicated context. See, e.g., George Herbert's poem, "Jordan (I)."

As lawyers will already know, but others may not, Brandeis is here drawing on an article of which he was a coauthor many years before. Brandeis and Warren, "The Right of Privacy," 4 *Harvard Law Review* 193 (1890).

13. See, e.g., Griswold v. Connecticut, 381 U.S. 479 (1965); Henry v. United States, 361 U.S. 347 (1967).

14. 389 U.S. 347 at 351 (1967).

15. For such an analysis, see Cunningham, "A Linguistic Analysis of the Meanings of 'Search' in the Fourth Amendment: A Search for Common Sense," 73 *Iowa Law Review* 541 (1988).

16. The first step of Justice Holmes's dissent in *Olmstead* is to identify what he sees to be the question of constitutional law presented here, on which he is studiously noncommittal. "While I do not deny it, I am not prepared to say that the penumbra of the Fourth and Fifth Amendments covers the defendant, although I fully agree that Courts are apt to err by sticking too closely to the words of a law where those words import a policy that goes beyond them."

But he doesn't have to decide this question, he says, for in his view the case can be disposed of on grounds he describes as nonconstitutional:

[A]part from the Constitution the Government ought not to use evidence obtained and only obtainable by a criminal act. There is no body of precedents by which we are bound, and which confines us to logical deduction from established rules. Therefore we must consider the two objects of desire, both of which we cannot have, and make up our minds which to choose. It is desirable that criminals should be detected, and to that end that all available evidence should be used. It also is desirable that the Government should not itself foster and pay for other crimes, when they are the means by which evidence is to be obtained. If it pays its officers for having got evidence by crime I do not see why it may not as well pay them for getting it in the same way, and I can attach no importance to protestations of disapproval if it knowingly accepts and pays and announces that in the future it will pay for the fruits. We have to choose, and for my part I think it a less evil that some criminals should escape than that the Government should play an ignoble part.

There is much of interest here, especially the eagerness with which Holmes faces the responsibility of individual decision: "for my part I think . . . " This is a refreshing change from the tone of many opinions which seek to disguise choice and responsibility alike under a pretense that the result is determined by other cases, or by the facts. But the very eagerness to reach this ground—the ground of pure choice, pure policy—is in my view excessive, for what does he mean by saying that this is not a constitutional question? What kind of question is it, and what is the Court's authority to decide it?

Holmes cuts through such questions as these to locate himself in a position from which he can decide what is better for society unconstrained by the decisions of others. To this extent this is an anti-legal opinion, for I think much of the life of the law lies in the way we identify and show respect for those constraints on will and reason alike which we call the law.

Chapter Seven

1. 401 U.S. 745 (1971).

2. The Federal Communications Act of 1934 provided that no unauthorized person should "intercept any communication and divulge or publish the existence . . . or meaning" of such communication to any person. The case holding that this statute required exclusion was *Nardone v. United States*, 302 U.S. 379 (1937).

3. 389 U.S. 347 (1967).

4. This notwithstanding the explicit cautionary language of the court: "[T]he Fourth Amendment cannot be translated into a general constitutional 'right to privacy.' That Amendment protects individual privacy against certain kinds of governmental intrusion, but its protections go further, and often have nothing to do with privacy at all. Other provisions of the Constitution protect personal privacy from other forms of governmental invasion. But the protection of the person's *general* right to privacy—his right to be let alone by other people—is, like the protection of his property and of his very life, left largely to the law of the individual states."

5. Hoffa v. United States, 385 U.S. 293, 302 (1966).

6. 385 U.S. 206 (1966).

7. 373 U.S. 427 (1963).

8. On Lee v. United States, 343 U.S. 747 (1952).

9. 388 U.S. 41 (1967).

10. 385 U.S. 323 (1966).

11. Why did Justice Douglas make no reference to this case, except in a footnote? I think the reason is that he had dissented in *Osborn*, believing that even under those circumstances the evidence should be excluded, and did not want to refer to it approvingly.

12. For an elaboration of the view that *Katz* added "no new dimension to the law," and should therefore be retroactive in its application, see Justice Harlan's opinion in *Desist v. United States*, 394 U.S. 244, 256 (1969).

13. 381 U.S. 479 (1965).

14. See Sanford Levinson, *Constitutional Faith*, ch. 1 (1988) for an elaboration of this comparison.

15. For fuller explication of this position see my article, "The Fourth Amendment as a Way of Talking About People: A Study of *Robinson* and *Matlock*," 1974 *Supreme Court Review* 165, 227–231.

16. And I have this to say against Harlan's opinion itself: that when he reaches the moment of decision, he articulates the question in a rather crude form of the method of cost-benefit analysis that has in its expanded form—

especially in its most elaborated form in the discourse of economics—been such a bane for the law.

Chapter Eight

1. 414 U.S. 218 (1973).

2. The text of the fourth amendment is reproduced above, pp. 141–42, and below, p. 181.

3. 116 U.S. 616 (1886).

4. The form of the amendment actually adopted by the House of Representatives in 1789 was somewhat different. The two clauses were connected this way: " . . . shall not be violated *by warrants issuing* without probable cause." (Emphasis added.) But the version received and ratified by the Senate and adopted by the states was the version we now have, the change having been made by the reporting committee. John Lasson, *History and Development of the Fourth Amendment to the United States Constitution*, p. 101 (1937).

5. One incentive to obtain a warrant might still remain, that of reducing exposure to criminal and civil liability. This was in fact one of the primary functions of the warrant procedure when it first evolved. See Matthew Hale, *History of the Pleas of the Crown*, vol. 2, chs. 10–13 (1736). This suggests another possible reading: that the officer is free to choose which sort of search or seizure to carry out, subject to the requirements of the warrant clause if a warrant is obtained, subject to presumably more restrictive trespass laws under common-law standards and to general constitutional criteria of "reasonableness" if not. A sensible body of law could be grounded on such a reading, but it has never been considered by the Court.

6. *See*, e.g., John Landynski, *Search and Seizure and the Supreme Court*, p. 43 (1966); Telford Taylor, *Two Studies in Constitutional Interpretation*, pp. 38–50 (1969).

7. Two important cases raised the role of state property law in defining the interests protected by the fourth amendment, one involving a landlord's right to enter a tenant's premises (Chapman v. United States, 365 U.S. 610 [1961]), and another involving a hotel clerk's power to consent to a police search of a rented hotel room (Stoner v. California, 376 U.S. 483 [1964]), but in both the Court evaded it. The hard question is to what degree, if at all, the state can authorize otherwise invalid searches by simply modifying its property law.

8. Henry v. United States, 361 U.S. 98 (1959).

9. Rios v. United States, 364 U.S. 253 (1960). For a more recent definition of arrest, see Dunaway v. New York, 442 U.S. 200 (1979).

10. 392 U.S. 1 (1968).

11. The Court does not make explicit that it is conceiving of some "seizures" that are less than "arrests," but some such doctrine seems necessary to the holding that a "frisk" is valid, for the frisk itself involves an interference with liberty.

The Court's implicit analysis does not work so well, as a practical or linguistic matter, with respect to "searches." What kind of search is less than a search? And it raises considerable questions both as to the place of the warrant requirement and its commands of probability and specificity. In what searches and seizures will probable cause and the warrant not be required, and by what criteria of reasonableness will they then be regulated?

For more recent cases dealing with what constitutes the "seizure" of a person, see United States v. Mendenhall, 440 U.S. 544 (1980); Florida v. Royer, 460 U.S. 491 (1983); I.N.S. v. Delgado, 466 U.S. 210 (1984); and Michigan v. Chesternut, 108 S. Ct. 1975 (1988). As for the grounds for such a seizure, see United States v. Cortez, 449 U.S. 411 (1981), and Brown v. Texas, 443 U.S. 47 (1979).

12. *Compare*, e.g., Spinelli v. United States, 393 U.S. 410 (1969), *with* United States v. Harris, 403 U.S. 573 (1971); and see Illinois v. Gates, 462 U.S. 213 (1983).

13. 387 U.S. 523 (1967). Subsequent cases somewhat complicate *Camara*. See especially Marshall v. Barlow's, Inc., 436 U.S. 307 (1978); Donovan v. Dewey, 452 U.S. 594 (1981); New York v. Burger, 482 U.S. 691 (1987); and Michigan v. Clifford, 464 U.S. 287 (1984). For a case undercutting the protection of *Camara* (available to the Court in *Robinson*), see United States v. Biswell, 406 U.S. 311 (1972).

14. Frank v. Maryland, 359 U.S. 360 (1959).

15. One's view of what circumstances should excuse the warrant requirement will depend in large part on one's view of the purpose and efficacy of the warrant mechanism itself, and on this point there have been some rather deep, though incompletely articulated, differences of opinion.

The classic statement is Justice Jackson's: "The point of the fourth amendment, which often is not grasped by zealous officers, is not that it denies law enforcement the support of the usual inferences which reasonable men draw from evidence. Its protection consists in requiring that those inferences be drawn by a neutral and detached magistrate instead of being judged by the officer engaged in the often competitive enterprise of ferreting out crime." Johnson v. United States, 333 U.S. 10, 13–14 (1948).

The rejoinder, implicit in some of the opinions discussed below, admits the value of judicial review of police decisions but sees little to be gained in having that review come before, rather than after, the intrusion. This view is supported by fears that the "independent magistrate" is in fact unlikely to be "independent" at all, but deeply committed to the police and their interests. Against this it is in turn argued, first, that one effect of the warrant procedure is to freeze the story of the officer or his informant at a point well ahead of the arrest or search. (Thus even if it is true that the only substantial judicial review takes place after the intrusion, that review will be far more accurate if it is based on facts asserted before the intrusion took place and not on a version possibly revised in the light of later discoveries.) Second, it is by no means realistic to assume that magistrates are never "independent," and, to the extent that they are so, certain impermissible intrusions will be prevented. Third, even where a magistrate is committed to the police view of the criminal process in general and of the case before him in particular, he still has an important function to perform: to advance the ultimate success of the intrusion and the admissibility of the evidence obtained, he will take pains to ensure that probable cause is adequately stated and that the other requirements of the warrant clause are met. Even deep-seated partisanship—if not coupled with an attitude of lawlessness—does not make the process of prior magistral review a pointless one. Finally—an argument that had great appeal to Justice Frankfurter—to require an officer to have a judicial warrant, however improperly granted, is to remain at least that symbolic step away from a police state, for the officer acts not on his authority but on that of a court and must tell the citizen so.

With respect to arrests, the Court has never required a warrant (though it has occasionally spoken of a "preference" for such a warrant). No persuasive reason has been given for the distinction between an arrest and a search—indeed, if there is to be a distinction, one might think it should go the other way—and it may rest on no stronger ground than the apparent historical circumstance that a warrant has generally not been required by the states or at common law for arrests for felonies and certain misdemeanors. See United States v. Watson, 423 U.S. 411 (1976). In Payton v. New York, 445 U.S. 573 (1980) the Court did require a warrant for arrest requiring entry to a house. For a classic discussion of this problem, see Barrett, "Personal Rights, Property Rights, and the Fourth Amendment," 1960 *Supreme Court Review* 46.

16. See, e.g., the plurality opinion of Mr. Justice Stewart in Coolidge v. New Hampshire, 403 U.S. 443, 455 (1971), and Arizona v. Hicks, 480 U.S. 321 (1987). It is also true that the warrant and probable cause requirements are both dispensed with where there is consent. See Schneckloth v. Bustamonte, 412 U.S. 218 (1973). For "third-party" consent, see, e.g., Matlock v. United States, 415 U.S. 164 (1973), discussed in my article in 1974 *Supreme Court Review* 165, 216–32.

17. Warden v. Hayden, 387 U.S. 294 (1967). But see Welsh v. Wisconsin, 466 U.S. 740 (1984).

18. Schmerber v. California, 384 U.S. 757 (1966).

19. Carroll v. United States, 267 U.S.132 (1925).

20. 399 U.S. 42 (1970).

21. In Coolidge v. New Hampshire, 403 U.S. 443, 461–62 (1971), Mr. Justice Stewart said: "The word 'automobile' is not a talisman in whose presence the Fourth Amendment fades away and disappears." But see Cady v. Dombrowski, 413 U.S. 433 (1973); Michigan v. Thomas, 458 U.S. 259 (1982); and United States v. Ross, 456 U.S. 798 (1982).

22. 339 U.S. 56 (1950). The fluctuating history of the permissible scope of such searches is presented in some detail in the opinions in this case.

23. 395 U.S. 752 (1969).

24. Testimony of the officer who arrested and searched Robinson in this case. United States v. Robinson, 414 U.S. 218, 251 (1973) (dissenting opinion of Marshall, J.).

25. It was never made clear whether the initial "routine spot check" was a truly random stopping of cars in a systematic way or simply the use of the policeman's hunch. There is no discussion of its propriety in the Supreme

Court. In the court of appeals, Judge Bazelon expressed the view that such procedures presented substantial constitutional problems. 471 F.2d 1085, at 1111 (D.C. Cir. 1972). Presumably the Supreme Court is to be taken not to have addressed the issue.

26. 447 F.2d 1215, 1217 (D.C. Cir. 1971). The defense originally argued that he had no right to ask for the draft card, but that issue was not faced by the appellate courts at any stage.

27. 471 F.2d 1082, 1088 (D.C. Cir. 1972). It is suggested in one of the opinions that Jenks then made a check of "criminal records" and discovered that Robinson had two prior narcotics convictions.

28. *Id*. at 1088 n. 3. The court of appeals did not deal with the defendant's allegations of improper motive because they found the search improper on other grounds. The Supreme Court said: "We think it is sufficient for purposes of our decision that respondent was lawfully arrested for an offense, and that Jenks' placing him in custody following that arrest was not a departure from established police department practice. . . . We leave for another day questions which would arise on facts different from these." 414 U.S. 218, 221 n. 1 (1973).

29. 414 U.S. 218, 221–22 n. 2 (1973).

30. 471 F.2d at 1089 n. 9; 414 U.S. 218, 251 (1973).

31. 471 F.2d at 1094 n. 17.

32. 414 U.S. 218, 235 (1973). Mr. Justice Powell put much the same point more bluntly in his concurrence: "I believe that an individual lawfully subjected to a custodial arrest retains no significant fourth amendment interest in the privacy of his person." *Id*. at 237.

33. The statement that the right has been "uniformly maintained" is, I believe, to be taken as a statement of the uniformity with which the general rule has been accepted, not as a statement that the generally stated right is without limit or qualification. Limits seem both stated and implied in the following language in the work by Bishop relied on by the Court in the passage quoted:

> [*T*]*he right of search for this purpose* [of finding weapons to prevent escape] *does not exist of course in every case*; as, for example, where the arrest is for mere disorderly drunkenness, and it is submitted to, and there is no ground to fear an attempt at escape. In like manner, in cases of larceny, *and others in which there is a probability of finding evidence of guilt on the prisoner's person*, he may be searched for them. (Emphasis added.) [1 Bishop, *Criminal Procedure*, p. 210 (3d ed. 1880).]

34. Ira Moore, *A Practical Treatise on Criminal Law*, p. 148 (1876).

35. Here is the language governing the frisk: "[T]he police officer must be able to point to specific and articulable facts which, taken together with rational inferences from those facts, reasonably warrant that intrusion." 392 U.S. 1, 21 (1968). "[T]he issue is whether a reasonably prudent man in the circumstances would be warranted in the belief that his safety or that of others was in danger." *Id*. at 27.

36. These are also difficulties with the *Terry* rule itself, of course. But, as suggested above, in a case where there is no probable cause to arrest, the

Court may properly feel that restrictions on the frisk are more important, lest the entire population be subject to the uncontrolled possibility of police frisk. *Robinson*, by contrast, assumes a contemporaneous valid arrest, and the class of persons exposed to any automatic search rule is correspondingly small. There is another facet to the distinction. In a large class of cases, at least, the state interest in the intrusion, and correspondingly the professional obligation of the policeman to proceed, is greater where there is probable cause to arrest than in a *Terry* investigation. More, that is, will be lost if the officer fails to act through uncertainty as to his safety or his right to protect himself.

37. The court of appeals and the Supreme Court seem to accept the following definition of a frisk, quoted in *Terry*, 392 U.S., 1, 17 n. 13 (1968): "[T]he officer must feel with sensitive fingers every portion of the prisoner's body. A thorough search must be made of the prisoner's arms and armpits, waistline and back, the groin and the area about the testicles, and the entire surface of the legs down to the feet." The Court is quoting Priar and Martin, "Searching and Disarming Criminals," 45 *Journal of Criminal Law and Police Science* 81 (1954).

38. In this sense, among others, the fourth amendment and the due process clause of the fourteenth amendment can be seen as intimately related, even if the particular criteria of the former were not thought to be "incorporated" in the latter. The interference by a police officer with a citizen's security and freedom—a search and seizure—is a deprivation of liberty or property to which the due process clause should apply by its express terms. Even on the state of the law antedating Wolf v. Colorado, 338 U.S. 25 (1949), and Mapp v. Ohio, 367 U.S. 643 (1961), a state would presumably not have been permitted to authorize searches and seizures without rational reference to its legitimate concerns. To the extent that *Robinson* establishes such an authority, it can be said to be inconsistent not only with the fourth amendment but also with the most fundamental conceptions of the due process clause and with the principle that the police are rationally answerable to the law.

39. For a consideration of other possible interpretations of the majority opinion, see the earlier version of this chapter that appeared in the 1974 *Supreme Court Review* 165, 205–209.

40. The Supreme Court has never suggested the use of such a limiting principle, but several commentators have argued that the power established in *Terry v. Ohio* should be so regulated, and it is commonly thought that Peters v. New York, 392 U.S. 40 (1968), a companion case to *Terry*, was decided as it was in order to avoid addressing the question. In *Camara* and its companion cases the question neither arose nor was adverted to. Judge Aldrich suggested that such a principle be applied in searches of air travelers, United States v. Skipwith, 482 F.2d 1272, 1280–81 (5th Cir. 1973) (Aldrich, J., dissenting), and several commentators favored it with respect to *Terry* frisks, e.g., Amsterdam, "Perspectives on the Fourth Amendment," 58 *Minnesota Law Review* 349, 427 (1974).

41. One could do worse for a starting point than the statement of the Supreme Court of New Hampshire in Closson v. Morrison, 47 N.H. 482 (1867), quoted above page 191. While the standard is framed in terms of

good faith or honest purpose, no doubt the relative reasonableness or unreasonableness of a claimed belief would properly be considered relevant by any trier of fact asked to determine motive. No legislation is necessary to permit such civil relief in the federal courts. Bivens v. Six Unknown Named Agents of Federal Bureau of Narcotics, 403 U.S. 388 (1971), *on remand*, 456 F.2d 1339 (2d Cir. 1972).

42. 116 U.S. 616, 630 (1886). Justice Black's concurrence in *Mapp v. Ohio*—necessary to a firm majority on the constitutional question involved—was expressly based on the view that the exclusionary rule was not merely a remedy devised to enforce a constitutional prohibition but emerged from the "close interrelationship" between the fourth and fifth amendments. 367 U.S. 643, 662 (1961). The best exposition of the interrelationship between the principles limiting search and seizure and the principle that a person cannot be compelled to incriminate himself is still the *Boyd* case, together with its English forebear Entick v. Carrington, 19 Howard State Trials 1030 (1765). For development of the argument that the fourth amendment was primarily directed against searches for evidence to be used in criminal prosecutions and forfeitures, see the opinion of Justice Frankfurter in Frank v. Maryland, 359 U.S. 360 (1959).

43. On this point compare *Heracles' Bow*, pp. 206–9.

Chapter Nine

1. For a concise statement by advocates of this position, see the Supplemental Brief for the United States as Amicus Curiae Supporting Reversal, p. 2, in Illinois v. Gates, 462 U.S. 213 (1982):

"Nothing in the Fourth Amendment or any other provision of the Constitution either directly or implicitly provides for the exclusion of illegally seized evidence from criminal trials. Instead, decisions of this Court over the last decade have made it clear that the exclusionary rule first enunciated in Weeks v. United States, 232 U.S. 383 (1914), and later extended to the states in Mapp v. Ohio, 367 U.S. 643 (1961), is a judicially-created remedy, the paramount and perhaps sole purpose of which is the deterrence of unlawful police conduct. As the deterrence rationale has achieved supremacy over earlier, now discarded justifications for the rule, the Court has recognized that it makes sense to apply the rule only to those situations in which its deterrent purpose will in fact be significantly advanced. Accordingly, the Court now employs a cost benefit analysis whenever it considers whether the rule should be applied to particular situations. When the costs of applying the rule are found to outweigh whatever deterrent effect it might achieve, the rule will not be imposed." [Citations omitted.]

2. 338 U.S. 25 (1949).

3. 367 U.S. 643 (1961).

4. See, e.g., Michigan v. DeFillipo, 443 U.S. 31, 38n. 3 (1979); United States v. Janis, 428 U.S. 433, 446 (1976).

5. See, e.g., Stone v. Powell, 428 U.S. 465, 485 (1976); Brown v. Illinois 422 U.S. 590, 599 (1975); United States v. Calandra, 414 U.S. 338, 359

(1974) (Brennan, J., dissenting) (quoting Elkins v. United States, 364 U.S. 206, 222 (1960)).

6. 116 U. S. 616 (1886).

7. 19 Howell's State Trials 1029, 95 Eng. Rep. 807 (P.C. 1765).

8. 1st Am. ed. Philadelphia (1847) at bk. II, ch. 18.

9. 255 U.S. 298, 309 (1921).

10. A case like *Warden v. Hayden*, 387 U.S. 294 (1967), involving the clothes worn in the commission of a crime, would presumably be a borderline case that could go either way.

11. United States v. Lefkowitz, 285 U.S. 452, 464–65 (1932).

12. 387 U.S. 294 (1967).

13. *Warden* also makes the problem of third-party searches both more difficult and more serious: under the earlier rule, the person on whose premises an item meeting the *Boyd-Gouled* requirements could be found was, however innocently, the possessor of something he was not entitled to possess, and a search of his premises for such items was therefore facially reasonable. Under *Warden*, however, one who perfectly rightly possesses items of his own purchase, and even of his own manufacture, may be subject to search and seizure if those items may be of use to the police or prosecution in the investigation or prosecution of others. See Zurcher v. Stanford Daily, 436 U.S. 547 (1978).

The Court in *Warden* was in part persuaded by a law review article which argued that the protection of "property" made no more sense, from the point of view of the interests it saw "actually" at stake, than the protection of items seized on "the even-numbered days of the month." Kaplan, "Search and Seizure: A No-Man's Land in the Criminal Law," 49 *California Law Review* 474, 479 (1961).

14. Edmund Burke, *Reflections on the Revolution in France*, p. 37 (T. Mahoney ed. 1955). On the role of law, especially property law, in the life of England, see William Blackstone's inaugural lecture, "On the Study of Law," printed at the beginning of most editions of the *Commentaries*.

15. On liberty and property and their relation to popular sovereignty, see generally Gordon Wood, *The Creation of the American Republic, 1776–1787*, pp. 214–22 (1969); Richard Hofstadter, *The American Political Tradition*, pp. 12–22 (1948). In this connection it is significant that each of the states had constitutional provisions similar both to the fourth amendment and to the fifth amendment's protection against compelled self-incrimination. This gives these provisions a different standing from the first amendment's prohibition against the establishment of religion, for example, for which there were few state counterparts and which can therefore be read as reserving to one sovereign the power denied to the other.

16. William Blackstone, *Commentaries* *2: "There is nothing which so generally strikes the imagination, and engages the affections of mankind, as the right of property; or that sole and despotic dominion which one man claims and exercises over the external things of the world, in the total exclusion of the right of any other individual in the universe."

17. 116 U.S. 616, 630 (1886). The kind of identity that the *Boyd* Court

sees between the person and his property, that is, makes it easy to regard the forcible production of one's property as the equivalent of compelling the individual to be a witness against himself. And when the government tries, as on the facts of *Boyd* itself, to reduce the obviousness of the fourth amendment intrusion by requiring the cooperation of the individual, the fifth amendment comes into play all the more.

18. 232 U.S. 383 (1914).

19. In *Boyd* the claimant produced the invoice under protest and objected to its admission in evidence. In holding the resulting judgment of forfeiture invalid for this reason, the Court was in fact holding that the claimant was entitled to the exclusion of the invoice. And while the Court does not expressly allude to the possibility of derivative evidence, it is hard to believe that such evidence as the testimony of the United States attorney as to what he saw during the examination, or copies made by him, would have been admitted either.

20. 232 U.S. at 393–94 (emphasis added).

21. 251 U.S. 385 (1920).

22. The Exclusionary Rule Bills: Hearings before the Subcomm. on Criminal Law of the Senate Comm. on the Judiciary on S. 101, S. 751, and S. 1995, 97th Cong., 1st & 2d Sess. 372–77 (1982) (testimony of Prof. Yale Kamisar).

23. See Camara v. Municipal Court, 387 U.S. 523 (1967), and the discussion of the civil-criminal distinction above in chapter 8.

24. In *Weeks* itself the Court ordered the return of certain letters and certificates but was silent as to the disposition of lottery tickets that had also been seized; yet in Amos v. United States, 255 U.S. 313 (1921), the Court ordered the return of illegally seized liquor on which tax had not been paid (referring to the bottles as defendant's "property"), notwithstanding the fact that this was apparently contraband.

25. 269 U.S. 20 (1925). That the exclusion was seen as a remedy for the violation of rights, rather than as a method of deterrence, is made plain by the Court's refusal to exclude the evidence from the trial of Agnello's codefendants, whose rights had not been violated by the search and seizure.

26. 338 U.S. 25, 27 (1949).

27. For an elaboration of this view, see Schrock & Welsh, "Up From *Calandra*: The Exclusionary Rule as a Constitutional Requirement," 59 *Minnesota Law Review* 251 (1974). But see Monaghan, "Foreword: Constitutional Common Law, The Supreme Court 1974 Term," 89 *Harvard Law Review* 1 (1975).

28. See Rochin v. California, 342 U.S. 165, 173 (1952) (states must "respect certain decencies of civilized conduct"). But see United States v. Payner, 434 F. Supp. 113, 132–33 (N.D. Ohio 1977), *affirmed*, 590 F.2d 206 (6th Cir. 1979), *reversed*, 447 U.S. 727 (1980). Here a flagrantly illegal search of one person produced evidence to be used against another. The district court in *Payner* granted the second person standing and ordered exclusion in order to insure that police practices as "outrageously illegal" as those in *Rochin* would be deterred in the future. But the Supreme Court reversed, on the grounds

that fourth amendment rights are personal. "Deterrence" is a rationale normally used to cut back protections; where, as here, it would expand them, the Court proceeds on another ground. One is reminded of a Black under the law of slavery, who was treated as property not a person, except—as in criminal cases—where this would have been to his advantage; then he was treated as a person after all.

29. 414 U.S. 338, 351 (1974). The idea of deterrence also leads naturally to the present nostrum, that the sanction should not be applied to "good faith and reasonable" conduct for many of the same reasons that strict liability deterrent measures are thought irrational or unfair in the criminal law. See United States v. Leon, 468 U.S. 897 (1984). This exemption may be harmless enough if the standard of "reasonableness" is that applied in criminal law, namely, that of one who knows and understands the law, which already makes allowance for reasonable errors (in the definition of probable cause, for example, or of the kind of exigency that excuses a search warrant). If, however, as its proponents evidently wish, a lower standard is applied, ignorance will be encouraged, and the courts will become involved in impossible efforts to determine double layers of reasonableness.

30. See, e.g., Sandalow, "Constitutional Interpretation," 79 *Michigan Law Review* 1033, 1054–55 (1981).

31. Even when employed by a legislature or a legislative commission, of course, cost-benefit analysis rests on weak and largely unexamined foundations and involves many of the ethical and political difficulties described in chapter 3. For an amusing instance of cost-benefit analysis running itself into the ground, see Commission on the Third London Airport, *Report* (1971), part of which is reprinted in *The Legal Imagination*, pp. 700–706 (1973). For an illuminating analysis of the ways in which risks—and benefits as well—are not objectively determined but culturally constituted, see Mary Douglas & Aaron B. Wildavsky, *Risk and Culture* (1982).

32. See Fisher v. United States, 425 U.S. 391, 407–408 (1976), and Andresen v. Maryland, 427 U.S. 463 (1976).

Chapter Ten

1. 443 U.S. 193 (1979).

2. 42 U.S.C. S2000 e-2(d).

3. In *Smith Hiatt*, 329 Mass. 488, 109 N.E.2d 133 (1952), the Massachusetts court held that a statute requiring notice of suit for injuries "founded upon the defective condition of [defendant's] premises, or of adjoining ways, when caused by snow or ice" applied to a case in which a guest slipped on ice that had fallen from the refrigerator to the kitchen floor. The legislature quickly amended the statute to add: "resulting from rain or snow and weather conditions," an amendment that it should not have been necessary for them to make.

4. Regents of the University of California v. Bakke, 438 U.S. 265 (1978). On this case see especially L. H. LaRue, "The Rhetoric of Powell's *Bakke*," 38 *Washington and Lee Law Review* 43 (1981). On *Weber*, see Lempert, "The Force

of Irony: On the Morality of Affirmative Action and *United Steelworkers v. Weber,"* 95 *Ethics* 85 (1984).

Chapter Eleven

1. It in fact begins as so many English borrowings from Latin do as the passive participle—"that phrase was *translate* from the Latin," someone says—then becomes a verb. (Cf. "act.")

2. Jose Ortega y Gasset, "The Difficulty of Reading," 28 *Diogenes* 1 (1959) and "Miseria y Esplendor de la Traduccion," in *Obras Completas*, vol. 5, p. 433 (7th ed. Madrid 1970). Compare George Steiner, *After Babel*, pp. 406–8 (1975). I owe my acquaintance with Ortega to Alton Becker.

Different translators may establish somewhat different kinds of relations with their primary texts, expressing different kinds of fidelity to them. At one end of the spectrum there is, for example, what we think of as the "literal" or "word-for-word" translation, the object of which is to help the student of the original language work through the text. At the other end is "imitation," most common in poetry, where the native writer uses a foreign or original work as a model, perhaps because it was a source of inspiration. Here the term "imitation" is used to acknowledge a debt, perhaps to claim an intellectual kinship with the great; it is also an invitation to a certain sort of reading, a way of saying to one who knows the original, "Read this, in light of that." Between these points lie "translations" proper.

For a classic statement of the differences among what he calls metaphrase, paraphrase, and imitation, see Dryden's Preface to *Ovid's Epistles* (1680) in *Of Dramatic Poesy and other Critical Essays*, vol. 1, p. 262 (Everyman ed. 1962).

3. Of course we can agree to limit our concerns to what is (relatively speaking) translatable, but that always involves a reduction of the full meaning of the text, and by no means always to its core. For it is a great mistake to think, as we often do, that a text has a "central" meaning, propositional in kind, which is surrounded by "peripheral" nuances or elegances, and that if we can approximate that central meaning we have got the heart of what is there. Such a view would make no sense at all of poetry for example, and it would structure every approach to the expressions of others in a false and rigid way. As we have seen to be the case with judicial opinions, what is most important about a particular text may lie in not in its apparently propositional content but in its modification of its own language, in the establishment of social relations with its reader, or, more properly, in the interaction of its several dimensions of meaning, which cannot be reduced to propositions at all.

4. For a fuller statement of a contextual theory of meaning, see the work of A. L. Becker, especially "Biography of a Sentence: A Burmese Proverb," in *Text, Play, and Story: The Construction and Reconstruction of Self and Society* (E. Bruner ed. 1983), p. 136 and *Beyond Translation* (forthcoming).

5. Lysias addresses the argument that there is an important distinction in the meaning of the two words—one meaning culpable homicide, the other

homicide *simpliciter*—by referring to the homicide procedure of the Areopagus, the most prestigious court in Athens, where a murder charge is framed in terms of *kteinein* not *androphonein*.

6. The Study says:

We have stressed the participation of the draftsman in the actual elaboration of the statute in order to underline what appears to be one of the most serious reasons for the inadequacy of the French version of federal statutes. The translator has not participated in the drafting. His sole function is to translate. He has been deprived of the opportunity given to the draftsman to familiarize himself with the true intention and purpose of the legislator and is thus at a disadvantage in attempting to convey this intention in another language. Secondly, not having participated in the drafting of the statute, he has had no opportunity to suggest changes of the English version to make both versions more nearly equivalent. As has been found in Quebec, where simultaneous drafting is done more frequently, the preparation at the same time of texts in two languages produces a type of feedback between versions which results in greater clarity and conformity between texts. At the present time the French version of a federal statute constitutes at best a literal translation of an English original drafted without any consideration for the intricacies of the French language or the difficulty of translating technical or legal terms which may not have an exact equivalent in the other language. (P. 112.)

For more on the Canadian experience, see Michael Beaupre, *Interpreting Bilingual Legislation* (1986).

7. For an even more complex account of law in a multilingual context, see L. J. Mark Cooray, *Changing the Language of the Law: The Sri Lanka Experience* (1985), where he describes the ways in which Sri Lanka has tried to establish Sinhala and, to a lesser degree, Tamil as the language of law. The trouble is, Cooray observes, that it is impossible to "think law" in Sinhala until a Sinhalese legal culture exists; yet that culture can come to exist only when law is done in Sinhalese. The only way to break this circle, he believes, is for the law to remain deeply bilingual for some time.

Think, for example, of a statute or case written in English that has authority within the Sri Lankan tradition: Can that be translated into Sinhalese without also translating the whole body of cases and statutes and professional understandings that create the context upon which the original acted and which therefore did much to shape its meaning? Each text implies the past against which it is written and cannot be deracinated without damage. Sinhalese legal language and legal thought can develop into something authentic and local, Cooray believes, only if they are for some time supported by competence in English; if they are so supported, something new and indigenous may indeed be created.

8. See, e.g., S. Rosenne, "The Meaning of 'Authentic Text' in Modern Treaty Law" (explicating The Vienna Convention of the Law of Treaties of May 23, 1969), in *Völkerrecht als Rechtsordnung: Internationale Gerichtsbarkeit Menschenrechte*, p. 759 (Bernhardt et al. eds. 1983); D. Wirth, "Multilingual

Treaty Interpretation and the Case of SALT II," 6 *Yale Studies in World Public Order* 429 (1980).

9. I owe this reference to Joseph Vining.

10. "On Linguistic Aspects of Translation," in Reuben Brower ed. *On Translation* p. 232 (1959). For an even stronger version of this claim see D. Davidson, "On the Very Idea of a Conceptual Scheme," which seems to assert it as a condition of the meaningfulness of a text that it be translatable, presumably into any human language whatever. Donald Davidson, *Inquiries into Truth and Interpretation*, Ch. 13 (1984).

11. I owe this example to Kenneth Dewoskin. Compare: "'[H]eart' in Greek must often be rendered by 'liver,' as in the Kabba-Laka language of French Equatorial Africa, by 'abdomen,' as in Conob, a Mayan language of Guatemala, and by 'throat,' as in some contexts in Marshalese, a language of the South Pacific. In languages in which 'gall' stands for wisdom and a 'hard heart' is a symbol of courage, the Bible translator is obliged to make certain adaptations or cause serious misunderstanding." Eugene A. Nida, *Language Structure and Translation*, p. 44 (1975).

On the translation of poetry in general, see the fine Introduction to *The Oxford Book of Greek Verse in Translation* by T. F. Higham (1938).

12. Compare Emile BenVeniste, *Indo-European Language and Society*, pp. 138, 358 (Palmer trans., 1973); Arthur W. H. Adkins, *Merit and Responsibility*, pp. 30–40 (1960).

13. To take one more example think of a simple sentence about "dog": William Empson has shown us that this simple and apparently natural term is in our language enormously complex, capturing or reflecting attitudes that run very deep indeed, which "chien" or "hund" would simply miss (*The Structure of Complex Words*, ch. 7 (1951). Compare here the observation in Ortega y Gasset that what one finds in a dictionary is not words—for words exist only in actual utterances—but abstracted "possibilities of meaning." J. Ortega y Gasset, *Man and People*, p. 235 (W. Trask trans. 1957).

Equally important, as I suggested in chapter 2, it is an abuse of most language uses to treat them as merely propositional in the first place. In the real world—as opposed to the kind of linguistics classroom where unreal and decontextualized sentences are often discussed as if they were the norm—texts have social and ethical dimensions of meaning, cultural motives, that cannot be replicated in other languages. (Of course in certain linguistics classrooms and some law classrooms too, attention is focused explicitly on those dimensions of meaning.)

We have a version of this problem in the law, where it is sometimes said that the purpose of the first amendment is to protect the expression of "ideas," especially political "ideas." The image of expression at work here is that of container and contents, or vehicle and substance: the core of what happens is that an "idea" that originates in my head is more or less well clothed in (or squeezed into) words, which convey "it" to you. What counts is the idea, the contents; the rest is style, form, container, merely aesthetic. One version of first amendment doctrine would protect only the "ideas" themselves and not their "manner" of expression; in its most extreme form this might insist on the translation of all utterances into a supposedly neutral language. All art would fall into the second category, that of pure form or style, either unprotected entirely, as without "ideas," or, if protected, only because it is harmless—not really about anything.

How about mathematics? Are not its "concepts" equally available to speakers of many languages? No, I would say, the meanings of mathematical texts are available only to the speakers of one language, mathematics. They cannot be translated into English or French; the meanings are to be found in mathematical texts themselves. The learning of mathematics is the learning of a language.

14. In this context think how impossible it is to feel the force of the taboo that is violated by swear words in a foreign language. To us they are just words, and while we know that others will be upset if we utter them, we have no internal forces prohibiting us from doing so.

Or think of the point Jaroslav Pelikan makes about the nature of Christian doctrinal disputes, arising from the fact the Christian tradition was "not dogmatic, but liturgical in form." (*The Vindication of Tradition*, p. 29 [1984]). The idea is that the central Christian experience has been, over centuries, the celebration of the Eucharist; debates over doctrine are to a large degree debates over the meaning of this central practice, which can never be wholly represented in doctrinal terms. In this sense the practice is primary, the doctrine secondary, always uncertain, qualified, tentative as the practice never is. (Pp.48–49.)

15. "The appeal . . . lies not from the pedantic scholar to the general public, which can only like or dislike Chapman's version, or Pope's, or Mr. Newman's, but cannot *judge* them; it lies from the pedantic scholar to the scholar who is not pedantic, who knows that Homer is Homer by his general effect, and not by his single words, and who demands but one thing in a translation—that it shall, as nearly as possible, reproduce for him the *general effect* of Homer." Matthew Arnold, *On Translating Homer*, p. 61 (1905).

16. For a fine example of this process, see Cristanne Miller, *Emily Dickinson: A Poet's Grammar* (1987), the explicit aim of which is to teach its reader how to inhabit Emily Dickinson's language. This is no easy task, for to contemporary and modern readers alike Dickinson's poems are odd both in diction and appearance: she turns nouns into verbs, fails to provide temporal endings for her verbs, uses dashes and capitals in an idiosyncratic way, and employs a vocabulary that strongly emphasizes certain ordinary words— such as "noon"—in extraordinary ways. She is often ambiguous to the point of vagueness. Miller shows us that the way to read this poetry is not as a set of discrete texts, each of which must rest on its own bottom, but as the work of a single mind, making its own ways of talking, its own language. The first task of the reader is to learn the language of the poet, the first task of the critic to help us to do so. Miller's object is not to resolve the ambiguities and indeterminancies of the poetry into clear statements (not to translate the poetry into prose), but to reduce and clarify them, to give them surer life as what they are. In Miller's view, then, the reader's aim should not be to repro-

duce the poetry in one's own language but to live with the poetry itself, in the form in which it was composed, more intelligently and fully.

17. See, e.g., William Frost, *Dryden and the Art of Translation*, p. 11 (1955).

Where sound is a major source of meaning translation is especially difficult; where it is the dominant or organizing principle, translation becomes hopeless. Pindar, for example, has been shown to build his poetry out of sounds in such a way, and so exclusively, that without the sound there is almost nothing left to translate. See Brower, "The Theban Eagle," 48 *Classical Philosophy* 25 (1948). Compare Gibbons, "Poetic Form and the Translator," 11 *Critical Inquiry* 654 (1985).

But even here we should be careful: in *After Babel* George Steiner gives us an example of a good translation of Gerard Manley Hopkins into French, which would seem impossible (p. 412), and Scott Moncrieff has done much to catch the rhythms of Proust's prose in English. And to look at it the other way round, the fact that we can make a good tale in English out of the story of the Odyssey does not mean that we are not losing something in its way as important as the music of Virgil or Dante.

18. There are simple ways to do some of this: the custom of including the original of Dante's Divine Comedy on the facing pages of translations, for example, makes one painfully aware that what one is reading is not the real thing. Or in class I have seen a gifted teacher read from an original, translating as he goes, while the students look at the English text before them; this lifts the translation off the page as it were, and teaches the students that the English words they have before them are not the words of Sophocles, say, or Homer, nor do they "correspond" to them.

Compare here Walter Benjamin's remark that "the interlinear version of the Scriptures is the prototype or ideal of all translation" (in "The Task of the Translator," *Illuminations*, p. 82 [1973]); George Steiner's observation that "literalism is not, as in traditional models, of translation, the naive, facile mode, but on the contrary, the ultimate" (in *After Babel*, p. 324 (1975); and Nabokov, "The clumsiest literal translation is a thousand times more valuable than the prettiest paraphrase" (in "Problems of Translation: *Onegin* in English," 22 *Partisan Review* 496 (1955). For translations that carry to something like a limit the obligation to render the familiar strange, see Browning's famous *Agamemnon* and Peter Boodberg, "Philological Notes on Chapter One of the *Lao Tzu*," in *Selected Works of Peter A. Boodberg*, p. 460 (Cohen ed. 1979). (I owe several of the references in this note, and elsewhere in this chapter too, to the excellent bibliography in Reuben Brower ed., *On Translation*, pp. 271–93 [1959].)

19. See especially his essay in Robert Alter and Frank Kermode, *The Literary Guide to the Bible*, p. 647 (1987). Compare Ullmann, "The *Pro* and *Contra* of Martin Buber's Root-Word Theory for Translation," in *Translations and Interpretation*, p. 93 (M. Batts, ed. 1975).

20. This phrase is from the introduction to Gerald Hammond, *The Making of the English Bible*, p. 12 (1982), a somewhat more polemical statement of his position.

21. Compare how carefully C. K. Scott Moncrieff traces the movements of Proust's prose to produce a text in English that has a sense of something else. Marcel Proust, *The Remembrance of Things Past* (Moncrieff trans. 1928).

22. One could sum up this image of verbal life this way: As we go through the world we acquire various bits of information, through "cognition," which we store somewhere in our brains. By a process so mysterious as to be indescribable, we also have what are known as ideas and values or attitudes. When we talk or write, we communicate these pieces of information, about facts or ideas or values, to others through a language which works through a process of naming: I use my words to label internal or external phenomena; you turn to the phenomena and apprehend them; at the end you have in your mind what I have in mine. My statements typically take the form of propositions, which can be either true or false. Rationality is defined as internal and external coherence: the propositions that I utter should correspond to the facts of the world and should be internally consistent. When we turn to the social world, we operate on the same assumptions about language; namely, that the social universe can be reproduced, at least in schematic form, in our theoretical discourse, which will be checked for accuracy by various kinds of empirical studies. The root metaphor is that of the machine, in which the various components perform functions that relate to each other in predictable ways: language, the mind, society are all machines.

This leads in turn to a bureaucratic vision of government; we talk as though we could create our social world from scratch, as though we were social architects working from a blueprint of our own devising, and as we talk this way our blueprint comes to substitute for the reality that it reflects. We assume, that is, that a process of representation, or translation, can go on perfectly well between the world and our discourse.

For a work that resists this view of language and law, and advocates the comparative study of law as a kind of translation, see Clifford Geertz, *Local Knowledge*, pp. 218, 232.

23. *The Translations of Ezra Pound*, p. 14 (Kenner ed. 1953).

Chapter Twelve

1. See Lawrance Thompson, *Robert Frost: The Early Years*, p. 333 (1966).

2. This is what the statute and judicial opinion offer their readers too, an opportunity for a certain kind of life.

3. This is of course an ideal not always attained, but its roots are deep in Islam. See, e.g., Roy Mottahadeh, *The Mantle of the Prophet*, pp. 199–203, 225 (1985); Bernard Weiss, "The Long Journey Towards God's Law: The Venture of *Usul al-fiqh*," pp. 6–10 (Lecture, University of Michigan Center for Near East Studies, 20 January 1988) and "Interpretation in Islamic Law: The Theory of Ijtihad," 26 *American Journal of Comparative Law*, 199, 203–5 (1978).

4. D. W. Winnicott, *The Spontaneous Gesture*, p. 34 (1987).

5. See generally George Steiner, *After Babel* (1975), especially ch. 6.

INDEX

Abstraction, 39–40, 97. *See also* Theory

Ackerman, Bruce, 274n.1

Adkins, Arthur W. H., *Merit and Responsibility*, 298n.12

Agnello v. United States, 209

Aleinikoff, T. A., 289n.3

Alter, Robert, and Frank Kermode, *The Literary Guide to the Bible*, 300n.19

Amos v. United States, 294n.24

Amsterdam, Anthony, 291n.40

Argument, legal: in *Dred Scott*, 124–26, 132; in *Prigg v. Pennsylvania*, 114–17, 132; ethics of, 124–26

Arizona v. Hicks 289n.16

Arnold, Matthew, *On Translating Homer*, 251–52, 299n.15

Art, as addressing both limits and resources, 265; law as, 18, 215–16, 224–25; nature of human life as, 264–67; of social reconstitution, 24; uniting justice and translation, 269. *See also* Integration; Translation

Art of writing, as comprising contraries, 33, 40, 42, 50, 75–79, 100. *See also* Integration; Translation

Aspiration, in the law. *See* Idealization

Attention: to our habits of mind, 25; to language, 32–33, 43–45; language as shaping, 49–51, 55–56, law as method of giving, 91; reading as focusing, 18

Augustine, St., *Confessions*, 272n.4

Authoritarianism: irrational character of authoritarianism, 196, 197; Rehnquist's authoritarian opinion in *Robinson v. United States*, 196; Taft's "literal" mode of reading as authoritarian, 143–48

Authority, created rhetorically in a judicial opinion, 217; defined in law by interpretation, 95–97; of "facts," 212–13; of "original intention," 218–19 and ch. 5 passim; of the past, 223; of "plain language," 143–48, 218–19; of precedent, 160–75 passim, 191–92, 246; in relation between past and present as reconstituted in judicial opinion, 167–72, 175, 216–18, and ch. 7 passim. *See also* Authoritarianism

Autopoiesis, 266

Balbus, Isaac D., *Marxism and Domination*, 274n.1, 276n.20

Barfield, Owen, *Poetic Diction*, 273n.6

Barker, Sir Ernest, on translating Aristotle's *Politics*, 248–50, 261

Barrett, Edward, 289n.15

Beaupre, Michael, *Interpreting Bilingual Legislation*, 2976

Becker, Alton, xvii, 90, 277n.21, 296n.2; *Beyond Translation* and

303

Becker, Alton (*continued*)
"Biography of a Sentence,"
271n.2, 273n.8, 283n.19, 296n.4
Becker, Gary, 275n.9; *The Economic Approach to Human Behavior*, 274n.1, 275n.8
Benjamin, Walter, *Illuminations*, 300n.18
BenVeniste, Emile, *Indo-European Language and Society*, 298n.12
Berger v. New York, 166
Berry, Wendell, on agricultural economics, 276n.14
Bible: King James, as model of translation, 253; New English, translation in, 246–53
Bishop, Joel, *Criminal Procedure*, 290n.33
Bivens v. Six Unknown Named Agents of Federal Bureau of Narcotics, 292n.41
Black, Hugo, 213, 224
Blackstone, William: on interpretation, 281n.9; on the nature of property, 206, 293n.16; on the study of law, 293n.14
Blaug, Mark, *The Methodology of Economics*, 274n.1
Boodberg, Peter, *Selected Works of Peter A. Boodberg*, 300n.18
Booth, Wayne C., xvii; *The Company We Keep*, 279n.9
Boyd v. United States, 200, 204, 206–08, 284n.4, 284n.5, 292n.42, 293n.17, 294n.19; as interpreted by Brandeis, 152
Brandeis, Louis D.: as judge, 173, 213, 217; opinion in *Olmstead v. United States*, 149–57; and the right of privacy, 285n.12
Brennan, William, 219
Brower, Reuben: on translating Pindar, 300n.17; *On Translation*, 298n.10, 300n.18
Burke, Edmund, *Reflections on the French Revolution:* as constitu-

tion-making, 100; on economics, 276n.19; on inheritance, 206, 293n.14

Calandra v. United States, 216
Camara v. Municipal Court, 190, 197–202 passim, 294n.23
Canada, Royal Commission on Bilingualism and Bi-culturalism, 241–44
Cardozo, Benjamin, 106, 213
Carroll v. United States, 289n.19
Cavell, Stanley: *Must We Mean What We Say?*, 271n.2; *This New Yet Unapproachable America*, 271n.2, 273n.6
Change, in language and the world, 22–25, 27–28, 68–70; Brandeis's view of, 149–51, 155–57; Douglas's view of, 166, 172; Harlan's view of, 169–72
Character, of court, as criterion for judgment, 102, 107, 108, 111–12; reciprocity with language, 22–25. *See also* Community; Judicial criticism
Closson v. Morrison, 191–92, 292n.41
Coase, Ronald, 275n.5, 275n.6, 277n.22
Coherence, poetic and propositional modes of compared, 32–33. *See also* Integration; Language
Communication, standard language of, 15–16, 301n.22. *See also* Language; Theory
Community: in Brandeis opinion, 157; as defined by language, 23, 35–36, 99–102, 177–80; economics as erasing, 66–67, 84–86; in judicial opinion, 99–101, 113, 124–26, 176; justice as, 197–202; enacted in our speech, 15–16, 18–19; as technical term, 99; in the university, 15–16, 35. *See also* Judicial opinion; Justice; Rhetoric

Composition: as central art of law, 136; life as, 20. *See also* Art; Integration; Translation

Concepts: as intellectual phenomena, 28–29; language of, xv, 25–33; and rhetorical topics, 229–30; tendency to nominalize, 272 n.4; undermined in the law, 277 n.24

Conrad, Joseph, *The Mirror of the Sea*, 71, 276 n.18

Constitution of the United States, conception of: in Brandeis's opinion in *Olmstead*, 150–57; in Douglas's opinion in *White*, 165–67; in Frankfurter's opinion in *Rochin*, 103–12; in Harlan's opinion in *White*, 167–71; in Marshall's opinion in *McCulloch*, 279 n.15; in Story's opinion in *Prigg*, 118–22; in Taft's opinion in *Olmstead*, 145–48; in Taney's opinion in *Dred Scott*, 131–37; in White's opinion in *White*, 162–65

Constitutive rhetoric, legal rule as form of, 94–100, 177–80, 203. *See also* Rhetoric

Construction of legal texts. *See* Interpretation

Conversation, legal, 80–82, 102, 145–46; quality of as criterion for judging judicial opinion, 91, 99–105, 109–12, 113, 121, 124, 141, 223. *See also* Judicial criticism; Judicial opinion

Coolidge v. New Hampshire, 289 n.16, 289 n.21

Cooray, Mark L. J., *Changing the Language of the Law*, 297 n.7

Cooter, Robert: and Rappoport, 277 n.25; and Ulen, *Law and Economics*, 273 n.1

Criticism: literary and judicial, 97–101; standards of judgment, drawn from experience, 265–66; as translation, 258, 259. *See also* Character; Conversation; De-

mocracy; Judicial criticism; Language

Culture: economics as, 27–28, 46–86 passim; language as, 27–28; law as, xii, 79–82, 215–18. *See also* Language; Translation

Cunningham, Clark, 285 n.15

Dante, *Divine Comedy*, 300 n.18

Davidson, Donald, *Inquiries into Truth and Interpretation*, 298

Declaration of Independence, equality in, 131

Definition, in economics, 54–57; in the *Federalist Papers*, 36–39; in *Prigg v. Pennsylvania*, 119

Defoe, Daniel, *Robinson Crusoe*, 31–32, 279 n.9

Democracy, in Brandeis opinion, 257; in Harlan opinion, 172–73; and the jury, 262; as test for quality of rhetorical community, 91, 100–01, 109–10. *See also* Criticism; Equality; Judicial criticism

Desist v. United States, 286 n.12

Deterrence, defectiveness of as ground for exclusionary rule, 210–13

Dewey, John, on democracy, 91, 105, 278 n.1

Dewoskin, Kenneth, xvii, 236, 298 n.11

Dickinson, Emily, learning language of, 299 n.16

Discourse, academic and professional, 8–12; as a competition in translation, 259; control by qualification, economics as an example, 75–79; economic, among economists, 60–61; legal, compulsory character of, 201–02; poetic, 4–8; propositional, as structurally coercive, 29. *See also* Language; Economics; Poetry

Douglas, Mary, and Aaron B. Wildavsky, *Risk and Culture*, 295 n.31

Douglas, William O., opinion in
White, 165–67, 172–75, 224
Douglass, Frederick, *The Life and
Writings of*, 280 n.3
Dred Scott v. Sandford, 123–32, 195,
218, 219, 280 n.2, 282 n.12. *See
also* Slavery
Dryden, John, on translation, 296 n.2
Due process, as requiring justifica-
tion of governmental action,
194–97; incorporation of the bill
of rights, 103–04

Easterbrook, Frank, 275 n.3,
275 n.8, 278 n.30
Economics: alternatives to modern,
72–75; Buddhist, 72–74; as a culture, 27–28; as erasing community, 84–86; as eroding law, 223–
24; inadequacy of as a method of
analyzing permanent resources,
83–84; integration of with other
discourses, 75–79; as an intellectual method, 15; justifying the
market, 61–65; as a language of
theory, 53–54; and law distinguished, 79–82; mathematical
image of the person in, 64–66;
and nature, 68–72, 83–84; as a
political system, 61–68; positive
and normative, 61; primacy
given to the human will by, 68–
74; psychology of, 75 n; relation
to other forms of thought, 46–
48; as a religion, 75 n; as a secondary mode of life, 68–70; as a
system of economic analysis, 68–
75; as a system of value, 56–61
Education: as criterion for judging
judicial opinion, 156–57; law as
mode of, 155, 223
Eisele, Thomas, 273 n.6
Emerson, Ralph Waldo, "The
Poet," xi
Empson, William, *The Structure of
Complex Words*, 198 n.13

Entick v. Carrington, 205, 292 n.42
Equality: commitment of legal
hearing to, 24; entailed in practice of translation, 264; implied
by reasoning in a judicial opinion, 125–26; in Declaration of Independence, 131; of dollars, in
economics, 66–68, 82–83; as object of human community, 269;
in relation between writer of judicial opinion and reader, 224–
25; in translator's ethic, 267. *See
also* Democracy; Ethics
Ethics: as affirming self and recognizing other, 24, 41–42, 230, 253,
257, 263–64; of argument, 124–
26; and a literary sense of language, 41–42; translation as,
257–269 passim
Eucharist, nature of practice and
theory, 299 n.14
Euclid v. Ambler Realty Co., 149
Exclusionary rule, 203–14 passim;
different meanings of when used
for different purposes, 213; diverse grounds for, 209; history
of, 203–10; property as basis for,
204–07; as remedy for procedural wrongs, 207–09; used to
enforce civil–criminal distinction, 198–202; in *Rochin v. California*, 104, 109, 104–12; in *Wolf
v. Colorado*, 104
Ex Parte Jackson, 152–53, 160
Expert testimony, and translation,
14, 261

Faulkner, William, *Absalom! Absa-
lom!*, 128, 282 n.14
Federalist Papers, 36–39, 138,
273 n.10
Fehrenbacher, Don E., *The Dred
Scott Case*, 282 n.12
Fidelity. *See* Interpretation;
Translation
Finkelman, Paul, 282 n.11

Fish, Stanley: *Is There a Text in This Class?*, 279n.8; law and community of interpreters, 99
Fisher v. United States, 295n.32
Fourth amendment: basic principles of, 153, 170, 186, 194–97; conception of in *Olmstead*, 143–55; distinction between particular and general principles of justification, 198–99; function of warrant requirement in, 188–89n.15; text of, 142. See also Exclusionary rule; Search and seizure
Frank v. Maryland, 288n.14, 292n.42
Frankfurter, Felix, 210, 216–17, 279n.12, 279n.13; opinion in *Rochin*, 101–12
Freud, Anna, 268
Friedman, Milton, 28, 272n.3, 275n.5
Friendship: and common languages, 261; across racial lines, 220–21
Frost, Robert, 40, 271n.2, 272n.4; "A Dust of Snow," 4–5; "a momentary stay against confusion," 21, 263; teaching the reading of poetry, 259
Frost, William, *Dryden and the Art of Translation*, 300, n.17
Fugitive Slave Act: of 1793, 114, 116–17; of 1850, 195

Geertz, Clifford, *Local Knowledge*, 271n.2, 301n.22
Gibbons, Reginald, 300n.17
Gillette, Clayton, 276n.16
Goffman, Erving, *Forms of Talk*, 271n.2
Gouled v. United States, 145, 205–08
Griswold v. Connecticut, 172
Gross national product, 28, 72, 74
Gudeman, Stephen, *Economics as Culture*, 274n.1

Gustafson, James, *Ethics from a Theocentric Perspective*, 276n.15

Hale, Matthew, *History of the Pleas of the Crown*, 287n.5
Hammond, Gerald: on translating the Bible, 253; *The Making of the English Bible*, 300n.20
Harlan, John Marshall, 213, 217, 224; opinion in *White*, 167–75
Harris, Marvin, *Patterns of Race in the Americas*, 282n.13
Havens, Leston, *Making Contact*, 271n.2
Heilbroner, Robert L., *The Nature and Logic of Capitalism*, 274n.1; 277n.20
Herbert, George, "Jordan II," 285n.12
Hiatt v. Smith, 295n.3
Higham, T. F., 298n.11
Historian, and judge, compared, 217
Hobbes, Thomas, *Leviathan*, x, 33, 47–48, 271n.1
Hoffa v. United States, 286n.5
Hofstadter, Richard, *The American Political Tradition*, 293n.15
Holmes, Oliver Wendell, 215, 224; dissent in *Olmstead*, 285n.16
Homer: translating, 251–52; the *Odyssey*, 237–38, 251
Hopkins, Gerald Manley, 300n.17
Human life, character of as art, 264–67; built on the gifts of others, 65–66; dependence on nature and community, 68–70, 82; as development, 65–66; image of as ground for Brandeis opinion, 150–51, 157; inadequacy of mathematics as a language for, 64–66; made as poetic or musical text is made, 266

Idealization, in the law, 121, 132, 137, 139

Ideal reader, in the law, 100–01
Illinois v. Gates, 292 n.1
Institutions, as places for a certain kind of talk, 80
Integration, xii, xiv; art of, 40, 214, 264–65; and art of lawyer, 224–25; of contraries, as principle of poetic structure, 33; of economic and other discourses, 75–79; in interdisciplinary work, 12–16; as model of literary and social composition, 3–21 passim; of particular and general, 39–40; in poetry, 4–8; social, 21; and translation, 263. *See also* Composition; Translation
Interdisciplinary work, "findings" and "methods" in, 13–15
Interpretation: as central art of law, 136; confidence in rhetorical process of, 245–46; fidelity to prior texts in, 246; legal, literary criticism and, 97–99; "literal" method (Chief Justice Taft), 143–48; as making meaning, 236, 239–41, 244–46; in Moslem law, 267, 268; of multi-lingual treaties, 244–46; use of "principles" in, 153–55, 169–70, 241; responsibility of, and evasive devices, 141, 212–13, 216–17, 246; text creates power of in reader, 159; translation and, 150–57, 239–41, 243. *See also* Language; Meaning; Translation

Jackson, Robert H., 213, 224
Jacobsen, Roman, on translation, 248
Johnson, Samuel, on hypocrisy, 138, 283 n.20
Johnson v. United States, 288 n.15
Judicial criticism, xv–xvi; the craft tradition, 94–97; quality of conversation, 141, 203; of character and community, 145–48, 164–

65, 197–202, 222–25; of kind of education, 148, 156–57, 171–72; and literary criticism, 97–101; methods of, 93–102; of opinion rather than result, 91–93, 95–96, 122–23, 156–59. *See also* Conversation; Character; Judicial opinion; Translation
Judicial opinion: compared with history, 217; as part of constitution, 156–57; as constitutive, 215–18, 179–80; as creating authority, 217; as creating community, 113, 164–65; as creating judicial character, 145–48; education in, 156–57, 171–72; educative character of, 92; ethical and political meaning of reasoning in, 125–26; facing responsibility of judgment in, 141, 212–13, 216–17, 246; as a form of life, 89, 215–25; as laying out precedent, 164–65; as model of thought for the lawyer, 90; nature of, xv, 89–90; openness in, 111, 167–71, 220, 224–25, 263; political character of, 222–25; as reconstituting the authoritative past, 167–72, 175, 216–18, and ch. 7 passim; as reflecting moral progress, 165–67; and result, xv–xvi, 91–93, 95–96, 122–23, 156–59; as rhetorically constituted, 113. *See also* Authority; Interpretation; Translation; *and names of individual judges*
Justice: as aspect of relations between people, 197–202, 217, 224, 233; as translation, 257–69

Kaplan, John, 293 n.13
Katz v. United States, 157, 160–75 passim, 213
Keats, John, "To Autumn," 7
Kelman, Mark, 274 n.1
Kennedy, Duncan, 274 n.1

Kenner, Hugh: on translation, 254;
   The Counterfeiters, 277 n.23
Klamer, Arjo, 274 n.1
Klein, Melanie, 268
Kottack, Conrad, *Anthropology*,
   282 n.13
Krier, James, 276 n.16

Landynski, John, *Search and Seizure
   and the Supreme Court*, 287 n.6
Language: as creating community,
   23, 35–36, 99–102, 177–80; as
   culture, 27–28; as dance or gesture, xi, xii; effects of use on the
   mind, 26–27, 49–50; of expert,
   14, 261; and friendship, 261;
   learning to give attention to, 44;
   learning by imitation, 36; literary
   sense of, xi–xii, 33–39, 89, 215–
   16; as a propositional code, ix–x,
   29, 31, 80–82, 229–31, 250–51,
   253–54, 259, 266, 301 n.22; reciprocity with character, 22–25,
   171; reconstitution of in text, 18–
   19, 216; as social and ethical action, ix, xi–xii, 17–19, 215–16,
   232–33; as transparent, ix, 29,
   80; universal, impossibility of,
   31–32, 80–81, 263–64; use of, as
   art, 26–27, 50. *See also* Definition; Discourse; Translation
Languages, differences among, 43–
   44, 234–35, 237–38
LaRue, L. H., 295 n.4
Lasson, John, *History and Development of the Fourth Amendment*,
   287 n.4
Law: as an art, xii, 18, 216–18;
   as central and marginal at
   once, 261–62; two chambers of
   mind and, 262; as mode of communal self-education and self-
   constitution, 174; as constituting
   community by conversation,
   141, 157, 223–24; as culture, xii,
   79–82; other disciplines and, 19;

distinguished from economics,
   79–82; idealization in, 132; as
   institution for the remaking of
   language, 24; interpreting authoritative texts, 91, 246; literature and, 16–20; and policy,
   distinguished, 95–97, 175, 212–
   13; separation of powers as a
   principle of, 80, 96–97, 223; as
   translation, 80–82, 217, 260–63.
   See also Ethics; Interpretation; Judicial opinion; Translation
Lawyers: as representative speakers, 18; virtue of suspension of
   judgment in, 224, 225
Leff, Arthur, 274 n.1
Legal discourse: compulsory character of, 179; transformation of,
   41. *See also* Law
Legal hearing, commitment to
   equality, 24. *See also* Equality
Legal realism, 95, 139; and *Prigg v.
   Pennsylvania*, 122–23, 132; as in-
   herently simplifying, 136–37,
   278 n.6; in Taft's opinion, 147
Lempert, Richard, 295 n.4
Levinson, Sanford, 286 n.14
Lewis v. United States, 162
Linder, S. B., *The Harried Leisure
   Class*, 274 n.1, 274 n.2
Literalism, as interpretative vice,
   143–48. *See also* Judicial criti-
   cism, Language
Literary discourse, xi–xii, 33–39,
   80–82, 89, 215–16; as noncoer-
   cive in character, 41–42
Literature, law and, 16–20. *See also*
   Language; Translation
Lopez v. United States, 160–75 passim
Lysias: "Against Theomnestus,"
   239–41; theory of meaning, 247

Macaulay, Thomas Babington, 9
Macey, Jonathan, 278 n.30
MacIntyre, Alasdair, *A Short His-
   tory of Ethics*, 30, 272 n.5

MacNeil, Ian, 274n.1
Maine, Henry, *Ancient Law*, 279n.14
Malinski v. New York, 106
Mapp v. Ohio, 204, 209–10, 216, 291n.38, 292n.42
Market, justifications for, 62–64. *See also* Economics
Marshall, John: on expounding the Constitution, 149; opinion in *McCulloch v. Maryland*, 279–80n.15
Marx, Karl, 72, 276n.20
Mathematics: as a language of its own, 299n.13; as an image of the person, 64–66; mathematical thought, 48
Matlock v. United States, 289n.16
McCloskey, Donald N.: *The Applied Theory of Price*, 274n.1; *The Rhetoric of Economics*, 274n.1, 275n.4, 271n.2
Meaning: aesthetic and political, 215; as "beyond" or "above" text, 247–48, 252; of exclusionary rule, 199–200 and ch. 9 passim; individuality of, 35–36; interpretation as making, 236, 239–41, 244–46; of judicial action, as test of excellence, 214, and ch. 4 passim; performative, in *Rochin v. California*, 105–09; poetic, 4–8; in relation between text and context, 137–38; of words, 34–35, 229–30, 247–48; of work, 70–71. *See also* Interpretation; Language; Translation
Michelman, Frank, 274n.1
Miller, Christanne, *Emily Dickinson: A Poet's Grammar*, 299n.16
Mind, limits of, art of translation as recognizing, 41–45, 80–82, 258–59, 264. *See also* Translation
Miranda v. Arizona, as socially constitutive, 196
Mishan, Ezra, 274n.1

Monaghan, Henry, 294n.27
Moncrieff, C. K. Scott, 300n.17, 301n.21
Money, shifting value of, 277n.26
Moore, Ira, 290n.34
Moslem law, interpretation in, 267–68
Mottahadeh, Roy, *The Mantle of the Prophet*, 301n.3

Nabokov, Vladimir, 300n.18
Nagel, Robert, *Constitutive Cultures*, 278n.3
Nardone v. United States, 286n.2
Nida, Eugene A., *Language Structure and Translation*, 298n.11

Olmstead v. United States, 141–59 passim, 160, 161, 164, 203, 213
On Lee v. United States, 160–75 passim, 286n.28
Order and disorder, in poetry, 7–8
"Original intention," 113–40; as erroneous method of interpretation, 113, 133–37, 219; as fictional, 134–37; as erasing intention to publish the text as authoritative, 135–36, 219; Story's method of reading, 118–21; Taney's method of reading, 129–31. *See also* Interpretation; Judicial opinion
Ortega y Gasset, Jose, 235, 296n.2; *Man and People*, 298n.13
Orwell, George, 275n.7
Osborn v. United States, 168–69

Paine, Thomas, *The Rights of Man*, 100
Payton v. New York, 289n.15
Pelikan, Jaroslav, *The Vindication of Tradition*, 299n.14
Peters v. New York, 291n.40
"Plain Meaning," as erroneous method of interpretation, 216–19 and ch. 6 passim. *See also* Inter-

pretation; Judicial opinion; Translation

Plato, 33, 45, 59, 100, 251

Poetry, as integrative, 4–8; built on simultaneous assertion and denial, 32–33; not translatable, 248, 257. *See also* Integration

Poirier, Richard, *The Renewal of Literature*, 271 n.2

Policy, distinguished from law, 95–97, 175, 212–13. *See also* Law

Positive and normative economics, relation between, 61 n. *See also* Economics

Posner, Richard A., 59 n, 275 n.11; *Economic Analysis of Law*, 273 n.1, 277 n.22; *The Economics of Justice*, 274 n.1

Powell, Lewis H., opinion in *Calandra*, 211, 282 n.9

Powers, separation of, as central idea of law, 80, 96–97, 121, 212–13, 223

Precedent, reading of, 160–75 passim. *See also* Authority; Judicial opinion

Priest, George, 274 n.1

Prigg v. Pennsylvania, 113–23, 218, 219

Principles, common-law adjudication by search for, 153, 169–70, 241

Privacy, as definition of search and seizure, 153–54, 161–62. *See also* Fourth amendment

Property, as basis for exclusionary rule, 204–07. *See also* Exclusionary rule

Propositions, not paradigmatic use of language, 298 n.13; as practices, 34, 39. *See also* Language

Proust, Marcel, *The Remembrance of Things Past*, 301 n.21

Race, friendship and, 220–21; language of in *Dred Scott*, 126–29, 132–33

Racism, rooted in desire, 128

Rationality, economic, 52–53; propositional view of, x, 29; narrow and broad view of, 40–41. *See also* Coherence; Language; Translation

Reader, ideal, as way of thinking about a text, 100–01

Reder, Melvin, 274 n.1

Regents of the University of California v. Bakke, 220, 295 n.4

Rehnquist, William, opinions of, 188–92, 219

Relativism, and translation, 263–65

Religion, nature of, 75 n

Rhetoric, constitutive: focus on character and community, 101–02, 108, 111–12; human life lived on rhetorical terms, 265–66; law as, xiv; as method of reading, xiv, 101–02; as mode of analysis of judicial opinions, 89–102. *See also* Character; Community; Interpretation; Language

Robinson, Ian, *The Survival of English*, 275 n.7

Robinson v. United States, 176–202 passim, 203

Rochin v. California, 102–13, 160, 203, 209, 213, 294 n.28

Rosenne, Shabtai, 297 n.8

Sahlins, Marshall, *Culture and Practical Reason*, 274 n.1; *Stone Age Economics*, 277 n.21

Sandalow, Terrance, 295 n.30

Schmerber v. California, 289 n.18

Schneckloth v. Bustamonte, 289 n.16

Schrock, Thomas, 294 n.27

Schumacher, E. F., "Small is Beautiful," 72–73, 274 n.1, 277 n.21

Science: and economics, 47, 51–54; false version of and language as code, x, 28–30, 41, 47–58, 98–99; and law, 212–13; as a model

Science (*continued*)
  for literary critics, 98; as a model
  of language and thought, 29
Scitovsky, T., *The Joyless Economy*,
  274n.1, 274n.2, 275n.9
Scott, Dred, the *Dred Scott* case,
  113, 123–32. See also *Dred Scott
  v. Sandford*
Search and seizure: for Brandeis,
  149–55; for Douglas, 165–67; for
  Harlan, 167–71; for Taft, 143–45;
  for White, 162–65; general principles of, 180–87. *See also* Fourth
  amendment
Self, affirmation of and recognition
  of other. *See* Ethics
Self-interest, and rationality in eco-
  nomics, 51–56; in Thucydides,
  59; language of, 59n, 84–86. *See
  also* Ethics
Sheppard, Claude-Armand, 241
*Silverthorne Lumber Co. v. United
  States*, 207
Slavery, in U.S. Constitution, 114–
  15, 117, 120, 123, 138. See also
  Dred Scott v. Sandford
Somerset's Case, 115–16
Sri Lanka, changing the language
  of the law in, 297n.7
Steiner, George, *After Babel*,
  296n.2, 300n.18, 301n.5
Stevens, Wallace, 33
Stigler, George J., 275n.8, 275n.9
Story, Joseph, 216; *Commentaries on
  the Constitution of the United States*,
  281n.9; opinion in *Prigg v. Penn-
  sylvania*, 114–23
Stroud, Barry, 272n.6
Swear words, taboo of lost in for-
  eign language, 299n.14
Swift v. Tyson, 282n.10
Swift, Jonathan, *A Tale of a Tub*,
  277n.23, 289n.4; on the true
  critic, 94

Taft, William Howard, 173, 216;

opinion in *Olmstead v. United
  States*, 143–48
Taney, Roger Brooke, 216; opinion
  in *Dred Scott*, 123–32
Tave, Stuart, *Some Words of Jane
  Austen*, 273n.11
Taylor, Telford, *Two Studies in Con-
  stitutional Interpretation*, 287n.6
Terry v. Ohio, 190, 193–95, 197–202
  passim, 291n.40
Theory: economics as a language
  of, 28, 53–54; and practice, 97–
  101, 132–37
Thompson, Lawrance, *Robert Frost:
  The Early Years*, 301n.1
Thoreau, Henry David, *Walden*,
  70–71, 276n.17
Thucydides, 11, 22–23, 59n, 272n.1
Time, in poetry, 6–7
Transformation, community in
  process of, 175; in the law, 41; in
  poetry, 6–7; as a result of integration, 77–79 and ch. 1 passim
Translation, 19–20; as an art of recognition, 203, 257–69; as art of
  composition in response to another, 19–20, 235–36, 246–48,
  252–53, 255–56; in Brandeis
  opinion, 152–57; criticism and,
  248–49; defects of usual talk
  about, 233–35, 246–48, 253–54;
  and drafting, 241–44; in economics and law, 80–82; as an
  ethical and political activity, 44,
  45, 255–56, 257–69 passim; and
  expert testimony in legal case,
  14, 261; indexical, 234–35; as necessary but instructive failure, 31,
  235, 255–57; fidelity to prior
  texts, 243–44, 257–58; and integration, 263–65; and interpretation, 236, 239, 241–44; as judicial
  method of Justice Harlan, 172–
  73; as justice, 230, 257–69; law
  as, 80–82, 217–18, 239–46, 260–
  63; and loss, 262–63; and limits

of mind and language, 258–59; and "metaphor," 233–35; as place between worlds, 230–32, 255; and relativism, 263–64; respect for other and assertion of self, 230, 259–60, 263–65; rhetorical meaning of, 233–34; as theme of this book, 225. *See also* Ethics; Interpretation; Language

Treaties, interpretation of multilingual, 244–46

Tribe, Lawrence, 274n.1

Uncertainty, radical, in law and life, 263–67

United States Constitution, due process clause, 103–04, 106–08; fugitive slave clause, 114–17. *See also* Constitution

United States v. Calandra, 211

United States v. Payner, 294n.28

United States v. Skipwith, 291n.40

United States v. Watson, 289n.15

United States v. White, 160–75 passim, 203

United Steel Workers of America v. Weber, 218–22

Value, economics of as a system of, 56–61, 69–70, 84–86

Vining, Joseph, xvii, 298n.9; *The Authoritative and the Authoritarian*, 289n.3

Virgil, *Aeneid*, 33, 247

Voluntariness and autonomy, in economics, 63–64, 67–68

Wagley, Charles, *Race and Class in Rural Brazil*, 282n.13

Warden v. Hayden, 205, 206, 289n.17, 293n.10

Weeks v. United States, 191, 207, 294n.24

Weems v. United States, 150

Weiss, Bernard, 301n.3

Welsh, Robert, 294n.27

West, Robin, 275n.11

White, Byron, 216; opinion in *United States v. White*, 162–65, 172–75

White, James Boyd, 278n.5, 286n.15; *Heracles' Bow*, 283n.18, 279n.7, 292n.43; *The Legal Imagination*, 17–18, 295n.31; *When Words Lose Their Meaning*, xiv, 18–19, 59, 99, 272n.2, 279n.15

Williamson, Oliver, 274n.1

Wilson, Edmund, on Emily Post, 17, 271n.2

Winnicott, D. W.: *Home Is Where We Start From*, 75n; *The Spontaneous Gesture*, 268, 301n.4

Wirth, D., 297n.8

Wittgenstein, Ludwig, *Philosophical Investigations*, ix, xii, 271n.2, 272n.6

Wolf v. Colorado, 103–04, 204, 209–10, 291n.38

Wood, Gordon, *The Creation of the American Republic*, 293n.15

Words: change in meaning over time, 32–35, 43, 240; defined by other terms, 119; definition of, 54–57, ("self-interest" and "rich" in economics), 36–39, ("deliberation" in the Federalist Papers); meanings of, denotative and connotative, 247–48, 250; nature of, 229–30; and sentences, 34. *See also* Definition; Interpretation; Language; Meaning

Writing: openness in, 224–25; as talking two ways at once, 26–27, 33. *See also* Integration

Zurcher v. Stanford Daily, 293n.13